Building a Showcase Culture

Powerful and Practical Keys for Manufacturing

Building a
Showcase Culture

Powerful and Practical Keys
For Manufacturing

Mark Lado

Published By

Global Manufacturing Services

ISBN: 978-1-7320475-0-1 (hardcover)
978-1-7320475-1-8 (softcover)
978-1-7320475-2-5 (e-book)

To my love,

Panjai

Forever in my heart

Table of Contents

LIST OF FIGURES

List of tables

Foreword

If you are reading this right now, you want to learn more about successful plant leadership, managing and/or improving plant operations, or quality. This book provides a wealth of information, tools and experienced-based knowledge that will help you run a manufacturing facility successfully — a true resource and toolkit to make you a better leader and elevate your facility to a competitive operation. Even if you are a seasoned manager, there are many refresher points in this book that will improve your manufacturing proficiency and your bottom line.

So, why am I writing this foreword? I have known the author, Mark Lado, for many years and have had the pleasure of having him work for me, both directly and indirectly in many roles. He was Quality Leader, Global Warranty Director, Plant Leader in China, and all around strong businessman. Mark led a start-up plant in China as that country was first experiencing tremendous growth. He set up the plant and grew it successfully, while instilling a unique and positive plant culture in a region of the world that did not have experience with basic process controls, quality plans, and shift patterns — these concepts were all quite foreign to the China team. Mark was excellent at finding strong solutions, even for the poorly defined issues.

This book was built from Mark's wealth of knowledge and 30+ years of experiences and provides the tools and guidance to become a leader in manufacturing. I recognize the value of this book as an excellent resource because I've had over 250 global manufacturing sites under my direct or indirect leadership over the last 15 years. As a senior leader for companies producing $18B to $30B in revenue, I have been responsible for Global Lean Manufacturing, Sourcing, Quality and Delivery, and have implemented two fully global production systems in Fortune 500 companies.

This book is broken down into four distinctive parts. You can read the entire book or concentrate on areas where you need help. This book follows a maturity model of plant excellence, starting with Orientation-plant basics. This area of the book also concentrates on your labor force, supervisor/leadership training, and establishing and utilizing Key Performance Indicators (KPIs).

The book then transitions into the Foundations of how to effectively build or improve the manufacturing facility infrastructure. Key areas of focus are the development of the organization, the facility itself, and the standard processes. In this section, key tools to success are demonstrated through principles such as Value Stream Maps, Standard Work and quality improvement processes. Additionally, focus on visual controls and people interaction are emphasized. If a plant does not utilize these tools, it will never have a successful operation.

In the third section of Mark's book, there is a heavy focus on operating rhythms. Having a consistent daily production rhythm in conjunction with a good communication plan is absolutely paramount to be a world class manufacturing site.

The book finishes with Competitiveness, which focuses on ensuring the site has a long-term strategic plan and vision. Having a true strategic roadmap with plans to organically grow is key, but again, tends to be a weakness at many sites, as people tend to focus on short-term metrics.

The fundamentals and processes presented in this book apply to raw material processing through to pioneering technologies like 3-D printing, ceramic matrix composites (CMCs), nano-technology, etc. The future may introduce more innovation, more digital technology, and a less labor-intensive environment, but the lessons in this book will stand the test of time for any manufacturing facility.

Good luck with your pursuit of establishing and running a world-class, factory showcase facility. Just taking time to look into this book indicates you have a curiosity to learn — an absolute essential for all leaders.

Bryce Currie
Vice President & General Manager
GE Aviation Delivery Operations

Preface

This book is intended for a variety of audiences, but especially those who want to become factory showcase leaders. Readers will learn various tools and techniques along a structured path and be able to apply them or evaluate their company's effectiveness. The information will be particularly useful for:

- Manufacturing Operation leaders
- Functional staff, supervisors and team leaders
- Students studying engineering, operations, supply chain, production planning, finance, human resources, quality, and business administration
- Entrepreneurs starting new manufacturing enterprises

The approach described in this book focuses on what is necessary for individuals to develop leadership capabilities in manufacturing either as a new hire, current employee, or developing manager. The chapters address the requirements to make it possible for employees to add greater value. In addition, the approach builds knowledge and collectively establishes a factory showcase culture. The reason for starting with Orientation is that the brick and mortar of most manufacturing companies is already in place, meaning something operational is already happening today in your company or a company you want to join. If your company is newly formed and not currently in production, begin by executing your business plan. If the destination is having a factory showcase culture, then the steps of the journey are:

Part 1 - Orientation is how your company introduces itself to New Hires and to other external people, such as customers, suppliers, contractors, etc. Orientation is visual, mindset, behavioral, and training based. It represents your company's standard operating practices for managing data using Key Performance Indicators (KPIs), which have to be learned, practiced, and honed for improvement.

Part 2 - Foundation is the core of a company's processes. It is a collection of various systems and practices that are the basis for your company's success. Foundation is purely operational in nature and builds upon the Orientation section. The Foundation section does not stand-alone — it must be used along with the other techniques.

Part 3 - Conditioning builds upon Orientation and Foundation. It's the culture of motivating people, using Daily Routines, data collection and analysis, auditing to ensure compliance, coordinating resources to take actions, and responding to various inputs using analytics.

Part 4 - Competitiveness is the way in which a company demonstrates its advantages by implementing short-term plans with long-term investments, strategies, and vision.

Why I wrote this book

I have been very fortunate to have worked in several different industries and in various manufacturing operations roles. I have extensive work-life experiences in Asia, Europe, and the USA, and have had several great mentors, as well as opportunities to work with some great companies.

My first professional position after graduating with a BS in Industrial Engineering Technology from SUNY Polytechnic was with GE Aerospace, where I had two mentors helping me learn about make versus buy, supplier development, supplier management, and how to use various inspection gages and equipment. I often reflect on these times, since they remind me how critical this was in my own development.

After several years at GE, I decided to obtain an MBA, since I wanted to gain business management knowledge and move up the corporate ladder. Earning my MBA from University of North Florida allowed me to work at Jabil Circuit, Saturn Electronics and Engineering, TRW Automotive (now ZF-TRW), and WABCO. TRW Automotive launched my global career and accelerated my learning from building new manufacturing facilities in several Asian countries to globally defining and developing a warranty management system.

My first international assignment was in Thailand. This is where I was first exposed to a hands-on, in-your-face global business environment. Every day, I was exposed to something I had never encountered previously in my studies or work experiences, from communicating with Thai people by drawing engineering diagrams on a whiteboard to taking three-wheeled motorcycle rickshaws across Bangkok to see customers and suppliers or just to get something to eat.

I was determined to succeed and behaved like a stereotypical American. To this day, I am still tough-minded, but much more open-minded. Here is where I learned to be culturally sensitive and adaptive to various situations. I was expected to participate in strategic management activities and be able to micro-manage various functional details as we started to build a new factory in the middle of a vast pineapple field an hour's drive from the city of Pattaya. Every day, I looked forward to testing my capabilities and seeing my previous day's work pan out to be a failure or success. On the weekends, I would reflect on the impact of those activities and decisions and assess whether I could have done something different. In addition, I studied the Thai language, and had time to recharge my mind for the next exciting week.

After several years in Thailand, I moved onto other projects in Australia, Malaysia, South Korea, Germany, UK, and the USA. I was becoming more of a global manufacturing operations leader, with key insights into various working cultures, as well as a growing understanding of various languages. While working globally, regionally, or within a certain country or factory, I was highly sensitive to the operation's culture, their management ways, prioritizing criteria, and how and in which ways I could adapt my management style to accomplish my goals and business key performance indicators.

As I was finishing a project in the UK and Germany, I accepted a general manager position in China. This is where I gained extensive hands-on application of the various tools and techniques written about in this book from working with American, Asian, and European customers and suppliers. I was able to manage a state-owned enterprise and initiate their first exports to Germany, as well as establish a new, significantly larger automotive parts manufacturing business.

Then I moved into a director's role in China, where I gained the experience of managing several factories and developed various skill sets essential to those manufacturing operations teams, including operational finance; business case analysis; Daily Routines; project management for building new sites; product launches; joint venture management; warehouse and distribution management; and management of wholly owned foreign investments.

Eventually, after 20 years of experiences around the world, I started a manufacturing operations management and quality improvement consulting company. Through these experiences, I have seen both successful and unsuccessful approaches for managing a factory.

The result of this wealth of experience is this prescriptive book. Managers and staff can use part of a section, an entire section, or the entire book as their manufacturing operations go-to book. Individuals can use it as a how-to guide for advancing into leadership roles. And students can gain a technical, practiced approach on various tools and techniques as well as learn how to implement them.

Introduction

Factory Showcase Culture

Anyone visiting a manufacturing facility gets their first impression from the street. Customers, suppliers, potential employees, and colleagues will judge your company by the external appearance of your facilities. Many manufacturing companies recognize the importance of curb appeal and put effort into ensuring that the exterior of their facilities and parking lots are safe, clean and well lit; have clear signage; and are generally appealing. Inside, these facilities involve more than just safety, cleanliness and general attractiveness — they embody high standards, with a focus on customer expectations such as high quality, reliability, on-time delivery, productivity, profitability, and frequent product and process innovations at competitive prices. Their workers are in tune with the customer demand rate, support staff reacts quickly to concerns, and the environment is conducive to empowerment and innovation. The local community is proud to have the company located there. The work culture is clearly positive, team oriented, and people want to work there, because they are appreciated. These factory "showcases" are not just physical demonstrations of a company's commitment to quality — they are a reflection of their management and manifestations of the essence of their culture.

Alternatively, some companies believe there is no value in having a factory showcase culture. It's too costly, too difficult to change, or they believe since they are currently profitable, they will remain profitable. These oblivious companies are living in a false and fragile environment. Their market share could erode at any moment, their employees do not have a vested interest, and their suppliers are unconcernedly filling orders. These companies face a bleak and eventual impending doom. Moreover, there are companies that recognize a change is needed and are struggling to be profitable and advance to the next level. Management is committed to success and believes they have a strong business foundation. They are using various KPIs and strategies to improve their business performance. However, some of the management and staff have doubts about their culture being changed into building a factory showcase culture. Their employees live and work in the now without having a destination in mind. It is essential to have the planned route and destination defined, communicated visually, audited, and regularly evaluated.

Management that has a factory showcase culture destination in mind stimulates ideas and encourages the employees to be entrepreneurs within the company. They cohesively develop business knowledge with all employees where everyone is accountable and committed to achieve the expectations. Every day, the entire company is building strength, confident they are fostering a factory showcase culture. Their customers recognize they are creating value for them, see this in their competitively priced and innovative products and services, and trust that the company has their interest in mind. And, their customers believe there is an alignment of strategies. The company's management mindset and commitments result in a total buy-in by all employees.

Part 1- Orientation

Every company, regardless of its number of employees or sales volume, benefits from having an orientation program. The purpose of an orientation program is to introduce newly hired personnel to the company in a standard, consistent, and controlled way. It is essential for all new personnel going through the orientation program to receive the same initial information; the only variability in the material should be presentation and perception differences. The perception of each new employee may be somewhat different, but the underlying materials are the same.

Orientation is critical to enabling new hires at all levels of the organization to understand the company's culture they are joining. By sharing information and candidly discussing the company's business processes, plans, issues, and goals, you accelerate new employees' ability to become productive and add value. This shortens the learning curve and speeds up their ability to contribute. If your company does not have a standard orientation program, use the following chapters to develop one.

Chapter 1 - New Hire First Day

The New Hire First Day is an opportunity for both employee and employer to showcase their best. Simply put, the employer has a responsibility to ensure the New Hire fits easily into their new role. The employee's responsibility is to understand quickly their new role, responsibility, expectations, and ability to add value.

As the new person at the company, you finally have your first job, are transferring from one company to another, or are changing from one industry to another. Whatever the reason for being a New Hire, you are enthusiastically ready for a fresh start on your career and life. The company needs to formally introduce itself via face-to-face meetings and a company handbook, and provide a training program.

First Day

How many of us remember our first professional day on the job? Do you recall how exciting it was to be a part of something new and so optimistic about the future? Were you willing to start work with 100% effort and passion?

In the worst case, many people spend their First Day in a new job filling out HR forms that could have been done at home, then sitting in various conference rooms listening to people talk about the company, policies, procedures, etc. By the time you leave on your First Day, you are wondering if tomorrow will be just as boring and when you can actually *do* something. Some companies have already learned to send the various forms to New Hires ahead of time, including policies and procedures, so they can read the material at their leisure.

A better scenario is that when the New Hire arrives at the company, someone warmly welcomes them and makes that person start to feel a part of the team or company from day one. During the initial moments of greeting, the New Hire receives an agenda for the first day, and someone guides them throughout the day. The guide could be a coach, trainer, mentor, or someone from their function or department. The agenda may be simple or include details about who to meet, where, and what is to be discussed.

Providing a warm greeting and a First Day agenda is a standardized way to orientate all New Hires. The best-case scenario is a First Week (or two) agenda, along with dates and times within the First Month to meet with more-senior people to help define the New Hire's 30-60-90-day targets, especially if the New Hire is a staff employee or manager.

It is vital that the First Day's agenda be an hourly schedule showing whom will be met, location and topic, and whether this activity is completed. The agenda may have some time and space for New Hires to observe the operations. The First Day is a formal introduction and opportunity to welcome the New Hire to the company and their colleagues, and to acclimate the New Hire to their new surroundings. As a minimum, the New Hire will have a face-to-face introduction with each manager and staff that they will be working with.

The agenda is the same for employee transfers, whether from a current site/ function/department to another function/department or even from one company site to another company site. There may be differences in the company handbook from site to site or in different countries, but the point is that the company handbook is a standardized orientation to the company.

The following table is an example for the New Hire's First Day, whether that new person is a director, manager, supervisor, or staff. This type of position is considered indirect labor as they support production operations of the factory and are not directly involved with material conversion into finished goods. These positions are also typically considered an exempt employee classification whereby they receive a salary and are not entitled to overtime pay. However, some indirect labor can be non-exempt and can receive overtime pay, such as a production supervisor or Quality inspector.

Table 1. 1 Indirect Labor - First day agenda

Time	Who	Location	Topic
08:00–08:30	Name, HR Officer	HR Office	HR forms
08:30–09:00	Name, HR Manager	HR Manager Office	Company introduction
09:00–10:00	Name, Functional Leader New Hire will work for	Functional Leader Office	Daily Routine, Functional responsibilities, expectations, introduction to colleagues, job description
10:00–12:15	Name, Functional Colleague 1	Factory	Factory walk and observations, and Environmental, Health, and Safety (EHS)
12:15–13:00	Lunch with Functional Colleague(s)	Cafeteria or outside	Getting to know one another -Open discussion
13:00–15:30	Name, Functional Colleague 2	Functional Leader office and various areas	Discussion of Key Performance Indicators (KPIs), company vision, mission, strategies, plans, key customers, products
15:30–16:00	Name, Functional Manager	Various areas	Introduce to other functions
16:00–17:00	Name, Functional Manager	Functional Leader office	Factory floor to observe shift handover and/or First Day closing and discussion for Second Day

Objectives
The generic objective for the new employee is to observe, understand, think, question, listen, retain, and repeat this cycle. Applying this objective day after day will ensure a successful orientation. The general objective for the various employer personnel is to convey information, make sure the New Hire understands the information presented; listens to the New Hire, and try to assess the New Hire's interest and capability. The employer must ensure the New Hire understands this vital information, this can be done through repeated statements, highlight key points, and questioning the New Hire.

Other physical objectives for the New Hire are to receive company identification badge and/or security access and work-related equipment. This may include a laptop, phone, and any personal protective equipment such as a uniform, steel-toe shoes, gloves, masks, hat, and place to put everything (whether a personal locker or desk). The employer must confirm the laptop and phone have all the needed applications installed and are ready for the employee to use as soon as they receive it. The employer must provide training on the applications and provide reference materials to ensure the employee understands the required applications. In some cases, this may take a few days of training. Therefore, the employer must provide a checklist to the employee with all the needed materials. The employee has the responsibility to confirm each line of the checklist has been thoroughly fulfilled and that they are satisfied with the materials and information provided. This seems rather basic and most companies can greatly improve their orientation with these simple and effective keys. The key is to give the right tools including software applications to the right people and to ensure they know how to use the tools correctly. This applies to all employees that are given new responsibilities or asked to use a new or different physical, analytical, or application tool.

The New Hire must learn the names, titles, and possibly general responsibilities of the various leaders and managers they have interacted with on the first day. Also, the New Hire must learn how employees recognize and greet each other, whether they are managers, staff, direct workers, temporary workers, contractors, customers, or suppliers in meetings, in the hallways, and on the factory floor. So, on the second day, the New Hire can start greeting the employees and start recognizing the leaders. Also, on the first day, someone ought to review the organization chart with the New Hire and inform them of the various leaders of the company with an emphasis on the functional area they will be working. The New Hire needs to receive a company handbook, participate in some functional meetings, and gain an overview of the company's products and processes while walking the factory floor. In addition, the New Hire should get a good sense of the operating work culture and general understanding of the company's EHS (Environmental, Health, and Safety) practices.

In many companies, it takes more than one day for a New Hire to get the hang of the new environment, work responsibilities, and culture. Towards the end of the first day, an agenda for the Second Day should be discussed with the New Hire. If during the first day the Daily Routine activity was not observed, then this must be a priority for the second day. The Second Day morning needs to include observation time for the Daily Routine activities on the factory floor (see Daily Routine in Chapter 24) as well as an observation or participation in other functional responsibilities such as meetings or even a Layered Process Audit, see Chapter 26 for more information. Day after day, it is vital the New Hire become more engaged with the employees and interactive with management.

Company Profile

Every new hire must receive a company profile on arrival for that first day of work. The company profile can be standalone information such as a booklet and can be included in the company handbook. The profile needs to be a handout, such as a printed presentation or brochure, that includes a facility photo, address, main contact number, vision statement, Quality and EHS policy statements, main products and their key features. Having the employee take home the handout is something like receiving a gift and the employee will most likely keep this as a reminder of their first day.

The profile also may include the main customers, general process information, organization or engineering and test capabilities, a list of quality certifications and customer awards. In addition, the profile can include an organizational chart, or even a site organization chart with names, so the new hire can get acquainted with the company faster.

Company Handbook

It is imperative that every company provides a company handbook to each employee on their first day of work. The company handbook is to be available and easily accessible on the company's internal systems. Updates are communicated via text message, email, and are posted in a conspicuous location such as in or nearby the cafeteria so everyone can see the revised changes. It is critical to update any changes to the company handbook in a timely manner. Some companies utilize an electronic signature by all employees to acknowledge they have received and read the updates.

For a newly formed company, this is one of the most important documented means of defining your company's culture, policies, rules, benefits, and conveying a variety of other information. Your newly hired employees need guidance, especially those who plan to advance into leadership roles. Developing a company handbook will take a considerable amount of time and will need input from all managers. The company handbook may have to be revised several times before being released to all employees and some content may need the company lawyer to review it.

Topics to include in the company handbook are:

- Company profile
- Company locations
- List of major customers
- Safety practices
- Equal opportunity statement
- Harassment policy
- Quality and EHS policies
- Conflict of interest policy
- Expense reporting policy
- Pay scale
- Use of communication devices
- Expectations to add value
- Manufacturing compliance policy
- Description of products
- Employee benefits or reference
- Employment at-will disclaimer
- Disciplinary procedure
- Smoking policy
- Drug and alcohol policy
- Hiring policies
- Non-disclosure agreement
- New job posting policy
- Termination policy
- Use of social media
- Expectations for innovation
- Policy Statements – Mission, Vision, Quality, Safety, Equal Opportunity Employment, etc.

Rules

Every company needs to have a set of defined rules, but many do not seem to have them documented in a formal company handbook. Rules are for addressing:

- Work clothing attire
- Work times
- Attendance requirements
- Work behaviors
- Possession of firearms
- Information posting
- Safety and security
- Use of company badge
- Parking locations
- Cafeteria cleanliness
- Use of company equipment
- Customer and supplier visits
- Contractor visits
- Use of telephones
- Overtime authorization
- Meetings
- Telephone etiquette
- Theft and vandalism
- Unsafe acts
- Call-ins for no show or late
- Emergency evacuation
- Emergency contact list
- Bathroom cleanliness
- Office and factory practices
- Use of company vehicles
- Expense reporting

What rules are there for the first time a New Hire enters the company?

Rules can start at the point that new employees park their cars in a designated lot, walk within lane markers, and use crosswalks to enter an employee entrance. Companies may require a badge swipe to enter the facility or guard identification check, or perhaps there is a limited- or no-security access checkpoint. At this time, an employee should be wearing the appropriate attire, including any personal protective equipment. Information about these steps should be given when a New Hire's employment is confirmed so that first day goes smoothly.

The company handbook can be critical to helping New Hires understand company culture and the rules that underlie that culture. In addition, the company handbook should be written in the language that the employees can understand. So, there may be multiple language company handbooks with one language designated as the primary, or an original company handbook and copies of the primary or original in other languages. Also, the language needs to be simple and clear, possibly include examples of "good" and "no good", and not legalese.

Putting rules into writing is essential for everyone in the factory, because managers can't be expected to enforce rules they don't know about and employees can't be expected to follow rules that are not documented. This all seems quite basic, but this is very important for the employee, supervisor, and other management.

Even employees with many years of experience will need guidance, especially if a company is considering a dramatic change to its culture. Minor culture changes also should be documented and shared throughout the company. Just because the company handbook is updated, doesn't necessarily mean everyone will immediately understand and follow or conduct practices in the new way. So, individual, group, computer-training-based programs, and/or frequent reminders will need to be developed and conducted to ensure everyone is at least aware of the changes. The management team may also want to praise and recognize employees for following the new practices.

All of this is important to developing the culture of ownership, control, and decision-making where employees feel valued and supported. It also might be a legal requirement in a manufacturing setting, where the company and its employees are expected to follow certain laws and regulations governing safety and quality control.

Job Description
The New Hire manager or direct boss needs to clearly communicate the Job Description to the New Hire. It is vital to have a clearly written Job Description that includes:

- Job Title
- Responsibilities
- Skills required
- Tools and equipment
- Travel requirements
- Expectations to add value
- Linkage to other roles
- Alignment to vision and mission
- Company's commitment
- Key Performance Indicators

- Role
- Knowledge required
- Qualifications required
- Working conditions
- Physical requirements
- Company's culture
- How position fits into the company
- Classification of job as exempt or non-exempt
- Percentage of time allocated to key responsibilities

Job Descriptions do not directly state compensation and benefits. Compensation and benefits are separate topics. The job description may define a work location, especially if there are multiple work locations or percentage of time for travel. Job Descriptions should be reviewed and possibly edited once a year to ensure they are an accurate reflection of the business needs. Specialized staffing agencies can be used to revise or help clarify Job Descriptions. Job Descriptions are not meant to be inclusive or comprehensive for every activity. The main reasons to define Job Descriptions are for:

- Potential and current employees to understand their role and responsibilities as defined above
- Recruiting
- Training
- Basis for performance reviews
- Market compensation comparison
- Basis for advancement criteria and career path
- Compliance requirements

One non-written main expectation is that New Hires know the names and contact information of their leaders, colleagues, and others that they will interface with. Introducing the New Hire to their immediate leaders, colleagues, and others can be done during the factory walks and at various meetings. If the company has a union, the labor contract key points need to be shared. This will reduce the likelihood of a union grievance.

Second Day
The company should expand on the First Day's introduction by involving the New Hire more in their new role. The company needs to provide an environment for the New Hire to feel they can start making a difference. The New Hire should feel comfortable and confident to offer their opinion.

A Second Day Agenda needs to allot the New Hire more time with their manager, mentor and colleagues. This is to ensure and support a comprehensive and standardized orientation. The agenda should include time in both the office and factory with a priority for the responsibilities and the Daily Routine requirements of the specific position. Daily Routines are further defined in Conditioning, Chapter 24. After the Daily Routine activities, the mentor and colleagues need to have a discussion about how the New Hire will contribute to the Daily Routine and any concerns either may have regarding the expectations.

Table 1. 2 Indirect Labor - Second day agenda

Time	Who	Location	Topic
08:00- 08:30	Name, Title, Function, Colleague 1	Functional office	Greetings and preparations for the day
08:30 - 09:00	Name, Title, Function, Colleague 1 or Functional Manager	Daily Routine location	Daily Routine (DR) observance
09:00 – 11:00	Name, Title, Function, Colleague 1	Factory	Observation of factory relative to the DR + previous day's discussion content
11:00 – 12:00	Name, Title, Function, Colleague 1	Functional office	Functional KPI reviews, or attendance at functional meeting
12:00 – 13:00	Lunch with Functional Colleague 1 and 2	Cafeteria or outside	General discussions
13:00- 14:00	Name, Title, Function A	Function office	Function Orientation 1
14:00- 15:00	Name, Title, Function B	Function office	Function Orientation 2
15:00- 16:00	Name, Title, Function C	Factory	Function Orientation 3
16:00- 17:00	Functional Manager	Function Leader office	First Day closing and discussion for the next days

Direct Labor

A direct labor worker is someone who actively is involved with the material conversion into finished goods. They are also considered non-exempt employees, as they are entitled to overtime pay. Here is an example of a First Day agenda for a direct labor worker. This agenda is a formal introduction to the company. Many companies do not have predefined schedules for direct labor, but this sets a precedent and standard.

Table 1. 3 Direct Labor - First day agenda

Time	Who	Location	Topic
08:00–08:30	HR Officer	HR office	HR Forms
08:30–09:00	HR Manager	HR Manager Office	Company introduction, Company profile, company handbook
09:00–09:30	Hiring Leader	Leader office	Job Description, introduction to colleagues and trainer
09:30–10:00	Environmental, Health, and Safety staff	Safety training area	Safety training, Personal Protective Equipment (PPE), and responsibilities
10:00–10:30	Supervisor or trainer	Functional office	Factory Walk
10:30 – 12:00	Supervisor or trainer	Factory floor	On-the-job training
12:00-12:30	Supervisor, co-workers	Cafeteria	Lunch
12:30-16:00	Supervisor, line leader, or trainer	Factory floor	On-the-job training
16:00-16:30	Supervisor, line leader, or trainer	Factory floor	First day closing and discussion for second day

Temporary Worker

The temporary worker should not be treated much differently from a direct labor worker, although there are differences. The temporary worker must meet with the local agency that hired them to understand their responsibilities. Once onsite, the temporary worker will go through the same First Day agenda as a direct labor employee (except the HR forms discussion would be eliminated as the employment agency would have handled this earlier). All other work activities, responsibilities and expectations are the same. Temporary workers may receive a modified company handbook that mainly focuses on the company rules. The temporary worker and direct labor worker should receive the same level of safety training and personal protective equipment. A temporary worker can be hired to perform direct labor activities as well as indirect labor activities.

The orientation program for Direct and Indirect labor employees should be the same except that the Direct Labor employee will spend more time in their newly hired area, while the Indirect Labor employee will have a more broadly based orientation. In addition, the Indirect Labor employee may also gain hands-on work experience in a variety of manufacturing operations throughout the factory, whereas the Direct Labor employee will stay in one area to build their skill level before moving onto other manufacturing areas.

Current Employee Orientation

If current employees did not go through an orientation program, then leadership should consider developing one. Every employee needs to be introduced to rules and expectations, as a minimum. The orientation program has to be defined in terms of all aspects of the company. Current employees should participate in the initial trials of any newly defined orientation program to look for potential issues and improvements before experimenting with New Hires. Also, at some frequency, current employees should audit the orientation program to ensure the materials are up to date and the conveyance of information is in-line with the company culture.

If management wants to make a cultural change, the leadership team must define the new culture with differences between the old and new culture and provide examples. Also, management needs to outwardly express their appreciation when new culture practices are observed. Just because leadership defines a new culture program does not mean that change will happen quickly. The change evolution will start with noticeable incremental changes, but there will always be a struggle or resistance by a few. Over time, momentum will gain for the new culture — especially when there is a level of trust and respect. The cultural change is accomplished by continuous practice and reinforcement. The management team has to be aligned and committed to the new culture.

On-the-Job Training Probationary Period

Typically, a New Hire's first full day of on-the-job training (OJT) occurs on the second day of employment, after orientation. OJT during the probationary period determines whether the New Hire is capable of performing the expected work, is reliable, conscientiousness, motivated to work, and meets any other company expectations or employee characteristics. Some companies have probationary periods are 30, 60, or 90 days. During the probationary period, if the New Hire violates any rules or is grossly unable to perform their expected work responsibilities, they usually are dismissed. If the New Hire is competent in the new work responsibilities, able to adapt to the culture and is achieving their goals, then they will pass the probationary period and become an employee. Other companies do not have probationary periods but do evaluate the New Hires on a frequent basis and terminate them if they are not able to perform the responsibilities as stated.

The OJT program must have a defined list of expectations and accomplishments that can be validated by an experienced certified employee or company trainer. OJT is for all levels of the organization and is on-going for advancement into greater roles and responsibilities. The New Hire should be evaluated on a daily basis. Feedback should be given in both "good" and "needs improvement" areas. This dialogue is helpful for both the New Hire and for assessing whether the New Hire is meeting the company's expectations.

Throughout the probationary period or on-boarding timing, the trainer or supervisor will provide feedback to the New Hire about whether they are meeting the basic job standards or not. In the case where the job standards are not being met, the New Hire may be dismissed. In some cases, the trainer or supervisor may provide additional time for the New Hire to master the basic job standards. When the employee is to be dismissed, Human Resources is alerted. The employee will have to sign the necessary security and dismissal releases prior to leaving the company. If the New Hire meets the basic standards, the next phase of OJT and work begins. Human Resources will retain all security and dismissal release records.

Chapter 2 - Shift Start and 5S

Shift Start

The start of the shift is an extremely important event — this is a critical time to efficiently transfer labor from one outgoing shift of workers to an incoming shift of workers. This needs to take place in a consistent, disciplined, and timely manner. In addition, workers should be on time and ready to start their days. Certain functional staff are required to coordinate their work schedule according to production, as some workers may have a staggered start times to provide support for both shifts. During the Orientation process, the New Hire will need to be on time every day. Indirect labor must also be ready to participate in their functional Daily Routine.

5S Daily Practice

5S methodology was originally developed in Japan and then was quickly adopted globally into manufacturing and various other industries. 5S is a daily structured practice that ensures the workspace is clean, clear of debris, organized, safe to work, and maintained. Most companies have some sort of documented and practiced shift or daily 5S routine for office and factory personnel. Companies with a documented and practiced 5S system are diligent about including scheduled audits to ensure compliance. Some companies include safety and spirit to make it a 7S program. The 5S components are:

Sort (Seiri)

- Identify and eliminate fixtures, tools, and other things not currently used for production.
- Prevent accumulation of any unnecessary items

Set in Order (Seiton)

- Organize fixtures, gages, and tools for quick and easy access
- Use shadow boards for easy identification and storage of necessary items

Shine (Seiso)

- Ensure work areas are clean and safe to work in
- Maintain a clean and safe area for the next shift

Standardize (Seiketsu)

- Define and visually display 5S standards
- Provide ways to identify and implement best 5S practices

Sustain (Shitsuke)

- Ensure 5S standards are being practiced every day in the office and factory
- Conduct 5S audits
- Provide on-going 5S training for all office and factory workers

A 5S program should have a training program for all New Hires including office staff. The training program can simply be a video. Ideally, there is an offline area for training that has a common factory manufacturing work-cell where the worker can perform some tasks to demonstrate proficiency in productivity, quality, and safety with a 5S understanding. The program should also include a 5S check sheet to ensure all items meet the 5S standard. Once the check sheet is completed, the worker can signal the trainer (team leader or supervisor) and indicate whether the area meets 5S. If not, the worker should write the concerns on the work area board and in the supervisor's note pad. Doing this in training helps all workers get accustomed to this type of daily practice.

Chapter 3 - Notepad

A conscientious employee keeps track of what's going on at all times by writing their observations, opinions, and ideas into a notepad. It's a good idea to provide the New Hire a notepad to start recording information. All indirect staff (especially supervisors) have to always carry notepads with them (either paper or electronic). They should bring them to meetings and walks on the factory floor. Some direct labor workers may also want to have a notepad or access to one. Initially, most people won't write things down because they don't know what to write down. Some guidance, coaching, and framework are needed to encourage this process.

Items to write down:

Concerns identified by anyone including employees, customer, suppliers, or contractors. Concerns may be related to product quality, productivity, cost, delivery, morale, safety, or any other situation that warrants a correction or improvement. The more details about it, the easier it is to understand the problem and then to correct it. The information to document expands on the 5Ws. Answer the 7Ws + 1H + Ps (What happened, Which, Where, When, Why, Who, What is happening now, How, and Photos?) using the following questions:

- What happened?
- Which material or part is affected?
- Where is the concern? Be specific as to the process operation location, machine, or location on the part.
- When did this happen? Include time, date, and shift.
- Why did this happen?
- Who identified the issue and who is working on the issue?
- What is happening now? Document troubleshooting activities, containment activities, escalation responses and reactions.
- How did this happen?
- Photos of the concern? photo of what is "good" and what is "no good"?

For every incident, there should be a folder or file, and it is important that reviews take place when the same incident or similar incident occurs. This helps to validate the effectiveness of the corrective action.

Things written in the notepad can include ideas on how to improve a situation in your functional area, or other areas such as customer service or administration. Ideas on innovation are also useful. These ideas can be refined over time, so sketching and capturing initial ideas is very important.

Label notepads with essential information on the inside and outside cover, such as:

- Notepad owner's name and telephone number.

- Other key contacts and telephone numbers (safety or medical, security, quality, maintenance, environmental, possibly a senior staff member or two at the facility).

- A template for the 7Ws +1H +Ps.

- Some Key Performance Indicators and their formulas (for ease of understanding and upgrading each other's knowledge). The KPI metrics might include: Safety, Health, Quality, Productivity, Downtime, number of personnel working that day and their locations, scrap, waste, etc.

Chapter 4 - Environmental, Health, and Safety Training (EHS)

EHS training is critical from the first day of employment. On the first day, the New Hire needs to understand the company's policies. Most importantly, the company should be sure the New Hire is trained in basic safety requirements and should be tested in the foundations, such as wearing personal protective equipment (PPE). To ensure the New Hire understands these requirements, they should be tested with some scenarios such as when and what to do when a safety concern is noticed. Safety practices and requirements vary for different industries, or even companies within the same industry.

Senior management should acknowledge that safety requirements are different for industries and locations, but basically these should cover how to put on and take off personal protective equipment (PPE), where PPE is supposed to be worn, and how employees should look when wearing it. Someone should demonstrate donning the PPE and how to store or discard items after usage. All New Hires also should be instructed in what to do in the event of a fire or severe weather incident. Also, the company needs to inform the New Hire about the protocol when traveling to and from work when there is a severe weather situation.

Safety guidelines and visual indicators need to show locations of safe areas and unsafe areas. Occupational Safety and Health Standards (OSHA) has a color code scheme that is used in most factories.

- Red – Fire protection equipment, dangerous areas, emergency stop buttons on equipment
- Orange – Signs and equipment that designate dangerous energized machines
- Yellow – Border markings, caution areas, light curtains on equipment, or specific hazards
- Green – Safe work areas, safety information, first aid

Other safety guidelines should identify safe working conditions for forklift drivers and employees that are nearby operating forklifts. For example, if you are driving a forklift and you approach other workers from behind, you must sound the horn and stop. The worker must acknowledge they have heard and see you before continuing on with driving the forklift. Or, if you are walking nearby someone operating a forklift, be sure to make eye contact with them. If the driver does not see you, do not walk behind the forklift and do not move closer to the forklift. Whenever you walk nearby someone operating a forklift, you should be a minimum of three feet away, or at least an arm's length distance from the forklift.

Safety also extends to being aware of your own situation and others nearby. Be aware of potential slip or trip hazards, or other potential safety issues. If you observe any potential slip or trip hazard, this needs to be taken care of immediately. Ensure a preventive action is in place so it doesn't repeat. Also, if someone is involved or observes any first aid incidents, they should be taken care of immediately and a preventive action should be put in place.

Safety is everyone's responsibility. Safety training must be offered regularly, such as weekly or monthly and must be conducted for New Hires. The company will retain all employee training records — especially for safety, as some safety programs need annual certification. For annual certification requirements, Human Resources, the employee, and the employee's functional manager should share a common training online calendar so training can be planned well in advance.

Chapter 5 - Supervisor and Leadership Training
On-The-Job-Training Plus Courses

Training is necessary to guarantee company processes, procedures, and guidelines are understood and practiced. This ensures the factory runs smoothly and performs as intended. There are different types of training that impacts all aspects of operations, including:

- Supervisor, management, and leadership development
- Compliance to laws, standards, policies, and procedures
- Technical for specific jobs and functions

Every employee needs to participate in their specific On-the-Job Training (OJT) supplemented by ongoing classroom style training, coaching and mentoring, and self-paced, self-directed, or instructor-led courses. The goal of classroom training can be to develop new skills, refresh current knowledge, or to obtain certifications or degrees. There are a variety of skills and competencies needed to be an effective manager and leader. According to John Kotter in "What Leaders Really Do", the difference between a manager and leader is:

Manager	Leader
- Planning and Budgeting	- Setting direction (vision and strategies)
- Organizing and Staffing	- Aligning people
- Controlling and Problem Solving	- Motivating people

In other words, the manager is responsible for the day-to-day business activities. Their job is to ensure the company's goals and objectives are accomplished using available resources, while the leader is responsible for long-term strategy and for motivating people to achieve the strategy. Management has the responsibility to identify and prioritize training for potential leaders and employees that are likely to advance to the next level, including successor candidates. Management will identify OJT opportunities and other coursework. The following are OJT and coursework topics to develop competencies in management and leadership:

Health, Wellness, Safety, and Environment
- Safety and Personal Protective Equipment (PPE)
- First Aid, Blood-borne Pathogens, and Cardiopulmonary Resuscitation (CPR)
- Hazardous Materials
- Machine Guarding
- Hazardous energy and fire extinguisher
- Slip and Fall Protection
- Sexual Harassment Prevention

- Substance Abuse Prevention
- Lock out / Tag out
- Forklift (material handling)
- Ergonomics (lifting and motions)
- Specific OSHA or state regulations
- Safety Data Sheets, including material safety
- Mental Health
- Health Care
- Diet and Exercise

Basics
- Active Listening, Communication
- Coaching and Mentoring
- Leadership, Motivation, and Team Development
- Employee Assessment and Training Needs Analysis
- Conflict Resolution
- Discipline and Documentation of Employee Issues
- Key Performance Indicator (KPI) Metrics
- Time Management
- Local Employment Legislation
- Labor Relations and Union Representation
- Ethics and Responsibilities
- Rules
- Customer Service

Computer and Business
- MRP, MRP II, or ERP Systems (Material Requirements Planning, Manufacturing Resource Planning, or Enterprise Resource Planning)
- Microsoft Office (Word, Excel, and PowerPoint)
- Making and giving presentations
- Basic Math, Basic Financials, Business case development

Manufacturing Essentials
- Basics of reading engineering drawings
- Company process certifications: cutting, extruding, forming, forging, stamping, painting, plating, soldering, stamping, welding, assembly, etc.

- Product Technology
- 7 Basic Quality Tools
- Root Cause Analysis, Corrective and Preventive Action (RCCA)
- Industrial Engineering practices or Value Analysis (VA)
- 5S
- Layered Process Audits (LPA)
- Value Stream Mapping (VSM)
- Process Failure Modes and Effects Analysis (Process FMEA), and Reverse PFMEA
- Quality Control Plan
- Lean and Six Sigma
- Quality Systems, ISO9000, IATF 16949, AS9100, and specific customer requirements

Training Content Review

The course list and training content should be reviewed and edited at least once a year. The review should consist of validating the training content and value, training service provider (internal/external), training schedule and frequency, list of employees to be trained, priorities for training, budget for each training session, and overall total training budget for supervisors. It is the responsibility of both management and employees to ensure OJT and training programs are identified, budgeted, planned, and effectively conducted. Defining a monthly training program is a good practice. The human resources function can help to identify and coordinate various training programs as well as to post or communicate upcoming training programs. In addition, the human resources function can keep track of the individual training records and help identify individuals needing various training, especially when training needs to be refreshed or certifications expire.

Being involved in OJT and attending coursework in the above training topics does not necessarily mean career advancement as a supervisor, manager, or leader. Other requirements for promotion include high performance capabilities, certain personality characteristics and behaviors, and business need for an advancement.

Supervisor Characteristics

How do you determine an effective supervisor? Is it by number of years working as a supervisor at the same position in the same area of the same factory, or is it by experience in different areas and positions within the factory, or is it based upon work experiences in different companies and different positions? Or, is it by evaluating the Key Performance Indicators for their responsible area for a specific time period, combined with the training levels of the people they supervise? Do you combine this with how they have developed themselves personally and professionally by accepting new projects and new challenges, and taking college level professional coursework? Also, is the person recognized among the direct labor and among the indirect staff as a key leader with certain exhibited characteristics and behaviors? The types of characteristics and behaviors of an effective supervisor or leader are:

- Listens well, comprehends issues, prioritizes, and verbalizes well
- Respectful, considerate, honest, ethical, non-political, trustworthy — i.e., a role model and mentor
- People-oriented, coaching style, timely, discipline-minded, mature, controlled ego
- Approachable, available, actively contacting people
- Motivated, punctual, diligent, accountable, positive attitude
- Strong work ethic
- Key Performance Indicator metric and time-management oriented
- Problem-solver, hands-on, improvement-oriented, flexible and open-minded
- Self-development oriented, teachable, team- and skill-builder, teacher, and organizer
- Technical-, operations-, data-driven; quantitative aptitude
- Seeks support and feedback, monitors workforce and operations' activities

Identifying and promoting an internal candidate for a supervisor position sometimes works better than recruiting a supervisor from outside the company. Developing direct labor into team leaders and then promoting them into being supervisors takes considerable support, leadership commitment, and most importantly takes a lot of time. In addition, management may also identify current supervisors or managers as a mentor for the potential supervisor and slowly give the potential supervisor additional responsibilities in a structured way. If one supervisor leaves the company, has a successor been developed? Is there a trainer or other team leader who can assume some or all the responsibilities? What other contingency plans needs to be executed during this interim period, such as an organization change or recruiting search? If you aim to be a supervisor or manager, aim to be trained and ready to step up if a leader should leave the company.

Leadership Development – Structure

Many companies have yet to realize the high value of focusing their management and leadership development programs to foster better supervisors. Instead, many company leadership development programs are aimed at specific cohorts of the organization, such as new college graduates, or staff who want to become functional managers, or plant managers who want to become directors. Clearly, there is a lot of value to developing the next-level leadership team. Addressing development needs of the direct labor team leaders and supervisors increases the potential to achieve greater value.

Management must define a structure for developing direct labor, team leaders, supervisors, and staff. The structure needs to define ways to develop employees into becoming leaders.

The structure should consider:

- How formal, semi-formal, or informal is the process
- Identification of the types of training, timing, and costs
- Budget, resources required, and Key Performance Indicators (KPIs)
- Different levels supporting various levels of the organization, including direct and indirect labor, supervisors, and managers
- Candidate selection committee personnel identification
- Candidate selection criteria
- Evaluation method and identification of possible candidates (short list or long and varied)
- Open discussions with candidates
- Management feedback to potential candidates
- On-the-Job Training – objectives, assignment, project, timing, personal accomplishments
- Candidate acknowledgement, acceptance, and commitment
- Candidate prioritization, training plan, and personal professional development roadmap, including possible mentor identification
- Mentoring or coaching structure, expectations, list of mentor and student participant matrix versus objectives, projects, and KPIs
- An environment that encourages and supports individuals wanting to gain more autonomy, be a part of different ad hoc teams, innovate, have job satisfaction, and develop an evolving company

Professional Development

All indirect labor employees and certain direct labor employees that want to excel should know their personal professional development needs for the year, as well as their functional Key Performance Indicators, their own personal KPIs, projects, plans, and expected value contributions. Development needs are formally discussed during annual assessments and informally throughout the year as necessary.

Indirect labor and management should have some defined projects that they are personally responsible to complete, either as a lead or participant. Developing competence is a challenge — some people are eager and want to be developed, while others are content with their current positions and would be satisfied with staying in the same role for years. Those who are eager to learn and take on challenges will be more promotable. For the not-so-eager group, the company should define its culture and programs not to accept mediocrity, or define an attrition program to slowly remove non-performers. More on attrition programs and non-performers is discussed in the section called People in Chapter 32 People. Keep in mind that just because someone is happy where they are, they can still be productive, effective, and valuable to the team and company. Not everyone can or should be a leader. But everyone can participate on a project.

Projects – Staff can take responsibility as a leader of a project or participate as a team member. In many cases, the staff will be on several different projects and may assume different roles, depending upon the maturity and status of the project. For any specific project, there should only be one leader. Leadership attributes should be practiced by the project members. Some staff may be reluctant to lead due to limited work experience, their confidence level, or personality characteristics, so providing encouragement and support is essential. Projects can be as simple as ensuring the office areas are cleaned and straightened every day to more complex ones, such as launching a new product line. Newly assigned projects will need regular follow-ups, even daily, while the work of more experienced staff can be reviewed on a weekly basis. All projects should be reviewed on at least a weekly basis against the project plan, budget, open issues, risks, and upcoming resource needs.

Skills – Management should know the skills that are needed for all of their subordinates. Also, management needs to know the organizational capabilities needed to achieve certain objectives. Based upon this information and the interests of the staff, a skills-based learning program can be developed. This skill development training program topic should be discussed during annual reviews or at the start of a new project. Most importantly, skills are developed and refined through OJT with support by managers, mentors, and coaches.

System Improvements – Various systems improvement activities can include reviewing and updating current functional practices, defining or fine-tuning part of a value stream, business process flow, or an activity within a specific function or department. A system improvement can have a very small scope, such as refining the way an automated program is shown on a laptop screen or mobile device display, or as large as an integrating business practices between the customers, business, and suppliers. System improvements should be an expectation for each functional area with a derived financial or tangible benefit and value.

Chapter 6 - Key Performance Indicator (KPI)
What is a KPI?

A Key Performance Indicator, or KPI, is a tool to help manage and develop objectives and activities. One common saying is that if you can measure it, you can manage it. The general manager should define the main KPIs that drive the business and all employees should understand and prioritize their work to meet or exceed these main KPIs. The management team will cascade these main KPIs into their functional area and develop more specific subsets of these KPIs. All employees need to understand the main KPIs and how these relate to making money for the business. Once the employees know this information, they can personally contribute their efforts. The desired result is for the company to sustain itself as a viable business and improve. So, it is important to introduce KPIs during the New Hire's Orientation.

KPIs are used for measuring the current status or effectiveness of a variety of business objectives and activities, such as safety, quality, cost, delivery, morale, sales, engineering, and many others, including project management.

KPIs are charted over time per hour, per shift, per day, per week, per month, etc., and are the basis for determining unfavorable or favorable trends. In addition, KPIs can be tracked using statistical process control charts and can be evaluated against a budget, plan, standard, or with another metric such as percent of sales. KPIs can be identified by function, work locations within a factory, specific product types, etc. Examples of KPIs are:

Safety

- OSHA recordable incident rate
- Lost time case rate
- Safety training hours
- Safety training certification readiness

Reliability

- Warranty cost as a percentage of sales, months in service, miles/kilometers, or hours of operation
- Service cost as a percentage of sales
- Service time per call
- Customer quantity returned by category (did not work as expected, broken)

Operations

- Overall Equipment Effectiveness (OEE) – a composite metric of Quality, machine uptime, and labor efficiency, see Chapter 29 for more information

- Availability – Percentage of production run time to total planned production time
- Performance - Throughput rate or process rate expressed as a percentage
- Quality - Percentage of the good product produced versus total number of product produced (the same as First Pass Yield)
- Labor Productivity – number of parts produced per planned number of parts or time period
- Mean Time to Repair (MTTR), Mean Time Between Failures (MTBF)
- Skilled Labor Matrix – employee skill-level percent versus total number of employees
- Direct labor headcount number versus total headcount or indirect-to-direct ratio

Morale

- Absenteeism or retention rate
- Job Satisfaction survey
- Engagement and Motivation survey
- Idea generation and implementation savings or profitability improvement
- Focus group participation %
- 90 Day Challenge participation %
- Incentives (bonus % year-on-year)

Launch

- Number of actions completed per planned items
- Phase completion rate per overall plan
- Man-hours per plan
- Delivery performance
- Cost performance

Supplier Quality

- Defective parts per million (dPPM), or defective parts per billion (dPPB)
- Percentage of defects received per total number of parts received for direct materials
- Rework and other efforts to avoid in-house manufacturing line stop

Supplier Delivery

- Direct material received on-time against total materials received
- Indirect material received on-time against total materials received
- Subcontracting services started on-time or completed on-time against plan

Cost or Profit

- Conversion cost as a percentage of sales, per part, per pound, etc.
- Labor or variable overhead cost as a percent of sales
- Warehousing cost as a percentage of sales
- Logistics cost as a percentage of sales
- Expense line items as a percentage of sales, per part, per weight, or other unit
- Profit as a percentage of sales, by group, product line, location, etc.
- Accounts payable, accounts receivable
- Cash flow and cash cycle
- Benefits, insurance costs as a percentage of sales, etc.
- Advertising costs as a percentage of sales
- Profit per employee, gross margin per product/per employee

Purchasing

- Material cost as a percentage of sales
- Productivity percentage by quarter, by year
- Material cost and/or Productivity as a percentage of total procurement, or by commodity
- Tooling costs as a percent of sales, by commodity, by project

Inventory

- Inventory turns
- Inventory days on hand
- Inventory type, amount, and percentage of total inventory – raw, work in-progress, finished goods, and material obsolescence
- Inventory aging: < 30, 60, 90, >120 days

Sales

- Number of quotes submitted

- New business awards (percentage of wins against number of quotes submitted)
- Product or commodity market sales
- Total sales: per employee product, per location
- Forecast accuracy: per month, per month+ 1 month, per month +2 months

Engineering

- Number of change notices per month and accumulation over project life
- Number of (new or percentage of standard part usage) items per product
- Number of development projects on-schedule, on-budget, test on-schedule per product and/or project
- Engineering costs per product or project versus budget

Customer Quality

- Defective parts per million (dPPM), parts per billion (dPPM), or incidents per product/project
- Tracking of effective corrective action implementation performance
- Number of customer concerns per month, by project, location, etc.
- Cost of nonconformance

Customer quality can be measured in different ways, such as in defective parts per million (dPPM), defective parts per billion (dPPB), percentage defective, or number of nonconformance tickets (NCTs) monthly for each customer. If there are many customers and products, the dPPM or dPPB, percentage defective or NCTs can be compared by product versus product, customer versus customer, region by region or a combination thereof.

dPPM is calculated as follows:

- dPPM = Number of Defective Materials/Total Number of Materials Shipped $\times$ 1 million
- dPPB = Number of Defective Materials/Total Number of Materials Shipped $\times$ 1 billion

NCT calculation is the total number of customer NCTs or corrective action requests received during each month.

Calculation of percentage defective is similar to that of dPPM and dPPB:

- Percentage Defective = Number of Defective Materials/Total Number of Materials Shipped $\times$ 100%

To calculate the dPPM, dPPB, or percentage defective for more than one product or customer, divide the sum of all the rejected quantities by the sum of all the materials shipped and multiply by 1 million or 1 billion respectively. Individual dPPM or dPPB should always be looked at first, followed by any summary for comparisons. This is because the summary can mask a product with a high dPPM or dPPB especially if other products have no defects with very high volumes.

The customer quality metrics should be reviewed daily during the operational Daily Routine meetings to communicate information and updates, especially for the start of the next shift. See "Daily Routine" in Chapter 45 for details.

There are some ways in which the dPPM or dPPB, and percentage defective are not true numbers. In some cases, the suppliers and customers have a good working relationship where as soon as the customer identifies a defective part, the supplier replaces it immediately with a good part. This sort of customer quality management is quite common in a variety of industries and regions. Basically, the customer accepts swapping of defective parts for good parts, as well as negotiations between supplier and customer, to ensure an NCT is not issued and the resulting scorecard shows a better score than would have been given for what actually occurred. The customer may be willing to accept such a compromise because of the quick response from the supplier. See quick-response quality control (QRQC) in Chapter 27. However, over the long term, this should be a rare circumstance. If this occurs, an internal root cause investigation and corrective action should be performed. For calculation of the "real" dPPM or dPPB, all NCT's have to be taken, not only those documented by customer. This is to ensure the company gets the full picture of its performance.

At the end of every month, customers may release their supplier scorecards. These reports may consist of the metrics above, plus warranty, pricing, audit status, corrective action status and more. The staff member from quality assurance should meet with the customer at least monthly and reconcile the numbers, so the same report metrics are accepted by both the customer and the supplier.

Customer Fulfillment
- On-time to customer request
- On-time to demand

One of the key customer metrics is customer on-time delivery or customer fulfillment rate. This metric can be defined in slightly different ways, but generally speaking, the metric is a continual performance metric in which every shipment counts and missing a delivery date (too early or too late) or making an incorrect shipment is a potential problem for the customer and may warrant a customer complaint.

In other words, every shipment made to every customer is measured, and the metric should be analyzed — especially if a delivery is not on time — to make corrections or improvements. Establishing a reliable logistics system is fundamental to having a consistent customer on-time delivery metric, even though the metric may not be satisfactory to the customer. This metric can be analyzed daily, monthly or weekly, or by specific customer, product or region. Typically, the metric is measured individually for each customer as a percentage of customer orders delivered on time, compared with the total number of orders received; for each customer as a percentage of the total number of parts received on time, compared with the total number of parts shipped; or the total number of line items shipped on time, compared with the total number of line items shipped over a specific period.

The "on-time" portion of the metric may be different for each customer, so reviewing each customer contract is essential to understanding the on-time delivery window. A delivery window is a range of time during which a shipment accepted by the customer is considered to be on time. If a delivery is not received by the customer within that specific time, the delivery is not on-time. Some customers can accept several days early and several days late, whereas other customers are much stricter regarding their receipts, such as certain automotive companies — some customers may require that parts be received at a particular hour of a certain day and placed within the delivery truck at a specific location and orientation, and may provide only a two-hour window for fulfillment of the order. It is important that your factory personnel generally know the manufacturing process priority, and team leaders and supervisors should know and continually meet the production takt, or at least focus on due date and timing of production planning work. Takt is the maximum amount of time at each operation step in which a product needs to be produced that equals the customer demand rate. Takt is defined with calculations and an example in Chapter 22.

Improving Customer Fulfillment
There are 8 steps for improving customer fulfillment:
1. Understand each customer's delivery expectations
2. Understand the customer's order planning process
3. Analyze customer delivery expectations versus past performance
4. Define the customer order acceptance criteria or rules, process, people and their responsibilities, and KPIs
5. Ensure proper implementation of the previous steps, include; on-going Layered Process Audits and Internal Audits
6. Have on-going monthly reviews of customer scorecards, KPIs, issues, corrective and preventive actions
7. Conduct a benchmark study at least once a year to analyze and update the value stream map and to confirm average lead times
8. Review all the steps above and modify them for use by your suppliers

The *first* step in improving the customer fulfillment metric is to understand customer delivery expectations for each product in the customer agreement (contract), including spare parts within the warranty service agreement. There may be other agreements and requirements as well, such as a project timing schedule or quality requirements, and various terms and conditions within each agreement. A matrix can be made for each customer, especially when there are multiple customers and products. This information then should be entered into an ERP system, and any changes to this information should be made through proper channels.

The *second* step is to understand the customer order planning process, release information content, forecast information, key customer contacts for purchasing, logistics, quality and production scheduling. This information may not be found in any agreement, and each customer or customer location may have different methods and surely will have different contact personnel. Knowing these contacts and building relationships will be of great help when urgent issues or problems arise.

The *third* step is to analyze these two steps versus the past performance and discuss how best to improve; information and communications. Manufacturing and logistics are 24/7, especially with a global customer base. A mix of ERP, spreadsheets, communication applications for phone text alerts or email alerts, desktop computer status reporting, and/or visual board presentation materials is needed. Also, ways to inform production about new products and new customers need to be developed, managed and controlled.

The *fourth* step is to define the customer order acceptance criteria or rules, process, people and their responsibilities, and KPIs. This step can be done internally in a workshop. A matrix of this information can be defined. Workshop attendees are to be from various functions, such as sales, supply chain, quality, manufacturing engineering, production, purchasing, IT, finance, product engineering and human resources. The workshop output details need to be updated in the ERP system and may need to use a product and process change notice, see Chapter 28 Change Management.

Once the workshop is completed and the process and KPIs are defined, all the operation staff should be trained, as well as any support staff such as warehouse or logistics. Topics should include the Daily Routine of the various functions, management escalation details and special circumstances. In all the situations in the list below, the customer(s) has to be contacted when the shipment is not going to be on time, to apologize, negotiate either different quantities or different timing, offer a similar product in stock, offer more of the product at a later date, arrange returning or disposing of unwanted materials, or even offer a coupon or discount for future orders. Rules and criteria regarding the circumstance including an apology and negotiations should be clearly stated in a standard operating procedure. The operating procedure must be clear as who is responsible for contacting and negotiating with the customer, timing, reaction, and follow-up activities.

Special circumstances include:

- Customer product requests not made within the defined or agreed-on lead time or not within the available capacity, such as an urgent requirement
- Long-term order changes due to weather or other forces of nature that affect supplier shipments, severe unplanned manufacturing downtime, or labor shortage
- Short-term order changes such as short shipments, where one line item or product quantity cannot be fulfilled for a specific order
- Over shipment – sending too much of one or more products
- Wrong shipment – sending something completely different from what the customer ordered, such as the wrong size package or a different package (e.g., the customer wants material in a 20-kilogram plastic bag, but it arrives in a 20-kilogram cardboard can); if the packaging is incorrect, the shipment is wrong
- Back-order log management
- Customer rejection of a shipment because the delivery is too early
- Packaging or goods damaged in transit to the customer, or damaged packaging or goods received by the customer

The *fifth* step is to ensure proper implementation of the previous steps, including having regular, layered process audits and internal audits, see Chapter 26. In addition, when KPIs are not met, the reactions, timing, corrective actions and preventive actions should be established so issues do not recur.

The *sixth* step is to have regular monthly reviews of customer scorecards, KPIs, issues, corrective and preventive actions, and to consider ways in which things can be done better within the documented process, including use of alternative logistics companies to improve the reliability of shipments. There may be two different reviews: one with the customer and one internally with a cross-functional team.

The customer reviews may include supply chain and quality, while the internal reviews would include a broader scope of functions. Many customers use some sort of monthly or quarterly scorecard to evaluate suppliers to maintain current business or be able to offer the opportunity to bid on new business. Thus, frequent reviews with customers ensure alignment and agreement, confirm that corrective actions are effective, and improve customer-supplier relationships. Being the worst supplier may cause the customer to be in your factory often, assessing and conducting meetings daily and having frequent meetings with senior customer management.

The *seventh* step is to conduct a benchmark study at least once a year to analyze and update the value stream map and to confirm average lead times. In addition, whenever a supply chain or manufacturing improvement affects lead-time or inventory stocks, that information must be updated in the ERP system.

The *eighth* step is to review all the steps above and modify them for use by your suppliers. The same requirements, practices, templates and meetings, as well as similar KPIs, should be implemented. Purchasing or supply chain should take the lead to define the process and requirements for suppliers. These steps can be rolled out to key direct material suppliers first, then other direct materials, then to indirect material suppliers. (Most manufacturing companies do not measure on-time delivery performance of indirect material suppliers.)

Many companies use quarterly sales, inventory, operations, planning and purchasing (SIOPP) or sales, inventory, operations, planning (SIOP) meeting results and update the ERP system accordingly. Participants at these SIOPP meetings review various functional improvements made over the past quarter, assess status of current productivity improvements, and discuss plans for improvements for the next quarter and beyond. Having specific SIOPP review meetings is important to systemically improve the on-time customer delivery metric.

Defining a KPI

The KPI (numerator and denominator) has to be clearly defined so accurate and timely data can be collected and analyzed. When defining a KPI, the following questions are helpful:

- What is the definition of the metric?
- What information can be derived for determining the status?
- What is the importance of the metric? (Why use the metric?)
- When is the metric created and what is the frequency for updating?
- Where does the numerator and denominator data come from?
- How do you validate the numerator and denominator data that is being captured (timing, comprehensive, accurate, repeatable acquisition)?
- Who collects the data, analyzes the data, and reports this metric?
- Where is this metric posted?
- Who will write the KPI instruction for use?
- Who will provide training to other users?
- Who will follow up or is accountable in case there are problems with the usage of the KPI?
- Who will determine or authorize that this is the correct metric?
- Most importantly, who will use this metric for improving the current status?

KPI Dashboard

A KPI Dashboard is a compilation of several KPIs that are displayed or distributed via text or email. A KPI dashboard can be paper-based, poster board, whiteboard, electronic with a digital display, or in a panel screen display so multiple people can view the real-time display at one time. A KPI Dashboard should be posted an area where people can influence and improve the KPIs.

The KPI Dashboard can be updated at any frequency such as every second or minute, but the minimum is to update it on a monthly basis. Most companies like to have hourly, shift, daily, and monthly dashboards in a variety of locations.

Hourly, daily, weekly, and/or monthly reviews should be conducted with relevant team members. For example, the previous evening's operation KPIs should be reviewed first thing in the morning with the operations team, including the outgoing supervisor. A monthly review should be conducted with the senior management team together with the individual departments or functions. They will review their current status and determine if any specific actions need to be taken to improve the KPI for the following month.

Chapter 7 - Financial Acumen

Business leaders must have a working knowledge of Finance and staff members that want to grow into leadership roles must learn about finance. At a minimum, the finance function has the responsibility to prepare the following reports — typically within a few days after the month ends:

- Income (Profit and Loss statement)
- Balance Sheet
- Cash Flow Statement

An income statement shows the sales or revenue, expenses, and profit. The balance sheet shows the assets, liabilities, and owner's equity. The cash flow statement shows a summary of the company's cash inflows and outflows via operating, investing, and financing activities. On a monthly basis, senior management reviews the financial statements to determine the company's viability and performance, how well the management team is employing its resources, and determines actions for improvement. Management does this by analyzing trends, percentages, ratios, variances, and any significant impacts line-by-line. Finance may also show several months or year-on-year data as well.

Local or online accounting classes like principles of accounting can be taken to learn the basic accounting concepts, steps of the accounting cycle, preparation of financial statements, and to develop understanding of various ratios. Managerial accounting teaches product costing, including the accumulated costs through production, budgeting, planning, forecasting, contribution margin analysis, break even analysis, and cost constraint analysis. Financial accounting helps senior management to learn and present managerial accounting details to investors or others outside the company.

Income Statement

The following shows an example of a monthly income statement for a manufacturing company. The top part of the statement shows the time frame (such as a specific month and year, or for a total year). The next section is for revenue or sales. Revenue is calculated by multiplying the price per unit and the quantity sold. If there are any additional sales, they would be summarized and added. If there are any discounts or returns, they would be summarized and subtracted to obtain a total net revenue line item. If there are multiple products and prices, these items will be summarized and a total revenue amount is shown. The next section shows the cost of goods sold. The cost of goods sold is composed of three main parts:

- Direct Materials
- Direct Labor
- Variable Overhead

Income Statement (Thousands $)		Month - XX
Revenue		**6271**
Cost of Goods Sold:		
Direct Material	1946	
Direct Labor	1102	
Variable Overhead	624	
Total Cost of Goods Sold		3672
Gross Profit		**2599**
Depreciation and Amortization	360	
Fixed Operating Expenses	1060	
Total Operating Expenses		1420
Operating Income		**1179**
Income tax		389
Net Profit		**790**

Figure 1. 1 Income Statement

Direct Material – Raw materials, components, and supplies consumed in the manufacture of a finished product. A finished product will have a list of these items and their associated quantities to make one unit of the finished product. This list is called the Bill of Material.

Direct Material as a percent of sales = Direct Material / Revenue x 100%

Example: $1,946 / $6,271 = 31%

Direct Labor – Employees or temporary contract workers involved in the transformation of raw materials into a finished product. The costs include regular hours, overtime hours, shift differentials, payroll taxes, and any related benefit costs.

Direct Labor as a percent of sales = Direct Labor / Revenue x 100%

Example: $1,102 / $6,271 = 17.6%

Variable Overhead – Manufacturing costs other than labor that vary with the production output. These costs can be packaging, utilities, production supplies, consumable tooling, logistics, and material handling.

Variable Overhead as percent of sales = Variable Overhead / Revenue x 100%
Example: $624 / $6,271 = 10%

Gross Profit – Revenue less the cost of goods sold. Gross profit is also called gross income or gross margin. Gross profit is earned from the core of the operating business. Gross Profit is a measure of management's effectiveness, as the managers have direct control over direct operating expenses and manufacturing capabilities and efficiencies.

Gross Profit Margin = Gross Profit / Revenue x 100%

Example: $2,599 / $6,271 = 41.4%

Depreciation and Amortization – An accounting method to prorate assets over their useful life. Depreciation is for tangible assets such as buildings and equipment. Amortization is for intangible assets such as patents. Depreciation and amortization are not expressed as a percent of sales as they remain relatively stable month to month.

Fixed Operating Expenses – Business costs that do not vary with the production output. This is also called fixed overhead. These costs can be related to equipment, tooling, leases, salaries, insurance, property taxes, salaried benefits, office expenses, salaried payroll taxes, administrative salaries and benefits, normal scrap, and other indirect staff costs such as quality staff salaries and benefits. Fixed Operating expenses are not represented as a percent of sales value as they remain relatively stable month to month.

Operating Income – Measure of profitability for a company. It is also referred to as earnings before interest and taxes (EBIT).

Operating Income Margin = Operating Income / Revenue x 100%

Example: $1,179 / $6,271 = 18.8%

Net Profit – Operating income less any extraordinary charges and income tax. Net Profit is also known as the bottom line or net income.

Net Profit Margin % = Net Profit / Revenue x 100%

Example: $790 / $6,271 = 12.6%

The income statement line item ratio percentages and/or amounts can be analyzed and plotted on a monthly chart to show whether they are increasing, decreasing, or remaining relatively the same. Significant changes would need to be further investigated. Also, percent changes from month to month can be charted. The formula compares as a percentage change the previous time frame to the current time frame.

Percentage change = [(previous month's value – current month's value) / previous month's value] x 100%

Income Statement Ratio

The following illustration shows income statement ratios month-by-month for the current year. Revenue has declined marginally in the first two months compared with the last months of the previous year, and ended with a slight overall quarterly improvement. Operating profit % change shows an unfavorable significant change in the first two months with a strong significant rebound recovery. Net profit % change shows significant favorable change starting the year and maintaining a strong favorable growth for the remaining quarters.

Income Statement % changes	Months			
	1	2	3	4
Revenue % change	-1.5%	-3.2%	5.8%	2.4%
Operating Profit % change	-15.9%	-23.6%	19.0%	9.3%
Net Profit % change	54.8%	15.7%	14.3%	14.5%

Figure 1. 2 Income Statement Ratio

Analyzing ratios, trends, and significant changes at the income statement level may make it difficult to understand the specific primary cause due to market changes, overall company structure changes, ability to sell the product, product availability, number of products produced at the company, each product's list of the bill of materials costs, product manufacturing location economics, labor or production scheduling impact, etc. One way to examine the income statement in more depth is using a financial variance analysis. Financial Variance Analysis is explained in Chapter 31.

Balance Sheet

The following figure shows a balance sheet of a manufacturing company. The balance sheet shows: Assets = Liabilities + Total Shareholder Equity

Assets are cash, receivables, inventories, properties, plant, equipment, and various other short- and long-term assets. Liabilities are accounts payable, accrued expenses, long-term debt, deferred taxes, and other short- and long-term debt. Equity is minority interest, preferred stock, and common equity.

Balance Sheet (Thousands $)	Month - XX
Current Assets	
Cash	2,587
Short Term Investments	120
Receivables	1,293
Inventories	1,386
Other Current Assests	128
Total Current Assets	5,514
Property, Plant and Equipment	2,568
Goodwill	3,518
Intangible Assets	3,381
Other Assets	96
Deferred Long Term Asset Charges	102
Total Assets	15,179
Current Liabilities	
Accounts Payable	1,029
Other Current Liabilities	1,079
Total Current Liabilities	2,108
Long Term Debt	3,694
Other Liabilities	613
Deferred Long Term Liability Charges	204
Total Liabilities	6,619
Stockholder's Equity	-
Common Stock	1
Preferred Stock	-
Retained Earnings	5,842
Capital Surplus	2,997
Other Stockholder Equity	(280)
Total Stockholder Equity	8,560

Figure 1. 3 Balance Sheet

Balance Sheet Ratio

Analyzing the balance sheet highlights the financial condition of the company. The balance sheet shows the amount of cash, cash equivalents, and assets owned. It also shows the amount of debt or liabilities owed. There are several ratios that help to understand the financial condition of the company such as:

Working capital – A measure of company's ability to pay its current liabilities with its current assets. Usually, a larger amount of working capital is better.

Working capital = current assets - current liabilities

Example: $5,514,000 - $2,108,000 = $3,406,000

Current ratio – Also called working capital ratio. Determines the ability to pay debt. It is a ratio that calculates the ability to pay off current liabilities with current assets. Current ratio = current assets / current liabilities

Example: $5,514 / $2,108 = 2.6.

Inventory turnover = cost of goods sold / average inventory. Average inventory is the beginning inventory plus ending inventory divided by 2. The example only shows ending inventory.

Example: $3,672 / $1,386 = 2.6

Number of days' sales in inventory = ending inventory balance divided by average daily cost of goods sold (COGS).

Average daily COGS = total COGS / number of days in the time period

Example: $1,386 / ($3,672 / 30) = 11.3

Inventory Days or Days in Inventory – A ratio that measures the average number of days the company holds its inventory before being sold.

Inventory Days = number of days during time period / Inventory Turnover

Example: 30 / 2.6 = 11.5

Days Sales Outstanding – Measures the effectiveness of collecting cash from customers.

Days Sales Outstanding = accounts receivable / average sales per day for the time period

Example: $1,293 / ($6,271 / 30) = 6.2

Each customer's contract payment terms need to be checked against the accounts receivable and cash received each month. This determines how well accounts receivable are being managed. An increasing ratio, a ratio greater than the contract payment term, or ratio greater than competitor's average shows either that customers have credit problems or that the company is weak in collecting cash from customers or is unable to.

Illustration – Balance Sheet Ratio

The following illustration shows a comparison between the company and its competitors from the previous year's annual reports. The company has a very strong liquidity ratio—nearly twice the amount of its competitors. However, the company is negatively impacted by a slightly lower inventory turnover and slightly higher number of days' sales in inventory (except for competitor D). The biggest advantage is the Days Sale Outstanding, which is on average 12 days lower than its competitors. This is an advantage unless it is hampering sales due to its credit policy being more rigorous compared to its competitors.

Ratio	Company	Competitors			
		A	B	C	D
Current Ratio	4.5	2.8	1.3	2.5	2
Inventory Turnover	3.8	5.4	5.9	5.0	2.7
# of days' sales in inventory	7.8	5.6	5.1	5.9	11.4
Inventory Days	47	67	71	73	137
Days Sale Outstanding	48	55	66	59	61

Figure 1. 4 Balance Sheet Ratio

Illustration – Days Sales Outstanding

The following illustration shows the company's Days Sales Outstanding for several customers with their payment terms, average customer payment, average minus term, and each month's calculation. All of the customers are paying marginally late, except for customer B paying significantly late each month. This can be attributable to poor customer relationship management, market practices, legacy situations, or a combination. Senior management must understand each customer's circumstances and take action. The weakness of this metric is that it does not show the amount of cash overdue. Finance can show the impact for each customer.

Customer	Average	Term	Avg - Term	Month			
				1	2	3	4
A	35	30	5	36	35	36	34
B	46	30	16	46	47	47	46
C	63	60	3	64	62	64	63
D	48	45	3	48	51	46	48
Others Avg	67	60	7	67	66	66	67

Figure 1. 5 Days Sales Outstanding

Cash Flow Statement

The following figure shows a cash flow statement. A cash flow statement consists of operating, investing, and financing activities. The operating section shows the inflow and outflow of cash from its primary activity of selling a product and services. The investing section shows cash spent or received from buying or selling assets such as plant and equipment. The financing section shows the cash inflow or outflow from gains or losses from investments in the financial market including proceeds from equity offerings or payments made on bonds or bank debt.

Cash Flow Statement (Thousands $)	Month - XX
Net Income	**788**
Operating Activities	
Depreciation	154
Adjustments to Net Income	78
Changes in Accounts Receivable	(7)
Changes in Liabilities	110
Changes in Inventories	(157)
Changes in Other Activities	(5)
Total Cash Flow from Operating Activities	**533**
Investing Activities	
Capital Expenditures	(158)
Investments	(2)
Other cash flows from investing	(15)
Total Cash Flow from Investing	**(175)**
Financing Activiies	
Dividends Paid	(78)
Sale Purchase of Stock	10
Net Borrowings	(252)
Other cash flow from investing	-
Total Cash Flow from Financing	**(320)**
Effect of Exchange Rate Changes	42
Change in Cash and Cash Equivalents	**80**

Figure 1. 6 Cash Flow Statement

Analyzing the cash flow statement shows how well the company is generating cash and using its cash. The cash flow statement shows the inflow and outflow of cash for that period and tracks movement of cash. For example, when selling a product, the customer may not make an immediate cash payment. Depending upon the customer payment terms, cash may be received sometime in the following months. Alternatively, making an insurance payment this month shows a cash outflow, but over the next few months there is no outflow of cash for insurance. An insurance premium typically is paid for months in advance. Any change to the income statement affects the cash flow statement. The first line on the cash flow statement is the net income (from the income statement).

Cash Flow Ratio

Cash flow ratios show liquidity, solvency, and business viability:

Operating Cash Flow ratio – Measures the ability to generate cash to pay off short-term debt. Having an operating cash flow ratio less than 100% indicates the company is not generating enough cash to pay off its short-term debt.

Operating cash flow ratio = cash flow from operations / current liabilities x 100%

Cash flow margin – Measures the ability to convert sales into cash. Cash is king and companies need to pay expenses, make purchases, and service debt. The higher the percentage, the more cash is available from sales. A negative ratio shows the company needs to borrow money or raise money from investors to keep the company operating.

Cash flow margin ratio = cash flow from operating cash flows / net sales x 100%

Illustration – Cash Flow Ratio competitor comparison

The following illustration shows a comparison between the company and its competitors. The company has a significantly weaker ability to generate cash from its sales than its competitors.

Ratio	Company	Competitors			
		A	B	C	D
Operating Cash Flow ratio	25%	53%	47%	61%	74%
Cash Flow margin ratio	8%	6%	13%	12%	18%

Figure 1. 7 Cash Flow Ratio Comparison

Other financial reports the management team review monthly are:

- Project Management status, especially budget versus actual costs
- Inventory-Finished Goods; Work in Progress (WIP); and Raw Materials
- Business plans and upcoming issues or changes in the coming months, such as capital expenditure status, new business award wins, new product launch start dates, sales contract expirations or business losses
- Financial Variance Analysis

During the senior management team meeting, action items are defined. Some of these action items may be confidential and only certain managers will take action and follow up. Other non-confidential action items may be communicated company-wide.

The important point is that at the end of the financial review meeting, all managers must leave the meeting with common statements about the financials of the company so they can immediately convey the business status with their staff. Each manager should have a meeting to inform their staff. This is professional, respectful, courteous, and reduces rumors and other idle chatter amongst the staff.

Chapter 8 - Seven Basic Quality Tools and Data-Driven Culture

Establishing a data-driven culture takes patience and the ability to develop the skill sets needed to collect, analyze, present, and take action. Learning the 7 Basic Quality Tools should be within a course on root cause analysis and corrective action.

An opinion about a root cause or how to solve a problem is just a hypothesis unless the solution is obvious. However, in many circumstances, even when the solution is obvious, the problem re-appears, sometimes in the same exact way or in a different area, function, or system.

The following tools are common in many companies in different industries. Companies need to develop and ensure all their employees participate in a root cause analysis and corrective action training that includes the 7 Basic Quality Tools. In addition, management should ensure everyone attend ongoing refresher classes internally, through a local college, or with the help of external trainers or consultants.

Another way for companies to use these tools is to have employees demonstrate them often in presentations as well as on the factory floor. Typically, most companies have monthly operations or business reports that include an example of something that has not gone according to plan, is currently not meeting target, or went wrong. This is an ideal time and place for employees to demonstrate their data analysis tool proficiency and develop their analytic and presentation skills. Alternatively, there are always issues on the factory floor where these tools can be applied, so direct labor personnel can explain the situation or status using these 7 Basic Quality Tools. The use of Basic Quality Tools is not limited to shop floor activities only. It is recommended to apply them in engineering, finance, human resources, logistics, maintenance, production planning, sales, and supply chain.

The following is not intended to be a course on Root Cause Analysis or on data analysis. Attend a course on root cause analysis to learn how to use these tools and practice them in different situations. Having employees participate in root cause analysis training and encouraging the use of tools when issues arise will help to establish a structured way to solve problems. Also, having a standard set of data analysis tools to use will help others learn, practice, and become more proficient at solving problems. Free templates of these tools can be found on American Society for Quality webpage.

The 7 Basic Quality tools are:
1. Check or tally sheet
2. Scatter diagram or X-Y graph
3. Histogram

4. Control charts

5. Pareto chart

6. Stratification

7. Cause and effect diagram

1. Check or Tally Sheet

A defined template form for collecting certain types of raw data that will be used for analysis. The data can be qualitative (pass/fail, good/no good, check marks, or tally marks), or quantitative showing actual measurements. A check or tally sheet can be quite simple, showing production and quality data for a machine from one shift, or can be more complex with multiple columns for data entry. A check or tally sheet should be simple to use, and if possible, standardized so that supervisors or direct labor can readily understand the importance of recording the data. Check or tally sheets can be on paper-based forms, whiteboards, or handheld devices; data can eventually be inputted into a computer for analysis. Also, note that check or tally sheets can be used in other functions as well, such as HR, Finance, Logistics, etc.

Questions to ask when developing a check or tally sheet:

- What type of data will be collected?
- How often will the data be collected?
- Who will be collecting the data?
- Where will the data be collected?
- How much time and cost will it take to inspect and record the data or is there an impact on the bottleneck process operation to collect data?
- What is the purpose of data collection?
- Is data being collected at the earliest point in the process?
- How much data needs to be collected to start analyzing it?
- Are people trained in collecting the data (measuring and recording)?
- What will the form look like to collect the data?
- What conditions are there to prevent the data from being collected? What can be done with the items being checked that cannot be measured? What happens when there is a problem collecting the data (e.g., data is not continuous)?

Illustration - Worker not available using Supervisor notepad

The following illustration shows a tally sheet that can be used by supervisors to track their daily number of people missing work by reason. This tally sheet can be written on the last pages of the supervisor notepad. For successive weeks or months, the tally sheets can be written and filled toward the center of the notepad. Even though HR may have a system for recording employees' arrival and departure times, it may not be capable of including call-ins, time of call, and reasons.

Table 1. 4 Call-in tally sheet

Shift -	Called		Not called	
Date	Will be Late	Won't come in	No show	Late
2/11	Carter, Luiz, Kal	Simon		James, Mona
2/12	Lori, Nora		Alfonzo	Paul, Lonny
2/13	Alex K, Alex B, Hemi, Kwon			Rachel, Jerry, Alan
2/14	Theresa, Maria, Rita, Bill H		Joana, Tonya	Jack, Lynn, Jackie, Jean

Illustration – Quality Defects recorded on paper

The following illustration shows a simple defect tally sheet that can be used in various work-cells to tally the number of defects by date for a number of different parts being produced. The direct labor person can use this form and throughout the shift, the supervisor and QC people can check the status. This type of tally sheet can be used in conjunction with other productivity sheets, such as an hourly productivity board.

Table 1. 5 Defect tally sheet

MONTH				Dimensions - above Spec or Below Spec				Packaging	Other	Day
Date	Scratches	Dings, Dents	Holes	Dim 12.5 AS	12. 5 BS	Dim 8 AS	Dim 8 BS	& Label	Defects	Total
1-Jan	丗丨	丨丨丨		丨丨			丨丨			13
2-Jan	丨丨	丗		丨丨丨丨			丨丨丨			14
3-Jan	丨丨丨丨		丨		丨		丨丨	丨	丨丨丨	12
4-Jan	丨丨丨	丨丨丨		丗			丨丨	丗丨丨		18
5-Jan	丨丨丨丨	丨丨丨丨		丨丨	丨		丨丨丨			14
8-Jan	丨丨丨		丨	丨丨		丨丨				8
9-Jan	丨丨	丨丨丨		丨丨		丨	丨丨		丨丨丨	14
10-Jan	丨丨丨	丗丨丨		丨丨丨	丨丨		丨丨丨			18
11-Jan	丨丨丨	丨丨丨丨	丨丨	丨丨丨丗			丨丨丨		丨丨丨丨	25

2. Scatter diagram or X-Y graph

A scatter diagram is a graph showing pairs of numerical data, with one variable on each axis. The purpose of using this type of graph is to show whether there is a relationship between two variables. If the variables have a strong relationship, there would be a straight line or curve indicating a strong correlation. The tighter the data or smoother a line, the higher the correlation, which means a very strong relationship between the two pairs of data. If the variables have a weak relationship, the data points plotted would be scattered with no pattern. This tool is useful to identify possible root causes such as a cause and effect. Typically, the independent variable will be the X-axis while the dependent variable will be plotted on the Y-axis.

Illustration - Generic

The following shows four simple X-Y plots with no correlations, moderate positive correlation, high positive correlation, and moderate negative correlation.

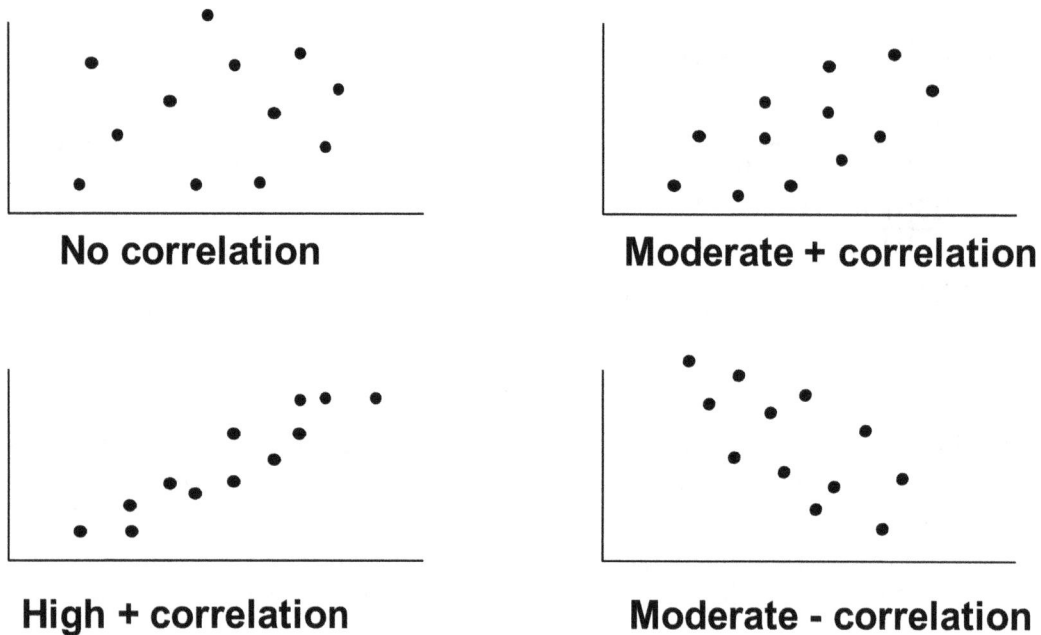

No correlation

Moderate + correlation

High + correlation

Moderate - correlation

Figure 1. 8 Positive and Negative Correlation

3. Histogram

A histogram can be used to graph data from the check sheet or can be used as a way to collect data as well. It is a graphical way to show the frequency distribution or represented shape of the data. The histogram can pictorially show whether the data is normally distributed as in a bell-shaped curve, or it can show the variability or range of data collected. The distribution may show other shapes as well, such as a bimodal distribution with two peaks. Distribution may be skewed, showing more data towards one end and tailing off at the other end. Understanding the distribution of data is very important in analyzing a situation or problem.

Illustration - Generic

The following illustration is a simple histogram showing the X-axis with groupings of measured or counted values and the Y-axis showing the frequency.

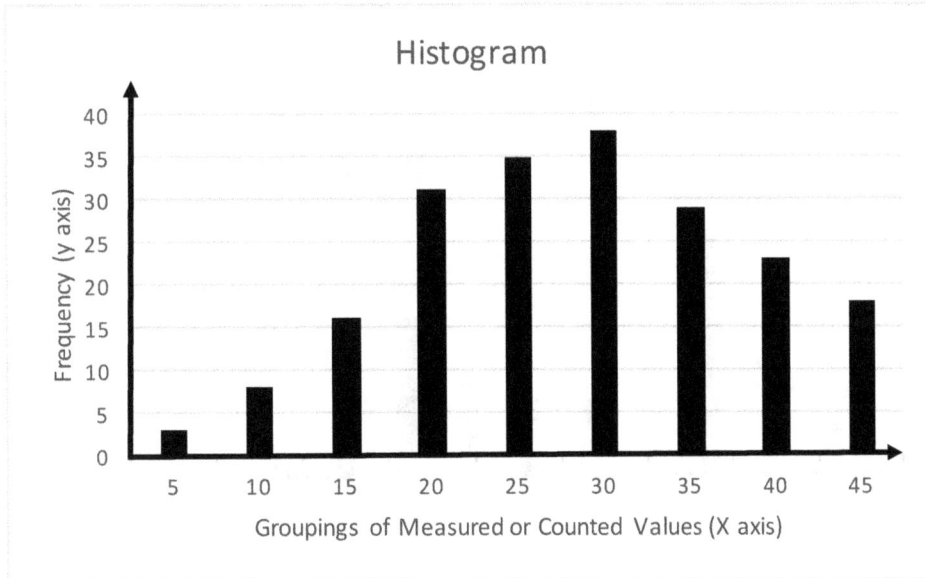

Figure 1. 9 Histogram - Generic

Illustration – Inspection data X-Y plot and histogram

The Dimension (Dim) 4.25MM graph below shows a run chart of 40 inspection measurement data points plotted on a graph and the second graph shows a histogram of the Dim 4.25 MM data. The first graph shows a slight downward trend of the data over time, while the histogram shows a bimodal distribution. Both graphs are useful to understand the data set, prompting further analysis.

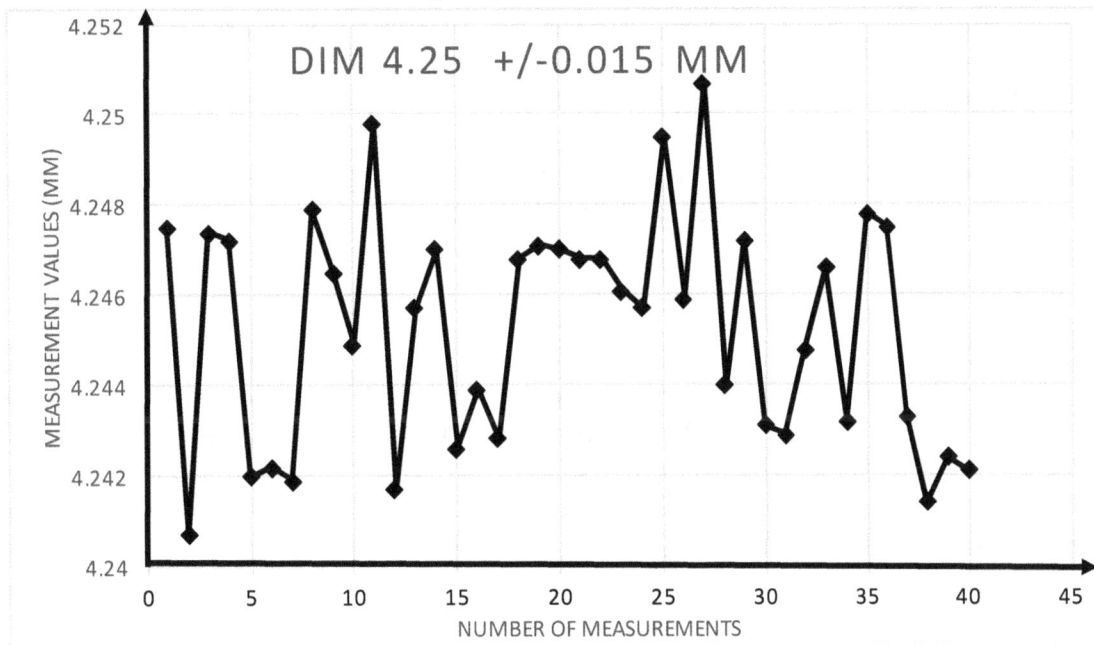

Figure 1. 10 X-Y Plot 4.25 MM

Dim 4.25 +/-0.015 MM
Histogram

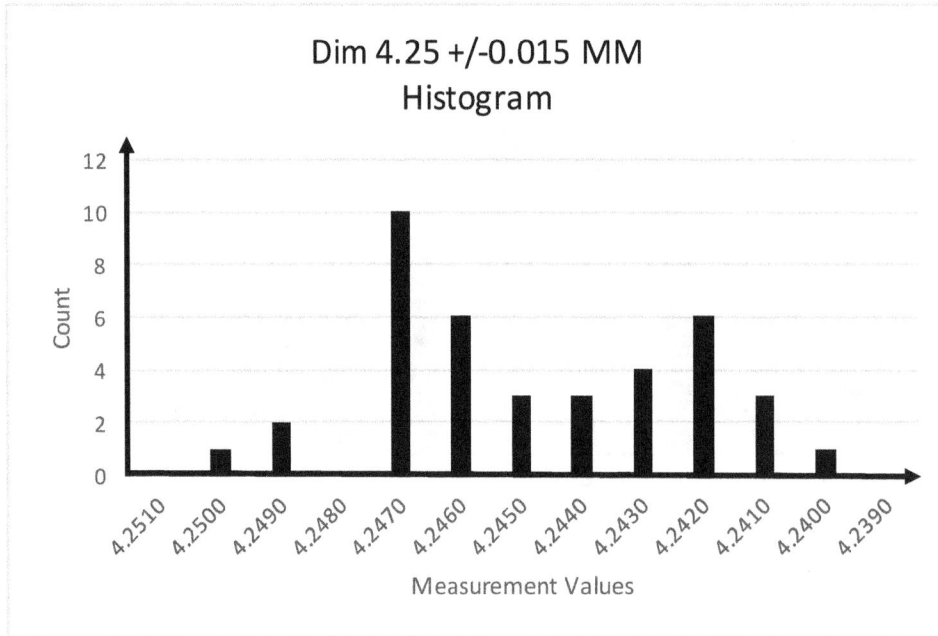

Figure 1. 11 Histogram 4.25 MM

4. Control Charts

A control chart is a graph that shows how a process varies over time. A control chart can show whether the process is stable, in control, or out of control using statistical tools such as mean, range, and some rules. The rules signify when a process is out of control. When the process is deemed out of control, the process needs to be analyzed to determine the special cause(s) for the out of control situation. These special cause(s) can then be further analyzed for the root cause. Then, a corrective action can be implemented to reduce or eliminate this out of control situation. Plotting the data is relatively easy to do, but learning which control chart to use, how to apply the control chart rules, and re-plotting requires some training and practice, as there are many different kinds of charts covering both attribute (qualitative) and variable (quantitative) data.

Illustration - Generic

The following control chart is a simple model showing Upper Control Limit (UCL), Lower Control Limit (LCL), and data plots illustrating both common and special causes. Common cause is the random distribution of the process caused by unknown factors, while a special cause is a shift in the process output caused by a specific process input factor.

Separating <u>common</u> and <u>special</u> causes

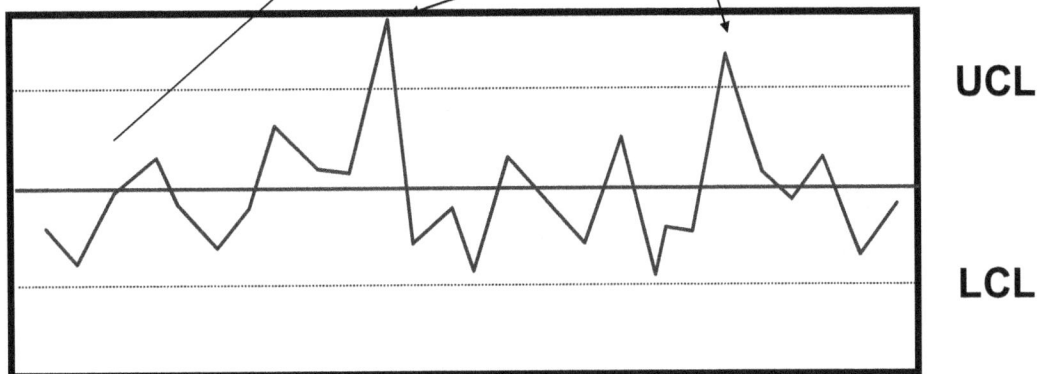

Figure 1. 12 Control Chart - Generic

Illustration – Inspection Data Control Chart

The following control chart shows Dimension 5.1mm being plotted consecutively in a production run. UCL and LCL are shown with dotted lines, while the Average is shown with a dashed line.

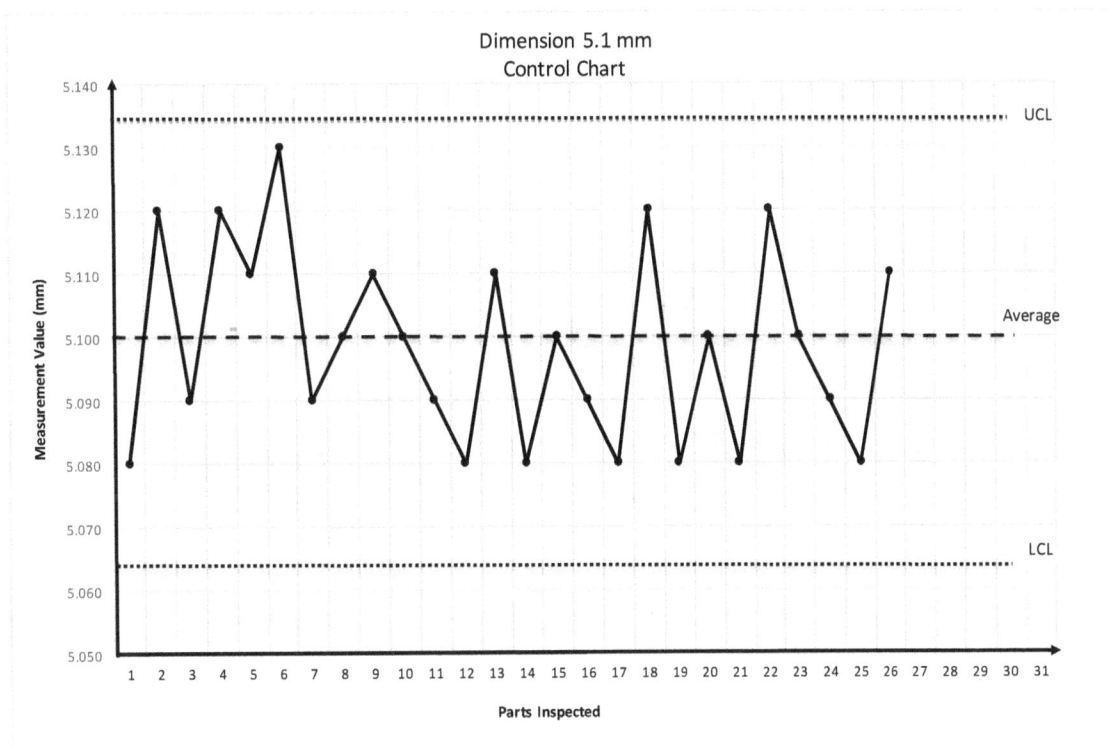

Figure 1. 13 Control Chart 5.1 mm

5. Pareto Chart

A Pareto is a bar graph showing factors in descending order of significance. This is one of the key graphs shown in operations' meetings, because it shows the most relevant factor for which actions can then be taken or discussed. Some basic questions to consider when using a Pareto is:

- What is the purpose of using a Pareto chart?
- Who is the audience and why are they interested in a Pareto (ranking) of factors?
- What are the factors and time period?
- What is the source data, and is it accurate, cohesive, comprehensive, and timely?
- What is the forum, location, and presentation format?
- Who is responsible for presenting and identifying any next steps?

Illustration - Generic

The following illustration shows a Pareto chart with the vital few and the useful many. The vital few failure types would be the first to be analyzed.

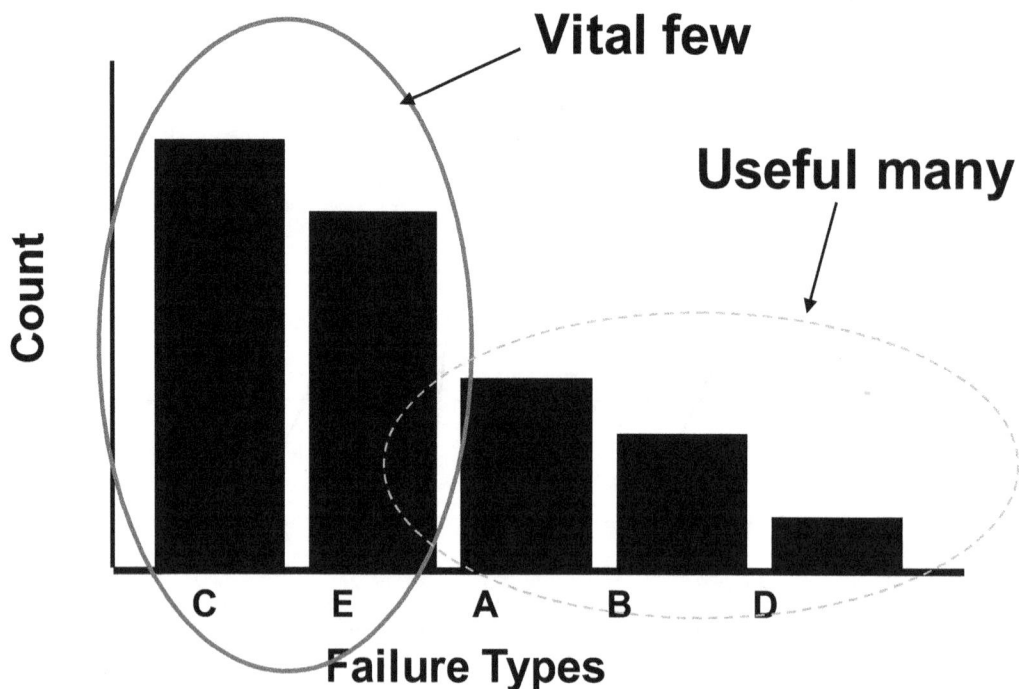

Figure 1. 14 Pareto Chart - Generic

Illustration – Pareto costs of poor quality

The following illustration shows a Pareto of costs of poor quality by manufacturing categories. This illustration also needs further analysis to understand the category definition and to analyze manufacturing scrap.

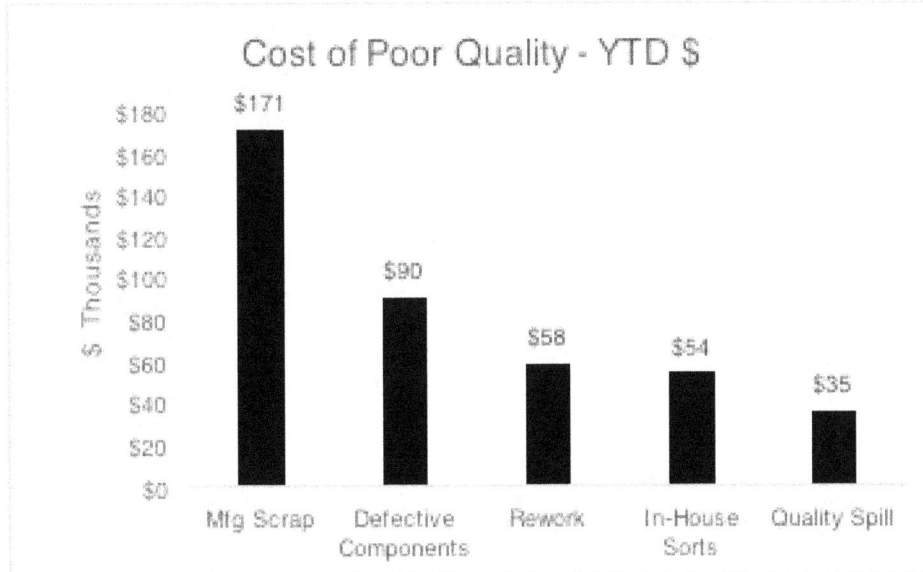

Figure 1. 15 Pareto – Cost of Poor Quality

6. Stratification

Stratification is a technique to arrange data into categories from a variety of data sources to observe patterns. These subgroups then can be analyzed separately. The analysis may yield a pattern or possible cause. For example, categories can be defined as 6M-man, machine, material, measurement, method, mother nature (environment); or in units of time, days of the week, shift, hours; customer, supplier, product, etc. This technique should be used by an employee or a team with problem-solving skills, as the data can be very broad, complex, or convoluted.

Illustration - Generic

The following shows a simple example of some data that has been stratified into 2 possible groups. Group 1 seems to be slightly negatively correlated with a smaller variance, while Group 2 shows no correlation with a larger variance.

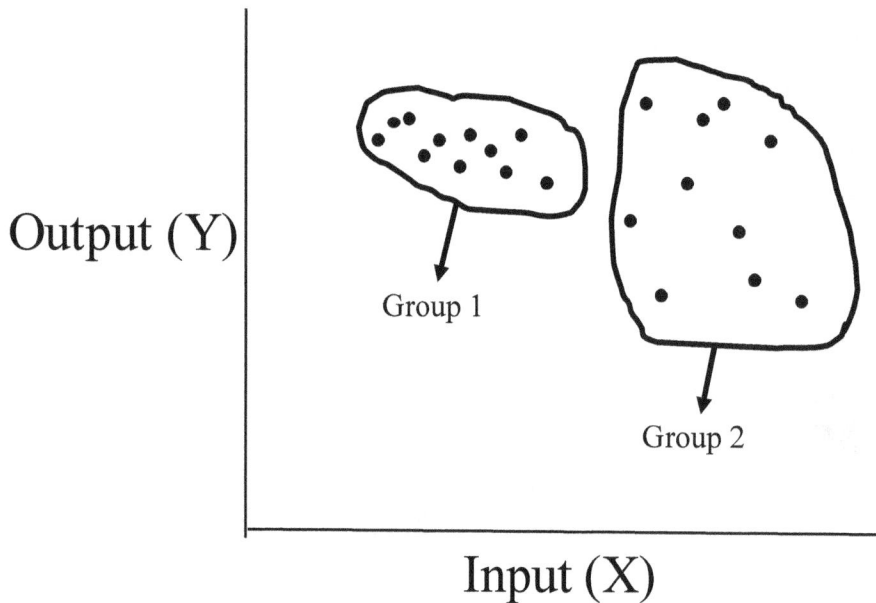

Figure 1. 16 Stratification - Generic

Illustration – Stratification of inspection data

The following illustration shows a data set composed of running a machine with two fixtures having a dimension 5.1 +/- 0.05. Parts are measured after machining from either fixture A or B and the results are inputted into a graph. Comparison between two fixtures shows there are differences between both fixtures and over time. Individual fixture data needs to be further analyzed.

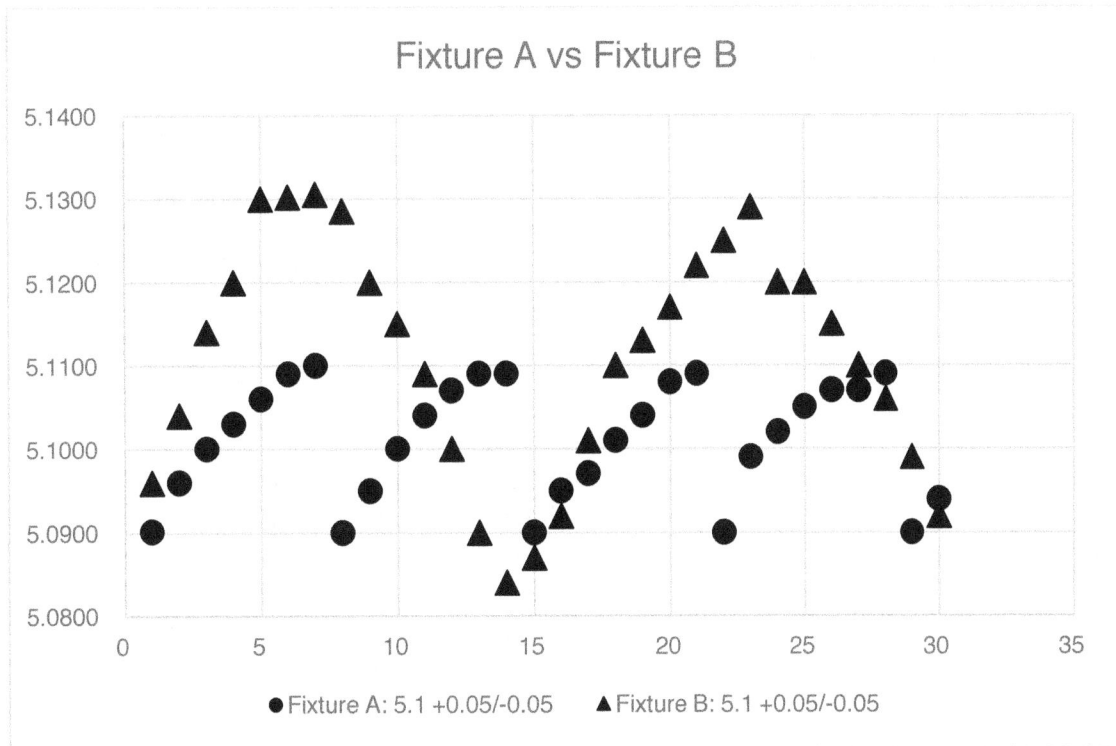

Figure 1. 17 Stratification - Fixture A vs. B

7. Cause-and-Effect Diagram

The Cause-and-Effect Diagram is also called an Ishikawa diagram or a Fishbone Diagram. The cause-and-effect diagram can show possible root causes for a problem by categories. Typically, categories are 6M- Man, Machine, Material, Measurement, Method, Mother Nature (environment). Other categories are 4P-People, Policies, Plant, and Procedures.

The basic process:

1. Team discusses and agrees on a specific problem statement, keeping the statement simple, clear, and concise. The problem statement will be at the head of the fishbone diagram (see below for an example).

2. The categories above will be the main bones of the fish skeleton. The group will then brainstorm possible causes of the problem with a short, clear, concise statement and put it in the appropriate category. A brainstorming session typically begins by having the leader say the problem statement and asking the group, "why does this happen"? Once people are stating some possible causes, the leader of the group will write those possible causes on a paper and place (tape or paste) them along the main category bone.

3. The leader can continue to repeat the problem statement and ask why does this happen to obtain more possible causes, then once ideas are exhausted, the leader can then start asking "why does this happen?" for each sub-bone category.

4. The questioning is repeated for each category and each sub-bone category until no one can answer the why question any longer. Typically, additional ideas are generated for possible causes during a second review of the entire cause and effect diagram.

5. Once the questioning reaches a point where no more statements can be made, then a plan can be made to investigate or conduct experiments to gain further knowledge. After some investigation and experiments are conducted, the cause-and-effect diagram may need updating. This cycle continues until a root cause is identified.

Illustration – Service

The following cause-and-effect diagram shows potential causes for a hotel room that is not available, categorized by People, Policies, Plant, and Procedures. To complete the fishbone diagram, the leader would follow the process above. At the head of the fish, the leader would write "room not available", then write the 4Ps above each main fish bone. Then, the leader would say they are going to ask questions for the Policy category. Then, the leader would ask the participants, "why is the room not available"? while they are pointing to the Policy fish bone. One participant may state "because of minimal training" while another participant might state "because of being overbooked".

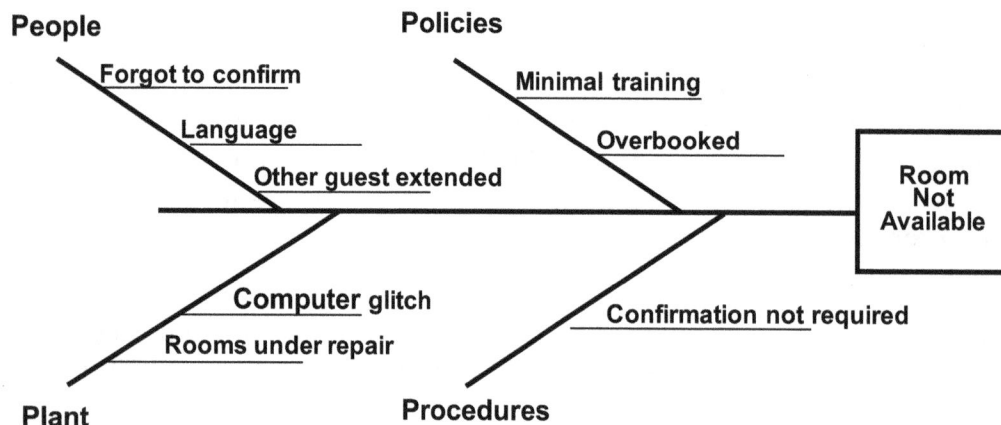

```
People                          Policies
    Forgot to confirm               Minimal training
        Language                        Overbooked
            Other guest extended                        ┌──────────┐
                                                        │  Room    │
                                                        │  Not     │
                                                        │Available │
            Computer glitch                 Confirmation not required
        Rooms under repair                              └──────────┘
Plant                           Procedures
```

Note: Machine, Manpower, Materials, Measurements, Methods, and Mother Nature (Environment) are categories for manufacturing processes.

Figure 1. 18 Cause and Effect Diagram - Generic

Illustration - Manufacturing

The following example shows a cause-and-effect diagram for a motor heater that fails thermal test. The categories are grouped by 6M. The common question to ask each category is "why does the motor heater fail thermal test"? A cause can then be placed for each category. Then the next series of questions can be asked – "Why does the motor heater fail thermal test"? Because of the cause just listed, then ask "why does this cause happen"? These questions continue until no further answers can be provided. Then, further analysis and tests may be needed to identify the most probable or root cause.

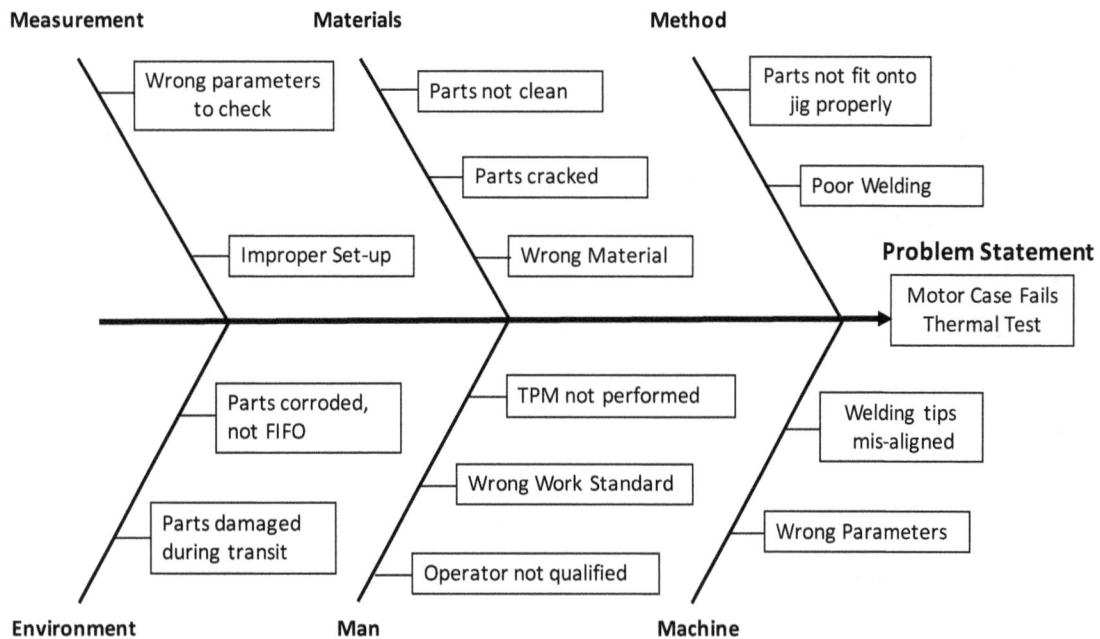

Figure 1. 19 Cause and Effect Diagram – Motor Case

Chapter 9 - Meetings, Emails, and Text Messaging

Meetings are conducted to have a discussion, brainstorm, make a decision, or share complex or emotionally charged information. When deciding whether to hold a meeting, consider other ways to communicate that may be as effective, quicker, and at lower cost, such as:

- Telephone call
- Text
- Text group chat
- Email
- Communications board posting
- Walk and talk
- Teleconference
- Hybrid teleconference with some face-to-face
- Face-to-face – no meeting room required
- Face-to face – meeting room required

Having an effective meeting requires as a minimum, the following:

1. Owner or leader
2. Purpose, intended goal, or expected outcome
3. Agenda
4. Note taker and time keeper
5. Attendees that are participative and have authority to make decisions
6. Start and stop on time

There are a few different types of meetings, such as:

Monthly

Monthly meetings are typically sit-down sessions in conference rooms or via teleconference with defined agendas, meeting leaders, and meeting note takers. Some examples:

- Business Performance – Operations, Financial, Project Management
- Product Development – Validation of Status, Risk Assessments
- Purchasing – Strategy meetings, supplier development, sourcing plans
- Sales – New business awards, business pursuit, and business case reviews

Daily

Daily meetings are typically short, stand-up sessions next to visual control boards, whiteboards or status boards. Most daily Operations meetings are stand-up (not sitting around a table). However, some companies still have daily sit-down Operations meetings. Typically, sit-down meetings last longer than stand-up meetings. Examples of the short, stand-up meetings are:

- Operations Status and Shift Handover

- Functional, Department, or Team Status

- Project Management (aka scrum) – A scrum meeting is a short daily meeting to bring everyone up to speed on the project status. Each member tells what they accomplished from the previous day, what they will be working on today, and states any concerns or obstacles so the leader can address or assign other resources to help. The scrum board is usually a whiteboard with some key milestones and typically updated with post-it notes while members are stating their project work status.

Impromptu or Irregular - Specific

Impromptu or irregularly scheduled meetings can be either sit-down or stand-up meetings depending on the topic, urgency, or importance. These impromptu or irregular meetings may or may not have an agenda, but are called to address a specific issue. Examples of these meetings are:

- Customer or Supplier – Quality or Delivery concern. These are typically stand-up due to the urgency and importance.

- Audits – Quality (external/internal), Environmental, Financial – These are typically sit-down and are planned months in advance. Agenda is specific to the particular audit topic with typically an opening statement, discussion on audit findings, then closing statements.

- Work team – Various functional or cross-functional team meetings. These meetings may be stand-up, in the work office area, conference room, or on the factory floor. These meetings are typically urgent as an important issue has come up. However, some work teams have regularly scheduled meetings throughout the week and they would be sit-down meetings.

Focus Group

Focus Group meetings are project and task oriented. These meetings can be scheduled anywhere, anytime — such as on the factory floor, in a functional team office or cubicle, in conference rooms, in a canteen, or at supplier facilities.

- Agenda, presentations, discussions, and work varies from meeting to meeting

Urgent

Urgent meetings are the same as impromptu meetings, as they are called at infrequent times throughout the day, night, or weekend. When there is an issue with critical and high priority severity, an urgent meeting is called. Participants are expected to be available, to contribute, and to re-prioritize their work to resolve an urgent matter. An urgent meeting may be called to address a customer complaint, an injury, or an internal safety violation.

A Quick Response Quality Control (QRQC) meeting is an example of an urgent meeting. All manufacturing companies should have a QRQC team. Leader, roles, and responsibility are defined well *before* an event occurs. Ideally, a procedure, organization chart, and communications matrix is defined and easily retrievable, by placing it in a text group chat such as in Skype, WeChat, Messenger, or other mobile phone communication system. The QRQC team ensures they can cover any urgent issue that arises seven days a week, 24 hours a day, 365 days a year, with backup employees defined. All QRQC team members and their backups will ensure their home, mobile/cellphone numbers, and alternative numbers are up to date so the team can be assembled quickly. See QRQC in Chapter 27 in the Conditioning section for more information.

Segments of a Meeting
The following describes the different segments of a meeting:
- Meeting Preparation
- Beginning and During the Meeting
- End of the Meeting
- After the Meeting
- Meeting Etiquette
- Meeting Action Items

Meeting Preparation:
- What is the purpose or objective of the meeting?
- Why is this meeting important?
- Will you and others be prepared for the meeting?
- Who needs to attend (identify the vital few)?
- What are the expectations of the participants?
- Was there a similar meeting like this in the past? What can be done better? When will the previous action items be reviewed to ensure the action items have been completed?

- Who is the leader? Who will write and distribute the action items?
- Can this be a short stand-up meeting?
- Is a meeting room available?
- Have you sent out an invitation and agenda to the vital few and have they accepted? If one of the vital few has a conflict, request a designee that has the same authority.
- If the meeting is a teleconference, be sure the telephone numbers will allow several people to participate and define who is the teleconference leader. If there are international participants, ensure the correct time zone for the meeting.

Beginning and During the Meeting

- Review the meeting etiquette quickly (see SPACER, below).
- Be sure to arrive several minutes early to ensure the meeting place is suitable for the meeting. (For example, ensure the presentation can be displayed with a projector, or that the whiteboards are clean and markers are ready to be used.)
- Start on time and deal with latecomers after the meeting.
- Put action items on a whiteboard and/or designate someone to write down action items throughout the meeting.

End of the Meeting

- Summarize the meeting.
- Review the action items and identify a person responsible and estimated timing to complete the action item(s).
- If a follow-up meeting is necessary, then schedule with everyone in attendance.
- Stay on the meeting schedule and agenda; if other items come up, take notes or action items.

After the Meeting

- Speak with latecomers, making it clear that this is disrespectful and a waste of everyone else's time. Is there a policy or warning given for people that are consistently being late?
- Immediately after the meeting, distribute the presentation and/or action items.
- Before the next meeting, follow up with any open action items to determine the status of each item.

Meeting Etiquette
- Companies need to provide training in how to conduct effective meetings.
- Leaders need to know how to run meetings efficiently.
- Every company should define and post its rules for conducting an effective meeting. Meeting rules can be posted in each meeting room or area and be included in the company handbook. Postings should have large enough font so everyone can read the rules from any part of the meeting room or where people are standing.
- Rules should be written in the language the employees participating understand. Consider having rules written in two or more languages.

SPACER rules can be used for meeting etiquette and should be openly stated at the beginning of the meeting, which should take just a minute or two. SPACER – Safety, Purpose, Agenda, Code of Conduct, Expectations, and Roles:

Safety –

Depending upon location of the meeting or if there are people unfamiliar with the location safety protocols, the leader will have to ensure all participants have and are wearing their PPE correctly and understand where the safety exits are and location to meet in case there is an emergency

Purpose –

Define no more than one purpose for the meeting. The purpose should be a simple and clear statement about the meeting

Agenda –

Clear, specific, timed, and visible

Distributed prior to the meeting so attendees can prepare information

Code of Conduct –

No laptops being used by attendees; only writing in notepads allowed

Phones on vibrate only; no texting during meeting

Start meeting on time, prepare needed materials, and arrive early

Only one person speaks at a time

Leave meeting room clean, as good or better than found

Expectations –

Everyone participates; leave ego and criticisms out of the meeting

Roles –

Define leader, timekeeper, and note taker

Meeting Action Items

Every meeting, unless it is a communications announcement, should have someone making note of action items. Each action item will be numbered consecutively with a description of the action to be taken, who is responsible for completing the action, an estimated time for completion of the action, a status identifier (such as Red: behind planned completion date; Yellow: in jeopardy of not meeting the planned completion date; Green: on schedule to be completed), a brief description of the status and next steps, and actual completion date. Other information can be taken about each action item, such as location or category (such as plant area or function), percent completion either by action item or overall.

Whiteboards

Every meeting area, including offices, should have a whiteboard with different-colored markers and an eraser at hand. Most people learn visually, so posting diagrams, agenda items, brainstorming ideas, etc., makes it easy for participants to see and understand important points or requirements. Some whiteboards are electronic so people from different geographic areas can participate. Whiteboards or paper poster boards can also be used in factory work-cells. More information about work-cell information displays can be found in Chapter 24, Daily Routine, in the Conditioning section.

Emails – Etiquette and Productivity

Emails should be brief, include only necessary information, and only distributed to those who need to receive them. Generally, emails that are longer than two paragraphs warrant a face-to-face meeting, telephone call, or short meeting. Also, instead of emails exchanging back and forth multiple times, consider if you could save time by just talking to the other parties via telephone call or teleconference. Companies should define rules for email writing, distributing, and replying, and include them in the company handbook.

Email Rules

1. Only include the people necessary to communicate about the subject, not everyone in the company, function, or team. Scrutinize who should be sent the message and who should be copied. Again, very few people should be copied.

2. The email subject line should be a clear, concise, description of the message content – the simplest summary possible.

3. First-time correspondence (especially to someone outside the company) should always be formal. Use Mr. or Mrs. with the surname or full name.

4. Every email message should have a signature (sigline) that includes the sender's name, company name and address, telephone/mobile number, and email address.

5. Don't use "Reply All" unless absolutely necessary.

6. Depending upon what the sender message contains, reply back with the requested information by using a different font color, especially if there are line items or questions to answer.

7. There are very few situations where an email should be forwarded. One is if a key team member was missing on distribution, another might be to let the boss know about some impending situation or important point.

There are many methods to significantly reduce email volume, such as:

- Not replying to "all" and not replying with just a "thank you."
- Not continuing, lengthening, or building the reply chain. Before adding to the chain, ask why this wasn't brought up and discussed at the meeting, or shouldn't be discussed in a meeting.
- Picking up the phone and have a conversation.
- Walking over to a colleague and have a chat in person, or talking over lunch, etc.

When workers in the same office are texting or emailing each other and can physically see each other, it is not adding value and is possibly interfering with business progress. Generally speaking, sending emails to fellow workers when they are presently in the same office or immediate work area is a waste of time. Focus on keeping communications productive and efficient by walking over to them and talking—in other words, have an impromptu meeting. However, there are certain times when emails need to be written that involve workers in the same work area.

Text Messaging and Phone Calls

Most people these days are constantly texting colleagues, friends, and family throughout the day, even during meetings. Developing personal discipline to review text messages only on the hour, as opposed to every time a message is received, will allow you to focus on current priorities. Text messaging to friends and family can be done before work, during lunch, breaks, or after work.

Phone calls to customers, suppliers, and colleagues should be encouraged over emails or text messaging. However, ongoing or multiple phone calls a day to friends and family during work hours should be frowned upon. Most importantly, while on the factory floor it is dangerous to talk or text on the phone. If a phone call or text message is needed, stop, be sure you are in a safe place, then proceed with taking the phone call or text message. Most companies have rules about usage and locations for phones and text messaging.

Chapter 10 – E-Commerce

E-Commerce is the buying and selling of goods, products, and services over the internet, including sharing of business information over the intranet and internet. Manufacturing companies today have access to potential new customers and potential employees via their websites, Facebook, Twitter, LinkedIn, Amazon, eBay, Alibaba, Taobao, and other online resources, including mobile social media applications. Company websites and other web applications can easily take orders as well as display company products and other information. Markets are available 24/7 and are more customer and relationship centric, as digital technology is a key driver and key differentiator.

A sales and marketing team greatly improves the opportunity for new and continued sales with a clever E-Commerce strategy. The Annual Operating Plan must define a budget and plans for the upcoming year's E-Commerce activities. All functions will have input into the E-Commerce budget and plans. All functional management, sales staff, and marketing staff need to be continually training on E-E-Commerce strategies, technologies, E-Customer interfaces, and generally the online global market.

E-Commerce's primary objective is to attract new customers, retain current customers, and build a stronger network of current customers. As a result of attracting customers, people want to work at the company. So, another objective of E-Commerce is to attract potential employees, while current employees have access to the company's business-to-employee (B2E) E-Commerce. Various company B2E applications include:

- Company locations, products, and services
- Company library and training programs
- Employee benefits and medical insurance information
- Latest company and industry news
- Links to various internal and external databases
- Organization information and job openings
- Stock price, stock market, and 401k investment information
- Special employee offers and customer offers
- Travel services

Potential recruits and New Hire employees most likely will only have a cursory knowledge of this information. So, the Orientation process needs to include training on the company's B2E, B2C (business-to-consumer), and B2B (business-to-business) E-Commerce network. Depending upon the New Hire's role, they may only receive a short briefing while others may have an E-Commerce orientation over several days.

Part 1 - Orientation Summary

Orientation is the first of four main sections of this book. Orientation is the way in which a company introduces itself to New Hires and others, such as customers, suppliers, contractors, auditors, etc. It is how New Hires quickly gain a comprehensive understanding of the company, including its mission, values, KPIs, and various business processes and expectations. Orientation is a must have business requirement that is visual, behavioral, and on-the-job training based. Orientation is the first and most important indication that the company has a Factory Showcase Culture.

As mentioned, every company has an Orientation process; however, there is a monumental difference between the Orientation at most companies and the activities and expectations defined in these chapters. Most companies think their Orientation process is sufficient and seems to work well, simply because that is the way they have been doing it for many years. But, times have significantly changed in the past decade, and things will continue to change. The information provided in these chapters applies to all industries and all manufacturing companies: large, small, international, and local.

The framework, processes, and details provided in these chapters should be evaluated against your company's current Orientation process. Next, identify the gaps or weaknesses. The gaps and weaknesses need to be clearly defined with a direct comparison between the information in these chapters and against the company's current documentation. Create a two-column matrix as a framework for comparison, then list each chapter with the main content and put the company's documentation next to it. A documented comparison will help other management clearly understand the gaps and will help to identify the next steps.

Part 2 - Foundation

Establishing a foundation for any structure or business is paramount for having it last a long time. The stronger the foundation, the more likely it will survive through natural, economic, or political hardships. In the case of a business, the stronger the foundation, the more likelihood for success. A manufacturing company's foundation includes many components including the organization structure and layout, manufacturing systems architecture, manufacturing footprint, visual management, managing for quality, process flow, production planning, and logistics. The following foundation elements should be the core of your company.

Chapter 11 - Organization, Layout, and Shift Planning

Defining a dynamic, productive, forward-looking team and a goal-oriented organization structure needs to be one of the company's top priorities. It is extremely important to determine who is on a team, what they are doing, how well are they doing it, what resources they need now and in the future, and in what ways management provides support.

Organization Structure

Read any lean management book and you will see that flatter organization structures are more efficient than others. However, the more people who report to a leader, the less effective the communication or less likely 1:1 interaction occurs. A 1:9 ratio of manager/ leader to staff/workers works well for communications and managing. Having a larger ratio hinders 1:1 communication and reduces 1:1 face time. However, there are some organization structures where the most senior person has 14 or more people reporting to them. This may work for some organizations whereby the senior manager delegates strategies, supports plans without micro-management, and the management team is strongly committed and aligned with company strategies. However, there are many organizations with larger than 1:9 ratio whereby this does not work well, and this can be seen from stagnant monthly and yearly financials.

Direct and Indirect Reporting

Direct reporting is where an employee has a primary report to their boss. Indirect reporting is where an employee has both a primary report to a boss and secondary report to two or more bosses. Having a direct and indirect reporting structure provides a platform for better communications across different functions. It also provides an opportunity for the indirect reporting staff to have a broader business scope of understanding by having two or more bosses. And, it provides a leader with a team that has a broader skill set. Basically, the direct and indirect reporting structure has one or more different functional staff reporting to a leader. There are many organizations that have this type of structure and this works well as long as the leadership is cooperative, supportive, and promotes open communication within and between functions. Also, there are many organizations that have direct and indirect reporting whereby there are many struggles and difficulties both with the management team and with the individual staff. The causes of this poor organization effectiveness are primarily due to low trust within the management team and weak cooperative commitment to achieve company strategies. Lesser causes are due to personality issues, lack of cross-functional and general business knowledge, and weak leadership skills.

Illustration – Direct and Indirect reporting

The following illustration shows a Direct and Indirect reporting organization structure. The General Manager and Director of Sales are shown at the same level in hierarchy, followed by the next level being the Quality Manager and Supply Chain

Manager, and the third lowest level shows a Planner and Sales Engineer. The Direct reporting is shown by a solid line and the Indirect reporting is shown by a dotted line. The Supply Chain Manager has a primary Direct reporting to the General Manager and the Supply Chain Manager has a secondary Indirect reporting to the Director of Sales.

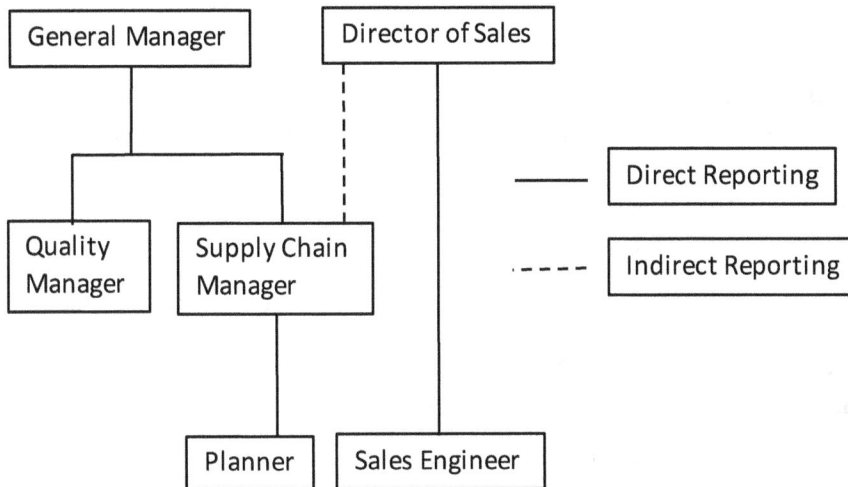

Figure 2. 1 Direct and Indirect Reporting

The daily issue in having a direct and indirect reporting structure is establishing and maintaining aligned priorities. Staff may get confused with directions and priorities given by their direct boss versus their indirect or functional boss. Common goals, objectives, KPIs, budget, time contributions, and priorities have to align with both the direct and indirect leaders and be communicated to the shared staff, along with regular reviews — preferably by both direct and indirect leaders. Problems inherently start to develop when communication is hindered, personal egos get involved, or trust is tested as the weaker, less-confident leader starts to cause problems. Constraints and conflicts will occur, so managers and staff must communicate the issues openly, clearly, unbiased, and timely so issues can be handled professionally, efficiently, and without causing undue high stress levels. Also, having regular reviews across all functions, with both direct and indirect reporting employees, keeps an agreed-on alignment in place.

Project-based and Ad hoc Structures
Typically, these are short-term, temporary-reporting structure relationships, that can last for a day or up to a couple years. The ad hoc structure can be a one-time, project-based structure such as when implementing an ERP system, or can be an ongoing repeated cycle, such as when there is a customer complaint, or new product to be manufactured. For example, the ad hoc structure may start as soon as a customer complaint is known and end when the customer complaint is effectively closed.

These project-, ad hoc-based structures work well to develop employees cross-functionally compared to more rigid structures, due to the varying interactions and various situations being confronted. However, being on multiple ad hoc teams adds stress and dilutes the individual's time for general functional responsibilities. A balance between rigid and ad hoc structures has to be evaluated consistently and managed by the leaders to develop stronger organization capabilities.

The organization structure and team composition evaluation can be performed on a monthly basis with the teams and individuals, by reviewing and discussing the project plan, issues, status, KPIs, action items, project progress, personal contributions, and any other obstacle or issue that has been or will be confronted.

When employees are not meeting expectations, one must ask why?
- Was there enough time allocated for the task?
- Did the employee(s) have the right skill sets?
- Did the employee(s) have different priorities?
- Did unexpected problems arise?
- Were enough resources allocated?
- Was the assignment and expectation clearly understood?

Not meeting expectations is unacceptable in any organization, so changes must be made. Leaders need to identify as early as possible when the expectation may not be achieved. In rare cases, the leaders may make changes to objectives, KPIs, and budgets as typically those goals are fixed throughout the planning cycle. See Annual Operating Plans in Chapter 35 in the Competitiveness section for more information.

Geographic, Product Line, or Value Stream Organization Structures
Organization structures vary widely, some are geography based; product line based; value stream based, or a combination of these. Geographic organization structures can be global, regional, country, state, county, or other territory-based. Geographic structures can also be customer oriented, by product line, or organized by processes within specific manufacturing facilities. In large, multi-national companies, factories typically are a combination of geographic and product line- or value stream-based. In smaller companies, the organization structure typically is simpler with less management levels and is organized as a value stream with defined products and customers as shown in the organization chart below.

Product-line and value-stream structures are typically determined by some commonality in manufacturing processes. There also could be more than one organization structure in one manufacturing facility, due to a variety of reasons such as: domestic and export business, different industries, or aligned by customers and products.

Illustration – Organization Chart

The following organization chart shows a typical manufacturing company with a 1:9 reporting ratio.

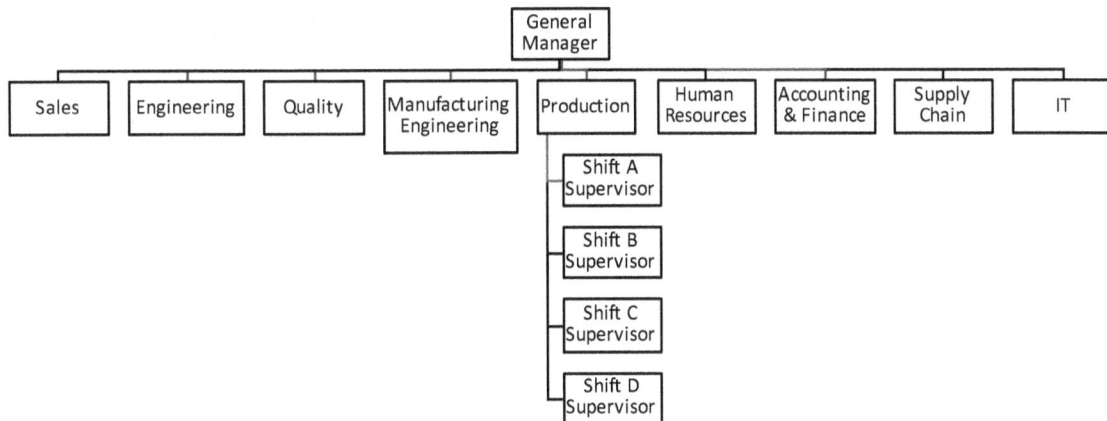

Figure 2. 2 Typical Factory Organization Chart

Companies may have roles and responsibilities that are larger in scope than just manufacturing. Some of these roles and responsibilities, with suggestions for reporting, include:

- Research and Development (R&D) and Testing – can be within Engineering
- Safety, Health, and Environment – can be within Human Resources (HR)
- Maintenance – can be within Manufacturing Engineering or under Production
- General Site Facilities (electric, gas, water, landscaping, building and roadway maintenance) – can be within Manufacturing Engineering
- Security (entrance to site, into buildings, and in buildings) – can be within HR
- Purchasing, Warehousing, and Logistics – can be within Supply Chain
- Project Management and New Product Launches – can be within Engineering,
- Packaging and Labeling – can be within Manufacturing Engineering or Supply Chain
- Import and Export – can be within Supply Chain
- Continuous Improvement or Kaizen leader – can be an assistant plant manager, or part of another function's staff member such as Manufacturing Engineering.

- Legal – can be outsourced
- Marketing – can be within Sales or even a separate function, depending upon the product sales amount and type of sales such as E-Commerce sales, size of the company, or size of the customer base
- E-Commerce – can be a composite of different functional managers with each manager having responsibility for a specific segment

4th Shift Organization Structure

The organization chart above shows 4-shifts (A, B, C, D). This chart does not show supporting functions for 2nd, 3rd, and 4th shift. If the company operates 24/7 or operates on several shifts, other functions should provide support especially when production is running. If the company's customers are primarily other manufacturing companies, then they should provide on-call support when the customer is running their production. Also, the company should identify support personnel if they operate globally or have customers in different time zones. Support can be managed in a variety of ways such as: on-site, on-call rotation, weekend duty rotation, online support, or even 3rd party customer service support.

Most importantly, leaders need to define clear responsibilities, response mechanism and timing, and escalation matrix for all production shifts. The escalation process is discussed in more detail in Chapter 27 and shown in an illustration. All management and supporting staff members must understand this matrix, which most likely will have to be reviewed on a quarterly basis for updates, either with personnel name and phone number changes; additional responsibilities or situations to be documented; information to be communicated; staff to be trained; and processes and results to be audited. If online support is defined, this also requires quarterly reviews to ensure the support personnel have the latest literature and ways in which to diagnose problems and support customers as well as to identify systemic problems so the next steps can be undertaken. Also, to ensure they are providing high quality prompt servicing.

As the company's customer base and geography broadens, expectations may change. The diversity of the company's product type may broaden and the company might need to expand into more manufacturing space or locations close to current customers or in another state or country. Alternatively, the products may become less competitive where new investments and innovative products are required, causing a need for different skill sets or creating different employment needs. The company may open into new markets or grow whereby the organization structure may broaden and change into other business units and value streams, such as:

Illustration – Business Unit Organization Chart

The following organization chart is a larger scale of multiple manufacturing plants and slightly different reporting structures. It shows the General manager having 6 direct reports, namely the 2 business unit managers, engineering, human resources, accounting and finance, and Information Technology. The 2 business unit managers have a plant manager and sales manager reporting to them. The 3 plant managers have operations staff managers: Quality, Manufacturing Engineering, Supply Chain, and Production.

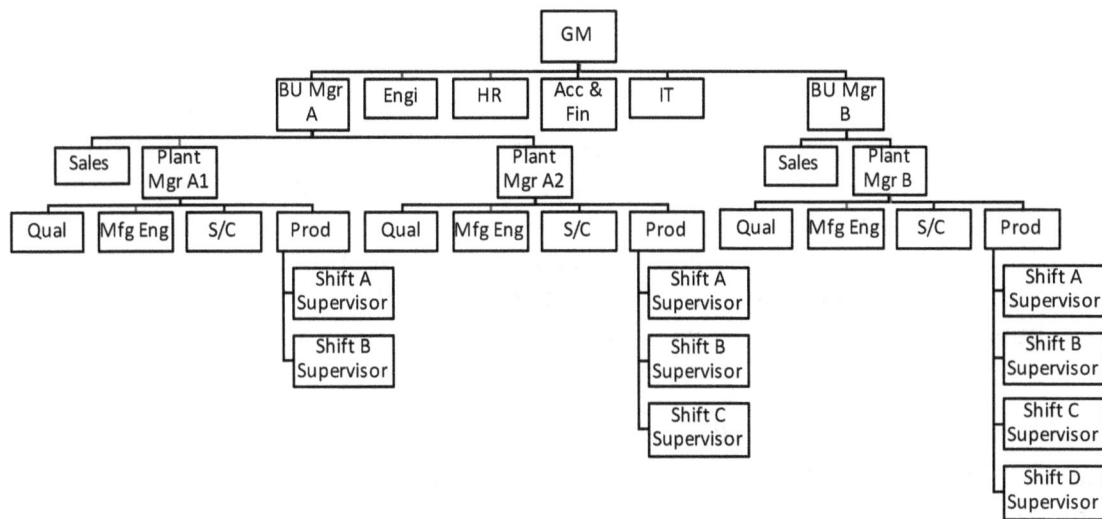

Figure 2. 3 Business Unit Organization Chart

There are strengths and weaknesses in any defined organization. The key is to keep the organization as flat as possible, use temporary organizations for projects or other short-term activities, promote flow of information, and most importantly value trust. It is imperative not to create functional organization silos where one function or group is isolated from others.

Office Layout

The type of office layout can greatly affect the performance and support on the factory floor. Moving the manufacturing operations support people close to or on the factory floor will greatly impact the factory performance. Also, having manufacturing operations support personnel work in an open office layout architecture gives them a highly visual and physical presence. The closer the staff are to the manufacturing operations activities, the more efficient or easier it is for staff to see a problem and provide support, and for the direct labor workers to search or contact the support staff. Also, having an open office architecture helps with office communications by knowing who is in the office or not, making it easy to walk to other office employees to have a conversation rather than waste time by exchanging emails.

Designing an office layout where operations staff are close to the factory floor while other functions are farther away is not difficult in a newly designed factory. Changing an existing building to accommodate a more open architecture may take some considerable planning, may encounter resistance, and may be somewhat costly. However, low cost ideas can be realized with encouragement, being open minded, and focus on a long-term goal of linking direct labor with supporting staff. Other ways to promote open communication between functions include combining two or more functions in the same room, while leaders occupy a different area, or converting a conference room into a team office.

Not everyone will like or support an office layout change, but some probably do not like the current layout. A change in the office environment to promote faster response to factory floor operations and improve face-to-face cross-functional dialogue needs more than just management directive and encouragement. However, depending upon your current business condition (growth rate increase), facility size, structure, and local building codes, there may be limited options for making an office layout change.

Illustration - Factory ground floor layout with offices

The following illustration shows a typical factory ground floor layout with offices attached. This layout shows Quality, Manufacturing Engineering, Supply Chain, and Production all sharing one large, common workspace area with ease of access to the factory floor; the space could have windows looking onto the factory floor. Sales and Human Resources are also on the first floor. In other types of layouts, the operations team can actually reside on the factory floor depending upon the manufacturing processes. This layout assumes there is a second floor that can contain bathrooms, conference rooms, other functional staff offices (Sales, Engineering, IT, Accounting & Finance), leadership offices, and the general manager's office.

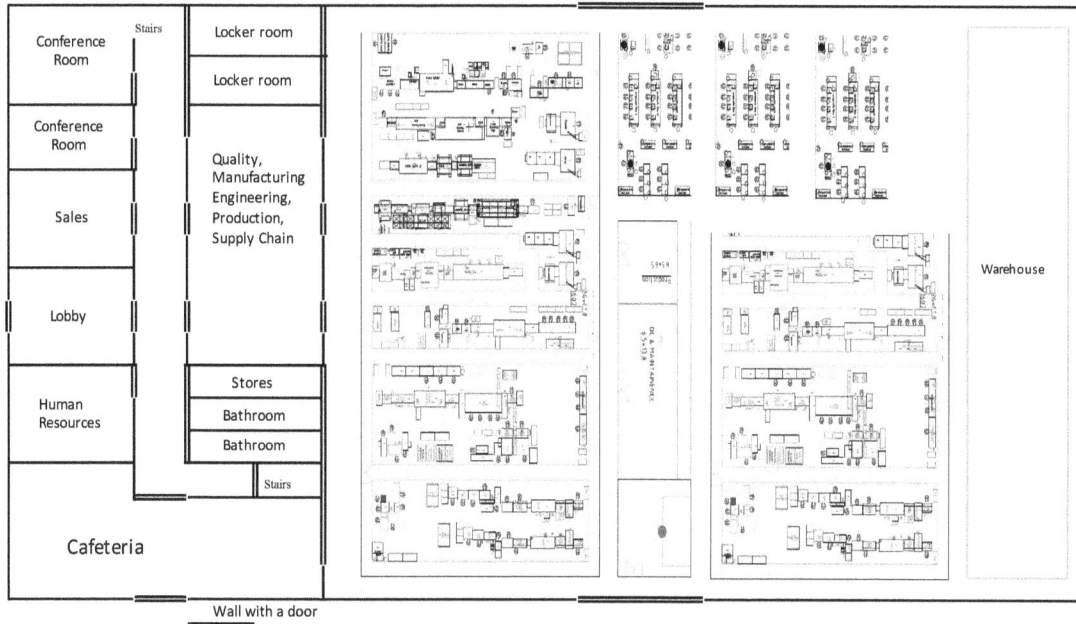

Figure 2. 4 Factory ground floor layout with offices

Office Layout Change

A cross-functional management team should be assembled to define objectives for new office layout. The general manager should establish a broad objective, such as to improve face-to-face daily communications or time based in minutes to recognize and respond to customer or operational issues. The team can then develop several options, including possible re-organization changes and estimated costs for renovation. Options can be further evaluated with advantages and disadvantages reflecting perspectives from customers, suppliers, factory staff, and other functional staff, or ranked according to the opinions of the management and staff. The general manager can request that a draft of the options be completed within a month and an options analysis with quotations be completed within two months. The team could then define a phased-in layout and organization change.

Desk Layout

The desk layout should be an open architecture without walls, and without (or minimal) cubicle height walls between desks. Some renovation work may be needed to remove some interior walls and some cubicles may not have the capability of reducing height, so new desks may need to be ordered.

Illustration – Desk Layouts

The following four figures show common ways to organize worker office desks. Layout "A" shows a desk on one end, which can be for a project leader, a supervisor for that team, or even a manager. Layout "A" includes two L-shaped desks. These desks can be for the most senior leaders of the team(s). "A" layout shows 20 people with 2 team leaders and 2 managers, while "B" layout shows 28 people with 4 team leaders.

Layouts "C" and "D" shows a series of 4 people to a square of L-shaped desks whereby each office worker faces toward the corner of a square. This type of desk arrangement can provide some larger personal space without affecting physical communication, especially if there are no walls between desks or between squares of desks. "D" layout shows a work table between two groups of desks. People working at these desks can swivel their chairs around and have a group meeting. This provides a highly efficient way to communicate without having to use a conference room for a meeting. "C" layout shows 24 people and "D" layout shows 16 people. Both of these figures do not show an apparent team leader or manager. However, team leaders and managers can be located anywhere in both figures.

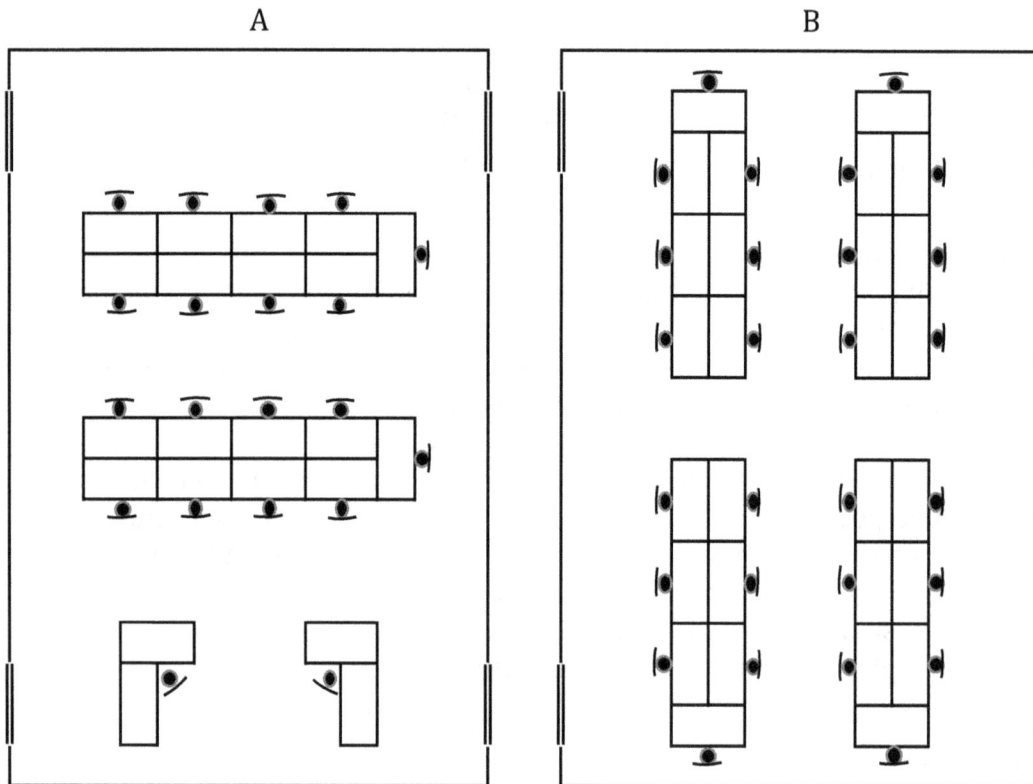

Figure 2. 5 Face to Face desk layout options-A and B

C   D

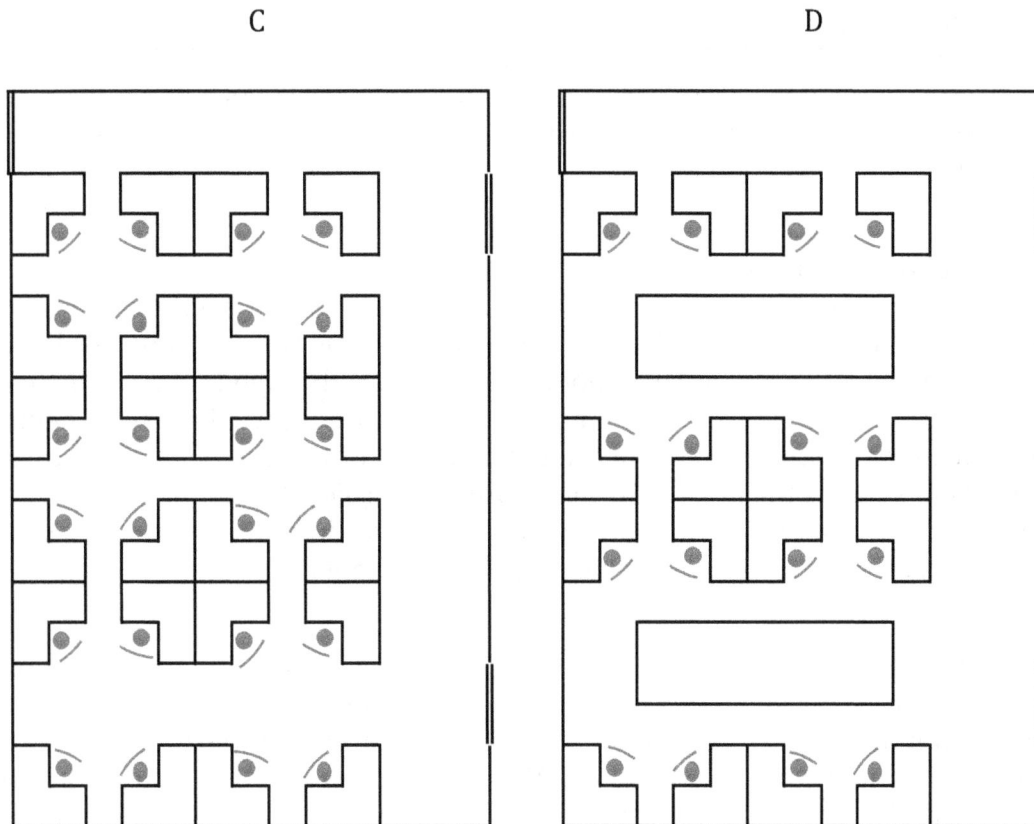

Figure 2. 6 Face to corner layout - options

Some companies have office layouts similar to the above with cubicle walls or desk barriers. Employees may enjoy working in this semi-private environment and would refuse to work in any sort of open architecture layout. This may be OK for those companies. However, for other companies, the culture could be tested and could possibly gain much benefit from greater physical interaction.

Organizing desks in different configurations will create some difficulties or challenges because people generally don't like change. People like walls between desks and generally are reluctant to share information openly, as they feel it creates job security to protect information. Others argue that without cubicle walls, there will be no privacy for personal phone calls and it will be difficult to do work because there will be too much noise. This culture can be tested during a short-term, urgent and high-profile project whereby daily or more frequent updates are needed. Also, surrounding walls can be insulated or textured, plants can be added between various desk sections, and signage can be hung from the ceiling to reduce noise.

Clearly, there are many barriers to overcome in changing office and desk layouts. One way to start is when there is a new project. Once the new project is announced and a team identified, the first objective is to identify a space for the team to work together, which could mean aligning their desks into a configuration that places desks next to or close to each other. Eventually, other projects will begin and new teams can be formed, or the rest of the office can be modified and adapted for a new configuration. This may be the simplest way to construct an open office architecture and get buy-in by the all staff.

Individual and Team Development

Identifying individuals to start a new project typically is rather challenging, since everyone is already busy, or at least everyone will tell you they are busy. Additional resources may be injected at some point in the project, but the initial project team members are usually from the current organization. A leader will have to be defined, and the leader and other functional leaders may offer or be asked to provide certain resources to support the project. In some cases, the project leader may not have the authority to select specific resources and may end up with resources that they would rather not have on their team, but that is part of the challenge.

The challenge is to develop individuals in a team environment to meet certain objectives. A project leader who is experienced will understand that it will take time to develop individuals to contribute as a team. If the project leader is new or the project has certain constraints and conflicts, a more senior person should act as a mentor to the project leader to ensure the project's objectives are met. The mentor or other leader also can make observations about the effectiveness of the project leader and team to determine whether other or more resources are needed, as well as offer advice to the project leader and individual team members.

Developing individuals and teams on projects requires regular reviews and time for feedback. Reviews are to validate project status, define further actions (especially if something is unfavorable), and evaluate each member's quality of contribution efforts including timing and adaptiveness to the team's culture. The project leader should give feedback to team members on a regular basis about their opinion of the project status and provide one-on-one individual reviews. Individual reviews can be short informal meetings with communication to the individual staff's functional leader, or jointly held with that leader. The reviews should discuss the individual staff's contribution or achievements, team value or team value level, and competencies — both strengths and weaknesses.

When the project team faces challenges, obstacles, or high-pressure situations, trust, competencies, and leadership will be tested. Negotiating skills must be honed and compromises made, especially during tense discussions or arguments. Communications may include others outside the company such as customers or suppliers. Effective leaders will encourage open, candid discussions with positive reinforcement while maintaining high expectations and professionalism. Encouragement can be a simple statement made at the beginning of a meeting to acknowledge the success of a member or team, treating the team to lunch, posting positive news on a visual display board, having an offsite gathering, or given privately during the individual's review. Alternatively, KPIs that are highly unfavorable or issues that are severely affecting a project must also be highlighted clearly on a visual display board, so everyone can focus more of their time and attention on these matters. Management, team, and individuals need to re-prioritize their daily efforts to contain and reverse the unfavorable condition.

The team's morale should be constantly assessed to ensure team members stay positive and productive. This can be done in their work area where the leader can hear, see, and sense the tone of team members' voices, see how often they update their visual boards, and observe how well and often they are interacting with each other. This is where the open office architecture really helps, allowing all the team members to see and provide help to each other.

Morale doesn't change overnight — it takes time and persistent effort to improve. Leaders can improve morale by paying attention to people's work and contributions; making simple, positive reinforcing statements about their work efforts, especially in front of others; providing visible tokens of appreciation, such as pizza or once in a while have catered coffee and donuts brought in for both staff and direct labor workers — especially when certain project milestones are met and are under budget. These appreciation tokens are for everyone in the company on all shifts to celebrate, not just for the select few.

Every team is likely to include relatively few members who, for some reason, are negative about the company or someone on the team, or have generally an indifferent attitude. These people can be like a disease and have to be identified early in the project planning phase. Confidential plans to re-position them elsewhere or even out of the company need to be made. Also, some leaders may not be aware of their staff's poor performance, especially if the leader is weak and ineffective. The general manager will need to know of this situation and at some point, make one large organizational change affecting several employees, including re-assignments, consolidation of responsibilities, change of titles, and/or terminations. Therefore, it is up to the general manager to regularly monitor performance and make changes.

Staffing Analysis
Determining the staff headcount number for each function or responsibility, including the headcount number for direct labor workers, should be part of monthly reviews. Indirect staff are employees who work in a function that supports production workers, such as those in Quality, HR, engineering, maintenance, logistics, etc. Direct labor workers are the employees who are transforming materials into finished goods — they are the contributing to product value. Many companies analyze their direct labor worker headcount numbers on a daily basis. Headcount numbers vary

depending upon customer production volumes needed, and the numbers are adjusted by hiring/dismissing temporary workers in the short term. These companies may use more than one recruiting agency to support their labor force and may even use the same agencies to help with hiring indirect staff. Temporary direct labor workers are generally used to fill production capacity gaps without having the current direct labor force incur overtime.

If your company is executing its business plan for establishing a factory, capacity planning is based upon forecasted production volumes over several years. The headcount number of indirect and direct labor workers correspond to that planning period. The business case would have to be clear about the headcount number of each functional staff, when they start, and their approximate total labor costs. In addition, the business case would define the headcount number of direct labor based upon certain production volumes. More information on business case development and analysis can be found in Chapter 36 in the Competitiveness section.

If your company is already in a production operation's mode, capacity should already be known against forecasted volumes to determine the headcount number of direct labor needed. However, the headcount number of indirect staff may or may not be sufficient to handle the current or expected upcoming business requirements. So, your company may be under capacity or overly burdened by having not enough or too many indirect staff.

How do you determine the optimal headcount number of indirect staff and their roles?

This is a vitally important question to regularly review, since indirect staff are fixed costs and generally are not correlated to production volumes unless there is a severe production volume decrease or increase. There are six ways to understand whether indirect labor costs are contributing to improving profitability, productivity and/or quality.

1. Evaluate productivity and quality improvements trends
2. Evaluate all business key performance indicators (KPIs) over time
3. Analyze fixed labor costs over time
4. Evaluate supplier material costs over time
5. Analyze how well indirect staff handle increasing level of responsibility and new projects
6. Fill organizational resource gaps quickly

1. Productivity and Quality trends

The *first* way to understand whether indirect labor costs are contributing to improving profitability, productivity and/or quality is to evaluate productivity and quality improvement trends. Indirect labor staff work with direct labor on various projects. They plot their productivity and quality improvements on a monthly, quarterly, and yearly basis. If the trend line is stagnant, or the percentage improvement change trend line shows an unfavorable direction over time, the indirect labor contribution value is becoming less effective. Functional management and indirect staff may not be focused on key productivity and quality KPIs. An evaluation should be initiated with the functional management to discuss issues for not achieving productivity and quality targets. This may be related to their own capabilities or to other issues such as operating performance culture decline, self-interests, or performing work on other administrative activities.

2. KPI trends

A *second* way to understand whether indirect labor costs are contributing to improving profitability, productivity and/or quality is to plot all business key performance indicators (KPIs) over time and analyze whether these metrics are stagnant, generally favorable, or generally unfavorable. Taking a macro view of KPIs can expose issues, mismanagement, and gaps in performance. If the overall trend is stagnant or unfavorable over time, management and indirect labor contribution value is becoming less effective. The general manager needs to have a candid discussion with each functional manager as a change needs to occur. Having regular financial and KPI reviews prompt these discussions and management should be held accountable. However, if there are certain special cause circumstances causing unfavorable trends, this may be accepted in the short term.

3. Fixed cost trend

A *third* way to understand whether indirect labor costs are contributing to improving profitability, productivity and/or quality is to analyze fixed labor costs as a percent of sales by month, quarter, or year. Indirect labor costs are fixed, so they do not vary with sales. However, if sales are changing at a moderate rate (either slightly increasing, decreasing, or stagnant) indirect labor contributions can be evaluated as a rough measure, as one of the main general expectations of indirect labor is to continually improve. In this case, a financial analysis of the projects need to be made to determine their effectiveness. Then, plans can be defined regarding indirect changes. For unfavorable cost trends, some of the following can be considered: postpone or cancel indirect hiring, reorganize functional responsibilities, determine which employees need to be challenged more or need training, restructure, or reduce management and indirect staff.

4. Supplier material cost trend

A *fourth* way to understand whether indirect labor costs are contributing to improving profitability, productivity and/or quality is to evaluate supplier material costs over time. This needs to be analyzed against the supplier's relative raw material commodity market prices along with the individual supplier's manufacturing cost productivity improvements against the purchasing contracts. Supplier costs and operation costs need to be analyzed together as the supplier cost reductions should not have a negative effect on operational productivity and quality. For example, supplier costs may have declined, but the related operational KPIs show productivity and quality unfavorable. This may be due to lower material quality, material composition change, higher variability of material dimensions, or a different raw material supplier. Whenever the supplier wants to make a change, they should submit a product and process change notification request along with some predetermined samples for engineering and operations to assess. The company can accept or reject the requested change. Ideally when the supplier makes a change, the supplier's cost decreases and there is a favorable operational effect, as expressed by this equation:

Supplier direct material costs reduced + Supplier quality KPI improved + Operations related productivity KPI improved + Operations KPI quality improved = Lower cost of goods sold

In this case, indirect staff are contributing to overall lower costs and this can be seen at the end of the month when accounting creates various financial statements. The detailed income statement line items for the cost of goods sold for direct materials would be favorable. Direct labor costs and variable overhead costs may be favorable as well.

Indirect staff value contribution can be gained from focused projects coordinated by purchasing, engineering and other staff working with individual direct material suppliers. When supplier costs are adjusted for raw material commodity market price and when they become stagnant or unfavorable over time, then purchasing and/or other indirect functional staff are not engaged with the suppliers. The purchasing function should lead these initiatives and should be held accountable for supplier productivity improvements.

5. Increasing level of responsibility

A *fifth* way to understand whether indirect labor costs are contributing to improving profitability, productivity and/or quality is to evaluate the indirect staff' contribution on how well they handle increasing level of responsibility and new projects. This type of evaluation requires an introspective review of the individual staff' accomplishments, activities against various business happenings, and the functional and individual Daily Routine activities. More information on Daily Routines can be found in Chapter 24 in the Conditioning section. For large multinational companies, there are software packages that can be used to manage much of this information, such as PeopleSoft. For mid-sized and smaller companies that do not have PeopleSoft or other HR related software packages, the company's senior management will need to define individual scorecards. These scorecards can then be updated during monthly and quarterly business reviews and used for annual employee performance reviews and other professional development needs. This may seem somewhat time consuming, but it forces management to be engaged and aware of which employees are high performers and which employees need attention.

Most companies review how well their staff handle increasing levels of responsibilities within their functions — but not across functions. Companies can be more profitable and gain greater knowledge by having employees trained cross-functionally. In this way, the current indirect staff can assume short- or long-term additional responsibilities when additional business requirements arise without increased costs. Also, if employees can communicate smoothly across functional silos and across geographic regions, productivity and efficiency can be improved. This requires leader(s) to look at the entire business scope and not just their functional area. It also requires coordination within the leadership for employee development. This is highly necessary, because workload in indirect functions varies from being underutilized to working significant overtime including weekends to accomplish certain tasks or projects.

If current business needs are being met with the current indirect staff, this may also be a problem of being over-staffed since productivity, profitability, and quality are expected to improve every year. This results in a scenario where fixed costs remain flat and variable costs do not meet plan. Current staff should be developed to assume greater responsibilities, as well as to ensure the company becomes more productive and profitable. If current staff cannot handle current business requirements and plans, the reason must be analyzed, and the management team should challenge themselves in terms of why they cannot meet the requirements and plans.

6. Organizational resource gap

Finally, when there is an organizational resource gap, it is important to fill it immediately. However, finding the right full-time replacement takes considerable time. Companies need to have succession plans and contingency plans for high performers and key employees. In addition, companies can consider using subcontracted services or interim management support while in the process of hiring a full-time employee. These services can support all functional areas, such as HR, IT, purchasing, engineering, production, quality, sales, and supply chain. Utilizing interim management services has many advantages:

- Immediate hands-on, highly skilled resource
- Able to provide an outsider's fresh perspective
- Provide an objective (non-political/unbiased) view

- Able to train various indirect staff due to their overall skill-set
- Help interview and develop full-time indirect staff and management
- Staff would appreciate outside support and recognize they are not a threat

Interim managers typically are independent consultants that are highly skilled in their field. Their extensive experiences allow them to enter into a chaotic work environment and quickly determine necessary actions. They can be hired by the day for a week, month, or several months and can be found through professional work groups, LinkedIn, or by word of mouth.

Shift Planning

There are various work shift patterns and schemes that can be searched online to determine which would work best. Common manufacturing schemes are:
- 1, 2, or 3 shifts per day or
- 4th shift covering operations 24/7

Shift schemes are fixed but may rotate throughout a month. Some shifts can be 8 hours while others are up to 12 hours for a specific day. Companies even develop their own unique shift program to accommodate seasonality and other business requirements. Note that any shift scheme change being considered may create significant unrest and may cause good people to resign. Therefore, shift scheme analysis should be handled in a confidential manner. If a shift change is to be implemented, this needs to be presented to all employees with the reasons for change and with advantages identified for both the company and employees. The following table shows a simple comparison of 4 shifts, including overtime hours and direct labor utilization rate.

Illustration – Various Shift Schemes

The following figure shows a group of 3 tables: Standard work week for number of work days per week for each shift, Overtime by hours per day for each shift, and % of work hours each week per total number of available hours during each week.

Table 2. 1 Various shift scheme work hours

Standard work week (days/week)					
Shifts	5 days			6 days	7 days
1	8 hrs/day	9 hrs/day	10 hrs/day	8 hrs/day	x
2	8 hrs/day	9 hrs/day	10 hrs/day	8 hrs/day	x
3	8 hrs/day	x	x	8 hrs/day	x
4	x	x	x	x	12 hrs/day

Shifts	Overtime (hrs/day)				
1	0	1	2	8	x
2	0	2	4	16	x
3	0	x	x	24	x
4	x	x	x	x	avg 2/week

Shifts	% of total week (hours worked each week/total hours in a week)				
1	24%	27%	30%	29%	x
2	48%	54%	60%	57%	x
3	71%	x	x	86%	x
4	x	x	x	x	100%

Standard work week table shows 5 days, 6 days, and 7 days per week for 1, 2, 3 and 4 shifts as well as working 8 hours, 9 hours, or 10 hours per day. Overtime table shows the number of overtime hours per day for each shift for each number of work days. For example, "0" overtime hours for 5 days a week working 8 hours per day. The % of total week table shows the percent of work hours per total hours in a week time. The 7 day work week shows an "x" for 1 to 3 shifts as companies do not have regular shift work for seven days a week.

For example, working 5 days per week on 1 shift contributes to using direct labor 24% of a total week of hours, that is 5 days per week times 8 hours per day divided by 7 days per week times 24 hours per day. So, the more days and hours worked contributes to using more direct labor time. This is an hourly based calculation and is used weekly by both manufacturing engineering and production planning, whereas Finance will use direct labor utilization costs. Direct labor utilization cost is calculated by total direct labor costs divided by total payroll costs. Direct labor utilization cost is reviewed on a monthly basis. Other cost metrics would be analyzed as well as such as unit part cost or direct labor cost per part.

When the direct labor utilization costs or other direct labor related cost metrics become unfavorable to plan, management should make a plan and take action to improve.

4th Shift

The following shift plan shows a scheme called 4th shift: 2-2-3-2-2-3. This scheme uses four teams working 12-hour shifts, covering 24/7. Each team works 2 consecutive day shifts, has 2 days off, works 3 consecutive day shifts, has 2 days off, works 2 consecutive day shifts, has 3 days off, then works 2 consecutive night shifts, has 2 days off, works 3 consecutive night shifts, has 2 days off, works 2 consecutive night shifts, has 3 days off. This is repeated every four weeks per the following schedule (D = Day Shift, O = Off Duty, N = Night Shift).

Illustration – 4th Shift Work Scheme

The following table shows a specific 4th Shift work scheme over a four-week period. Each shift shows whether they work Days (D), Nights (N), or are Off duty (O). There are a few different 4th shift work schemes.

Table 2. 2 Shift scheme for a 4th Shift

	Week 1	Week 2	Week 3	Week 4
Shift A	DDOODDD	OODDOOO	NNOONNN	OONNOOO
Shift B	OONNOOO	DDOODDD	OODDOOO	NNOONNN
Shift C	OODDOOO	NNOONNN	OONNOOO	DDOODDD
Shift D	NNOONNN	OONNOOO	DDOODDD	OODDOOO

The shifts need a fixed start and stop time, and a definition of when the work week begins, such as the Sunday night shift starts the week working from 8 p.m. to 8 a.m. and the day shift is 8 a.m. to 8 p.m. Monthly work calendars are posted, available in the company handbook, and usually on the company's intranet so workers can see the upcoming work shifts.

This 4th shift scheme has the advantage that the employees work either two or three days consecutively and have a three-day weekend every other weekend. The disadvantage is the work shift is 12 hours. A 4th shift scheme has the highest utilization of assets (factory is running 24/7), so it works well for highly capitalized manufacturing companies, especially those that have continuous process flow. For continuous flow processes, shutting the process down for an hour is extremely costly as materials may seize the machines, spoil, or may cause a serious or hazardous situation. The disadvantage of this scheme are long shift hours (12 hours), and requires on average 2 hours of overtime per week.

When companies experience an increase in business volume, they often try to initially start adding overtime to a current shift scheme to meet the new requirements before adopting a different work shift scheme. At some point, overtime increases and becomes fixed for longer work days, and eventually weekend overtime work becomes standard. At some point of increasing overtime, labor costs increase to a level that becomes a detriment to profitability. Also, other key performance indicators may be affected as well, such as safety incidences or first aid issues increase, quality or productivity levels drop, absenteeism increases, or customer and employee satisfaction drop. During monthly reviews, the key performance indicators show unfavorable trends, which can be extrapolated to show that a different work shift scheme or new way to operate is needed to reverse the unfavorable KPIs.

Example

A manufacturing company currently works three shifts at 8 hours each shift, Monday through Friday, and is currently meeting customer demand, but sometimes has to postpone deliveries. The company has started to work a partial overtime shift on Saturday. The company has been investing in new equipment, conducting monthly improvement events, and has a low customer quality defect rate.

In the short term, working a partial Saturday shift would continue until partial Saturdays cannot meet demand. Other shift planning options are defined, analyzed, selected, and presented to all employees. In addition, the company may consider expanding its capacity by upgrading or adding new processes. Adding incremental capacity is explained in Chapter 13, Manufacturing Footprint in Foundations, and Capacity Planning is explained in Chapter 37 in the Competitiveness section. There may of course be a combination of shift planning, process re-design, and procurement of new machines to increase overall capacity. Once a plan is defined for increasing capacity, this would be presented to all employees. Then, if it includes a shift plan change, a training session for employees would be conducted, and finally the new shift plan can be implemented.

A company leader would take responsibility to kick off this project and select a cross-functional team. The leader will then schedule and lead various meetings to ensure the objectives are met. Typically, this would either be the general manager or operations leader. This project would have a high priority, because customer or consumer needs and demands are not being met and other unfavorable KPIs are occurring. Also, employees may already have encountered increased stress due to working overtime while working six days a week. The leader may direct the team to study changing the work schedule to a 4th shift scheme. There are several questions to be addressed by the project team such as:

- Which 4th shift scheme to use?
- How to change the current three shifts to four shifts — which supervisors and employees will be on each shift?
- How many new direct labor and indirect labor will have to be hired?

- Are there possible internal candidates that want to become team leaders and supervisors for the 4th shift?
- What is the timing for the shift change?
- How will the indirect staff support the change to four shifts?
- What other supplier, internal, and customer service support is needed, including material movements and logistics?

If there is only one cross-functional indirect support team to support the 4th shift scheme, this may not be enough resources, so additional resources may be required or other teams may need to be formed. Generally, expanding the one cross-functional indirect team is the better option, since employees will want self-control, want to be a part of the solution, and want to contribute to the company success. Having a combination of new inexperienced employees with more senior staff is a least risky way to support a new oncoming shift.

Once the project team announces it is going to a 4th shift, many employees will want to know how this will affect them personally. A very clear plan detailing who goes on which shift, when this will start, and who the shift leaders are should be clear in the initial announcement or announced within a very short time after the initial announcement. In addition, the cross-functional project team will have to identify new open positions such as a shift supervisor and other direct and indirect labor positions.

Best Shift Plan Work Scheme
There has been extensive research on work shift schemes in many different industries and in many different countries. No one single shift scheme is best. Every shift scheme has advantages and disadvantages for both the employer and employee. Management can prepare a matrix that shows advantages and disadvantages of the current work shift plan versus various options from both the employee and employer perspective and then decide the next step.

Having employees participate in defining work shift schemes has a greater acceptance rate. However, there will always be some employees who are reluctant to change, while others won't have a problem. Before implementing a work shift change, it is important to distribute an advance notice that includes several formal meetings with employees. Companies with unions will have to discuss and agree upon the new work shift plan before it is implemented. Besides defining the advantages and disadvantages, other important aspects have to be considered, such as indirect support staffing requirements on nights and weekends, new hire and training fulfillments on the different shifts, use of temporary or contract workers, identifying a capable response team covering all work shift schemes, security of accessing the various parts of the facility, raw material and finished goods movements, as well as addressing other incremental capacity increases and investments. Also, if payroll dates and times have to change, this also must be communicated. Once all of this is finalized, the company handbook would need to be updated and training programs amended. In summary, any modifications to a work shift scheme must be communicated to all employees.

RASIC Matrix

RASIC is a management tool used for identifying functional or individual roles for a specific activity of a project. RASIC stands for Responsible, Accountable, Support, Inform, and Consult. The definitions of each component are below; each definition can be applied to a specific person or functional part of the organization such as the Supply Chain function:

- Responsible – Functional leader, project leader, or individual that is designated as the lead for the action, implementation, and completing the task or project

- Accountable – Functional leader or individual that has the authority to approve or reject the task or project, establishes requirements such as a technical expert

- Support – Function(s) or individual(s) that actively participate in the task or project

- Inform – Function(s) or individual(s) that provide inputs and require updates of the task or project including decisions made about the activity or project.

- Consult– Function or individual that provides advice but are not actively participating in the activity or project.

RASIC is one of the best tools to use in a cross functional organization that has direct and indirect reporting structures. For example, a RASIC matrix can be used for various large and small projects such as building a new factory, acquiring a business, divesting a business, launching a new product, implementing a ERP or other software system, or used in conjunction with a Value Stream Map to reduce overall lead times, buying a new machine, etc. Also, a RASIC matrix can also be used as a baseline to establish a contract between different business entities such as a Joint Venture or for two or more companies involved in working to achieve a certain business outcome. The main disadvantage of a RASIC matrix is that it does not determine the amount of time required or timing of resources needed for a specific activity of a project.

Illustration – RASIC Matrix

The following table shows a RASIC matrix of a project showing Phase 2, Industrialization. This table shows a condensed number of line items as typically there are many more line items during this phase. In addition, there may be other functions that need to be included in the RASIC matrix.

Table 2. 3 RASIC table - Industrialization phase

Phase 2 - Industrialization	Project Leader	Product Eng	Mfg Eng	Quality	Production	Logistics	Purchasing
Project milestone plan	R/A	S	S	S	I	I	S
Project-Functional Matrix	R/A	S	S	S	S	S	S
Final technical product data	A	R		I/C			
Control plan	A	S	S	R			C
Equipment capacity plan	A		R	I	I		
Demand Planning Process	A				R	I	I
Material Order	A	S		S		I	R
Labor readiness			A	S	R		
Change Management Process	A	S	S	R	S	S	S
Sample plan and delivery dates	R				A	I	I
Samples delivery quantity and dates					A	R	I
Submit PPAP	A	S	S	R	I	I	C
Start of Production	R	S	S	A	S	S	S

Key Steps to Establish a RASIC Matrix

1. A project leader has a meeting with key individuals and starts to make a list of the various tasks/activities for a project using a whiteboard and/or spreadsheet. After completing the list of activities, columns are placed to the right of the activities to construct a matrix or table.

2. The list of activities will typically be the first column. The other column headers can be different functions, companies, or individual names to be involved in the project. Key individuals will assign a RASIC role for each specific activity using the letters R, A, S, I, and C. Each activity should have only one "R" and only one "A". Having more than one "R" or "A" for each activity causes confusion amongst the support team. However, there can be more than one "A" for project gate or project phase review. Also, each activity must have an "R", or this activity will not be managed. Also, for a specific activity an "R" and "S" can be put together for one specific function, company, or individual. Finally, multiple activities can be marked with "S" and "I".

3. Using the matrix, conduct a simulation run to ensure the activities are logical, there aren't any missing steps, and the RASIC designations are correct. The simulation can follow a business process for a specific product, issue, or event from the start to end where the people identified in the RASIC matrix can concur or not with their identified role. Amend the RASIC matrix during this time to ensure correct roles are identified.

4. After the simulation is completed, the project lead and key individuals will then make an announcement to others in the organization by having a larger meeting with the individuals defined in the RASIC matrix to review the RASIC. Then, each function or individual can sort the spreadsheet for their specific role for each activity and highlight certain activities for their role.

5. Job Descriptions may then need to be updated. The functional leader may then need to provide training based upon these updates.

Chapter 12 - Manufacturing System and Architecture

Every manufacturing facility has either Computer Numerical Control (CNC), Numerical Control (NC), Programmable Logic Control (PLC) Systems, manual equipment, or numerous combinations of these machines and systems organized in varying degrees of productivities, efficiencies, and material flows.

Also, machine controls may use different technologies, configurations, and software versions. Some machines may be state of the art, while others have obsolete controls but are still functional and are running production. Communications may exist between multiple machines while others may not be linked or even have an interface. Machines may have the same controller but the software may be of different versions, so they may not communicate with each other.

Understanding the current machine layout and manufacturing system architecture is important because, over time, new products and processes may be introduced. Current products and processes may become obsolete, processes may need to change, and repairs, replacement, upgrades, and reconfigurations will be needed at some point to the various machines, controllers, and overall system.

These changes may involve the same model, a different model, or even a different technology, so it is important to understand the current equipment (process) layout and manufacturing system architecture details, as well as develop a future equipment (process) layout and manufacturing architecture technology and controls roadmap. In addition, the site or facility infrastructure equipment requires maintenance, upgrades, and improvements, so the infrastructure should also be included in the current and future roadmap.

Process Layout

The layout of the machines in the factory is discussed later in the Foundation section, since this is a core of Operations. There are many objectives, constraints, and influencing factors to consider in defining process layouts. Influencing factors to consider are: customer perspectives, material movements, people movements, people work space size, machine accessibility, machine portability, and internal and external environmental and safety factors (noise, emissions, temperature, etc.), size of production area needed, and support staff work area required (as this may limit production volume).

Main factors to consider are: manpower headcount and skill-sets, number of machines and type of machines, material flow, production volume, number of different products, manufacturing method, tooling, gaging, internal process costs versus external costs, productivity per hour or shift required, quality levels, work hours per shift, work days per week, and other key performance indicators.

Specifically, the following list should help with creating effective layouts and for building new machines, workstations, or processes.

Building New Machines and Process Layout
1. Establish layout for ease of people working, material movements and accessibility to the machines.
2. Establish a process layout that is flexible whereby different production volumes use different number of direct labor people.
3. Establish a work-cell layout shape, such as an "L", "U", straight line, or combination of these shapes, minimizing any obstacles within the worker area and providing visibility of each worker to other workers within the layout as best as possible.
4. Establish one-piece flow or continuous flow with minimal work in process between processing steps.
5. Establish one direction of material flow and define material flows that feed into main aisles. For example, U-shaped work-cells on both sides of an aisle.
6. Establish layout with the fewest environmental concerns.
7. Make the machine or process easy to set up, changeover, and potentially be able to physically move the equipment to another work area.
8. Use equipment that has a narrow floor footprint that faces the worker, such as narrow and long, not wide. This will minimize the distance for the worker to move materials from process step to process step.
9. Link machines-material loading and unloading at same height level for ergonomic benefits.
10. Enable quick gaging checks and communications between machines for broadcasting when an issue is identified.
11. Balance machine cycle times for all the different machines required based upon customer demand, meeting takt time. Takt is available production time divided by customer demand.
12. Use multi-purpose machines rather than purpose-built machines.
13. Design and build equipment with scalability in mind. Define a range of production volumes with associated production and overhead costs for a processing line or work-cell including a break-even analysis.
14. Use machines that maximize processing time to optimize tool head movements.
15. Use a semi-automated or automated signaling device that is Wi-Fi compatible and upgradeable. The signaling device can be activated when there is a machine problem, material unavailable, defect produced, or safety issue. This is called an Andon system — a Japanese term meaning a notification system that lets others know when a machine has a problem — within smallest unit of process operation to prevent moving defects to the next process.

16. Identify equipment within the layout that is the cycle-time constraint. Post the current cycle time and takt time prominently for each product. Utilize hourly productivity metric to ensure overall process meets takt time.

17. Identify equipment in the layout that produces the highest number of quality defects and post quality alerts and identify mistake or error-proofing devices to prevent defects moving to the next process operation step.

18. Identify Standardized Work instructions and post simple and clear pictorial instructions adjacent to the locations where work is performed. Standardized Work defines the most efficient way to produce a product at a consistent rate of production. See Standardized Work in Chapter 22 for more information.

19. Place machines with ease of performing preventive maintenance checks in mind, ease of access to wearable and replaceable parts, ease of access for lubrication, ease of discharging water from air lines, and ease of access for cleaning and removal of process debris.

20. Build machines with quick changeover in mind for both tool and fixture changes, including work in-process holders.

21. Place tool Shadow Boards within reach of operator's need of use. Shadow Boards are boards that hold tools whereby when a tool is removed the outline of the tool is shown so it is clear which tool goes where or is missing.

22. Build fixtures and jigs to allow different products to be produced with easy installation, removal, and storage.

23. Build fixtures and jigs with mistake-proof or error-proof devices to prevent producing defects and prevent from producing the wrong product.

24. Build and place equipment with the understanding that upgrades or other modifications will be needed for hardware, communications, or software. Ensure the manufacturing controls and architecture meets current and future requirements.

25. Build and install equipment for ease of use by an operator.

26. Build and install equipment with internal lighting, temperature control, humidity, oil mist collector, and dust control.

27. Provide simple assembly constructions for holding trays or boxes of components within reach and for ease of work by operator. Component trays or boxes should be loaded into workstations without interrupting work and the layout should make it possible to empty trays or boxes without interrupting work.

28. Build/install equipment for ease of conducting various tool life studies.

29. Build/install equipment with primary and secondary safety devices and display the various safety labels in prominent locations on machine.

30. Ensure all commissioned and qualified equipment has asset tags and have a general understanding of where these would be placed on each piece of equipment.

31. Build assembly equipment that can be easily modified for other configurations and ease of handling different assembly jigs and fixtures.

32. Build assembly equipment with an understanding of ergonomics, material weights and sizes, distance, heights, and arm and hand movements.

33. Build assembly equipment with the lowest level of automation balanced with cost, productivity, and quality that meet or exceed customer requirements.

34. Define manufacturing standards for the above — both generic and specific for each process.

35. Establish layouts to consider whether any process operation is outsourced and how this material will move to an external supplier and be re-introduced into internal process operations with a known, qualified quality level.

36. Before building equipment and establishing a layout, make a computer simulation or consider a cardboard model of the machines, and place it into the proposed layout. This will help all involved understand many key details that might be missed due to the complexity of manufacturing operations, number of machines required, workspace environment, and infrastructure requirements.

Illustration – Machining Process Layout

The following figure shows a machining process layout with a:

- 4 shift operation
- 12 hours each shift, Day shift 08:00-20:00 and Night shift 20:00-08:00
- 7 days a week production
- Shift production target is 200 pcs per shift
- One Direct Labor is responsible for machining a specific part moving from Operation 10 through to Operation 50
- Direct Labor performs Quality inspection checks, performs Total Preventive Maintenance activities, and performs 5S before, during and after shift activities

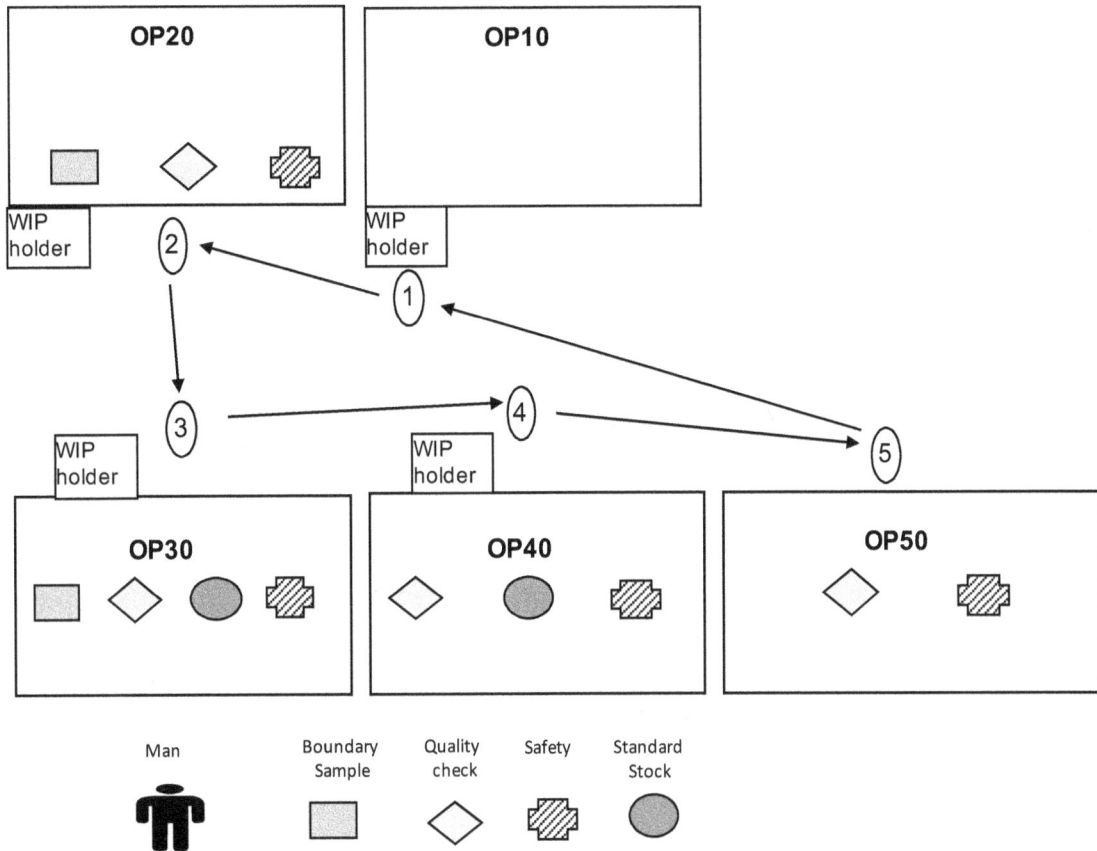

Figure 2. 7 Machining process layout

Buying New Machines

Building and buying machines requires more than just manufacturing engineers writing requirements and specifications. Inputs and requirements are needed from quality, supply chain, and production staff that will be using the equipment. In addition, finance needs to be involved — especially in support of performing due diligence. After selecting possible suppliers and before sending out a Request for Quote (RFQ) package, schedule a supplier visit to ensure the supplier has the technical capabilities needed to meet the expected requirements. Also, visits should be made to companies who are using such or equivalent machines already, ask for weakness and strengths, and compare with own potential use/requirement. In addition, there should be a request to each supplier of their financial viability and a request to provide a list of references that can be contacted.

When defining an RFQ, the following should be included in the package to the machine build suppliers:

1. Non-Disclosure and Confidentiality Agreement, to ensure control over proprietary information. These documents are prepared by the company's legal advisor. The lawyer needs to review and approve other documents including the purchase order standard terms and conditions.

2. A clear description of the company's need and expectations for the machine(s).

3. Product name(s) and description, basic product function and usage of the product with the final end customer, production volume for each product, expected cycle time and takt time, and defined quality level or acceptance for various part dimensions.

4. Product drawings with material specifications and any other specifications for the operation processes being quoted. A request to provide a Machine PFMEA, see Chapter 17 for more information about Potential Failure Mode and Effects Analysis.

5. Confirmation that the supplier has a document control system in place in case there are any revisions to the drawings, specifications, or RFQ.

6. Quantitative definition of layout and machine build requirements. These requirements can be discussed in great detail before the supplier submits a proposal.

7. Defined payment terms and conditions for payment, such as 30% upon purchase order issuance; 30% upon equipment qualified at supplier; 30% upon commissioned, qualified, and accepted at customer location; 10% upon 6 months in service without experiencing any significant downtime, quality, or other significant performance issue. A significant event detail needs to be clearly defined.

8. Definition of a general project timing plan and financial penalties for missing or delaying any of the agreed-upon milestone dates.

9. Project gate review dates, RFQ due date, and supplier acknowledgement of receipt.

Equipment maker should provide the following in response to an RFQ:

1. Schematics and details for the machine(s), including materials and component specifications, machine footprint size, weight, power requirements, air pressure requirements, wiring diagrams, machine accuracy, controller details, accessories, replaceable parts, machine guarding, material inputs, material outputs for "good" and "no good", tool movement and means for changing tools, tool types and details, fixture design, part holding details, and performance specifications. This includes computer modeling to show loading forces and location of part holding and supports.

2. A machine program to train users, which should be editable for engineers to make changes.

3. An initial set of tools, tool supplier contact information, tool specifications, tool speeds and feeds, and tool paths. Also, an estimated tool life study for each tool.

4. List of quality inspection gages or equipment needed to confirm part dimensions meet requirements. Supplier should ensure a gage repeatability and reproducibility (gage R&R) study is conducted and is acceptable.

Alternatively, the supplier will need to ensure the proposed layout does not affect or constrict inspection points within the process.

5. A definition of and commitment to meeting process performance requirements: cycle time, tool life costs, changeover times especially for multiple products, Total Productive Maintenance time and activities documented or system program defined, and quality level.

6. Coolant specifications, filling locations, chip removal location and means of removal, or other debris location points; emission levels and control checking points including alarms when conditions are not suitable for operation.

7. List of spare parts and training on how to replace machine wearable parts.

8. Detailed machine qualification procedure and physical validation at supplier location, including conducting preliminary process capability studies.

9. Commitment to commission machine at customer site and conduct preliminary process capability studies aimed at meeting expected quality levels.

10. Definition of the necessary means to connect with the current Manufacturing Execution System (MES), linkage to other internal systems such as ERP, quality inspection databases, and provide support personnel and time or time per hour to support the communication's linkage.

11. Cost package including accepting the financial terms and conditions. Follow-up correspondence may include a detailed cost or itemized package.

After the RFQ has been submitted to several suppliers, the suppliers will have a certain amount of time to submit their proposals. During the proposal development time, the suppliers may need several technical or other clarifications. The company should create a Frequently Asked Question sheet (FAQs) with answers to ensure all suppliers have the same understanding; this also documents knowledge gaps in designing the process.

Once the suppliers' quotes start to arrive, a matrix needs to be made to compare the proposals equitably. Even if a standard RFQ sheet and cost template is provided to suppliers, suppliers often modify or make amendments to the template. The matrix helps to consolidate information for ease of comparison and analysis.

Once the selection of suppliers has been narrowed to a few, you may invite those suppliers to make formal presentations or visit their facility and walk through each proposal with their teams. During this walk, be sure to understand who on their team is dedicated to support your proposal, what their role and length of time will be, and what other resources will be needed, including timing of resources and work areas for building the machine(s). Confirm their technical capabilities, evaluate their current production availability, and assess their work capacity to complete the RFQ on-time. At this time, the supplier should have already provided a statement of their financial viability from their banking institution.

After reviewing each of the supplier facilities and formal presentations, a final round of negotiations should take place. Then a decision will be made by the company's manufacturing, technical, quality, EHS, and financial team. A purchase order can then be issued to the chosen supplier, along with a telephone call to congratulate them and begin joint planning of a project kickoff at their facility.

Once the purchase order is given, the project team from both the company and the supplier should meet weekly to discuss and review the project plan and open action items. The company may also have internal activities such as facility infrastructure changes or improvements to install the new process equipment. The manufacturing footprint and quality systems will need to be updated with the new list of equipment. In addition, the company project team members should define the logistics for receiving and installing the new equipment, along with an inventory buildup and production plan — especially if other process equipment needs to be temporarily halted. The above business process activity can be customized for procuring one machine or multiple pieces of equipment.

The above process for buying machines is very similar to purchasing direct materials needed to make a finished goods product to be sold to a customer. Direct materials are raw materials, parts, and/or components utilized to make a final finished product.

Manufacturing System Architecture
Along with having a manufacturing footprint, each facility should update its manufacturing system architecture footprint regularly, such as major changes, or at least once a year. The manufacturing system architecture footprint is specific for each production machine (whereas the manufacturing footprint is for a process or work-cell that may have multiple equipment). Other ancillary and non-production machines should have similar structures of control, but those are not typically updated yearly since there are few updates made to this equipment; however, if there are upgrades or changes made, then the footprint needs to be updated.

There should be a file for each machine containing the latest machine program, as well as a system to retain historic machine programs. Computer backups should be made on a regular, frequent schedule and supported by the IT function.

The manufacturing system architecture footprint should have, at a minimum, the following information:
- Business unit, factory identification, and/or value stream name

- Work cell name, machine name and machine identification number (finance department should have a specific asset number for each machine)
- Machine maker name and model name
- Machine description or other specific key criteria
- Machine controller brand name and model number
- Controller version level, configuration and/or other information
- Controller software name and software version level
- Controller software program name and revision level
- Controller date of installation (latest installation date)
- Acquisition, depreciation, maintenance, and/or calibration costs
- Any other information for reference purposes; backup location can also be noted

Facility Infrastructure

Various other facility infrastructure systems and controls also have to be documented, controlled, maintained, and identified. These include electricity, water, wastewater, gas, fire sprinkler and suppression systems, communications devices and lines, Wi-Fi, security devices and systems both inside and outside, safety devices and systems, data processing systems, logistics and warehousing systems, and any other devices or systems used to support operations. In addition, annual Industrial Hygiene surveys may be needed to assess an employee's exposure to chemical, biological, and physical hazards. The results of these surveys may require improvements to procedures, or investment to reduce or eliminate these exposures.

Chapter 13 - Manufacturing Footprint

Every manufacturing facility should define a manufacturing footprint and a summary of its overall product and process capacities and capabilities, along with any certifications, permits, and customer awards. Many companies post a summary of this information in their entrance or lobby area. The manufacturing footprint is used primarily for planning purposes, but is also used for various comparison analyses. The manufacturing footprint should be defined in a spreadsheet and regularly updated with information. The summary should include items such as:

- Country, province, state, city (especially when there are multiple facilities)
- Manufacturing site location name, business unit or value stream name
- List of Finished Goods (names) with production volumes, previous year, current year, and forecasted volumes

The detailed manufacturing footprint is defined by work-cells and would include every process type such as plastic molding, forging, heat treatment, machining, assembly, painting, welding, etc. The list has the work-cell name or identification, product types or product names that are being processed, location in the factory if a large factory, or multiple building identifications. If products are similar in nature, then the corresponding values can be averaged, or a weighted average can be used. However, if products do not have similar values due to size, weight, features, materials, and tolerances, then they would have to be defined separately.

- Theoretical current production capacity
- Actual or average current production capacity over some time period
- Overall Equipment Effectiveness percentage:
    - Availability
    - Performance
    - Quality level (average defect parts per million, Cp/Cpk for critical characteristic, and/or tolerance range)

- Average tool cost per unit of production (if machining) over some time period
- Average maintenance cost per unit of production over some time period
- Average other consumable cost per unit of production over some time period
- Average total cost per unit of production over some time period and/or volume
- Work cell cycle time (typically, machine with highest cycle time)
- Estimated, budgeted, or approved capital expenditure spending for current year. Notes can be defined for upgrades or for adding other improved capabilities that impact safety, quality, cost, delivery.

- Number of machines in each work-cell

- Manufacturing work-cell physical size (square feet or square meters)

- Number of direct labor operators per shift

- Estimated capital expenditure for replacement of entire work-cell (amount can be in local currency with notation)

- Current depreciated book value

- Original date of machine installation (subsequent modifications or upgrades can be noted)

There are several reasons for having a current manufacturing footprint that identifies current manufacturing process details, which include capacities, process capabilities, technologies and utilization rates. The footprint reasons are listed and discussed in the subsections that follow.

- Evaluating incremental capacity
- Link to product technology roadmap
- Benchmarking
- Evaluating underutilized capacity
- Replacing current processes with advanced technology
- Capturing requirements for new business opportunities
- Acquiring technologies and vertical integration

Evaluating Incremental Capacity

Manufacturing engineering analyzes current Overall Equipment Effectiveness metrics, capacity, and direct labor shift scheme against forecasted demand to determine the constraints and actions to reduce potential issues. Overall Equipment Effectiveness metric is explained in Chapter 29, Total Productive Maintenance, in the Conditioning section. Manufacturing engineering may make some assumptions to use additional idle equipment, buy new equipment, consolidate processes, rearrange equipment, or combine this with a different direct labor work scheme such as adding overtime to meet incremental capacity needs.

In addition, forecasted product demands should be analyzed against current utilization rates to determine whether new investments are needed to meet the forecasted demand. In many cases, if demand increases, short-term capacities can increase to match, as already stated with overtime. However, at some point, longer-term, more-permanent solutions may be necessary, including process improvements, process re-design, new equipment, or different work shift scheme.

Incremental process capability investment needs are difficult to assess and keep track of, because this factor is related to the reliability of the equipment and product tolerance width. Maintaining equipment is paramount to ensure stable, long-term capacity and capable processes. Wearable machine parts and other machine electronics will need replacement, which may positively affect capacity and capability.

Another related point concerns customer requests for changes to the product (e.g., a request for an engineering or product re-design). These changes must be thoroughly studied for their impact on capacity and process capability. In some cases, a change request may affect the capacity and process capability, especially if a customer request is associated with tighter specification requirement or more complicated design requirement.

Link to Product Technology Roadmap

A product technology roadmap is a technical comparison plan of the items currently produced; products under development; competitors' products; and process or other technologies greatly affecting the product. The plan can be a graphical description of the various products over the coming five to ten years. Marketing, R&D and engineering are responsible for developing, maintaining and regularly presenting updates to this plan. This roadmap can identify linkages and non-linkages with current manufacturing processes and their capabilities. Highlighting these linkages and non-linkages is a way to show technical competitiveness and possible paths for business growth. One criterion for evaluating new business pursuits should be to evaluate the product technology roadmap with the current manufacturing footprint, because one new business venture win can significantly change the direction of future investments and core technologies.

This evaluation is conducted during the business case development. Business case development is further explained in Chapter 36, Pursuing New Business, in the Competitiveness section. If the pursuit of new business is aligned in some framework with the product technology roadmap, then this criterion would be satisfied.

Benchmarking

Benchmarking requires an understanding of not only the product features and performance, as well as the manufacturing processes. It is important to define using product features, performance and manufacturing processes on the product technology roadmap. The map can be illustrated by technology levels, specific features, performance criteria, critical manufacturing processes (including process capabilities), and time.

Benchmarking also can be performed against similar processes among different factories, work areas/cells for capacity, process capabilities and costs, and can be used as a base for improvement plans. It is very important to realize the company's overall competitiveness locally and globally. Obtaining data from related companies is not difficult. However, obtaining this data from competitors is extremely difficult.

In many cases products from competitors may be bought from the market and be stripped down and compared with its own products. In some cases, the company's customers can provide an insight into the competitiveness position. Also, external consultants can provide an independent assessment of the company's competitiveness.

Evaluating Under-utilized Capacity

Defining current and forecasted capacity requirements and then determining available capacity for other purposes or even reconfigurations or consolidations is a major undertaking and requires a manufacturing footprint as the basis for the planning. In addition, when business contracts expire and volumes decline, under-utilized capacity needs to be evaluated for repurposing, outsourcing, or selling. Also, the level of available capacity can be used temporarily or permanently for other new business pursuits, but this needs to be analyzed case by case using business case modeling.

For example, a proposal for pursuing new business shows a slow increase over several months. Current processes can possibly be used on an overtime basis, such as weekend work. Another example is if several processes have an available capacity of 20 percent or more, these processes may be considered. However, if there is significant fluctuating demand, these processes may not be dedicated fully for potential new business. Detailed analysis of the current manufacturing footprint, along with requirements for any new business proposal can determine whether current capacity can be used or not, and for what length of time. This type of analysis is practical, low-cost, and a capacity-driven model.

Replacing Current Processes with Advanced Technology

Companies evaluate needs for new advanced manufacturing technologies in slightly different ways — customer-, cost and profit-, quality-driven, or a combination of these options. A company may be looking to replace older, less-efficient, less-capable and less-reliable equipment with new, advanced technologies. This company may want to replace its technologies over a long period and may want to align its manufacturing technologies in several ways.

For example, the company may strive for standardization of manufacturing software programs (machine programs, machine-to-machine interfaces, CAD/CAM linkage, enterprise resource planning [ERP] interfaces), standardization among an affiliation of supplier manufacturing technologies (the company may use the latest equipment from known, currently used equipment suppliers), or flexibility and modularizing of equipment so machines can be moved into various work-cell configurations, with several factory layout iterations over years of upgrades.

In addition, older equipment can be sold, used internally in a prototype or for maintenance services, or dismantled and used for spare parts. Another important point to consider is that when older equipment is replaced with newer equipment, the older equipment may not be fully depreciated, adding a cost burden to company financials.

Capturing Requirements for New Business Opportunities

Capturing process requirements is critical when pursuing new business opportunities. The manufacturing footprint should be updated and highlighted with these new business requirements, even when still in the pursuit phase. Once the new business opportunity is confirmed or not, the manufacturing footprint would be updated. If the company wins new business, the highlighted manufacturing equipment needs to be verified and any new capacity (re-design, new equipment, etc.) needs to be qualified on the manufacturing floor and validated. Whenever a company loses business or does not win the new business opportunity, the manufacturing footprint needs to be updated. The capacities planned for that specific business should be removed from the manufacturing footprint.

Each week — or at a minimum, each month — manufacturing engineering or process team must update this footprint based on awards for winning new business, expiration of customer contracts, continuous improvement events and RFQ submissions. Also, process improvements need to be recorded in the manufacturing footprint after they have been validated, perhaps after one month of running production. The footprint is not a tool for recording the variability of throughput day by day, week by week, or month by month. That variability can be tracked using an Overall Equipment Effectiveness metric or other operation's metrics. Also, when a SMED workshop (single-minute exchange of die) is conducted, improvements can be validated after a month. Then, the manufacturing footprint is updated.

Acquiring Technologies and Vertical Integration

During due diligence for acquiring technologies or integrating vertically, a manufacturing footprint is typically assessed. The assessment is a fit for manufacturing and profitability economies. The before-and-after manufacturing footprint views of the acquisition or integration may provide some clear advantages that were unknown previously. Alternatively, due diligence may uncover technologies or manufacturing systems far different from those currently being used, so certain perceived advantages may be difficult to achieve or too costly to implement.

Some examples include different software controllers, manufacturing equipment with foundations that are difficult to move or reconfigure, manufacturing equipment with lower process capabilities, manufacturing equipment with smaller or larger work capacities (such as press tonnage), and dated manufacturing equipment that is high maintenance or for which parts are no longer available. Acquiring or vertically integrating also requires a business case analysis. The business case is updated and analyzed with new sets of information, including knowledge of the manufacturing footprint, and analysis of the before-and-after capabilities and capacities.

Chapter 14 - Visual Management

Visual management is a process for prominently displaying important business-related information for people to see, notice, and understand in a quick and purposeful way. Visual management can be in the form of electronic displays, panel chart boards, paper charts, markers on whiteboards, markers on poster boards or signs, and, to a lesser degree, painted lines, painted areas, labels, or other marking or colors that have specific meaning.

Benefits of Visual Management

a. Improve safety, quality, productivity, profitability, delivery, and morale

b. Reduce inventory

c. Decrease downtime

d. Identify problems or deviation from standards more quickly

e. Escalate problems in a clear and transparent manner

f. Improve control

g. Strengthen employees' pride in their work

h. Promote stronger communication among staff and workers

i. Increase employee engagement

j. Empower employees to improve their work areas

k. Establish a culture that is highly organized where high performance expectations are practiced

l. Create a positive impression for customers, suppliers, and other visitors

Visual Control Boards

Many companies post visual control boards in offices, factory floors, conference rooms, hallways, etc. Typically, these visual control boards are updated on an hourly, daily, or monthly schedule. Usually one person or position has the responsibility to keep specific boards up to date and accurate. The type, amount, and timeliness of information posted is indicative of that employee's responsibility, business needs, and business status.

The design of the visual boards may have a common theme, such as company logo in the same place on every board; use of company colors; use of a common typeface, color, and size for the board's title. Other features can be standardized, such as the size of the board, information content (specific spreadsheet or graph type), and location and orientation of information on the board.

The following questions can be used to evaluate the effectiveness of each of your company's use of visual boards:

- How informative or helpful is this visual board?

- How can this information be modified to be more informative?

- Who is the audience and are all intended audience members aware of this?

- Is the information displayed in a prominent location for the audience?

- Is the information updated on a timely basis or does the information need a higher refresh rate (information recorded once an hour, once a shift, etc.)?

- Who updates the information (specifically dates, times, names)? Is there a back-up person identified?

- Can the information be displayed more simply but as effectively?

- What response or action is the audience expected to take?

- If the audience wants to make a comment about the information, is there a location to do so?

- Should other languages be added to communicate with the audience?

- What other information can be communicated and how can this be displayed?

- If there are several information postings or boards, are they presented in a logical, process-oriented, and functional way?

- How easily and quickly is the information obtained? Can the information be automatically obtained and posted electronically? Is there a cost-benefit for doing so?

A status board should be formatted with these considerations in mind:

- Is the information stating a status, such as current versus plan?

- Is the information being recorded in the best timeframe interval (e.g., is it currently by day, but would be more relevant by shift, or by hour)?

- Is the status easily known by using colors?
  - Green: meet or exceed goal
  - Yellow: not meeting goal but better than previous period(s)
  - Red: not meeting goal

- Are the "good" and "bad" statuses displayed so differences can be seen?

- Is there a comparison between performance last year and this year, last month and this month, last shift and this shift, or hour by hour?

- Are there notes to show a reason for any significant change?

Office, Cafeteria, and Hallways
Visual boards in these areas usually are different from ones elsewhere in the company since these boards are broader in scope, they can be arranged by function, business process activity, upcoming events or history, recognitions, or business performance and KPIs. For example, some boards may be a summary of production status, upcoming projects to participate in, job postings, employee benefits, news

announcements, etc. In addition, functional boards may contain the Daily Routine (DR) activities by day, by project, by person, and status.

Offices, cafeteria, and hallways may not be able to accommodate all of this information, but plans can be made to prioritize the important business information that should be communicated and actively kept up to date.

Factory and Warehouse Visual Boards

There are many different kinds of visual boards in factories and in work-cells. Some examples include 5S, Audits, Continuous Improvement Projects (Kaizen), Cost of Quality, Delivery, Daily Routine (DR), Financial (cost), Hourly Productivity, Manufacturing Performance, Material Receipt/Shipment, Kanban, Monthly Plans, Morale, Organizational, Process or Value Stream, Production Planning, Project, Procedural, Quality (QRQC), Safety, Shadow, Story, Total Productive Maintenance (TPM), Training, Warranty, and Yearly Plans. Other types of boards can be used to show a deviation or special cause from a standard, plan, or target.

Illustration – Monthly Plan Board

The following example shows a Supply Chain monthly plan visual control board. Basically, two large whiteboard calendars are posted on a wall within the Supply Chain work area and placed where their Daily Routine meeting is held. The current month and next month's plans are defined by calendar date with someone's name next to the task for defining ownership. Different colored markers can be designated for customers, suppliers, or individual staff. During the Daily Routine meeting the whiteboard is updated, then after the meeting an electronic version is updated so everyone — anytime and anywhere — can see the functional or even operation's upcoming key events. Many more items can be inputted into the calendar, as this is for all Supply Chain personnel to use and to see where work can be re-distributed. Acronyms for supplier names and business meetings are needed for ease of reading. Some of the acronyms used below are: LPA-Layered Process Audit, B/C Prep-Business Case preparation, WSM-Worst Supplier Meeting, and MOM-Monthly Operations Meeting.

Table 2. 4 Visual monthly planning board

Current Month -

	1	2 Project Meetings	3	4 LPA Audit	5	6
7	8 B/C Prep	9 Project Meetings	10	11 Internal monthly review	12 Submit monthly report WSM	13
14	15 B/C Prep Supplier Audit	16 Project Meetings Supplier Audit	17 MOM Supplier Audit	18 Supplier Audit	19 1-1 Meetings WSM	20
21	22 B/C Prep Supplier Audit	23 Project Meetings Supplier Audit	24 SIOP Meeting Supplier Audit	25 LPA Audit	26 1-1 Meetings	27
28	29 B/C Prep	30 Project Meetings	31			

Next Month -

				1 LPA Audit	2	3
4	5 B/C Prep	6 Project Meetings	7	8 Internal monthly review	9 Submit monthly report WSM	10
11	12 B/C Prep Supplier Audit	13 Project Meetings Supplier Audit	14 MOM Supplier Audit	15	16 1-1 Meetings WSM	17
18	19 B/C Prep Supplier Audit	20 Project Meetings Supplier Audit	21 SIOP Meeting Supplier Audit	22 LPA Audit	23 1-1 Meetings	24
25	26 B/C Prep	27 Project Meetings	28	29	30	

Illustration – Visual Control Safety Board

A safety board can be located at the entrance to the manufacturing factory floor, in the canteen, or in a main hallway where it is easy for everyone to take notice. Previous year's information also can be identified in this chart. The layout of the factory can show the various types of incidences with markers, a year-to-date performance graph, a list of upcoming training events, and previous audit findings. Other Safety information can also be regularly updated on these types of boards. The Operation's Daily Routine meeting should have a brief stop at this board for any updates.

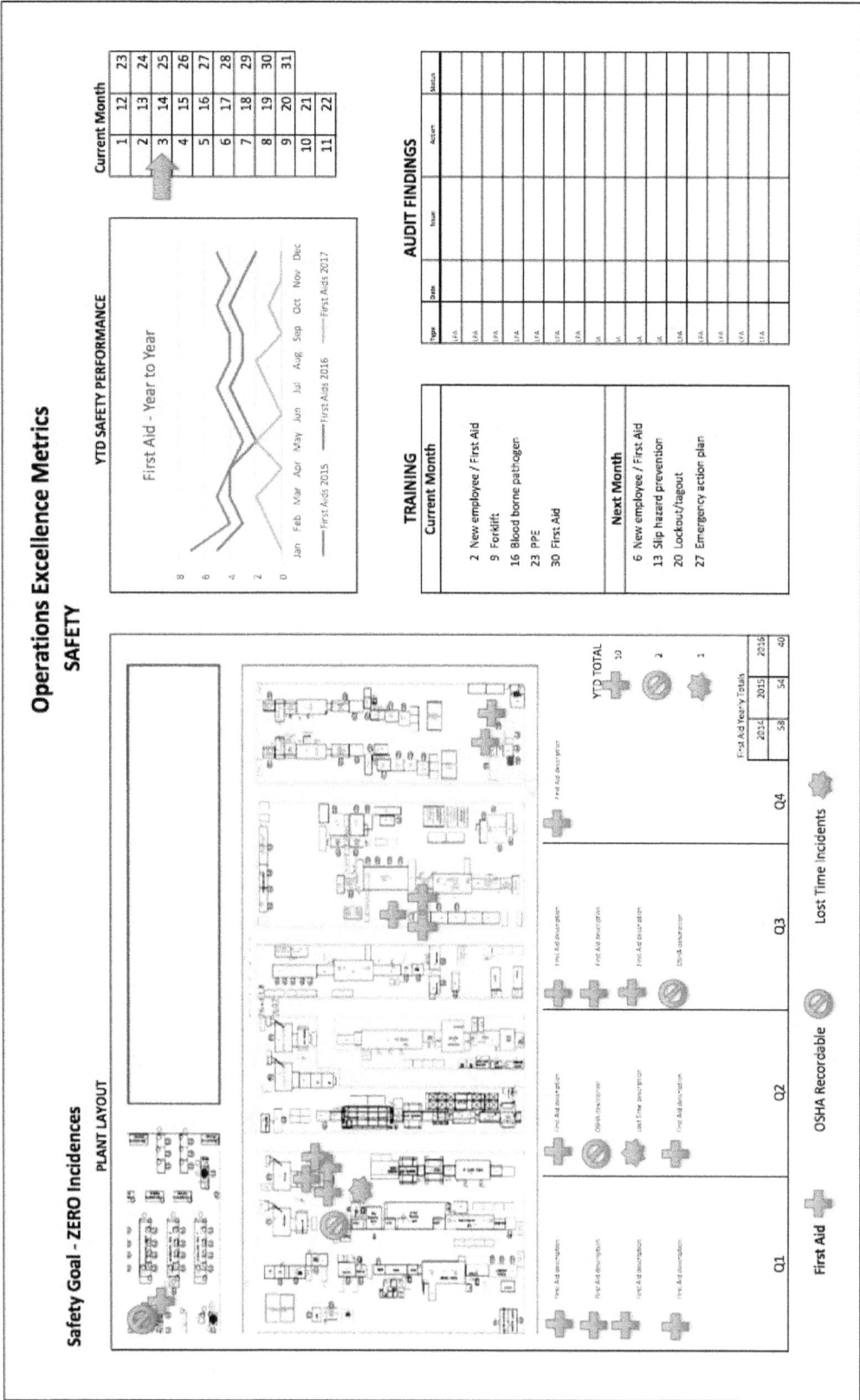

Figure 2. 8 Visual Control Safety Board

Illustration – Visual Control Productivity Chart

An hourly productivity chart can be located inside every manufacturing operation's work-cell and updated every hour by the operator, then confirmed by a supervisor. This chart can also be in electronic format so information can be broadcasted and displayed anywhere, and ongoing productivity and quality activity results can be measured over time.

Workcell Hour	Target	Actual	Defect Analysis Reason 1	Reason 2	Reason 3	Reason 4	Reason 5	Reason 6	Action Plan	Status (RYG)
1	30	29	5S issue on station	Night shift					Mgmt needs to talk with supervisors	Y
2	60	56	tester issue	miss connections	connector plug	worn			Update PM plan, change connectors after X number of parts	Y
3	90	76	Same	Same	Same	Same			Same	
4	120	106								
5	150	136								
6	180									
7	210									
8	240									
9	270									
10	300									
TOTAL	300									

Figure 2. 9 Visual Control - Hourly Productivity Chart

Illustration – Key Performance Indicator Board

The following board can be placed nearby each manufacturing work-cell. This type of visual control board would contain all operations KPIs for a specific work-cell or group of work-cells that support a product family. Hourly related metrics are posted and used within the work-cell and typically are located nearby the last production operation. This board shows 4 main KPIs; Safety & Training, Quality, Customer Fulfillment, and Continuous Improvement. The subsets within each main KPI may be specific for one work-cell, product family, or the entire factory. However, depending on the various customers, products, and processes, the subset KPIs may be different.

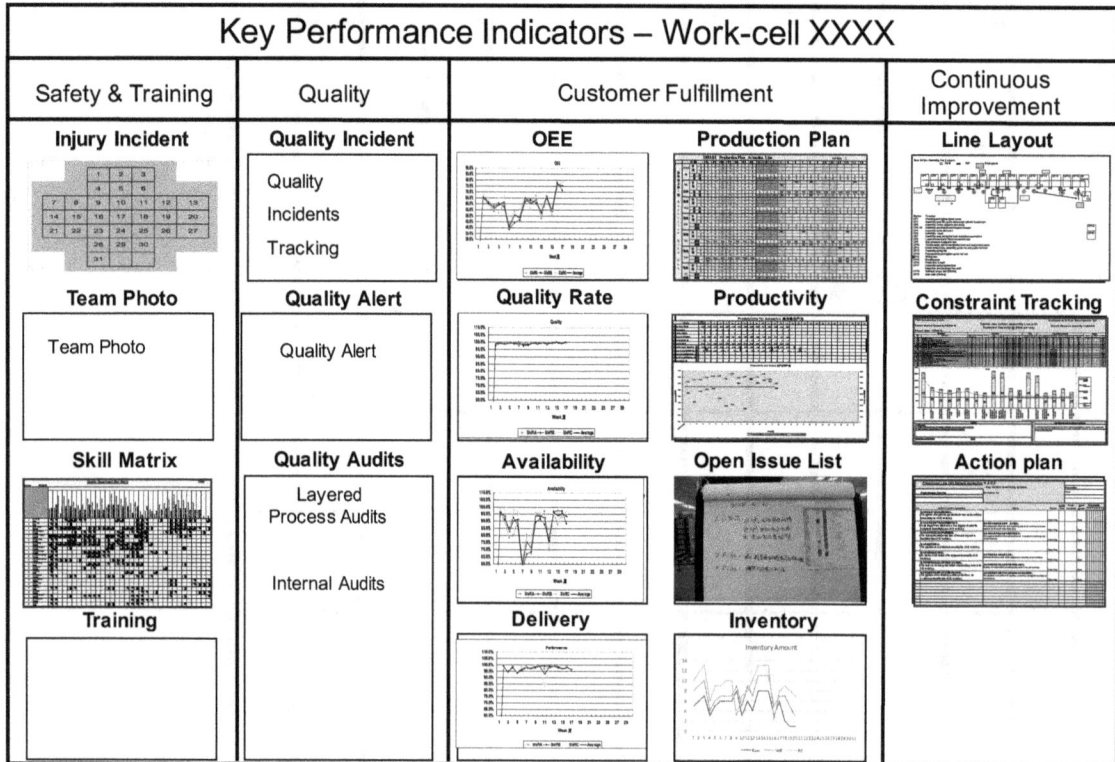

Figure 2. 10 Visual Control – KPI Board

Illustration – Visual Control- Direct Labor Skills Matrix

The following figure shows a skills matrix for a specific work area, for a specific shift, and for either permanent direct labor workers or temporary workers. This matrix is established by the Team Leader and is validated by the supervisor and other operation's members each month. The Team Leader is responsible to:

- Train workers- both permanent and temporary workers
- Validate the worker's skill capabilities
- Ensure the skill level matches the work they are performing or is performing work under supervision of a trainer

Table 2. 5 Direct Labor Skills Matrix

Shift 1 (2) 3   Skills Matrix   (Permanent) / Temporary

Workcell	Station #	1	2	3	4	5	6	7	8	9	10	11	12	13	14	15
	OP #	420	430	440	450	460	470	480	490	500						
Final Assembly- Large Carrier	Station Name	Chassis Base	Fan Motor and screw	PCBA and screw	Wire connect	Cover and screw	Final Assembly	Functional Test 1	Functional Test 2	Inspection and Package						
Name																
Josh (TL-Mar)		●	●	●	●	●	●	●	●	●	⊕	⊕	⊕	⊕	⊕	⊕
Sona		●	●	●	●	●	●	●	●	●	⊕	⊕	⊕	⊕	⊕	⊕
Jasmine		◕	◕	◕	◕	◕	◕	◕	◕	◕	⊕	⊕	⊕	⊕	⊕	⊕
Debra		◕	◕	◕	◕	⊕	⊕	⊕	⊕	⊕	⊕	⊕	⊕	⊕	⊕	⊕
Zaki		◕	◕	◕	◑	◑	◑	◑	◑	⊕	⊕	⊕	⊕	⊕	⊕	⊕
Liam		◕	◕	◑	◑	◑	◑	◑	⊕	⊕	⊕	⊕	⊕	⊕	⊕	⊕
Olivia		◑	◔	◔	◑	⊕	◑	◔	◑	⊕	⊕	⊕	⊕	⊕	⊕	⊕
Ava		◑	◑	◑	⊕	⊕	⊕	⊕	⊕	⊕	⊕	⊕	⊕	⊕	⊕	⊕
Aiden		◑	◑	◔	⊕	◔	⊕	⊕	⊕	⊕	⊕	⊕	⊕	⊕	⊕	⊕
Carter		◑	⊕	⊕	⊕	⊕	⊕	⊕	⊕	⊕	⊕	⊕	⊕	⊕	⊕	⊕
		⊕	⊕	⊕	⊕	⊕	⊕	⊕	⊕	⊕	⊕	⊕	⊕	⊕	⊕	⊕
		⊕	⊕	⊕	⊕	⊕	⊕	⊕	⊕	⊕	⊕	⊕	⊕	⊕	⊕	⊕
		⊕	⊕	⊕	⊕	⊕	⊕	⊕	⊕	⊕	⊕	⊕	⊕	⊕	⊕	⊕
		⊕	⊕	⊕	⊕	⊕	⊕	⊕	⊕	⊕	⊕	⊕	⊕	⊕	⊕	⊕
		⊕	⊕	⊕	⊕	⊕	⊕	⊕	⊕	⊕	⊕	⊕	⊕	⊕	⊕	⊕

Team Leader Name		ML	ML	ML									
Validated By:		Jan	Feb	Mar	Apr	May	Jun	Jul	Aug	Sep	Oct	Nov	Dec
Supervisor (initials)	Week 1	KAB	KAB	JP									
	Week 2	KAB	KAB	JP									
	Week 3	KAB	KAB	JP									
	Week 4	KAB	KAB	JP									
	Week 5	KAB		JP									
Supervisor	Initials	JJ	JJ	JJ									
Production Manager	Initials	AS	AS	AS									
Quality Manager		WG	WG	WG									

Legend:
- ◔ Learning Job, must have someone approve work
- ◑ Meets Takt and Quality Knows All Key Points
- ◕ Expert, Can perform rework or repairs
- ● OJT Trainer

Office Signs

Mandatory signs include entrance; exit; fire extinguisher; directions (with destinations and arrows); office area name; function; safety or personal protective equipment areas; evacuation routes; and room names such as conference room names. Specific cubicles or desks can be identified with employee photo, name, title, contact information, and possibly a personal creative message that meets the communications requirements in the company handbook.

Color Scheme

A color scheme can be used to identify various areas of the factory. Office areas may have carpet or colored tile floor that is typically a different color than the factory floor. The factory floor may have different colors to designate specific work areas or separating certain areas due to environmental or processing conditions. Transitions from office areas into the factory, safety and PPE signs should be posted and these transition areas should be painted in a way whereby people entering or leaving will not be injured when doors swing open. Also, colored floor areas can be designated for forklifts, autonomous vehicles, and material storage areas. Material flow can also be defined with painted arrows and with signs. The areas in and around the factory site should have signage, markings, lighting, and supplementary security safeguards:

- Chemical, oil, gas storage
- Cross walks
- Parking areas
- Handicapped parking
- Electric car charging stations
- Waste
- Smoking area
- Low structure height
- Piping

- LNG, LPG storage
- Roadways and intersections
- Direction arrows
- Building numbers
- Accessibility ramps
- Material storage
- Flammable area
- Weight limits
- Truck lanes

Chapter 15 - Managing Quality

Managing Quality is a challenging activity, as everyone in the company has responsibility for Quality. This is similar to Safety in that it is everyone's responsibility to work in a safe environment.

Upon entering a factory, quality is noticeable, is a deliberate goal of the workers, and is practiced within a structure. The structure is documented formally in the Quality Management System, which includes an established mindset and behaviors that are continuously trained, evaluated, and improved upon. There are many components of a Quality Management System such as:

- Quality Policy
- Quality Planning
- Quality Control
- Quality Assurance
- Reliability & Warranty
- Supplier Quality
- Customer Quality
- Quality Improvement

Illustration – Quality Management System

A Quality Management System consists of many formally documented integrated business processes and controls. The following diagram depicts the concept of a Quality Management System with the center of focus being Quality Improvement. The 4 arrows show Deming's process of: Plan, Do, Check, and Act affecting all components.

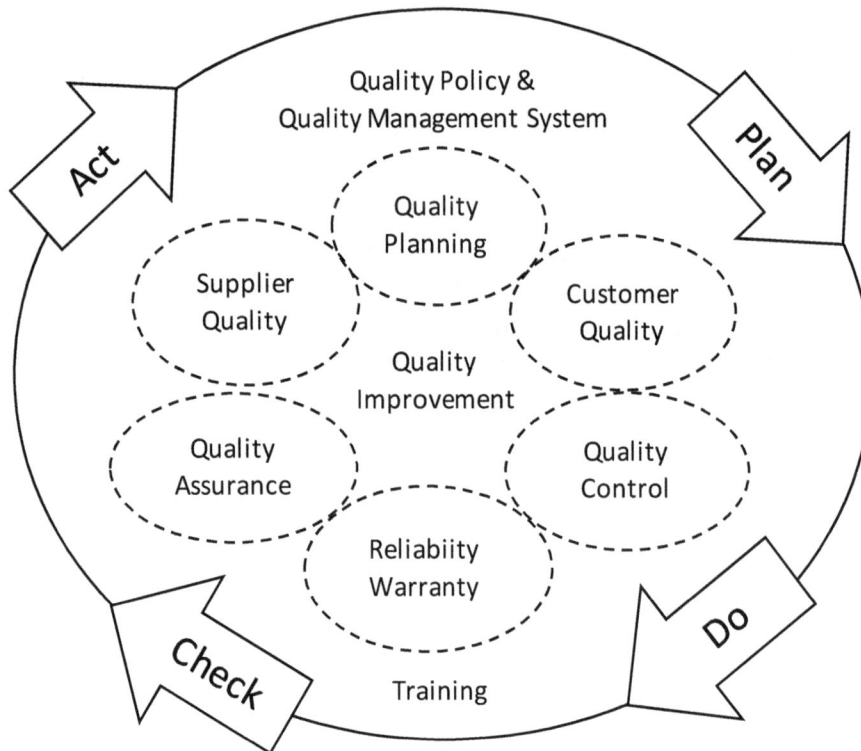

Figure 2. 11 Quality Management System

Quality Management System

A Quality Management System documents all business processes and changes. To ensure the business process is practiced and effective, various audits will be conducted, including use of third-party auditors. A quality system can be audited and certified against international quality management system requirements such as ISO9001, IATF 16949, or AS9100. The quality function within the company has the responsibility of ensuring the system is compliant with these standards and will help develop policies, procedures, standards, work instruction, visual aids, and various training programs and audits.

Everyone in the organization needs to be continuously trained and routinely practice their procedures relative to the quality system, depending upon their job scope and responsibilities. The procedures should be available both in bound manuals and electronically with a simple, easy way of accessing the information. Someone in the quality organization should pursue various quality certifications, including becoming a Lead Auditor, so that proper internal audits (internal quality management reviews, layered process audits, skip-level audits, and dock audits) can be defined and conducted in a structured, effective way. Audits are discussed in much greater detail in Chapter 26 in the Conditioning section.

Quality Policy

A Quality Policy is defined by a company's top management team and is basically the umbrella covering the Quality Management System structure. Management defines the direction for Quality and the company's strategies and objectives are aligned to it. Management needs to ensure the Quality Policy is communicated to all employees, is a part of the Orientation process, and the employees understand how their job affects quality and success of the company. The Quality Policy statement needs to be consistent with the scope of the Quality Management System. Also, the Quality Policy needs to cover the following and be a commitment to ensure; customer satisfaction, continuous improvement, and defect prevention. This is a requirement for ISO 9001, AS9100, and IATF 16949 and may be a requirement of your customers.

Quality Planning

Quality Planning is a process for product realization that defines all the requirements for inputs and outputs. Most automotive manufacturing companies use the Automotive Industry Action Group (AIAG) *Advanced Product Quality Planning and Control Plan (APQP) Manual* for Quality Planning. However, these guidelines can be used for any manufacturing company, in any industry, in any part of the world. If the organization is relatively small, the management team will decide who will be the project leader for a specific project. If the organization is quite large, there may be a dedicated project management or program management function. For any project utilizing a Quality Planning process, the project leader typically has a greater role in Quality Planning than the Quality function.

Companies that develop a product realization process have highly repeatable outcomes. A product realization process includes procedures, checklists, customer reviews, internal reviews, and supplier reviews. Every project that uses a Quality Planning guideline provides an inherent confidence in the output, provides opportunities for employees to gain knowledge, and provides an opportunity to further strengthen the company's Quality Planning process. The main phases or stages of a product realization process are:

- New Business Pursuit
- Plan and Define Program
- Product and Process Design
- Industrialization
- Production Validation
- Feedback, Assessment, and Corrective Action

Key Points for Quality Planning

1. There is a defined Advanced Product Quality Planning (APQP) process that the employees practice when developing and launching new products.

2. The project leader and team have experience with the APQP inputs, process, and outputs, or want to be trained for a specific input, process, and output.

3. Management identifies and provides resources and training as needed for the project team.

4. The project leader and team are accountable for the project completion and have a desire to use a documented APQP process.

5. The project plan is comprehensive, covering all product and process phases with cross-functional support defined with milestone phase review target dates.

6. Phase or stage exit reviews are conducted diligently, in accordance with the project plan. The status for each output is documented with evidence that demonstrates the output is completed. This also provides a historic record for building knowledge and provides a certain level of confidence to move onto the next phase or stage. Outputs not completed according to the project plan are summarized into action plans. Outputs behind schedule are indicated with a red color on the project status plan and have a higher priority when scheduling resources to work.

7. Phase or stage exit reviews are conducted by the project leader, project team, functional and senior managers, and with technical experts.

8. Functional and senior managers decide whether to move on to the next project phase or stage with contingencies, risks and actions defined. Management can also decide to stay on the current phase or stage with various other support and priorities given.

9. Project phase or stage exit reports are reviewed with senior management soon after the project has completed a phase or stage.

10. Action items during the project phase or stage reviews are monitored for closure.

11. Quality planning documentation and supporting evidence is controlled, retained, and easily retrievable. Historic APQP documents and evidence may be reviewed to gain knowledge and to avoid repeating problems.

Quality Control

Very simply, Quality Control (QC) is a documented business process to ensure requirements are met. QC can be done by an inspection or test, either with or without instruments, gages, tooling, equipment, and automation. For each of a company's products, processes, and services, requirements are defined by specific characteristics with known values and tolerances. While the business process is active, the products, processes, and services are then checked in some way to ensure they meet the requirements. QC should be in all functional areas, including production, logistics, HR, purchasing, engineering, finance, etc. The QC in these functional areas should be documented and performed according to their documented practices.

QC activities and practices are documented in various procedures, defining Who does What and When. In production, a QC Plan is developed in great detail for each product. It contains specific QC information and answers the following questions:

- What product or process characteristics should be inspected/tested?
- What will be used to determine whether the product or process characteristic meets the requirements?
- Where in the process should a check, inspection, or test occur?
- What is the frequency for the check, inspection, or test?
- Who or what will do the inspection/test?
- How should inspection/testing be done?
- What to do with the inspection/test data?
- What happens to the part after it has been tested and passed? What happens when the part fails?
- Is the part identified and traceable to show the part has been inspected/tested at each specific inspection/test location?

Quality Control Standard Content

A Process Quality Control Standard Operation Sheet, Work Standard, Standard Operation, Work Instruction, or Standardized Work Instruction Sheet defines step-by-step instructions for a specific activity or set of activities. These documents are very similar in definition but are used in widely differently ways in practice. These documents are controlled and maintained by Quality to ensure the latest document is available. These documents can be found in various locations around the factory where the activity consistency is expected. These documents can be found in all functional areas, not just limited to manufacturing operations. However, the format for these documents may vary in different areas such as in human resources versus on the factory floor. For activities involving moving materials or transforming materials on the factory floor, these documents may include the following:

- Document name, number, revision, approval, and dates
- Launch status; production, pre-production, prototype
- Work area and station identification
- Part number, part name, operation number, operation name, and operation description
- Identification of the product being produced
- Raw materials needed and/or amount of Work in-process
- Safety points and Personal Protective Equipment (PPE) required
- Step-by-step process actions with diagrams or photos
- Material and staffing movement with photos or sketches of each step

- Key product and process points (each key product and process point should include the product or process values with tolerances)
- Inspection details and criteria for acceptance
- Frequency of inspection/test (can be based on time or quantity produced)

The process quality control sheet also may reference other information — 5S activities, daily preventive maintenance, changeover process instructions, and indicator of whether this process operation is the bottleneck (constraint). If this process operation is the bottleneck, use a specific color or icon on the document and post a label on the machine.

If there are any inspection activities defined in these documents, then this inspection data most likely will be collected via a QC data sheet or by electronic means. This data collection information may contain the above information plus:

- Inspection values - quantitative or qualitative
- Inspection status such as Good versus No Good, or Pass/Fail
- Process characteristics setting and range, and actual values
- Name of worker that inspects or tests the materials or products and/or name of worker at the specific operation
- Date and time of the produced material or part
- Raw material batch, lot, or serial number
- Traceability information for materials and parts that have finished the workstation or work-cell, such as serial number, batch, lot, time and date

Illustration – Process Quality Control Standard Operations Sheet

Process Control Quality Control can be in the form of step-by-step instructions on a computer screen, or on paper. For a computer screen, the current step details and whether the step has been completed correctly is shown, then the next step is shown until the process has been completed correctly. QC data can be recorded manually or automatically. Mistake-proof systems can also be shown electronically or on paper. Additional visual aids can be posted, too. However, be careful about posting documents all over a workstation or area because no one will read them if there are many documents. Ideally, standardized work documents are posted on the side or back of the workstation that include process quality control checks. Standardized Work is discussed in Chapter 22.

Process Quality Control Standard Operation Sheet S

Date :
Revision :
Responsible :
Number :

Control Plan Number

Customer: | Model/Project: | Part/Process Description: | Part No.: | SOS No. : | Station : | Status: x Production / Pre-Launch / Prototype

No.	Operation Sequence	Main Operation Steps.	Diagram / Photograph	Key	Quality Care Points
1.1	Pick up housing with Right Hand fitted with bleedscrew		Fig 1	1	Visually check the bleed screw is fitted properly
1.2	Using both hands, locate housing into jig, with bore facing up. F			2	Visually check the seal is not damaged and is located the seal groove
1.3	Pick up a seal with Right Hand and locate into seal groove in bo Use Left hand and finger to ensure seal is within groove			3	Visually check the boot is located into the boot groove
1.4	Pick up boot with Right Hand, and locate into housing boot groov		Fig 2		
2.1	Using both hands, pick up housing from jig, truen housing 180 degrees, so the bore is facing downwards		Fig 3		
2.2	Using both hands, place bore of housing onto the male fixture, th push down firmly and twist the housing to ensure the boot is in th groove, see Fig 2			4	Push housing down onto the male fixture, and twist to ensure the boot is located correctly
3.1	Using both hands, pick up the housing off the male fixture and lo into piston, Assy fixture Fig. 5				
3.2	Using Right Hand, pick up a piston from the piston tray.				

| Operator Skill Level Required | U | Calibrated Equipment Required | Y | Number of Mistake Proofs. | - | Number of Boundary Samples | - | In Process Checks | ✓ | Work In-process | 10 | Changeover 1st Off, Last Off | Y | | Safety | SAFETY EQUIPMENT |

ALL REJECT/SUSPECT PRODUCT(S) TO BE IDENTIFIED AND SEGREGATED

| APPROVAL | Manufacturing: Sign & print name | Quality: Sign & print name | Production Support: Sign & print name | Ear Protection | Gloves | Shoes ✓ | Glasses | Other (specify) work clothes |

Figure 2. 12 Process Quality Control Sheet

What actions, if any, have to be taken based upon the inspection/test?

If the requirements are satisfactorily met, then the next operation can be started.

If the requirements are not met, then a deviation or problem is detected, and one or more of the following actions can be taken:

- Continue running the process (if authorized).
- Stop the process.
- Contact a lead operator, maintenance, engineer, or supervisor.
- Adjust the process within acceptable ranges or, if outside the acceptable range, a documented deviation and approval process should be followed.
- Start a root cause analysis.
- Define a containment action and identify when the first product was made that had a deviation or problem, and all products up until the process is corrected.
- Define a corrective action.

QC Self-Check

To ensure waste is minimized, QC should be conducted at each process step and throughout the process, including mistake proofing. If the process operations are manual, there should be self- and successive checks for each manual operation. Even if the process is semi-automated or automated, self-checks can be performed. By having self-check and successive checks, any deviation or reject can be instantly detected and corrected if possible. This also provides an opportunity to identify improvements, such as implementing mistake proofing.

QC Self-Check - Illustration

The following illustration can be used in all functions and business processes. For business processes other than manufacturing parts, the "Red Bin / Reject Box" can be return to sender with a comment as to the reason for rejection. The sender can then learn from the reject, modify the activity and re-submit. Also, the sender can evaluate their process activity to identify the root cause of the rejection and make any necessary corrective action.

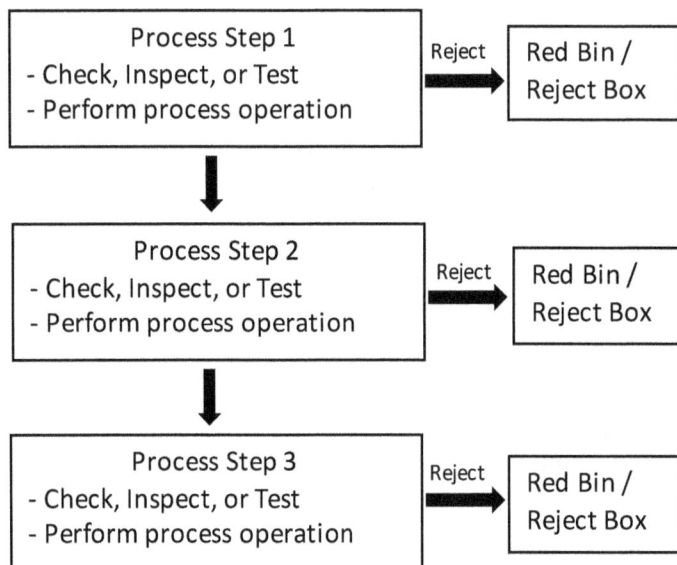

```
┌─────────────────────────────┐
│      Process Step 1         │  Reject  ┌──────────────┐
│ - Check, Inspect, or Test   │ ───────> │  Red Bin /   │
│ - Perform process operation │          │  Reject Box  │
└─────────────────────────────┘          └──────────────┘
              │
              ▼
┌─────────────────────────────┐
│      Process Step 2         │  Reject  ┌──────────────┐
│ - Check, Inspect, or Test   │ ───────> │  Red Bin /   │
│ - Perform process operation │          │  Reject Box  │
└─────────────────────────────┘          └──────────────┘
              │
              ▼
┌─────────────────────────────┐
│      Process Step 3         │  Reject  ┌──────────────┐
│ - Check, Inspect, or Test   │ ───────> │  Red Bin /   │
│ - Perform process operation │          │  Reject Box  │
└─────────────────────────────┘          └──────────────┘
```

Figure 2. 13 Quality Control Check

Master Parts

To ensure a standard quality level, Master Parts — both good and no-good — are commonly displayed and compared against current production throughout the process flow, from receiving to shipping at a specified frequency, such as start of shift and end of shift. Master Parts can be used to distinguish a variety of visual defect flaws, but also can be used for comparison testing for leakage and other functional issues. Master Parts are typically better to use for comparison than printed color visual aids or computer displays.

When establishing a Master Parts system, the good and no-good parts need to be taken care of so damage, rust, or even loss of these parts does not occur. Typically, the quality function will take this responsibility. At each process operation or work-cell, a Master Parts program can be put in place to ensure subsequent operations do not have defects. Quality should review Finished Good Master Parts with their customers to ensure an acceptable quality level. However, for consumer products or any other large customer base, Master Parts can be developed and agreed upon by a cross-functional team, such as with engineering, marketing, sales, and quality.

Workers can compare good and no-good parts against the parts they just produced, such as the first piece produced on a shift, one piece per hour, and/or last piece per shift. With very large or heavy parts, cross-sections of the Master Parts can be displayed for comparison. Alternatively, the Master Parts can be hung or secured on workstation shelves or somewhere else within the workspace area. If the Master Parts are used for functional testing, they can be used to qualify the tester before the first part being produced by every shift.

If the functional test does not have the same readings as the Master Part, there may be an issue for the functional tester to correct before production resumes. Master Parts should be treated just like inspection gages and equipment and controlled and evaluated on a regular cycle such as in a gage calibration program.

Quality Assurance
Quality Assurance (QA) is a process to prevent defects and avoid problems during the Quality Planning phase, while QC is a process for on-going production and for servicing to the customer. QA is an act of giving confidence to the Quality System in meeting customer requirements. There are a variety of Quality Assurance tools, techniques, and management activities that are described in detail including:

Auditing	Chapter 26
Gage Repeatability & Reproducibility Study	Chapter 18
People	Chapter 32
Plan For Every Part	Chapter 16
Potential Failure Modes and Effects Analysis	Chapter 17
Process Capability Study	Chapter 18
Process Control Plan	Chapter 18
RASIC Matrix	Chapter 11
Seven Basic Quality Tools	Chapter 8
Standardized Work	Chapter 22
Total Productive Maintenance	Chapter 29

Quality Assurance techniques are also utilized during the hiring and onboarding of new people with the Orientation process. The potential recruit analysis and job interviewing process utilizes checklists. The onboarding process utilizes a daily agenda and checklist to ensure the New Hire completes each step of the Orientation process, including understanding their role and Job Description.

Reliability and Warranty

It is very important for the company to assess its product reliability and warranty activities. Product reliability is initially tested during the product realization process by subjecting the parts in various environments, conditions, stresses, and other performance criteria — this includes dropping parts to see if they still function as required. Once the product is in the market, the true reliability is tested. Customer service typically receives first-hand information about product issues in the field via online reviews, emails, or customer service phone calls. However, quality, engineering, or sales may also receive emails or phone calls directly regarding product failures in the market. In some capacity, engineering, sales, customer service, supply chain, and quality will be involved in gathering product failures and failure-related information from the market. Market data and failed parts are then analyzed to determine the failure mode and potential causes of failure. Then quality and engineering will decide the next steps, such as introducing an upcoming product or process change with additional quality control actions. The customer may also provide benchmarking reliability information that engineering needs to analyze.

Supplier Quality and Responsibilities

Supplier Quality needs to be managed effectively by all manufacturing companies as this impacts customer delivery, customer quality, company reputation, and of course profitability. Supplier Quality activities are linked with several functions including: finance, manufacturing engineering, product engineering, production, purchasing, quality, and the supply chain organization. Supplier Quality typically is not a standalone function and its responsibilities fall directly or indirectly under purchasing, quality, or supply chain. The role designation name varies between companies such as Supplier Quality Assurance (SQA), Supplier Quality Engineering (SQE), Supplier Development Engineers (SDE), or Supplier Technical Assistance (STA). The main areas of responsibility for Supplier Quality are:

- Identification and qualification of suppliers
- Supplier selection
- Supplier product realization process
- Supplier part and process validation
- Supplier on-going production, monitoring, and evaluation

Illustration – Supplier Quality activity

The following flowchart shows the main activities for Supplier Quality as being Supplier Development Process and Supplier Management Process. Detailed descriptions for each of the two main processes are defined below. Purchasing typically leads the Supplier Development Process and shares responsibility with the Quality organization for the Supplier Management Process.

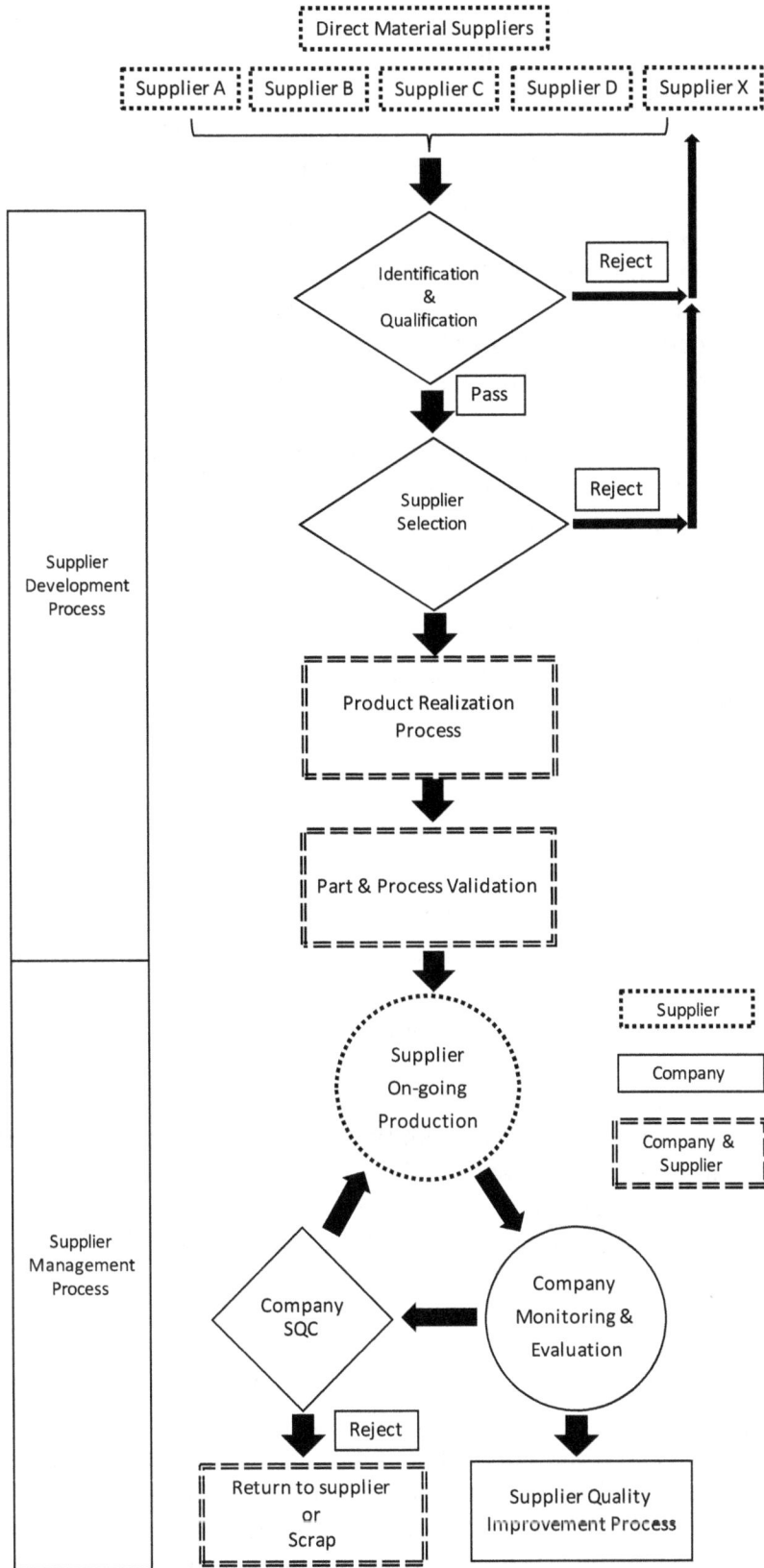

Figure 2. 14 Supply Quality Process

Identification and qualification of suppliers

One of the main responsibilities of Purchasing is to identify and qualify suppliers as well as to ensure they provide on-going supply of competitively priced raw materials and parts. Purchasing may have Supplier Development Engineers (SDE) or Supplier Quality Engineers (SQE) within the Purchasing organization function. SDEs and SQEs in many companies have the same responsibilities. The main difference between SDE and SQE is the SDE has responsibility within the Supplier Development process and the SQE has responsibility within the Supplier Management Process. SDE ensures the identification and qualification process through to Part & Process Validation Process follows the company's procedures. SDEs provide and coordinate technical assistance to the suppliers. For new suppliers, SDEs have significant work-load involvement from the qualification of suppliers to product and process validation. For current suppliers, SDEs spend significant time with suppliers during the industrialization and product and process validation with meetings either on-site or off-site. Also, SDEs are involved with the analysis of whether supplier's strategies are aligned with the company. This analysis is typically conducted during both the identification and qualification process and in the supplier surveillance and evaluation process. The supplier's strategies may be documented as policies, objectives, certifications, patent awards, and may include physical demonstrations of investments in product development, manufacturing process technologies, and the supplier's capacities and capabilities.

Supplier selection

Supplier Development Engineers (SDE) have responsibility to help assess and validate the cost analysis process phase. And, SDEs are involved with ensuring the supplier and company have current risk and contingency plans for supplier parts. SDEs will validate the supplier's Request For Quote (RFQ) financials by reviewing this — typically on-site for large projects. For smaller projects, purchasing may just review the RFQ process cost details or may include SDEs for assistance. Purchasing will populate a standardized criteria template from the various suppliers that submitted an RFQ with all associated inputs from the various functions. Then, either Purchasing or a cross-functional team will analyze and decide which supplier or suppliers win the business. Purchasing will inform the supplier of their win, expectations, re-affirm the timing, and re-affirm the commitment to the supplier quality requirements.

Supplier product realization process

Once the business award has been given to the supplier, the supplier needs to kick off their product realization process activities. The supplier must have a designated project leader and team. SDEs will ensure the supplier fulfills all their requirements by visiting the supplier often to confirm the project is meeting the intended plan, evaluating quality planning documentation off-site, participating in the supplier's project reviews, and having frequent dialogues throughout the project. SDEs may have to train the supplier with product realization process requirements, QA documentation submission requirements, and technical requirements over the entire product and process validation timing. During this part of the process, the supplier is making prototype parts. The prototype parts will be inspected, evaluated for assembly fit, and functionally tested by different company functions, such as engineering, manufacturing engineering, and supplier quality.

Supplier part and process validation

The key deliverables of the supplier's product realization process are determined by the company's supplier quality requirements. Supplier Development Engineers work with the supplier to ensure they understand the requirements for the submission and commit to a flawless launch of the new product. The submission package may consist of some or all of the following:

- Initial part submission documentation
- Parts – prototype, pre-production, initial production parts, and master parts
- Parts with dimensional inspection layouts
- Process control plan
- Various QC and QA documentation
- Manufacturing readiness reports
- Process capacity and capability study reports
- Laboratory and test reports
- Packaging and logistics information

SDE works with other functions and analyzes whether the submitted materials meet all requirements and define action plans for requirements not met. The submission package can either receive an interim approval, approval, or rejection. If the supplier is given a submission approval, the supplier can then proceed with delivering production parts according to a safe launch production plan schedule. If an interim approval is provided, the supplier can ship production parts for a limited time or quantity with certain conditions, such as increased inspections and tests until full approval is granted. If the submission is rejected, the supplier and SDE need to define an action item plan to correct all discrepancies. These actions would have a very high priority for completion. During the initial supply of production parts, the SDE and Supplier Quality Engineer (SQE) are involved to ensure a flawless launch. The company may define specific safe launch criteria to ensure no defects are passed to the next operation and when defects are detected, they are clearly identified and controlled. The SDE may directly be involved on-site with the supplier's root cause and corrective action process. Also, during the submission process and safe launch activities, the SDE will involve the SQE.

Supplier on-going production, monitoring, and evaluation

Supplier on-going production, monitoring and evaluation consists of several activities, including; company supplier quality control, defect materials returned or scrapped, and supplier improvement process. Once the supplier has received some form of initial part submission approval, the supplier can then produce and deliver according to the company's supply chain schedule. Each shipment and all parts being shipped will be monitored in some way with both the supply chain and SQEs. For any shipments that do not meet the company's expectation, the company will immediately notify the supplier and the supplier is expected to establish a root cause and corrective action. For suspect and defect parts produced, parts in-transit, and parts at the company, the supplier is expected to define a containment action plan that ensures all defective material is identified and quarantined as quickly as possible. Some companies have requirements of 24 hours to identify and implement a containment action. Typically, both the company and supplier are aware of the material discrepancy severity and containment actions taking place. SQE and the supplier's management should provide at least daily reports until corrective actions have been implemented and verified by the supplier. And, once a month or at least once a quarter, SQE should issue a status report to all manufacturing part suppliers. The status report or balanced scorecard for a specific time period includes any status and concerns for the supplier's management team to address. The report or scorecard may include a rolling 12 month's trend chart of the following:

- Supplier defective parts per million or defective parts per billion
- Quality issues, alerts, and status
- On-time delivery performance and status
- Part realization process and submission status
- Overdue action items and status
- Costs of poor quality (cost chargebacks to supplier)
- Productivity improvements (cost reduction) status
- Overall business status rating. Ratings can be colored coded with numbers or letters and may indicate whether the supplier can't be awarded new business, can be awarded new business with conditions, or can be awarded new business

The worst performing suppliers will be identified based upon quality and delivery criteria. The bottom 5–10 worst suppliers are required to present their improvement plans. Some companies require the supplier's management to formally present their corrective and improvement plans on a monthly basis. All suppliers should be required to regularly submit their Quality Improvement Plan and Status. However, some companies do not have this expectation of their suppliers. Companies pursuing a factory showcase culture evaluate their supplier improvement activities on-site on a regular basis with frequent off-site reviews. The improvement plans typically consist of the following categories; Safety, Quality, Cost, Inventory, Lead-Time, Delivery, and System including significant business changes and innovations.

Customer Quality

Customer Quality is important to ensure the customer is satisfied with the development and on-going supply of products and that the company is servicing the needs of the customer. The sales and quality function should both have an understanding of customer quality requirements, but the quality function should have a more thorough understanding of the technical and supply requirements. Customer Quality impacts all elements of the Quality Management System including specifics such as:

- Customer satisfaction surveys
- Performance monitoring
- Quick Response Quality Control
- Customer service

Customer satisfaction surveys are routinely given to various customers and cover a broad range of topics including innovation, price, quality, delivery, product reliability, responsiveness and various other qualitative topics. Senior management or the Quality function will inquire either anonymously or directly with various functions and positions at the customer level, then will analyze the information. Having this information available prior to the upcoming year's operating plan development can help clarify and prioritize strategies. Company management should review the survey questions in advance to ensure they cover a broad range of topics, the questions are clear, understandable, allow for comments, and the number of questions are reasonable to answer in a few minutes.

Performance monitoring is essential to ensure there is no decline in quality, delivery, service, or other customer expectations month to month. Whenever there is a customer concern, the company should react based upon their Quick Response Quality Control procedure. This is defined in more detail in Chapter 27 in the Conditioning section. Customer performance monitoring is typically managed by the Quality function and reviewed monthly with the management team. Reliability/Warranty information feedback can also be included in the performance monitoring.

Quality Improvement

Many companies have a formal documented quality improvement processes that specify using a variety of analytical tools and processes such as 7 QC Tools, Lean Six Sigma, Benchmarking, and Breakthrough. Undocumented and informal quality improvement processes also are often implemented, but every manufacturing related change or improvement should have a documented Product and Process Change Notice.

A basic description of quality improvement tools and processes includes:

- 7 basic quality tools – defined in the Orientation section.
- Lean Six Sigma – reducing or eliminating waste by Defining, Measuring, Analyzing, Implementing, and Controlling (DMAIC).
- Benchmarking – comparing or evaluating products and processes against best in class.
- Continuous Improvement – making many small, incremental stepped improvements, conducted by anyone in the company.
- Breakthrough – making a significant leap in improvements conducted by a focused group of both internal and external support personnel.

Managing for quality is 24/7, so the quality organization has to communicate the current status of activity constantly, from supplier quality to operations to customer warranty, as well as participate and/or coordinate many quality activities. These communications, postings, and meeting updates have to be clear, concise, and easily understood as to the status. Management has to support training the quality organization, as the Quality organization needs to be knowledgeable and competent in a wide variety of tools, techniques, and latest customer and industry requirements. Quality is a very important function that must be integrated into all aspects of the business and into all functions. A yearly training needs assessment should be performed for every person in the quality organization.

Chapter 16 - Process Flow and Plan For Every Part (PFEP)

Many companies have process flowcharts that define the physical path a product takes from receiving through shipping. Defining and then walking the product path is critical to understanding how to make the process simpler, more efficient, or to add more value in the process. Shortening the path and reducing the time it takes for the product to travel through the factory reduces overall costs. That means, basically, removing non-value adding activities.

Product, Process, People, and Information Flow

Defining the product, process, people movements, and information flow is important for improving productivity, quality, communication and feedback, cost, safety, process knowledge, lead times, and many other factors. When defining the process flow for a specific product, consider the following questions:

Product

- Are materials handled and moved from one operation step to the next in a smooth and efficient manner? Is there a better way? Can value be added, or non-value-added activities reduced?

- Do materials move from one operation to a staging area before the next value-added operation is made? If so, why? Can the staging area be removed or reduced in size?

- Is material scheduled and processed according to a customer demand pull system or Just In Time (JIT)? JIT originates from the Toyota Production System where the objective is to reduce the total process cycle time and improve the response times from customers through to suppliers.

- Is a significant amount of material in process? Can this amount be reduced or packaged differently so there are fewer movements?

- Do materials move in the shortest path from receiving to each operation to shipping, or is there more-efficient route to take?

- How are materials identified and controlled when they are good, have a suspect quality problem, or are no-good?

Process

- Do the machines and layout meet the requirements mentioned earlier (see Building New Machines and Process Layout)?

- Is the process organized to ensure that production flows continuously?

- Are disruptions in the process documented for reason and time?

People

- Are there defined responses when something abnormal is encountered? Or do workers just react to process abnormalities, so there can be different reactions based upon a specific abnormality?

- Are direct labor workers performing their operations in a repeatable and consistent manner?

- Do direct workers know how much time is required for each operation or to produce a part?

- How often does the team leader and supervisor see each direct worker's work area and output, and discuss any issues?

- On a daily basis, in what ways do the support staff and management interact with direct labor workers?

- What are the triggers and response times for the support staff to be engaged when materials are unavailable, machines are down, or there are other production problems?

- Do all direct labor workers know the safety, production, and quality targets for their work station and their shift?

Information

- What information is communicated upstream when there is a problem? How is this information recorded and visually presented so others can see the status?

- When a concern is identified, is there a known escalation process and timing?

- What information is used for end-of-shift/start-of-shift communications?

- What and when is information presented to the workers to know what they have to produce?

- At what frequency do direct labor workers input their production data? Does the information need to be timelier to make decisions?

- Are visual control boards utilized within the work-cell?

- Do visual control boards show a history of improvements? If not, what are the reasons for not improving this work area?

Plan for Every Part (PFEP)

Having a Plan for Every Part (PFEP) is key to creating a lean, efficient material handling system. Also, having a PFEP can support optimizing inventory, including reducing potential material obsolescence and using First In First Out (FIFO). Developing a PFEP can be started at any time, whether in a project planning phase or in a production phase that is already underway. However, starting early in the product realization (Quality Planning) process is best for ease of implementation. Implementing a PFEP in full production mode may cause a production interruption due to not everyone being informed, new places for storage, or another change that was not communicated effectively. A PFEP should be constantly reviewed, updated, controlled, and communicated to everyone.

There are many factors to consider and control when defining and implementing a PFEP. While improvements or supply chain changes are being made, the PFEP can be reviewed and updated as needed, since all operational information regarding the PFEP is documented in one place, this makes the change control process more robust and efficient. The key points are to have a product and process change system in place that captures any changes made in the PFEP. It should be required to have the PFEP as a master file within the MRP or ERP system and stored electronically. The following is a list of factors to collect for a PFEP:

Part

- Commodity, part number, part name, and description
- Number of parts needed to make one assembly unit (may need a separate matrix for defining the quantities needed for multiple finished goods and for different finished good volumes)
- Annual, monthly, weekly, daily, shift, and hourly usage
- Part dimensions (overall length, width, and height, or volume)
- Part weight

Point of Use (POU) container

- POU container dimensions (length, width, height) and container volume
- Number of parts per POU container
- Total weight of POU package and part
- Type of POU container material and description (cardboard, plastic, metal, pallet, foldable, returnable, etc.)
- POU label content information, and RFID
- Container ownership (supplier, internal, customer)

Re-packaging (if re-packaging, then define)

- Container brought from supplier to POU in operations or re-packaged
- Re-package label/POU label content information
- Radio frequency identification (RFID) type, size, location
- RFID affixed to part or container
- Re-packaging area
- Re-package container dimensions and volume
- Responsibility for re-packaging
- Frequency for re-packaging parts
- Handling, safety, and personal protective equipment requirements
- Re-packaging material type

Kanban

A production pull scheduling system where manufacturing is managed as make to order in a replenishment cycle using Kanban cards or signals. Kanban cards or signals order materials to be produced as needed and moved throughout the supply chain from customer to supplier.

- Is the part in Kanban?
- Number of Kanban cards?
- Minimum and maximum number of re-packaged containers at POU
- POU space required
- POU material feed description (manual, forklift, roller conveyor, workstation back load, etc.)
- POU locations (may need a matrix for multiple work-cells in different locations)
- Trigger (description of how withdrawal is taken)

Storage

- Safety stock quantity of supplier parts
- Storage location of containers with supplier parts
- Storage location for re-packaging containers
- Storage location of re-packaged parts
- Re-order point for re-packaged containers (none if re-usable)
- Cleaning frequency for re-usable container
- Responsibility for cleaning re-usable container
- Manufacturing supermarket location and size of location for part. A manufacturing supermarket is similar to a consumer supermarket store as parts are stored nearby the manufacturing for ease of withdrawal and for return during changeovers. Supermarket materials are transferred out of a receiving warehouse and onto the factory floor nearby the POU. This material is identified as Work In Process (WIP) inventory.
- Manufacturing supermarket minimum and maximum quantities

Supplier

- Supplier name (make a list for each supplier), city, state, country
- Item supplied
- Frequency of delivery, shipment size (number of parts per box, per pallet)
- Container or box weigh, box dimensions

- Standard order quantity, lead-time to order, transit time,
- Transport carrier(s)

Key Steps for Making a Plan For Every Part (PFEP)
There are 6 steps for establishing a PFEP:
1. Choose 1 finished goods product
2. Identify replenishment activities
3. Identify movement method
4. Identify replenishment improvement options
5. Implement replenishment improvements
6. Conduct trial period

Step 1 – Choose 1 finished goods product

This may be an overwhelming task to perform on all products in your factory, so make a list of all product families and volumes. From all the product families, choose one that has high volume. Obtain the Bill of Materials (BOM), process flowchart, and plant layout. A bill of materials is a list of all the raw materials and components, and their associated quantities to make one finished product. Start to collect information into a matrix for the above details and decide how best to control this information (preferably electronically). Try to start working with one of the BOM finished goods parts, then work your way through all of the BOM raw materials and component parts. Some of this information may not be known or may vary, so make a note in the matrix for that item. At some point, you may need to hold a meeting with other operations team members to complete the information, or the team will have to make a decision on how best to define the above information. Also, note common BOM component parts or parts that are included in multiple finished goods.

Step 2 –Identify replenishment activities

Identify the locations and space required in the warehouse for the incoming supplier materials and the finished goods products. Identify which aisles are used in the factory for replenishing the manufacturing areas, replenishment quantities, and frequency (times and time between replenishing) to fill the manufacturing area of use, as well as to return or discard the used packaging. Locations for component parts and finished goods parts may or may not have specific designated locations. Replenishment frequencies and amounts may vary. Replenishment data should be collected from all shifts for at least one day. When a warehouse uses an automated database, the warehouse locations may be dynamic so there is no specific recurring material location. For non-automated warehouses, generally it is easier to specify locations for materials. Supermarkets on the factory floor should have designated locations and minimum and maximum amounts for materials. Supermarkets with kanban or other trigger mechanisms for replenishment needs to be documented.

When moving raw materials from the warehouse to the factory floor, note the route taken throughout the different shifts as it may be different depending on who is the material movement person. The factory floor locations (bins, racks, areas) should have signage identifying various materials. Also, all manufacturing work areas should be clearly identified with name of work area, finished product part name, number, or even product line or customer. Colors, diagrams, or photos of materials can also be used for distinguishing differences and for ease of identification. These areas must be kept clean and clear for material movements, need to be sized for ease of use, and safe for stacking (if stacking is allowed, maximum height needs to be visually defined). Also, during this step, either for one product family or multiple product families, consider defining a purchased part or raw material supermarket near the work area(s). Having a manufacturing supermarket nearby the work area reduces any potential work area stock-outs and supports an efficient way to move and store materials during changeover. A manufacturing supermarket is a storage location for work in process materials located nearby the manufacturing work-cell.

Step 3 – Identify movement methods

Identify ways in which the materials are currently being moved to the POU and (approximate) amount or quantities of materials — for example, via forklift, electric carts, handcarts, or other means. Consider reducing the travel distance, using different aisles, supermarkets, or minimizing the use of forklifts. Forklifts require large aisles and space to turn and are a potential safety concern with people working and walking alongside them.

Step 4 – Identify replenishment improvement options

Study and define options for minimizing handling of materials to the point of use (POU) by combining different materials, quantities, frequencies for replenishing, and identifying the pull trigger signals. Also, define the cycle time for one replenishment cycle of each option. The replenishment cycle or pitch can be calculated based on takt time using a standard container quantity. Packaging type, size, quantities, movement method, storage locations, and aisles may have to be modified for the different options, and/or the manufacturing work areas may have to be configured differently. The timing of movements can be considered a specific time for specific parts, just as a bus schedule has a defined location and times for passenger pickups and drop offs. Variability of the movements and timing needs to be analyzed over a period of time as buffer materials may need to be established. Work-cells should never be starved for materials and materials moving in and out of work-cells should be an external activity during the manufacturing changeover.

Step 5 – Implement replenishment improvements

Determine which option and improvements work best from a cross-functional perspective, specifically with the direct labor workers and material movement workers. Identify advantages and disadvantages for each option, then determine the better choice. Ensure the replenishment route and details for replenishing are fully defined by using a Standardized Work Combination Sheet and training people accordingly. The greater the replenishment cycles per shift, the less inventory on the factory floor, and the greater flexibility and control for demand changes. Training should be conducted and managed closely to ensure the new standardized work is practiced exactly.

Step 6 – Conduct trial period

Prior to defining the trial period, analyze other products in the same product family as they may have many shared materials and processes. A decision should be made to either complete the PFEP for all products in the same product family or just perform a trial on one part in the product family. There are no strict rules or practices when defining a PFEP.

Define a trial period, ensure a cross-functional team is available, and take notes during every replenishment route. Action items at the end of every shift and day have to be defined, communicated visually, and closed out before the next shift or day. The trial period may be as short as one batch, a few days, or one week. The objective is to have an improved, documented, and efficient material handling system from supplier through manufacturing to customer. Once the trial period is completed, note the improvements made, then select the next product family and repeat steps 1-6.

Chapter 17 - Potential Failure Mode Effects Analysis and Control Plan

The automotive industry — specifically the Automotive Industry Action Group (AIAG) — has published many helpful manufacturing related manuals and various other publications. Their Potential Failure Mode Effects Analysis (PFMEA) and Control Plan manual should be read and utilized by all manufacturing companies. Manufacturing companies that are non-automotive can utilize many of the tools, techniques, methods, and systems identified by AIAG.

The purpose of a Failure Mode Effects Analysis (FMEA) is to systematically identify high-priority failures and define controls or improvements to reduce or eliminate those potential failures. There are four types of FMEAs to become familiar with:

System FMEA: interactions between systems and how they might fail.

Design FMEA: how the product design might fail.

Process FMEA: how the process operations might make the product fail.

Machine FMEA: how machinery that performs the process operations might fail.

The following describes the use of a Process FMEA and Control Plan. Once a Process FMEA is completed, this becomes the basis for developing a Control Plan. Both Process FMEA and Control Plan should be defined and updated for the progressive stages of product and process development from the prototype stage to pre-production stage to on-going production. Both Process FMEA and Control Plan spreadsheet templates are available on the Internet along with information on how to fill out a PFMEA and Control Plan. An example of one company's Process FMEA and Control Plan is shown below:

Key Steps to Establish a Process FMEA and Control Plan

1. A project leader assembles a cross-functional team. The cross-functional team should include product engineering, manufacturing engineering, quality, production personnel (including experienced operators, team leaders, or supervisors), logistics, maintenance, purchasing, supplier quality, and any other resources or expert personnel who may be requested to participate. As mentioned previously, keeping the team to nine or fewer would be best for communications.

2. The project leader should have an understanding of the team's competence in using an FMEA. The project leader may want to have the cross-functional team attend an FMEA training course before participating in an actual FMEA. Alternatively, if team members have some FMEA experience, then perhaps just a review of an FMEA will be helpful — a simple presentation of an hour or so may provide everyone with a baseline of the same knowledge.

3. For current production, the project leader should present the team with information about the product or product variants, use by the consumer, features, key product characteristics, process steps and machines, production volumes,

cycle times, customer demand rate, and layout. For new products, the project leader should present information about the proposed process details previously mentioned.

4. For current production, the project leader has the team walk through the process, step-by-step using a process flow chart or process map. If a process flowchart or process map has not been completed, the team should prepare this while walking the process. The team will observe parts being produced at each process on the factory floor. For new products, the team will need to define the process flow. Prototype parts, prototype processes, or other simulation methods can be used to understand the process operation details.

5. For current production, once the process has been walked, a PFMEA template can start being populated. The PFMEA should be developed on the factory floor with an observation of the process running. The basic understanding is the PFMEA template is completed at each process step, one row at a time. For new products, the PFMEA is started with proposed process details and any other simulation information, prototype parts, or other supporting production relation information.

6. Once the PFMEA is completed, an audit should be conducted to ensure the PFMEA is accurate and complete. Then, the Control Plan can be started. For current production, the PFMEA will be used as the basis for developing the Control Plan. This is best done walking the process once more to populate the Control Plan template. For new products, the PFMEA will be used to create the Control Plan and will be updated throughout the process development and industrialization phase.

7. Conduct a Reverse PFMEA on the work stations with the highest RPNs (risk priority numbers). A reverse PFMEA validates the process controls with all failure modes as well as to identify new potential failure modes. A risk priority number is a calculation based on the following formula: RPN = severity x occurrence x detection where each of the three factors have a scale 1-10. Severity is ranked as 1= least safety concern and 10 = highest safety risk or dangerous condition. Occurrence is ranked as 1 being a very low probability of occurring and 10 occurring with an extremely high frequency. Detection assesses the chance of the failure being detected with a ranking of 1 being the highest chance of detection and 10 being the lowest chance of detection. RPN factor scales typically are a standard within the company where some customers have pre-defined scales.

8. Once the Control Plan is completed, an audit should be conducted to confirm the process details have been captured correctly. This needs to be done several times throughout the process development and industrialization phase.

Illustration – Potential Failure Modes and Effects Analysis (PFMEA)

The following figure shows a Process FMEA for a printed circuit board assembly (PCBA) operation #30, screen printing. Each PCBA operation would have descriptions completed including actions taken with updated Risk Priority Numbers (RPN). The Process FMEA will continue to be updated throughout the process development and through the product life which could be over several years. Reviews and audits are regularly conducted on Process FMEAs as well as Process FMEAs are reviewed when defects or process issues occur.

Potential Failure Mode and Effects Analysis
(Process FMEA)

Part Name: _____

Model Year(s) / Program(s) _____

Core Team: _____

Part Number(s): _____

PFMEA Date: _____

PFMEA (orginal date) _____

PFMEA Num _____

Page _____ of _____

Process Step/ Function	Requirement	Potential Failure Mode	Potential Effect(s) of Failure	SEV	CLASS	Potential Cause(s) of Failure	Controls Prevention	OCC	Controls Detection	DET	RPN	Recommended Action	Responsibility & Target Completion Date	Actions Taken Completion Date	SEV	OCC	DET	RPN
OP30 Solder Paste- Printing	IPC 7527 Class 1	Solder paste volume not meet requirement	Customer risk : 0Km or field returns (random bad functionality) Internal risk : Warranty cost, Potential failures during the testing process, random bad functionality, scraps	7		Paste : Temperature high	1.Solder paste warm up system control 2.Shop floor temperature Control.	2		3	42	Thermocouple in paste container inside temp control box	Date A	completed	7	1	1	7
						Paste: Storage temperature out-of-range reduces shelf life and rheology breakdown	1. Automatic temp control/alarm for storage	2		3	42	Thermocouple temp profile management system	Date B	completed	7	1	1	7
						Paste: Expired solder paste cause rheology breakdown	1.Solder paste warm up system control	2		3	42	scan before and after temp box	Date C	completed	7	1	1	7
						Equipment: Damaged stencil	1. Stencil check before every time using 2.stencil maintenance	2	1. 3D Solder Paste Inspection 2.X-Ray 3.In-circuit test, Master Part, Functional Test	4	56	use of stencil sleeve for each stencil when not in use	Date A	completed	7	2	2	28
					SC/CC	Equipment: Worn stencil	1.Stencil using time control and TPM	2		4	56	photo scan of stencil before adding solder paste to confirm	Date D	completed	7	2	2	28
						Maintenance: Squeegee damaged	1. TPM	2		4	56	1. None						
						Maintenance: Machine issue	1.TPM 2. PM per month	2		4	56	1. None						
						Process: Operator does not clean up excess solder on stencil	1.Clean the stencil per hour	2		4	56	1. None						
						Program: Stencil Auto wiping frequency is too low; Cause paste to build up inside apertures	1. Program update: frequency to every 3 prints	2		4	56	Add LVDT to control movement	Date E	completed	7	1	1	7
						Program: Print Speed too slow, too much time to fill apertures	1. Fix the print speed.	2		4	56	1. None						

Figure 2. 15 Process FMEA

Illustration – Process Quality Control Plan

The following Process Quality Control Plan is for the same process operation defined in the Process FMEA. The Process Quality Control Plan is also regularly reviewed, assessed, and updated throughout the process development through the product life and when issues are encountered with the process or product.

Part/ Process Number	Process Name/ Operation Description	Machine, Device Jig, Tools For Mfg.	No.	Characteristic Product	Characteristic Process	Special Char. Class.	Product/Process Specification/Tolerance	Evaluation/ Measurement Technique	Sample Size	Sample Freq	Control Method	Reaction Plan
30	Solder Paste printing	Screen Printer; Machine ID; Stencil #; Block #; Roller Rack #; Sleeve		Correct solder paste		SC	Alpha OM338 PT	Scan	Once	DR Shift start up	Operator, scan barcode tube container	Change to correct material, contact material handling
					Solder paste warm up time		Warm up temp. control X-Y deg (minimum 4 hours)	Solder paster warm-up control system	All	Continuous	Solder paste control system	stop line and inform supervisor
					Solder paste air exposed time		Room temp. without open: <14days; After open: <3 days; On stencil: <3 hrs	Visual check and check sheet	Once	Each tube	SOS # Operator follow Solder paste printing control	SOS# Solder paste printing control
					Correct stencil	SC	STEN- XXXX STEN- YYYYY	1st part inspection	Once	Change-Over/ Shift Start-Up		Use correct stencil. Contact Supervisor if not correct stencil
					Clean Stencil		Stencil Cleaner Operation SOS	Visual Check & Machine check	Once	After each break	SOS # Operator follow Solder paste printing control	Re-clean stencil
					Stencil status		Visual, Physical Check, and Photo analysis	Visual check Surface Tension measurement Photo	Once	1st piece, last piece per shift		Stop using and inform technician
					Correct program		Correct program name: ABCDE, ACDEFG	1st piece	Once	Change-Over/ Shift Start-Up	1st piece, checksheet	stop line and inform supervisor
					Correct parameter setting		Squeegee force: 6 +/-.75 Kgs; Squeegee speed: 40 +/- 10mm/sec; Auto wiper Freq.: every piece	1st piece	Once	Change-Over/ Shift Start-Up	1st piece, checksheet	Inform technician to adjust
				Solder paste height; Solder paste volume		SC	Stencil Tolerance (+/- 25%); Pads stencil (+60% ~ -30%)	auto-check by SPI	All	100%	SPI system control MES record Capability study Cpk>1.67	Inform technician to adjust; Scrap PCB
					Solder paste position		PCB CAD file	auto-check by SPI	All	100%	SPI system control MES record	Inform technician to adjust; Scrap PCB
					Air pressure		90 +/- 5 PSI; Auto adding solder paste: 30-40 PSI	Visual check	Once	Daily	DR TPM- AAAA	Inform technician to adjust

Figure 2. 16 Process Control Plan

The Process Failure Mode and Effects Analysis and Process Quality Control Plan above are examples of process control information and are not meant to be a training guide. The above information is presented to broadly illustrate that a team defines specific information for each step of the manufacturing process and that this information needs to be documented, controlled, and regularly validated and updated. The documents can be in written in single or dual languages. Whenever there is a product or process change or improvements made to the process, both the

PFMEA and Control Plan would be updated accordingly. It is absolutely necessary that the P-FMEA, the Control Plan and related records filled on the factory floor are linked, ideally by document management system.

Chapter 18 – Process Capability and Gage R&R Studies

Process capability and gage repeatability and reproducibility studies should be conducted for new product launches, product or process changes, or on a regularly scheduled cycle (such as annually). The quality team should have reference materials, software, statistics knowledge, and measurement systems experience when setting up, conducting, and analyzing the measurement data for a process capability study, and gage repeatability and reproducibility study. It can be difficult to assess whether the quality team has sufficient knowledge and experience to properly conduct either study. The minimum criteria for conducting these studies are also rather difficult to define, but at a minimum, someone on the quality team should have participated in a Statistical Process Control (SPC) and Measurement Systems Analysis (MSA) training course, be certified or degreed as a quality technician or engineer, or have experience completing a process capability and gage repeatability and reproducibility study previously. The following information is a greatly abbreviated overview of these studies and is not sufficient to conduct either study. However, the questions that follow are important to ask in validating how well the studies are conducted.

Process Capability Studies

Process capability studies (most commonly identified as Pp, Ppk, Cp, Cpk) and gage repeatability and reproducibility (commonly known as Gage R&R) are well-documented in Automotive Industry Action Group (AIAG) publications. For new processes or product launches, a process capability study known as Pp and Ppk should be conducted. Pp and Ppk is a capability measurement of the process performance or measurement of the process spread. A Pp and Ppk study is conducted because there is not a lot of historical data available. Pp and Ppk uses the standard deviation, while Cp and Cpk calculation use an estimate of the standard deviation (R-bar/d2). Pp and Ppk calculations are similar to Cp and Cpk. A Cpk study is a capability measurement of the process within specification. If Ppk=Cpk, the process is likely in statistical control whereas if Ppk does not equal Cpk, the process is unlikely to be in statistical control.

A Cpk study can be conducted if the process is under statistical control. A Cp and Cpk study should regularly be conducted for all critical, significant, or special product and process characteristics. These characteristics are typically defined and agreed on by the customer and project team, along with the definition understanding and symbol usage on drawings for dimensions or requirements needing to meet a specific statistical capability. Process capability studies also can be conducted for any characteristic that affects the product's form, fit, or function.

Gage R&R

To validate Pp, Ppk, Cp, and Cpk results, a Gage R&R analysis should be conducted before performing the capability study. A Gage R&R measures the total variation of the measurement system, including the measurement device and the people using it.

Knowing the total measurement system variation validates the capability result for the specific characteristic being measured.

Once the Process FMEA and Control Plan are complete, the most critical and significant characteristics should be identified, unless the customer and company project team have already defined them. If the team has not defined them, look at the process operations in the Process FMEA and sort them by Risk Priority Number (RPN) greater than 80 or severity ranking of 8 or greater. Actions should be planned and taken to reduce the highest RPNs. Then, look at the Control Plan for each of those process operation steps and identify those affected product or process characteristics and the measurement device for those characteristics. This list of characteristics will be used for the Gage R&R studies and process capability studies.

Process Capability and Gage R&R Key Points

There are many key points to consider to ensure a Gage R&R and a process capability study can be conducted properly. Some points are not well-documented in the industry and may or may not apply to your specific manufacturing processes:

1. Has a Gage R&R and/or Pp, Ppk, Cp, Cpk study already been conducted? That is, is this a duplicate process, has a product or process change occurred, or has a process improvement been made? If this is a duplicate process, a Gage R&R may not be needed, but a process capability study should be conducted.

2. Is the measurement device new? All measurement devices have to be calibrated and controlled in an environment that does not affect its measurement ability. A Gage R&R should be conducted.

3. Are workers using the measurement device trained or certified and have experience? Train inexperienced workers and/or validate their capability using the measurement device. Then, conduct a Gage R&R.

4. Are parts available above, within, and lower than the specification tolerance for the product characteristics being studied? Ideally, the entire measurement range should be analyzed during the Gage R&R study. If parts are available, they should be identified or marked (such as numbering them 1-10). Numbering the parts helps to identify them if they are mixed together. Under certain circumstances, parts may be modified so the entire measurement range can be analyzed, meaning the part dimensions or specification can be purposely altered to conduct a Gage R&R and then be disposed of properly.

5. Does at least one quality or other staff have Gage R&R training and/or experienced in conducting Gage R&Rs? Typically, the quality organization would have one or more individuals trained and experienced in conducting Gage R&Rs. AIAG has a Measurement Systems Analysis (MSA) manual that can support Gage R&R education and be used as a reference source.

6. When conducting Gage R&R studies, are part measurements performed in a random order, where the measurement operator does not have bias? Re-arranging the order of parts to be measured is important to ensure the measurement being taken is not biased by the operator measuring the part.

7. Is a Gage R&R spreadsheet template or software available, such as Minitab? The measurement data collected during the Gage R&R study should be inputted into a Gage R&R template spreadsheet or other software.

8. Is Gage R&R total variation within an acceptable range? Gage R&R analysis results can be affected by many factors, such as operator variation, measurement device, environmental conditions during measurements, or another extraneous factor. A quality person should make the initial assessment to determine whether a specific factor influenced the Gage R&R study and correct as needed. The quality manager, management team, and/or customer should be the final authority in determining the suitability for use of the measurement device.

9. What is the Total Gage R&R variation percentage?

% Total Variation	Gage Usage
1 ~ 9%	Acceptable
10 ~ 30%	Marginally acceptable, may need improvement
> 30%	Not Acceptable

10. What to do if the Gage R&R is marginal or not within the acceptable range? There are several possibilities to consider, such as: improving the operator's capability at using the measurement device, use a different measurement device, use the current device but modify the method by checking a specific location or section of the part, modify its usage such as using a jig for holding the part or measurement device, improve the environmental conditions for inspection, modify the measurement device itself especially if it is a special-purpose measuring device, or consider using a go, no-go attribute gage.

11. When should process capability studies be conducted? A process capability study should be conducted before and after any product or process change, and annually, to confirm the process is validated and under control. Also, for any new products being produced. Process capability studies also need to be conducted when a new raw material or component supplier is used.

12. Are there multiple fixtures on a specific machine where the parts will be processed? Each fixture should have a corresponding process capability study performed, due to the manufacturing fixture variations, machine, or machine program influence.

13. Can a Cp and Cpk study be conducted on a large production run? Identify sub-groups of samples, such as every (X) number of parts every (Y) minutes. A statistical process control chart can also be used as a part of this study.

14. Is the capability study conducted under observable and/or controlled conditions? Having the quality and manufacturing engineering staff observing the capability

study is important to ensure other factors are not introduced or known, such as rework being performed, machine maintenance issues, tool usage issues, use of untrained operators, or not recording rejected or suspect parts as part of the study.

15. During the capability study, is a control chart being used? A real-time control chart during a capability study is helpful to ensure the process is stable and under control. Having the process under statistical control also ensures that no special cause variations occur.

16. During the capability study, are parts, materials, or containers being marked for identification? All parts, materials, and containers should be at least temporarily marked for measuring and controlled to prevent mixing with other materials for possible re-inspection at a later date. For example, identify parts produced consecutively so they can be identified during measurement and after for re-measurement, if needed, or for analyzing beginning and end-of-study variation.

17. Will materials or parts be sold after the capability study? Materials and parts may need different handling methods, especially if they have to be taken outside normal routing to be measured. Also, marking on the parts may be unacceptable to the customer.

18. Are the capability results acceptable? It may be necessary to tabulate Pp, Ppk, Cp, Cpk data and results and report them to the customer for acceptance and approval. When the process capability results do not meet the acceptable criteria (such as less than 1.67), a team should be assembled to investigate this issue and define proposed solutions for improvement.

Illustration – Process Capability Study – Pp and Ppk Study

Process Capability Analysis Sheet

Study Date:

Part/Drawing#				Specification/Tolerance		3.3 +/-1.1 mm			
Batch Number				Gauge		digital caliper			
Process Name				M/C Operator		Jason			
Op #/Machine #				Inspector		Lee			
Lower Specification	2.2	mm		Upper Specification	4.4	mm			
No.	Value	No.	Value	No.	Value	No.	Value	No.	Value
1	3.260	11	3.200	21	3.220	31		41	
2	2.980	12	3.660	22	3.420	32		42	
3	3.400	13	3.450	23	3.390	33		43	
4	3.620	14	3.130	24	2.940	34		44	
5	3.180	15	3.630	25	3.100	35		45	
6	3.190	16	3.360	26	3.280	36		46	
7	3.110	17	2.950	27	3.310	37		47	
8	3.140	18	3.320	28	3.450	38		48	
9	3.640	19	3.110	29	3.220	39		49	
10	3.150	20	3.450	30	2.950	40		50	

Mean value of sample $\bar{X}$ = 3.2737

Standard deviation of sample σ_s = $\dfrac{\sqrt{\sum (xi - \bar{x})^2}}{(n-1)}$ = 0.2082

PpU = $\dfrac{USL - \bar{X}}{3\sigma_s}$ = 1.80

PpL = $\dfrac{\bar{X} - LSL}{3\sigma_s}$ = 1.72

Ppk = MIN(Ppu,Ppl) = 1.72

Pp = $\dfrac{USL - LSL}{6\sigma_s}$ = 1.76

Final Decision = Pp,Ppk > 1.67 ⟶ Acceptable = Acceptable

Doc #		**Responsibility**	**Conducted by**	**Checked by**	**Approved by**
Rev #					
Date #					
Owner		**Title**			

Figure 2. 17 Process Capability Study

Illustration – Gage Repeatability & Reproducibility Study

Gage Repeatability and Reproducibility Study (Gage R&R)

Part Number & Name : _____
Characteristics : Depth
Specification Limits : 113.65-114.15mm

Gage Name : Depth Gauge
Gage No. : _____
Gage Type : 0-200mm

Date: _____
Performed By: _____
Approved By: _____

Part Number	Appraiser 1 (Donny)					Appraiser 2 (Maria)					Appraiser 3 (Callie)					Part Average
	Measurements			$\bar{X}$	R	Measurements			$\bar{X}$	R	Measurements			$\bar{X}$	R	
	1	2	3			1	2	3			1	2	3			
1	113.92	113.92	113.92	113.920	0.000	113.92	113.92	113.9	113.913	0.020	113.92	113.9	113.92	113.913	0.020	113.916
2	113.9	113.88	113.92	113.893	0.020	113.89	113.9	113.89	113.893	0.010	113.9	113.9	113.88	113.893	0.020	113.893
3	113.9	113.9	113.92	113.907	0.020	113.9	113.92	113.92	113.913	0.020	113.9	113.92	113.9	113.907	0.020	113.909
4	113.9	113.9	113.9	113.900	0.000	113.91	113.89	113.9	113.900	0.020	113.9	113.9	113.92	113.907	0.020	113.902
5	113.9	113.88	113.9	113.893	0.020	113.9	113.9	113.88	113.893	0.020	113.9	113.9	113.9	113.900	0.000	113.896
6	113.9	113.92	113.91	113.910	0.020	113.9	113.9	113.9	113.900	0.000	113.9	113.92	113.9	113.907	0.020	113.906
7	113.92	113.92	113.9	113.913	0.020	113.92	113.9	113.9	113.907	0.020	113.9	113.9	113.9	113.900	0.000	113.907
8	113.92	113.9	113.9	113.907	0.020	113.91	113.91	113.92	113.913	0.010	113.92	113.92	113.9	113.913	0.020	113.911
9	113.92	113.9	113.9	113.907	0.020	113.9	113.92	113.9	113.907	0.020	113.92	113.9	113.9	113.907	0.020	113.907
10	113.92	113.92	113.92	113.920	0.000	113.92	113.92	113.9	113.913	0.020	113.92	113.9	113.92	113.913	0.020	113.916

Average	X_1 = 113.9070	X_2 = 113.9053	X_3 = 113.9060	$\bar{\bar{X}}$ = 113.9061
Range	R_1 = 0.0140	R_2 = 0.0160	R_3 = 0.0160	R_p = 0.0222

R = (R1 + R2 + R3) / No. of Appraisers = 0.0153
X_{diff} = (Max. of X_1,X_2,X_3 - Min. of X_1,X_2,X_3) = 0.0017
UCL$_R$ = R * D$_4$ (D$_4$ = 3.27 OR 2.58 for 2 and 3 measurements) = 0.0396
LCL$_R$ = R * D$_3$ (D$_3$ = 0 for up to 7 trials) = 0.000

If R & R as **% of Tolerance** is required, enter Tolerance Range ---> [0.5000]

Repeatability - Equipment Variation (EV) = (R * K$_1$) = 0.0468
(K$_1$ = 4.56 OR 3.05 for 2 and 3 Measurements respectively)

Reproducibility - Appraiser (AV) Variation = $\sqrt{\left[\left(X_{diff} * K_2 \right)^2 - \left(EV^2 / n*r \right) \right]}$

AV = 0.0000
(K$_2$ = 3.65 OR 2.70 for 2 or 3 Appraisers)
n = Number of Parts, r = Number of Measurements

Total Process Variation, TPV is determined from Sample Values

$$TPV = \sqrt{\left(R\&R^2 + PV^2 \right)}$$

TPV = 0.0590

Parts	K$_3$
5	2.08
6	1.93
7	1.82
8	1.74
9	1.67
10	1.62

Repeatability & Reproducibility, $R\&R = \sqrt{\left(EV^2 + AV^2 \right)}$

R & R = 0.0468

Part Variation (PV) = R$_p$ * K$_3$ = 0.0360
(Value of K$_3$ taken from the given table)

% Gage R & R :

	% of Tolerance	% of Total Process Variation (TPV)
EV =	9.35	79.24
AV =	0.00	0.00
PV =	7.20	61.00
R & R =	9.35	79.24

Note 1 : Data can be entered only in the columns marked 1, 2, 3 and Cell for Tolerance Range and top header section. (All those cells which are shaded light blue)

Note 2 : Study require any combination of 2 or 3 Appraisers, 2 or 3 Measurements and any parts from 5 to 10 .

Note 3 : (% R & R Interpretation - Lower of % Tolerance and % Total Process Variation- TPV)
Under 10% error - Measurement system is acceptable;
Between 10 - 30 % error - Marginal (May be acceptable based upon importance of application, cost of gage, cost of repairs, etc.;
More than 30% error - Needs improvement. Make every effort to identify the problems and have them corrected

Results of this Gage R&R Study: MEASUREMENT SYSTEM IS ACCEPTABLE

Figure 2. 18 Gage R&R Study

Chapter 19 - Production Planning

Most medium to large manufacturing companies are using Material Requirements Planning (MRP) systems or Enterprise Resource Planning (ERP) for production planning, scheduling, inventory management, and other activities. The main function of these systems is to manage customer orders from procuring raw materials through manufacturing to shipping products. For smaller companies, the order management system may be managed visually in combination with multiple spreadsheets. Other companies use an MRP/ERP system with multiple spreadsheets and with visual triggers. Companies often experience difficulties with their production planning at some point, resulting in lower sales and/or lower profitability. The cause is having one or more of the following:

- High inventory

- Missed or postponed customer deliveries

- High overtime

- Excessive use of premium freight

- Low Overall Equipment Effectiveness (OEE) performance-Low availability, performance and/or Quality, defined in Chapter 29.

- Poor management, low competence, commitment, or dedication

- System and configuration issues

Supply chain has many factors and complexities for the production planners to manage on an hourly, daily, weekly, and monthly basis. MRP/ERP systems rely on a defined or fixed set of dependencies, but it is the variability of these factors and other inherent complexities that are undefined or difficult to define. Manual planning, make-to-order systems, or pull-based manufacturing execution systems rely on a future that looks exactly like past orders and similar demand schedules. However, forecasts may not be like historic demand and consumer interests may change, making inventories obsolete. In the event of an increased demand beyond previous demand schedules using a manual, make-to-order, or pull system, the supply chain may not have materials available. Some suppliers cannot react quickly to a pull signal without some sort of forward planning and inventory stores due to long lead times for raw materials.

Key issues to understand are how well does the system manage variability?

- Varying factors and magnitude

- Reaction and timing

- Actions and effects

Varying Factors and Magnitude

As previously stated in Chapter 16, Process Flow and Plan For Every Part, implementing a PFEP will improve productivity, quality, communication, feedback, cost, safety, process knowledge, and lead times. The PFEP answers many questions categorized by product, process, people, and information. The operation's team can make better decisions when the PFEP is combined with the following details and associated variability into the order management and planning system:

- Data portals for orders and shipments, including data accuracy and timeliness for data inputs for customers and suppliers

- Order frequency, delivery receipt frequency, lead-times, and volumes for customers and suppliers

- Import and export shipping schedules, customs clearance timing, transportation routings for customers and suppliers

- Packaging and labeling requirements for customers and suppliers

- Order fulfillment rate for customers and suppliers by part

- Customer order processing: first-in/first-out, and grouping by similar processes, work-cells, least changeover time, product family, or other types of groupings

- Product manufacturing times and manufacturing product changeover times (may be quite complex for continuous flow manufacturing)

- Finished goods inventory, customer-required inventories, inventories on hand such as safety stock inventories, finished goods, work in process, and raw materials inventories

- Product manufacturing capacities, Overall Equipment Effectiveness (OEE), including specific process operation constraints such as cycle time, quality rate, and labor efficiency

- Current production schedule, schedule flexibility, and overall availability of materials, machine time, and labor

- Production batch, lot size, or individual piece production run quantities or volumes

- Priorities, rules, algorithms, or models for running production

- Production Part Approval Process (PPAP) process routings (not all process routings may be usable unless they have been approved by the customer; this is typical in the automotive manufacturing parts industry)

- Various strategies and projects impacting supply chain performance

Reaction and Timing

The key question for reaction and timing is: How quickly can the order management and planning system react to a shortage or other change from a customer order through planning to procurement to receiving materials to manufacturing to customer delivery? Companies rarely perform a deep dive analysis into this question as it is very difficult and time consuming. Most companies have defined their business process for order management and planning and have identified a time component for each process step. However, very few companies regularly audit each of these business process steps and timing with historic known events. The following questions can be asked to gain an understanding of the reaction, timing, and what improvements can be made:

- What was the event?
- When was the event known?
- When could have the event be known?
- What risk mitigation analysis was performed?
  - Were options defined with issues, risks, timing, resources, and costs?
  - What criteria was used to select the best option?
  - Are the criteria the same for all customers? If not, how do the decision makers or production planners know this information?
- What business process steps were taken?
- What business process steps were missed? Why?
- How to evaluate the timing for this event? And, how to improve?
  - Do you measure the timing difference between when the event could have been known and when the event was known?
  - Do you measure when the event occurred to reaction taken, then compare against the business process steps and expected timing?
  - Do you measure the overall business process timing for this event?

Production Planning Weekly Schedule
Many companies try to have a regimented weekly planning process with a Daily Routine meeting and mandatory production planning meetings on certain days of the week. The following is a typical production planning format for each day of the week. The meeting formats should be aligned with the meeting etiquette, defined in Chapter 9. Nearly every meeting defined below will be an hour or less unless some major issue or unforeseen circumstance arises. In addition, the following can be developed into a production planning Daily Routine, see Chapter 24 for more information.

Monday (late morning): Operations review of last week's performance. Action items should be defined with a lead responsible person and expected timing for completion. These action items are functional high priorities and the management team has to focus its attention on managing their resources accordingly.

Monday (evening): Sales to finalize current week's orders and following week's orders. The following week's orders may or may not be confirmed. However, some customers provide a firm two-week order or even three- to four-week firm orders.

Sales should also update any forecasted information. Sales and the supply chain team should frequently (at least once a week, if not more often) have contact with customers via email, phone calls, and in-person follow-up once a month or quarter to build and maintain a strong relationship and to ensure any customer changes will be communicated quickly.

Tuesday (morning): Operations team meeting to review current production plan against planned shipments and identify issues, risks, and action items. One person will take the lead responsibility to perform the task typically within 24 to 48 hours. Action item follow-up information may be communicated to all via whiteboards on display in the operations office, emails, or various forms of text messaging. In some cases, this information may be reported on an hourly basis.

Tuesday (afternoon): Attend project management meetings and other functional meetings. Perform functional responsibilities.

Wednesday (morning): Attend project management meetings and other functional meetings. Perform functional responsibilities.

Wednesday (afternoon): Production forecast meetings once a month. These meetings analyze the following month's forecasts and review forecast accuracies (current month +1 month, +2 months, +3 months, etc.) against the previous month's meeting forecasts and are typically longer than 1 hour. Typically, sales will lead this meeting and discuss any significant changes to the previous forecasts and the operations team will make necessary changes.

Thursday: Attend functional meetings. Confirm production plan is being executed as planned, research unfavorable items to plan, and fine tune production plan details. Participate in customer and supplier meetings, audits, and training.

Friday: Operations team meeting to discuss the next four days of production, similar to the Tuesday morning meeting. This meeting should also review the status of the previously defined action items. Open action items at this point must be assessed for whether to upgrade, downgrade, or keep the same level of risk. Typically, risk is identified with a red, yellow, or green identifier for the action item. When risks are upgraded to either yellow or red, the items must be communicated to the management team. In many companies, some of the management team attends these Friday sessions too, since these are intended for addressing and assessing open action items that were not closed out during the week. Analyzing these action items over time can lead to identifying not just special-cause issues, but systemic issues as well. Solving systemic issues typically involves the management team defining a special project's team.

Key Points for Effective Production Planning

Translating the above issues, activities, and variabilities into an order management and planning system requires:

- Plant management and staff who are engaged and attentive to direct labor (people), process, and product issues.

- Visual management — boards, KPIs, signals, and triggers such as Andon, Kanban, or material staging area readiness queues; and manufacturing supermarkets refreshed at known or signaled rates

- Active participation in Daily Routine meetings

- Active participation in production planning meetings

- Displayed product value stream maps, regular reviews, and audits of: MRP/ERP supply chain and production-related master file input data, PFEP, make-to-order/demand-driven processing system, spreadsheet fixed values, value stream details such as capacities and capabilities for each part number

- Operations team's desire to open issues, post issues, and the team's competency of root cause analysis

- Operations team's desire to ensure issues are not repeated by reviewing the root cause and corrective action across other similar parts produced

- Operations team with the resources and capability to identify and reduce risks, and close out open issues

- Operations team regularly conducting training programs with direct labor

- Operation's team motivation to learn new skills, willingness to apply them, and provide an environment to implement the changes

- Operation's team ability to understand the MRP/ERP and multiple spreadsheet logic and be regularly trained, especially when templates are modified. Relying on one or two people to manage the planning process via spreadsheets is dangerous

- Operation's team ability to candidly perform a deep dive analysis into their order management and planning system at least quarterly. Then, update and communicate the changes in the order management system.

Chapter 20 - Logistics

Logistics should be an integral part of any manufacturing operation. Logistics involves inbound and outbound transportation and handling of materials and parts including data communications, order fulfillment, warehousing, inventory management, supply/demand planning, third-party management, and fourth-party management. Material handling activities include the methods for receiving, un-packaging, re-packaging, and moving materials and parts within the factory for processing. In addition, logistics involves labeling and distribution to various customers on time. However, logistics in most manufacturing companies are overlooked or are the responsibility of multiple functions, such as supply chain, purchasing, materials, production, receiving, shipping, and/or sales. In some manufacturing companies, a supply chain function has a broad scope of responsibility covering purchasing, sourcing, and logistics from suppliers through manufacturing to customers.

The costs of logistics are often overlooked in the financial income statement because these costs as a percentage of sales are relatively low, sometimes less than 6 percent. Logistics costs are typically shown as a financial line item for costs associated with delivering a finished product to customers because many companies have their suppliers pay for freight to their manufacturing locations. Logistics are often overlooked by management even though management has a high expectation for reliable, on-time deliveries — whether receiving from suppliers or shipping to customers.

Typically, the general manager does not have a strong logistics background and has not worked in the logistics function. In addition, manufacturing companies use various types of systems, such as MRP or ERP, and third-party logistic interfaces. Systems are often combined with spreadsheets for logistics activities, such as receiving, production control and shipping. These systems and spreadsheet extensions usually do not provide a real-time report on the current and upcoming issues, status, and plans. So, management and the logistics team need to develop analytical tools and reports. A results summary, key highlights, and KPIs should be visually displayed, electronically available, and presented with some frequency. Manage logistics well by developing a real-time issues status board, broadcasting this via text messages, and visually displaying it on computer desktops and other electronic boards.

Internal and External Logistics

Internal logistics are material movements within the company premises, which can include offsite warehouses for temporarily storing materials and products. External logistics are material or product movements from a supplier to a receiving operation or from a shipping operation to a customer, distribution center or other company that may provide additional process operations.

Each manufacturing location's management team may determine its internal and external logistics responsibilities — usually under one function, but many companies separate internal and external logistics responsibilities. In larger companies, the executive management team defines the organizational structure and responsibilities, while individual manufacturing facilities focus on their own responsibilities. Whether in a small or large company, the one function that can encompass internal and external logistics is the supply chain. External logistics are quite complex because of the various suppliers and modes of transportation involving incoming and outgoing materials and products. Transportation includes trucking, rail, sea freight, air freight, warehousing, distribution, and third- or fourth-party companies providing various services, such as importing and exporting activities from and to various countries. Other risks and factors to manage for external logistics are weather, seasons, natural events, political unrest, social implications, economic risks, currency risks, time zones, language, custom's duty management, digital communication linkages, lead-time reliability, and the overall depth and breadth of the entire supplier base.

Third-party logistics service companies typically provide external logistic services, including preparing customs documentation and managing imports and exports, and can provide additional services, such as warehousing, distribution center management, inventory management, decanting and repackaging of materials, delivering materials to points of use at manufacturing work-cells, and procurement of various materials. A fourth-party logistics provider manages third-party logistics services — sometimes manufacturing companies outsource their logistics activities to several third-party logistics providers and contract a fourth party as the lead logistics provider to manage all the third-party activities. Use of various third-party logistics is quite common among small and large companies; fourth-party logistics companies are rarely used by small companies.

Key Steps to Improve Internal and External Logistics
Any of the following steps can be undertaken by the supply chain or logistics functions or can even be considered in a 90 day challenge. Project team members outside the supply chain and logistics function should also participate. Chapter 38 defines a 90 day Challenge with more details. In addition, resources such as trainers or consultants can provide additional input or be a part of a 90 day challenge. There are 7 steps to improve internal and external logistics:

1. Develop an understanding of the various internal and external logistics activities and responsibilities

2. Understand and define the details for each part movement – establish a plan for every part (PFEP)

3. Compare third-party logistics costs with internally managed costs

4. Study packaging schemes and identification

5. Evaluate the receiving, internal movement, warehousing, and shipping areas for cost, quality, productivity and safety improvements

6. Pursue various negotiations with suppliers, customers and third- and fourth-party logistics providers

7. Consolidate all the activities in the previous six steps and create monthly and quarterly plans showing the expected improvements, lead person, status and overall indicator of meeting the plan

The *first step* is to develop an understanding of the various internal and external logistics activities and responsibilities. This understanding can be achieved via a value stream map with support information from a RASIC matrix (responsibility, accountability, support, inform, control) or, more simply, a list of functional responsibilities, KPIs, organization charts, systems, database modules, business process flowcharts, and spreadsheets. Defining Daily Routine meeting objectives and deliverables (daily, weekly, monthly) may be helpful as well. In addition, procedures using swim-lane diagrams can help clarify the process flow, timing and responsibility. After analyzing this information, a realignment of current responsibilities or plans for restructuring may be needed.

A *second step* is to understand and define the details for each part movement — the plan for every part (PFEP). This is especially important if one of the objectives is to use third-party service providers for some specific parts or activities. Using a PFEP to compare internal costs against various third-party service providers is fairly straightforward but may require some coordination to compare details for each incoming material, including costs, timing and information flow. Other quantitative and qualitative information to compare is:

- Material lead-time reliability
- Quality of services
- Response quickness and accuracy
- Overall competency and breadth of service coverage
- Third-party service support requirements and expectations

The above items can be further defined during the due diligence and quoting phase of identifying a third-party service provider. Generating statements and questions is fairly common during this stage. And, specific questions will help to compare different providers as each may have unique answers with improvement opportunities. The PFEP should be updated and analyzed internally first, before discussion of possible options or engagements by a third-party service provider.

A *third step* is to become familiar with the scope of services that third-party logistics companies offer. Comparisons of third-party logistics costs with internally managed costs are sometimes biased on the part of the manufacturing company because of impact of staff's changing roles and responsibilities or downsizing. However, these comparisons are still valuable and should be considered at least for benchmarking services and costs. In addition, examining ways in which to receive or integrate data can make the overall logistics function more efficient. It also might be of benefit to have a third-party or even a fourth-party logistics service provider help design a logistics network for both domestic and international suppliers and customers.

A *fourth step* is to study packaging schemes. These schemes for customer, internal and supplier packaging may involve packaging design; package label design; packaging procurement; decanting of supplier packaging materials; separation of pallets, cardboard and plastic wrapping in supplier packaging; returnable packaging (which may be received by a facility, customer or supplier); a location for packaging and cleaning; internal packaging movements; customer packaging; and pallets.

Another important aspect in packaging schemes is identification and status of materials and parts. This information has to be visual, clear, and simply presented, and will be consulted at various processing locations (receiving stage area, receiving warehouse, manufacturing supermarkets, work-cells, shipping warehouse, shipping stage area and so on). Identification should appear at least on the pallet. Individual parts within a pallet can be labeled as well, or their location within the container or box can be indicated visually and/or with a barcode. Identification can include traceable information such as location of manufacture, details about process operations (product and process characteristics, test results, and timing), supplier information, and specific information about parts (part number, revision, weight, date of manufacturing or expiration, color and so forth).

Packaging typically utilizes some type of pallets. Pallets can be made of wood (including heat-treated wood for export), plastic, aluminum or steel. Wooden pallets can be designated for certain uses and must be controlled inside the factory because of fire safety and local regulations (for example, the number of pallets in certain areas of a building may be restricted). Materials and parts placed on pallets, or within other packages on pallets, are prepared in a way to prevent material or part damage and to make movement of materials easier. Pallets can be stacked with or without boxes within trailers for transport. Materials and parts in boxes on pallets may have additional protective coatings, wrappings or boxes; be secured with plastic ties; have plastic separators or other barriers, such as oil or rust inhibitors; or be wax-dipped, bound or sealed with desiccant or in a way to prevent oxidation, contamination or part damage.

There are many aspects to consider when designing a package, such as the primary purpose of the package, secondary usage (re-use or recycle), and disposal. Packaging typically is made of paper, cardboard, plastics, various plastic laminations, wood, aluminum, steel or combinations. The primary purpose may be single or multiple use, transport within the country or export to other countries. It is important to take into account overall weight load, strength for stacking or transport, overall package dimensions, material or part orientation within the package, identification and labeling, ease of handling, decanting or use by the customer, and optimization for movement (ground transportation, air, and shipping), such as stacking inside a container or trailer. In some cases, customer and supplier packaging design may need approval because of local legislation regarding packaging handling, use, disposal, or even esthetics. Packaging should meet all regulations and be designed with overall lowest cost in mind.

Packaging can be stored in various locations in and around the factory, including offsite locations. These locations are for supplier parts, supplier packaging materials that have been decanted, various internal containers and pallets, disposal areas for different packaging wastes, and customer pallets. Such places can use a covered roof or storage; have metal racks to store materials at various heights; have large trailers, containers or compactors stationed by receiving/shipping docks, at or within work-cells. Locations should be specific and clearly defined because there can be different packaging types within an area. Both empty and full locations should be delineated — for example, with painted lines, posted signs, rail, or chain-link fences.

Space is needed for cleaning internal or returnable packaging and for repairing packaging, especially returnable packaging. Returnable packaging may be used for internal movements or for shipping to or from customers and suppliers. Returnable packaging has to be cleaned, so specific areas should be designated for uncleaned returnable containers, cleaning, and returnable packaging that has been cleaned. Cleaning instructions are needed because in many cases, temporary or part-time workers perform this task, which is not a daily activity, so they may not be trained or familiar with the materials. The packaging cleaning operation is overlooked in most factory layouts and often takes place in a non-ideal location, leading to customer complaints.

Logistics costs should include all material movements: shipping by suppliers, moving materials throughout the factory and shipping to customers. However, material movements within the factory are typically not accumulated within logistics. For any specific product, there may be different logistics costs owing to different customer locations. Also, some raw materials may not have any logistics costs, if the supplier pays. Finally, there may be no specific strategy or financial template for logistics and packaging for domestic or international suppliers or customers.

Each new business opportunity may have its own unique costs. Some companies have standardized their requirements for inbound materials, such as a delivery free on-board (FOB) shipping point, where there is no charge to the buyer to place the material in a logistics carrier's vehicle, trailer or container and the buyer assumes all responsibility during shipment for any damage or loss.

Packaging costs should include everything in this discussion of the fourth step, including design, use, repair, replacement and eventual disposal. Typically, these costs are captured in the original business case. If the business is awarded, these costs are managed by conducting monthly reviews of profit-and-loss financial statements. Finance will decide how the packaging costs are allocated and presented.

A *fifth step* can be to evaluate the receiving, internal movement, warehousing, and shipping areas for cost, quality, productivity and safety improvements. Using the PFEP and understanding the material movements and timing can help in determining more efficient material movement and methods to move materials. For example, forklift routings stopping at certain places to drop off or pick up materials at certain times with the use of indicator lights, computer displays, radio communications or other means by which forklift drivers are informed of certain urgent material movement needs or upcoming pickups and drop-offs. For large premises, a truck routing map, list of contacts, and schedule for dock loading and unloading can improve safety, productivity and reliability of movements. Another example is to consider the use of roller carts with or without the use of short roller conveyors. This would replace the use of materials on pallets or materials in boxes to move between work-cells.

A *sixth step* can be to pursue various negotiations with suppliers, customers and third- and fourth-party logistics providers. Consider negotiating with suppliers and customers for a different packaging type, a method that leads to using full truckloads rather than partially full truckloads, different carriers, and possibly consolidation centers or other ways to reduce logistics costs, improve reliability of shipments, and reduce transit times. Negotiate with suppliers and customers to package materials more densely and maximize use of container or trailer space to reduce overall logistics cost per unit. Alternatively, negotiate with suppliers and customers regarding ownership of the inventory, such as FOB versus cost, insurance and freight (CIF), or consider changing payment terms. Generally speaking, buying FOB for international trade can be less expensive because the purchaser has responsibility for defining the freight forwarder. Using CIF might permit additional logistics markup and add some administration costs. However, using FOB, CIF or other international commercial terms (incoterms) affects costs, risks, responsibilities and ownership. That means using a third party, a fourth party or even consultants is highly beneficial for conducting annual training; performing, quoting or coordinating logistics analysis; or even doing audits to ensure compliance or identifying possible risks, issues or improvements. Finally, arrangements can be made to have the supplier own the inventory until the company uses the inventory within their manufacturing process.

A *seventh step* is to consolidate all the activities in the previous six steps and create monthly and quarterly plan showing the expected improvements, lead person, status and overall indicator of meeting the plan, such as a red-yellow-green identification for each specific activity. During each monthly review, plan results are presented and the plan is then updated or revised as needed.

Chapter 21 - Value Stream Mapping

Defining the material and information flow from the customers all the way through to the suppliers and compiling this information in one document is known as a value stream map (VSM). The value stream mapping exercise is a high-level visualization of a product family showing value-added and non-value-added activities in the factory, but also with information about the supply chain, from suppliers to customers. One key book to reference is "Learning to See: Value Stream Mapping to Add Value and Eliminate Muda" by Mike Rother and John Shook, and "Seeing the Whole Value Stream" by Dan Jones and Jim Womack.

There are many benefits to developing a VSM, such as:

- Helps to visualize a product family's processes within the factory
- Shows the linkage between material and information flow for a product family
- Shows some process performance indicators for a product or product family
- Provides a training platform for current business activities
- Provides insight for identifying sources of waste; non-value-added activities and time
- Provides a visual display of opportunities for reducing operation variations
- Helps identify upcoming improvement projects for the entire workforce; can highlight various sections of the map for potential projects or to focus on constraints or other issues
- Provides a basis for defining a future value stream, planning changes to the business, and developing annual plans
- Can compare different product family value streams

Value Stream Usage

If the company has not yet developed and displayed openly its product value stream map(s), this should be a priority. A cross-functional team should be assembled to take the following steps to define a value stream map. If the company has already defined a VSM, these questions will help improve its functionality:

1. Define plan to make and post a VSM for all product families (products and services). Priority to define and post a VSM can be ranked by similar products and processes, volume, and profitability. The team may want to develop VSMs only for the top one or two product families and go through several iterations of improvements before tackling the company's entire line of products and services. Most factories have fewer than five product families/VSMs.

2. Ensure that the VSMs are posted in a conspicuous place where the operations teams see them often and easily. When VSMs are posted in areas where people walk by or congregate, they are more likely to be noticed and encourage a higher willingness to participate in discussions involving the operations.

3. Once VSMs are completed, months should not have to go by before improvements are made. The key is to document and display incremental improvements to develop momentum for continuous improvements. Engage the team immediately, discuss issues or improvement opportunities, and write these on the VSM or on a board next to the VSM.

4. When analyzing a VSM, what should you look for? There are many observations to make when analyzing a VSM. Observations can be summarized to determine which process should have a continuous improvement or kaizen event, or the observations can be categorized into 1 of the 7 kinds of waste. The 7 Kinds of Waste are also known as DOTWIMP: Defects, Overproduction, Transportation, Waiting, Inventory, Motion, and Processing. Additional wastes can be included, such as HR Utilization and Lost Time Accidents. A Pareto of these categories can then be made to decide which category to focus on for improvement, or which category can contribute the highest return with the lowest investment. The categories can also define expected improvement contributions relative to safety, quality, cost, delivery, and morale.

5. When improvement projects, studies, or experiments are undertaken, they should be written on the value stream map and results posted near it. The team should be constantly challenged for productivity, quality, safety, delivery, lead-time reductions, inventory reductions, etc. Baseline metrics should be defined in the VSM and challenged for improvement. Documenting these activities provides increased knowledge and can be potentially used for other work areas.

6. Upcoming product and process changes should be noted on the value stream map, along with Before and After changes. When the VSM becomes difficult to read due to many changes, a new VSM should be created and posted. Alternatively, the current VSM could show the Before change and the future VSM show the After change — unless, of course, changes are occurring so often that stability and control are questionable.

7. Post a future value stream map next to the current value stream with improvements listed or defined and marked with colored handwritten loops to focus attention on them. It is important to give the operations team a direction and vision of where to focus the next opportunities or what KPIs to focus on. The future VSM may also contain a monthly project planning diagram showing the current status versus planned improvements.

8. If VSMs are used in annual operating plans, then a summary of the comparisons between the current and future VSMs can be shown (actual results and next year's targets), including the current and future VSMs (future value stream can be shown as a project-based monthly plan). This leads to comprehensive, factory-based understanding, direction, and management control of business operations.

9. Use a VSM for training. Management should use the VSM often as a tool for educating the operations team and to provide focus and clarity when discussing issues and opportunities. Management should constantly talk in terms of continuous flow, velocity, value, and identification and removal or reduction of waste. Velocity can be defined as the time from receipt of the customer order to

ordering raw materials, then processing through the factory, then delivery to the customer.

10. Require a VSM for capital expenditure requests. Doing so visually demonstrates the whole business, not just one part of the business. Not all capital expenditure requests need a VSM. A VSM is not needed for capital expenditures, site and facility infrastructure, quality equipment, maintenance, and IT.

Key Steps for Creating a Value Stream Map

1. Define a team for collecting data and defining the current value stream map. The team should be fewer than six people per product family. The team should be cross-functional and have the ability to obtain various operational data sets. If the team is unable to obtain some data, they can ask more-experienced people.

2. Have the team select a product family and scope of work. Selecting the product family may be quite simple for small to medium-sized factories that may only have one or two product families, but more difficult for a larger factory. Ideally, the team should make a matrix of all the products and process operation number and names (for example: Product XYZ, Operation #120 cutting). A product family may consist of one or more products. Making a matrix using the product process flowcharts and adding volume for each product can help define different product families. Items in a product family should have similar, if not identical, processes. Some processes may be different due to product variation itself, but if more than 75% of the processes are the same, these can be combined into one product family. Once the product family has been selected, the process flowcharts, process routing sheets, plant layout, production schedules, operator attendance list, and/or operator training matrix must be collected. This information will be used for walking through the process to understand each activity and where direct laborers are working. Define the scope of work, such as from supplier to customer, or from Operation #120 to #500.

3. Have the team meet to discuss the following tasks and then walk the process from shipping to receiving and collect various data at each product location and process step. The first walk should be to collect information. Try to keep the data collection simple by using one piece of paper for each process location or process step. The information collected should be: number of customers, customer volume requirements, customer product mix, frequency of delivery, number of shifts customers operate, quantity and pack size, information that the customer provides about contact and frequency, description of the activity or process, cycle time (average), changeover or set-up time (average time), available time, uptime (average), yield rate (average), quality rate (average), EPE (every part every time period: how often that product family is produced in a specific operation), batch size or average amount of product being produced in a specific operation, number of product variations, number of shifts, number of people, inventory between process operations, how material moves between process activities, information and frequency of information for each process activity, number of suppliers, information given to supplier, frequency of information, etc. The average times can

be calculated based upon observation of a few cycles of the process activity. At the bottom of the paper, allow some space for adding notes or comments section for any special circumstances identified, outsourcing of any process, or documentation of activities, and time involved for other activities that the operators are doing while the machine(s) are ready to be loaded or unloaded. If an operator follows a routine path to load/unload parts, this has to be noted. If the operator waits at the machine while the machine is in operation, this also should be noted.

4. As the information is being gathered for each process, post it on a wall where the team has been working to show the product flow. The wall can be somewhere within the operation's team office or other temporary location. The information may have to be consolidated, summarized, and drawn into standardized process activity boxes. The process activity boxes should include: cycle time, changeover time, number of people, available work times, machine uptime, EPE (every part every X). If there is inventory at each process this should be collected and drawn into the triangle shape. You may also want to use Post-it® notes and a whiteboard to record action items. As more of the process activity blocks are put together and posted on a wall, the entire product family process will appear.

5. Both shipping and receiving information will be summarized and displayed with icons that represent shipping, trucking, or air for logistics. Receiving and shipping information including frequency, pack size and quantities will need to be summarized.

6. The information flows will need to be defined and shown as either arrows or process activity boxes. The scheduling information signals should include forecast frequency, daily or weekly schedules, MRP/ERP, and thin arrows from the scheduling to the various process operation activity boxes that control production.

7. A timeline will then need to be drawn under all process activity boxes and inventory triangles, with takt time to be defined and summarized into a customer block. For each inventory triangle amount, it should be divided by the daily customer requirement, lead-times for supplier and customers to be defined, value-added times should be defined under each process activity box, then sum total all production time (including lead-time and sum total the value-added time).

8. Eventually, this map should be re-constructed on a wall where others can readily see the product flow and timing for each operation. Next, this product flow map or value stream map should be summarized in one page, so it can be used in presentations, annual plans, or other email communications. Common icons can be used for ease of understanding. (These common icons can be found online for use in spreadsheets or can be hand-drawn on the template sheets.) Post-it® notes are helpful here since the icon can be on the note.

9. Analyze the value stream and compare it against MRP master file data. Once the entire value stream is clearly shown, other operations team members should be invited to see it so they can understand it. Some information may be missing or opportunities for improvement or issues could be identified. Walking the process again with the updated value stream is helpful for confirmation and to define a variety of other observations. This may have to be done several times and with

different operations members due to misunderstandings, errors in constructing the map, or responding to opportunities for improvement that surface immediately. Comparing the collected data to the MRP/ERP master file is important for confirmation, although more data checks may be needed. Typically, there are differences between the MRP/ERP system and the data collected. This information has to be discussed by the operations team and actions have to be taken, such as collecting more data or making a change in the MRP/ERP system using a product and process change notice system.

10. Define improvement opportunities; define pacemaker process operation (process constraint) and analyze the production scheduling trigger for it, define pull signals, identify ways to produce a mix of parts at the pacemaker process; reduce batch sizes; minimize scrap, reduce changeover times; reduce lead times, reduce non-value add activities, etc. Once a list of improvement opportunities is defined then these can be analyzed and prioritized for implementation. Different teams may be identified for each opportunity with expected dates of completion and reviews weekly.

11. During the weekly production planning review meetings, issues such as missed deliveries, material not available, overtime, production scheduling changes, etc., should be highlighted or marked on the VSM as specific process activities. As mentioned previously, action items will be defined during those meetings and followed up for closure at consecutive meetings. The main reason to have the VSM available is that not all operation and support staff may understand where the problem occurred in the process. When issues are repeated in certain process activities, either the corrective action was not 100% completed, root cause was not clearly identified, the process activity was disrupted, or other problems occurred. This is another value of a VSM, to identify and reduce process operation variations. However, most companies do not perform a deep dive or spend sufficient time determining where in the process the problem occurred, so time after the time, the same issues are repeated.

12. Repeat steps 1-10 for all other product families. Be sure there is enough space on a wall to post the various product family Value Stream Maps. Ideally, having all value streams in one room may make it easier to compare; however, this may cause confusion with notes and maps posted on all walls. Another way is to use different conference rooms for each type of product family value stream. This way, everyone can stay focused on specific value stream issues and improvements.

Illustration - Value Stream Map – Product XXX

The following illustration shows a value stream map for a specific product XXX. The legends have information such as the VSM team names, revision description of changes, customer volume and takt time, list of improvement action plans, summary of value-added and non-valued activity times, and highlighted constraints.

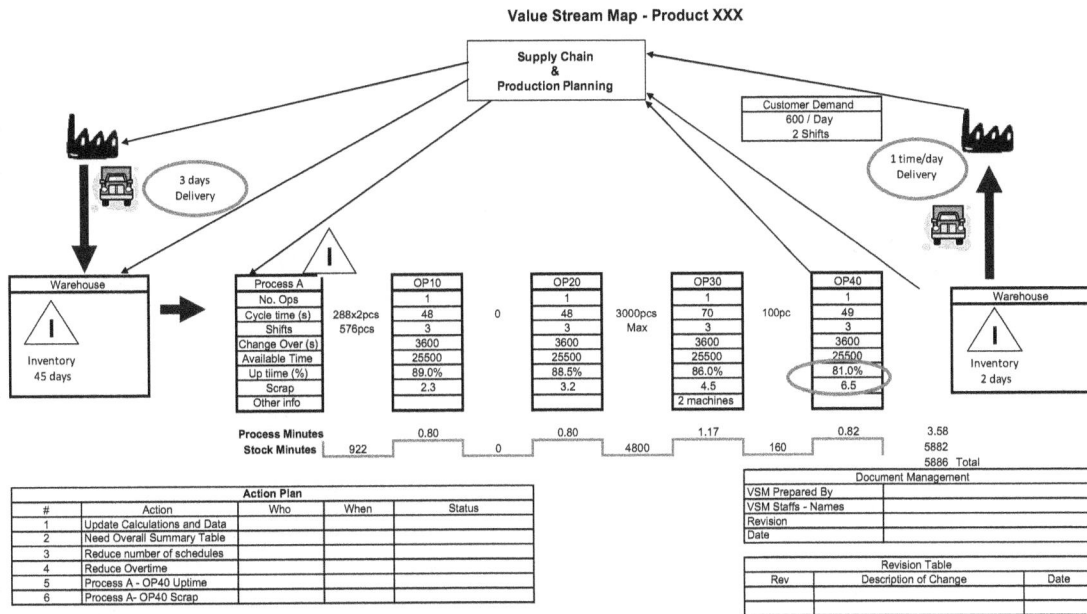

Figure 2. 19 Value Stream Map – Product XXX

Illustration - Value Stream Map – Product XYZ

The following Value Stream Map is for Product XYZ. This Value Stream Map is far more sophisticated but still has the same type of information such as the VSM team names, revision description of changes, customer volume and takt time, list of improvement action plans, summary of value-added and non-valued activity times, and highlighted constraints.

169

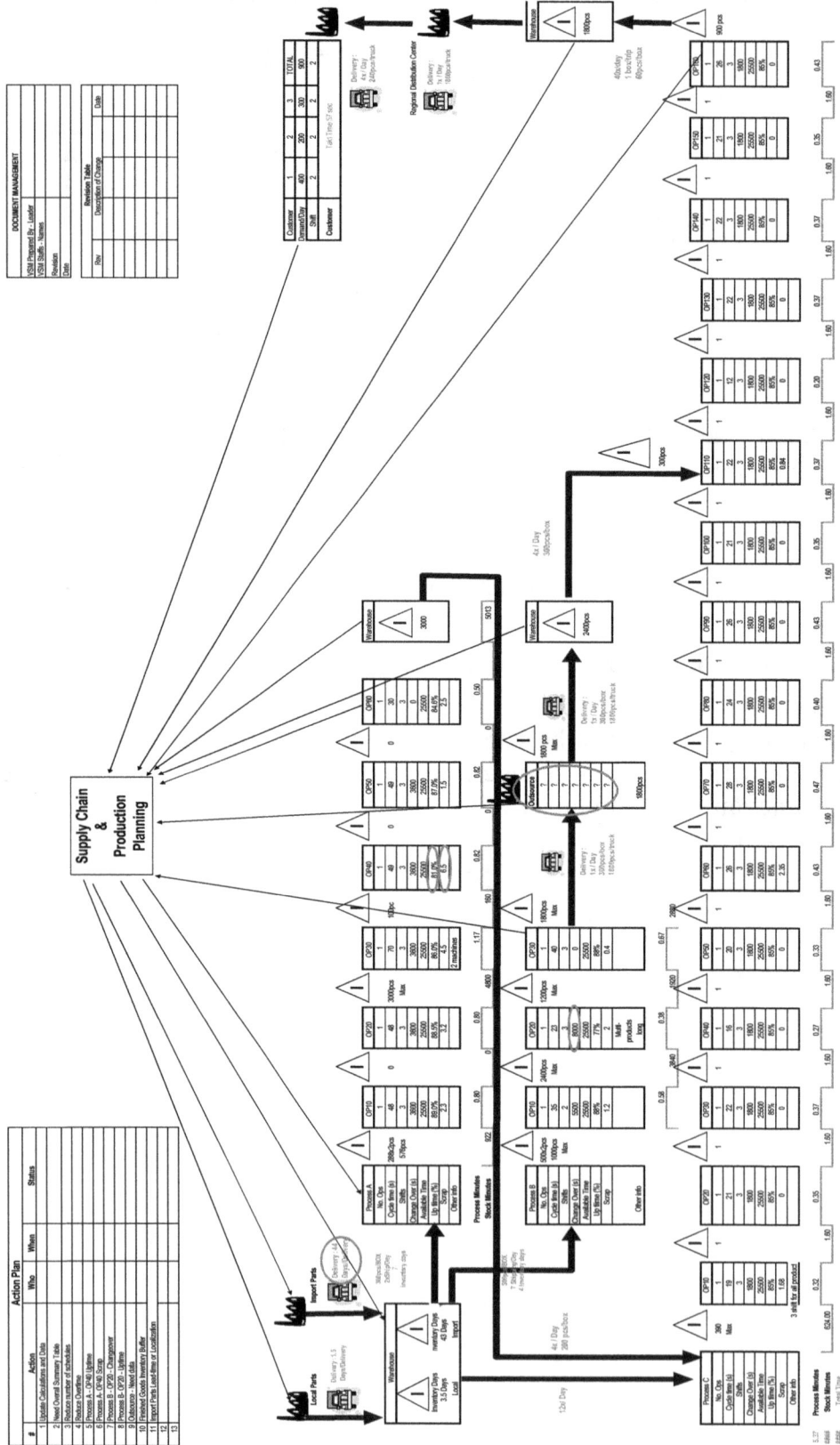

Figure 2. 20 Value Stream Map

Chapter 22 - Standardized Work

People are often confused by Standardized Work and Work Standards, and what they should use and follow in their factories. Standardized Work is a documented, precise work sequence that must be followed to meet takt, or the rate needed to meet customer demand, ensure the required inventory is available to keep the process running smoothly, and ensure there is sufficient production capacity within the work-cell. Takt is available production time divided by customer demand.

Work Standard versus Standardized Work

A Work Standard is a documented standard operating work instruction or procedure. A Work Standard may also contain descriptive and visual sequences. While both Standardized Work and Work Standards are similar in name and definition, Standardized Work is the basis for continuous improvement and is aimed at the staff and management, while Work Standards are mainly aimed at the direct labor workers who are performing work. Another way to understand the difference is that Work Standards are the basis for doing something consistently, while Standardized Work enhances this by having the work done according to a precise sequence of events within a certain time period (takt) and at a continual rate with standard inventory available.

Illustration – Production Capacity

The following figure shows an example of evaluating production capacity for a specific work-cell. Operations are listed with defined cycle times and other machine details, available work time, production output details including identifying bottleneck if applicable, and a status to indicate whether there is under or over capacity. This chart is required for development of a Standardized Work sequence. The following chart shows the customer daily requirement of 640 parts and a weekly potential capacity of 3,200 parts. The bottleneck or constraining operation is the inspection operation, being under capacity by 13 pieces. Action items can be detailed on the chart to show the history of improvements and can be used to follow up with either an operations review or project review. The action items stated in the figure:

1. Improve Process Capability for OP #20 and OP #30, to reduce rework and scrap. Responsibility Name, Date to be completed by.

2. Improve Uptime for OP #20, OP#30, OP#50, and OP#60. Responsibility Name, Date to be completed by.

3. Review the inspection measuring program to determine which product features can be removed based upon the process capability results, and/or edit the inspection measuring program to reduce the inspection frequency based upon the process capability. Responsibility Name, Date to be completed by.

Workcell # and Name-   Date ____   Part name & number ____   Customer Daily Requirement **640**

Days Available: 5   Potential Capacity **3,200**

Operation		Machine					Time					Production Output						Status		
Oper. No.	Description	Cycle Time Sec/Cycle	Pcs/Cycle	Sec/Pc	Gross Pc/Hr/Mach	# of Mach.	Uptime %	Re-work %	Scrap %	Standard Hrs/Day*	Gross Time Per Day	Gross Capacity	Operation Capacity	Constraint Operations	System Capacity	Daily Req'd for Customer Level	Potential Capacity Increase	Above Requirement	Below Requirement	Over/Under
OP10	Rough cutting	26	0.5	52	69	1	76%	0.2%	3.3%	19.85	24	1652	1008	OK	1008	700	654	308	0	Over
OP20	Top side - machining	130	2	65	55	1	79%	1.5%	0.5%	19.85	24	1329	851	OK	851	697	478	155	0	Over
OP30	Bottom side - machining	128	2	64	56	1	79%	1.5%	0.5%	19.85	24	1350	854	OK	854	688	466	166	0	Over
OP40	Groove	78	1	68	53	1	84%	1.5%	0.5%	19.85	24	1271	865	OK	865	679	405	187	0	Over
OP50	Drill and Tap	80	1	66	55	1	79%	0.5%	1.3%	19.85	24	1308	840	OK	840	670	469	170	0	Over
OP60	Drill and Tap	74	1	70	51	1	79%	0.8%	1.0%	19.85	24	1234	794	OK	794	663	440	131	0	Over
OP70	Wash	45	1	45	80	1	85%	0.0%	0.0%	19.85	24	1920	1350	OK	1350	663	570	687	0	Over
OP80	Inspect	102	2	96	38	1	85%	0.8%	3.5%	19.85	24	900	627	Bottleneck	627	640	273	0	13	Under
OP90	Laser Marking, Scan, and Package	40	1	40	90	1	90%	0.0%	0.0%	19.85	24	2160	1608	OK	1608	640	552	968	0	Over

Constraint tracking sheet

Legend: Below Requirement; Operation Capacity; Potential Capacity Increase; Customer Daily Requirement XXX; System Capacity

Action Items - What, Responsibility, Timing, Status

1. Improve the Process Capability for OP #20 and OP #30, to reduce the rework and scrap. Responsibility Name, Date to be completed by.
2. Improve the Uptime for OP #20, OP#30, OP#50, and OP#60. Responsibility Name, Date to be completed by.
3. Review the inspection measuring program to determine which product features can be removed based upon the process capability results, or edit the program to reduce the inspection frequency based upon the process capability. Responsibility Name, Date to be completed by.

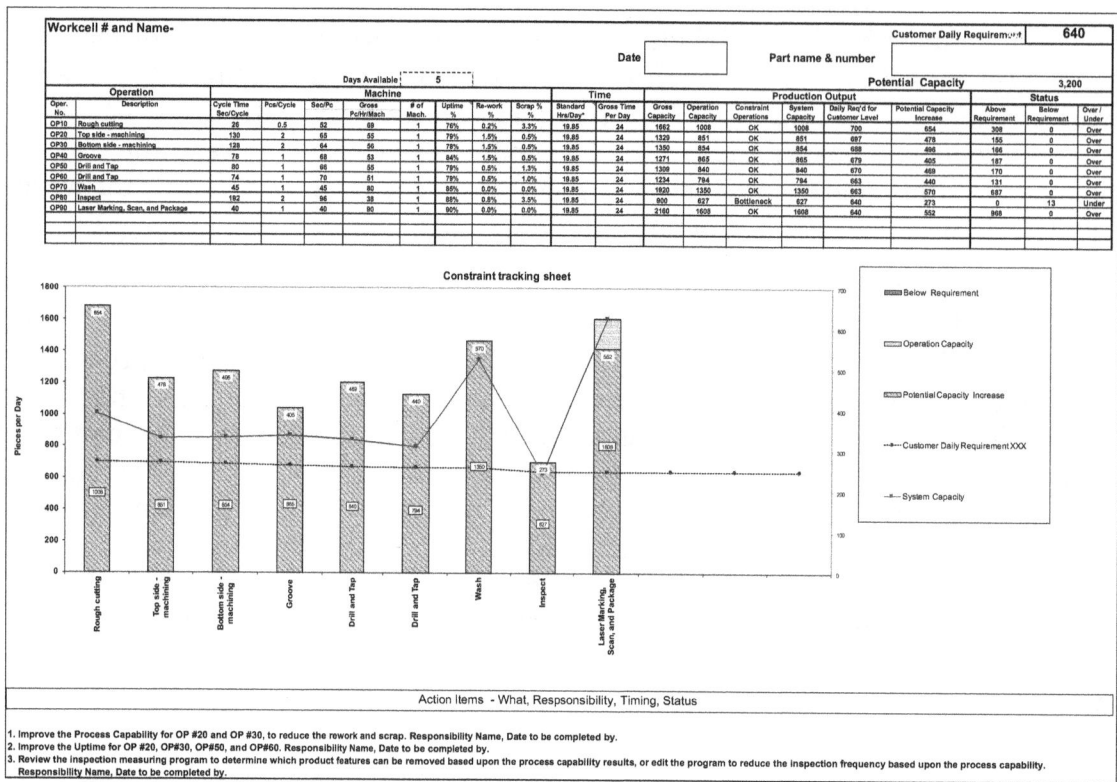

Figure 2. 21 Production Capacity

Illustration – Takt Time

A simple example of Takt follows: A manufacturing company works three 8-hour shifts with each shift having one lunch break of 30 minutes and two 15-minute breaks. The company also has a requirement of participating in Daily Routine of 5 minutes per shift, Total Preventive Maintenance of 5 minutes per shift, conducting 5S activities of 5 minutes, shift change of 5 minutes per shift, and set-up time of 3 minutes at one time per shift.

Takt Time Calculation
Annual Average

Work-cell _____	Prepared by: _____
Issue Date: _____	Approved by: _____

TIME AVAILABLE CALCULATION

Hours per Shift
| 8 | x 60 min x 60 sec = | 28,800 | Seconds |

minus

Lunch	1,800	Seconds
TPM	300	Seconds
Break	1,800	Seconds
Daily Routine	300	Seconds
5 S	300	Seconds
Shift Change	300	Seconds
Total Non-Work Time	4,800	Seconds

equals
| *Time Available w/out Set-Up* | 24,000 | Seconds |

minus
| Set-Up | 180 | Seconds |

equals
| *TIME AVAILABLE* | 23,820 | Seconds |

DEMAND CALCULATION

| UNITS per YEAR | WORKDAYS per YEAR | | |
| 160,000 | / | 250 | = | 640 | UNITS per DAY |

| Past due backlog units | Days to eliminate | + |
| | / | | = | | UNITS per DAY |

equals
DAILY DEMAND
| 640 | UNITS per DAY |

| *DAILY DEMAND* | # OF SHIFTS** | *DEMAND* |
| 640 | / | 3 | = | 213 | UNITS per SHIFT |

| # OF STATIONS** | UNITS PER STATION |
| 1 | = | 213 |

PER SHIFT - PER STATION
| TIME AVAILABLE | DEMAND | | *Takt Time* |
| 23,820 | / | 213 | = | 111.6 | Sec. |

Figure 2. 22 Takt time calculation

Standardized Work Sheet

A Standardized Work sheet defines each work element with a time to execute that element of the process activity. By adding up the work elements for a specific process activity, the total work time must be equal to or less than 112 seconds. If the total time for a specific process activity is greater than the takt time, then a Line Balancing exercise should take place. A Line Balance exercise would re-evaluate and change the work elements, so the operation time becomes less than or meets the takt time. In other words, some work elements of the process constraint would move to other operations. This would reduce the process constraint time while increasing other operations time.

Illustration – Line Balance

The following example shows a Line Balance for Operation #40, 50, and 60. Work Elements (WE) are shown as time blocks for each operation. The BEFORE activity shows cycle time exceeding takt time with OP#50. When one or more operations exceeds takt time, this causes the process to not meet the customer demand, meaning missed shipments, less sales, and potentially loss of a business opportunity. Also, the

BEFORE activity shows OP#40 and OP#60 having some non-value-added time, meaning no production work is being done. The AFTER activity shows 3 work elements from OP#50 moving to OP#40 and OP#60, where all 3 operations are now less than takt time. Also, the AFTER activity shows an improvement of productivity as the cycle time has been reduced, and material flow is also improved as the flow is smoother.

Process development

Moving work elements for both machining and assembly operations between different stations is part of the process design and development. There should be a cross-functional team that includes suppliers of the machines, tools, and fixtures to conceptually define each process operation's work elements, then simulate those details using computer-aided design and manufacturing method tools. These software tools can visually show a 3-dimensional view of each individual process work element with estimated times and movements of direct labor workers.

Current production

Moving work elements for both machining and assembly operations between the different stations is typically not a simple study due to many considerations, such as machining-part orientation and machining program logic (if there are multiple machining stations, they may have different machining datum). Alternatively, machining operations work elements may not have to move, as a tool-life study can be conducted by comparing different tools or different tool suppliers to yield an overall tool-cost savings with lesser cycle time.

Assembly- The work stations have defined specific part orientation, operator ergonomics, and component to component assembly logic. If the work elements can be moved without impacting quality, then this process change should be processed according to the product and process change system. Also, moving work elements may happen with use of different fixtures, tooling, direct labor, component part presentation movements, or assembly station movement.

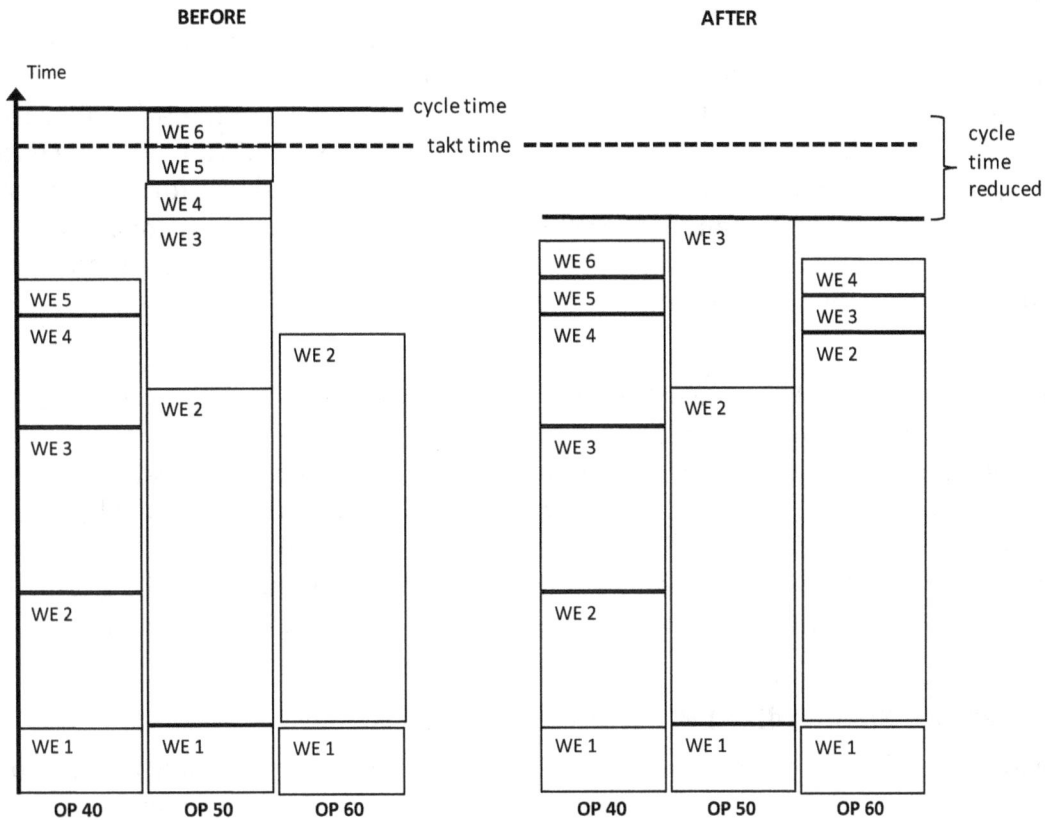

Figure 2. 23 Line Balance

Management and staff should observe the work elements being practiced by direct labor according to the Standardized Work sheet. Understanding these elements and sequences can be a basis for management and support teams to improve the process in safety, quality, and productivity (more units produced per time period), as well as reduce inventory.

Most companies have Work Standards for their manufacturing operations and for supporting functions. They also can be refined or upgraded. Developing Standardized Work requires the operations team to be much more involved on the factory floor, studying and defining the sequential work elements along with the time to perform the work, and inventory for continually running the process.

For example, one shift may follow a Work Standard one way for a given time and another shift may follow the Work Standard, but with a different time and possibly a different quality or inventory level. Someone from the operations team can highlight the better Work Standard practices, obtain a time for this, update the Work Standards, and train the other shifts to follow the new practice. Another operations person may work on changing the formats of the Work Standards to include the precise operation sequence with timing and inventory requirements and then post this in place of the current Work Standard. This new document can be the first attempt at developing Standardized Work and used to train all of the direct staff. All operation's staff should know about the conversion from Work Standards to Standardized Work, and participate in both Standardized Work training and in developing a Standardized Work for a specific process. At some point, all Work Standards throughout the entire factory can be upgraded to the new Standardized Work sheet format for each operation. It is very important for direct labor operators to be deeply involved in the precise sequence of work elements to ensure that better or best practices are documented and then relayed to the other shifts.

Another option is to hold a workshop with the work-cell direct labor operators to discuss the precise work elements. Developing a simple simulation to visualize the work elements will help, especially when the machines are not yet available for use for a new product or purpose. As the operations team moves from work-cell to work-cell, they can upgrade Work Standards to Standardized Work. KPIs would start trending favorably as better or best practices are implemented. Upgrading to Standardized Work gives a stepping stone to the next level of improvement.

Illustration – Standardized Work Sheet

The following figure shows a Standardized Work sheet for a typical machining work-cell. Assembly work stations will have more detail describing the order of assembly component-by-component with either the right or left hand for specific components. Also, the Standardized Work sheet may show the layout of the component parts presentation locations. The work-cell shows one direct labor operator moving parts from OP#10 through OP#90. There are many features shown such as:

- Each machine foot print, operation number and name
- Raw material and finished goods inventory location
- Work-in-process inventory shown as black dots
- Operator movement shown as an arrow
- Quality Control Table for the operator to visually or mechanically inspect a part
- KPI board for the operator to write the status and issues
- Symbols at specific operations to indicate inspection, safety, or ergonomic point
- Key Quality and Safety Points and specific requirements
- Work Elements and timing for manual, automatic machine, walk, and summary
- Takt Time
- Revision Control

Standardized Work Sheet

Cust/Proj:		Part Name:				
Workcell:		Part Number(s):				

OP #	Work Elements	Element time			Process layout and material flow diagram
		Manual	Auto	Walk	
OP10	pick up 1 part, orientate with grooves facing up, place on fixture, cycle, blow-off part and fixture, re-position part on other fixture, cycle, blow off part, unload and place onto conveyor, blow-off fixture	10.3	52.0	2.0	
OP20	Load 2 parts into fixture with grooves facing DOWN, cycle, blowoff part, unload, blow-off fixture	8.9	66.0	2.0	
OP30	Load 2 parts into fixture with grooves facing UP, cycle, blowoff part, unload, blowoff fixture, visual check	8.9	64.0	2.0	
OP40	Load 1 part into fixture with grooves facing UP, cycle, blowoff part, unload, blowoff fixture, visual check	6.2	66.0	2.0	
OP50	Load 1 part into fixture with grooves facing UP, cycle, blowoff part, unload, blowoff fixture, visual check	6.2	66.0	2.0	
OP60	Load 1 part into fixture with grooves facing DOWN, cycle, blowoff part, unload, blowoff fixture, visual check	6.2	70.0	2.0	
OP70	Load/Unload Washer, visual check	3.1	45.0	3.0	
OP80	Load 2 parts on mag plate, cycle for inspection	2.2	98.0	2.0	
OP90	Laser mark, scan, and package	2.2	40.0	3.0	

Key Quality and Safety Points
- Be careful, parts will have sharp burrs
- Visually check part for damage
- Reject parts for any visual concern :
- Tool marks, chatter, pitting, non-fill
- cuts, damage, or other visual issue

TAKT Time	111.6	sec	Total Manual Work	64.2 / 20.0 sec
			Total Cycle Time	74.2 sec
			Parts per cycle	1

Revision Control
Doc #	
Rev Level	
Date	
Launch Status	
Approval	
Approval	

Safety Requirements
- Safety glasses
- Kevlar gloves
- Steel toe shoes

Requirements
Safety Check	Verify light curtains work. No slip hazard around machines
Quality Check	Inspect master parts at beginning of shift
5S	Perform at beginning of shift
TPM	Conduct at beginning of shift and after meal break
Data Recording	Record hourly productivity on whiteboard
Material Handling	Signal flag at start of new pallet.
Escalate	Contact supervisor after 3 rejects

Figure 2. 24 Standardized Work Instructions

Illustration – Standardized Work Combination Table

The Standardized Work Combination Table is a management tool that shows the operation process sequence with detailed timing including manual, machine, and walking times. It is important to visually show the specific timing to identify opportunities for improvement such as excess waiting times, overloading of work, and to identify the location of a worker at any point in takt time.

Table 2. 6 Standardized Work Combination Table

Standardized Work Combination Table

Cust/Proj		Workcell	Operation Type	Part Name						Current Pcs/Hr	31.6	Run Pcs/H	32.2			Waiting Time
				Part Number's								TAKT TIME	112			Manual Work Time / Walking Time

SYM	NO.	Work Element	Element Time			
			Man ual	Mac hine	Wal king	
	10	Rough Cutting	10	52	2	
	20	Top Side - Machining	9	65	2	
	30	Bottom Side- Machining	9	64	2	
	40	Groove	6	68	2	
	50	Drill and Tap	6	66	2	
	60	Drill and Tap	6	70	2	
✚	70	Wash	3	45	3	
◇	80	Inspect	2	96	2	
	90	Laser mark, scan, pack	2	40	3	
		TOTAL	74.2	54	566	20

✚ Safety   ◇ Inspection

Revision					Change History	
Manufacturing Eng.	Quality	Production	Date	Revision	Change Description	

Key Points about Standardized Work

How does Standardized Work reduce variation?

Standardized Work defines, in clear detail, the motions or step-by-step activities for a specific operation. For example: "Pick up part with right hand, confirm that there are 4 tapped holes without any burrs, inspect the bearing race groove, then position onto fixture with bearing race groove facing up. The time it takes to perform this work element would be 2.3 seconds to pick up part, and 3 seconds to visually inspect holes and bearing race, then 3 seconds to place part in fixture. Inventory before the machine is 1 part". Standardized Work defines this level of detail to ensure the operation is performed precisely and consistently, part after part, and provides timing for inspection and placement. By performing work in such detail, it provides few opportunities for variation and reduces defects from passing to the next operation.

Does a revision to Standardized Work have to show the previous cycle time, inventory, and quality level?

A revision box is a good feature to include to show the progressive improvements to a specific operation. Only a summary of each previous change needs to be shown. A revision box shows the frequency of when improvements are made. Priorities to improve Standardized Work at specific work stations can be ranked by high risk priority numbers (RPN) from the process failure modes and effects analysis, from layered process audit findings, from customer complaints, and from high defect rates at subsequent operations.

How often should Standardized Work sheets be updated?

There is no prescribed interval for improving any particular operation, but there should be some level of improvement at least once a year in each work-cell or process line and in one of the seven kinds of waste. The 7 kinds of waste are: defects, overproduction, transporting, waiting, unnecessary inventory, excess motion, and inappropriate processing. Also, any change in the 6M (Man, Machine, Material, Method, Measurement, Mother Nature) plus individual input from direct labor and staff should require a review and update.

Other functions, such as receiving, shipping, customer service, and purchasing, probably have Work Standards. Should they also have Standardized Work sheets?

At a minimum, all manufacturing operations and supporting activities should have Work Standards. Developing Standardized Work guidelines for manufacturing should be the first pursuit; supporting functions should be a secondary pursuit, but there is likely more variability with support functions and Work Standards are typically sufficient.

Which is better for training new direct labor workers, Standardized Work or Work Standards?

A company's goal should be Standardized Work. Ideally, any new direct labor operator would be trained using Standardized Work with someone — such as another senior certified operator — delegated as their trainer, with a team leader or supervisor to oversee their work and ensure they are following the Standardized Work precisely. Off-line training is essential to mastering specific motions and skills such as soldering or welding. Offline training ensures a New Hire has the capability, competence, and confidence to meet online manufacturing operations requirements.

Common questions when observing a manufacturing operation or examining Standardized Work include the following. Observations can be written in a Notepad and/or photos taken:

- Is there a Standardized Work document available for this specific operation and is it easy for support staff to locate?
- Are the exact same operator movements occurring for the operation from part to part? (Determine this by observing the operator movements for five or more consecutive parts being produced and note any deviations or differences.)

- Is the work element timing being met? Is the cycle time the same for each successive unit?

- Are quality checks being performed the exact same way?

- Is anything disrupting the material flow or operation activity?

- Is the environment safe for conducting this activity (no sharp corners on work tables or fixtures, no pinch points, no trip or slip hazards, well-lit, etc.)?

- Has the direct labor worker confirmed that safety devices work correctly for this operation (light curtains, dual palm press buttons that must be depressed at the same time for the process to run, etc.)?

- What does the direct labor worker do if a defect is identified — what are the next steps and timing?

- What happens when the operation cannot keep up with takt time or the productivity goal per hour?

- How often does the supervisor stop by to check this operation to see whether there are any problems?

- How often do support staff ask the operator about the status or discuss ways in which safety, quality, or productivity can be improved?

- Is there a specific documented activity when the shift starts and stops? If so, is this consistent from shift to shift?

- Are productivity boards and other documents updated as per time standard?

- Is changeover process activity and timing conducted exactly per the standard?

- Are the shift start and shift end activities conducted exactly per the standard such as performing Total Productive Maintenance (TPM), tasks confirming Master Parts or 1st piece and last piece parts have been inspected and validated?

- Are Direct Labor workers wearing their appropriate Personal Protective Equipment (PPE)correctly?

- Are any 7 kinds of waste observed (Defects, Overproduction, Transportation, Wait, Inventory, Movement, Processing)?

- Are the Direct Labor workers trained to perform these tasks?

Standardized Work – Practical Scenarios

It is important to recognize potential issues and respond to them in a consistent manner utilizing policies, rules, and other documented practices. Here are a few practical scenarios to address:

What happens when a worker is observed not following Standardized Work sheet work elements?

After you observe a deviation from Standardized Work and confirm it by checking more than one unit, whether you speak with the direct labor operator, line leader, or supervisor depends on the company's operating culture. Normally, a line leader or supervisor would be notified first, and promptly. The line leader would immediately want to know whether the deviation from Standardized Work potentially caused any defects to be produced so a containment action can be put in place. The line leader would then have a discussion with the operator to understand the reason for not following the Standardized Work element instruction, then escalate the issue to the supervisor, then identify and locate the work done by the operator. The operator should not be allowed to continue performing work at that station until they follow the Standardized Work as stated.

Can direct labor workers challenge or dispute the work elements in the Standardized Work sheet? If so, is this handled in a positive, constructive, and improvement-oriented way by both the operator and supporting staff?

Direct labor workers can challenge Standardized Work elements — as long as they do so in an improvement way, not in a refusal-to-work way. The worker should inform the line leader about the improvement idea and investigate it at that level first, since they work in that area all the time. Some companies have an improvement sheet in each work-cell for workers to write notes. Once the line leader believes the suggestion is an improved method, it is time to contact the supervisor and the operations team. Changes to the work elements cannot be made until the operations team has approved them, as the customer may need to review and approve the change as well. The direct labor or line leader do not have authority to change the Standardized Work elements, but they do have responsibility to identify changes.

If a quality problem occurs downstream, can the team decide to make a temporary deviation to follow in addition to the Standardized Work?

First, does the team have authority to approve a deviation? Making a deviation from an approved process needs to go through a formal change process and may require customer approval. Deviations to the process must be fully investigated to determine whether it is a temporary or permanent situation. In either case, a formal review of the deviation request has to be analyzed. Then the operations team will decide to approve or not (perhaps with customer approval). The team is typically composed of cross-functional supporting staff that are responsible for that product being produced (in other words, staff not responsible for that area cannot approve the deviation). Any deviations must be documented and approved, and training must be conducted for the direct labor workers and team leaders involved on all shifts.

Can management inform the direct labor workers to make more parts faster when they are following Standardized Work?

The operation has to follow the Standardized Work activity and timing precisely. Management should challenge the team — both support staff and operators — to make improvements, in a positive, encouraging, and constructive way. Management should not direct supervisors, team leaders, or direct labor workers to make more parts faster when they are following Standardized Work. Management should always challenge both the operation's staff and direct labor to work on improving the productivity, quality, safety, etc.

Is it necessary to change all Work Standards to Standardized Work?

At some point, all manufacturing operations should upgrade their Work Standards to Standardized Work. Priority and a project timing plan should be made and displayed so support staff and direct workers become aware of the new practices to follow, and improvement expectations. Standardized Work training should be provided to all operation's staff, supervisors, team leaders, and eventually to all direct labor workers. Changing from Work Standards to Standardized Work is not an administrative exercise, it is a mindset, behavior, and ultimately a cultural change. However, manufacturing operations such as job shops, prototype work-cells, and custom fabricated works do not need Standardized Work, but they do need Work Standards.

Part 2 - Foundation Summary

Both organizational and manufacturing topics were discussed to establish, maintain, and strengthen a company's foundation. These critical foundation elements define the structure needed to develop the company into becoming a Factory Showcase Culture. These elements are vital for cutting-edge technologies as well as for mature industrialized processes, including high and low product mix and volume. These elements can be established during an entrepreneur's product conception or when the general manager and management team decide to modify their vision and mission statements to strengthen their company's foundation. Basically, these elements can be introduced and implemented at any time. While there is no specific time any particular element should be implemented, not working on these elements shows little care. Just as the ambitious employee who wants to advance and promote their career must be committed, it takes commitment for management to foster a vibrant and successful company.

After the general manager and management team determine this new direction, priorities and objectives can be defined. The next step is to educate employees in these topics. The employees need to have a basic knowledge, competency, and be able to trust management and work as a team to achieve these new expectations. Training programs that are hands-on, application oriented, and on the factory floor will lead to greater and quicker benefits than online or offsite programs. Plus, engaging staff and factory floor employees with training on new business processes, practices, and new ways to interact will be more readily accepted. Employees will be willing to continue when they have input and can see value. However, changing the organization structure, office layout, or desk layout is inherently more challenging than having employees implement a new business process.

Part 3 - Conditioning

Conditioning is built upon the two previous sections, Orientation and Foundation. It's the culture of Daily Routines, data collection, analysis, reporting, coordinating resources to take actions, and responding to various inputs using analytics. Conditioning is about using tools, techniques and management systems on an hourly, daily, and weekly basis. This includes auditing, process line stop and escalation, total productive maintenance (TPM), and — most importantly — people management. Conditioning also is about your own personal health, wellness, and work life/balance. Conditioning takes place on the factory floor, from every direct labor worker to the supporting staff and to management.

Chapter 23 - Daily Routine (DR)

You probably have a daily routine for every work day, or at least start out by working to a plan. An hour or so later, that plan may change due to unexpected issues, phone calls, unplanned meetings, etc. Having a Daily Routine (DR) system in place will keep you, your staff, and everyone else in the company working toward your stated goals while promoting an efficient way of communicating information.

Simply stated, a DR system typically involves all staff, including the general manager, with a set of fixed activities practiced daily in a disciplined way according to a timeframe. In addition to that fixed set of daily activities, other activities might have to be started and completed on specific dates, such as month-end closing and reporting. Corporate office personnel (those people not working in the manufacturing facility) have to understand that manufacturing operations support staff must finish their DR responsibilities before taking phone calls from corporate or addressing their emails. The priority for the manufacturing operations team or any value-stream organization team is to start their DR on time at the beginning of the shift and work through the fixed set of activities without interruption, unless a safety or severe manufacturing disruption occurs.

The following table contains a summary of DR activities for a manufacturing operation. Detailed DR guidelines are defined by level, scope, and timing, starting with the direct labor worker.

Table 3. 1 Daily Routine levels

Level	People	Scope	Timing or Time required
1	Direct labor worker to line leader	Operating station or work-cell performance info, preventive safety	15 min before end of shift, <1min
2	Line leader to supervisor	Line performance info, 6M issues, preventive safety	15 min before end of shift (after level 1), <5 min total
3	Supervisor to supervisor	Shift performance, 6M issues, production plan status and changeovers, preventive safety, first aid, OSHA incidences, incoming manpower issues (call-ins)	10 min before end of shift (after level 2), <15 min
4	Supervisor to operations team, including management	Shift performance, 6M issues, production plan status and changeovers, safety, first aid, OSHA incidences	30 min after shift starts (after level 3), < 30 min

4A	Night and weekend supervisor to (on-call) management	Phone call, email or management on-call report: shift performance, 6M issues, production plan status and changeovers, safety, first aid, OSHA incidences	End of shift (after level 3), <30 min
5	Various functional teams	Previous shift/day issues update, impending issues, external visits	Before or after Level 4; ideally, information can be brought to the level 4 meeting, < 30 min
6	General or Plant Manager to corporate operations leader	Phone call or email with daily performance, 6M issues, customer status, supplier issues, financials, safety, first aid, OSHA incidences	Next day after completion of DR, < 10min
7	Various functional individual staff members	Tailored specifically for each staff's daily activities	Entire shift

Manufacturing Operations
Level 1, Direct Labor to Line Leader

Direct Labor workers need to be trained from their very first day on the job as explained in the Orientation section. At the end of the shift, each Direct Labor worker must clearly state, in a professional, business-like way, the status of their workstations from when they started their last specific operations activity. The line leader or supervisor may have moved the direct labor workers to different operations or work-cells or have had them perform other miscellaneous work throughout their shift, so it is important to keep accurate track of people and production. All direct labor workers must obtain the required information themselves to avoid any misunderstandings or wrong communications to the next level.

Each direct labor worker will have a brief face-to-face conversation with the line leader or supervisor and provide the following information unless other ways have been defined to collect this information such as automated controls reports or use of work-cell productivity boards:

Productivity/Throughput for all products produced during shift for the location they worked. This can be a sum total by product name, number or volume for amount of time in question for a specific work location, with the reasons for the amount not meeting the productivity goal per hour or per shift.

Amount of downtime and possible cause, number of defects, or other time loss, such as a containment action to inspect or perform some checking activity. Downtime should identify the specific machine and activity that was not able to run according to the required Standardized Work element.

Suspect defective materials should be inspected and confirmed by others, such as quality technicians or engineers. If this is a new type of defect, it must be retained and shown to all other shift personnel working at this workstation, and updates must be made to the training materials as needed. Typically, a stand near the DR board, productivity board, quality board or some designated area is used to display the tagged defective parts/materials. If the defective part is too large for display, samples of it can be retained, tagged and displayed, or photos can be posted.

Inventory remaining at a work-cell can be a sum total or total by station, depending on the size and number of work stations within a work-cell.

Potential safety issues or other work area concerns (lighting, equipment, tooling, gages, materials, containers, abnormal noise). These may have already been identified earlier in the shift and responsive actions may be in process or have been completed. It is in everyone's best interest to communicate safety issues as soon as someone recognizes the potential for such concerns, and they should be escalated to the point where an action is defined. Other information that should be reported, although this should be a rare occasion, includes total productive maintenance activities or 5S not completed as per expected requirements.

Level 2, Line Leader to Supervisor
The line leader will have a face-to-face brief conversation with the supervisor stating the production summary information they obtained from the direct labor workers. Large companies will have a designated place for the line leader to meet with the supervisor. It is the responsibility of the line leader to find and communicate their shift report in a clear, concise, timely, and accurate manner. In addition, line leaders most likely will have to return to their work area to finish shift paperwork, provide a communications handover to the next shift line leader, and ensure the work area is ready for the next shift. The communication exchange is to ensure the incoming line leader is aware of the work area readiness and any issues.

Typically, there is a standard format to collect production information to ensure the information is complete and performed efficiently. Some companies may not have line leaders, so the same applies when the supervisor has face-to-face meetings with all direct labor workers. If there is no line leader, then the supervisor needs to meet with all direct labor at the end of the shift. If there are too many direct labor workers to meet with, the supervisor and operations team need to define a way in which end of shift communications can be performed efficiently.

Level 3, Supervisor to Supervisor

A new shift should not start until there has been a formal transfer of responsibility between the outgoing supervisor and incoming supervisor. This is known as the shift changeover, which is the primary means for communicating between shifts and needs to be clearly defined in the Supervisor Daily Routine. The shift changeover is one of the most important changes that occurs every day. Incoming shift supervisors should not start their shifts until they have been properly briefed by the outgoing supervisors about what occurred on the previous shift.

The outgoing supervisor should inform the incoming supervisor of the current and planned production activities, and production and quality status of actual to plan results, as well as any issues encountered and their status. The outgoing supervisor should use their notepad to record this discussion. The incoming supervisor may want to write some of these issues into their own notepad. Some companies use one notepad or electronic device, so the outgoing supervisor gives the incoming supervisor the notepad and they review it together.

The main point here is that the incoming supervisor is sufficiently briefed to be ready for the start of the shift without any surprises. One of the best ways to transfer this information is to take a walk along a predefined route around the work areas so both supervisors can ensure a comprehensive and accurate transfer. Depending upon the number of people working in a factory, there may be more than one operations supervisor. So, each area supervisor would meet with their counterpart.

The outgoing supervisor will summarize all of the line leaders' inputs and inform the incoming supervisor. The outgoing supervisor may provide an overall factory productivity/throughput summary and report on main processes performance, or delineate process performances that did not meet the expected plan, including a summary of downtime.

Supervisor information exchange timing depends upon how well the information is presented to the incoming supervisor and the number of issues encountered. However, it should take between 10–20 minutes. If the facility is too large to cover within 20 minutes, then the walk-around route can specify different routes for each shift, and whichever route is taken can be written on the shift transfer notepad or posted outside of the supervisor work area. The summary may highlight the top work-cells/machines with the longest downtime, along with causes and actions taken or in process. There also should be a discussion of the suspect defective material or parts, by asking, "Is this a new defect type? Is there a trend or special cause that produced this suspect defect material or parts?"

If a new defect type, trend, or special cause has been identified, the incoming supervisor will need the details to provide to the incoming direct labor workers, as well as inform the operations team and management. If the incoming shift is an off-shift for the operations team, such as a night shift, then the incoming supervisor will have to closely pay attention to that particular work-cell/machine. The supervisor may need to escalate certain issues during their shift, see Escalation Process in Chapter 27.

The outgoing supervisor will inform the incoming supervisor of any other deviation or issue in a 6M way (man, machine, material, measurement, method, mother nature/environment), including production output results against plan and status by work-cell or machine and, most likely, by part number, name or other product identifier. A summary of the inventory status and any potential safety concerns will also be included. Typically, automated spreadsheets or handwritten check sheets identifying the major schedule variations are created by the outgoing supervisor for the incoming supervisor.

Level 4, Supervisor to Operations Team

Once the outgoing supervisor and incoming supervisor have had their walk-route information exchange, the outgoing supervisor provides a briefing to the incoming operations team. If this is a start to a new work week day, then the plant manager, production manager, manufacturing engineering manager, quality manager, and supply manager attend this briefing. Other managers may attend on occasion to gain an understanding of what is currently happening in operations. The incoming supervisor does not have to attend this meeting; their focus is to ensure a successful startup of their shift by ensuring the right people are in the right place so they can start working.

Depending upon the shift transfer times and work days, the operations team and management typically are only available for one update each weekday. However, some companies have supporting staff and management available for each shift change. In a four-shift operation, each shift rotates throughout the week, so the outgoing supervisor is able to meet with the operations team and management several times a week.

The Level 4 DR will take place at a designated time and place every day, typically 30 minutes after the weekday shift starts. These are standing meetings — that is, no need for a conference room with chairs. The outgoing supervisor will start the briefing on time. The plant manager ensures the operations team has the discipline and respect to be ready for this important briefing. The outgoing supervisor presents the shift highlights with various Key Performance Indicators (KPIs), consolidated and displayed prominently where many — ideally all — employees can see them. In some companies, the KPIs are displayed along a wall so DR attendees can walk from KPI board to KPI board, with the outgoing supervisor taking the lead.

During this DR, action items will either be written on a whiteboard or recorded electronically and then posted to all operations team members and management soon after the DR is over. Each action item should clearly specify an action to be taken, which person or functional team is responsible for the action, and when the action must or can be completed. Typically, action items are updated with a status before the end of each working shift so the next shift can see what, if any, progress has been made.

There should be a designated action item writer for these actions. Typically, the plant manager will state the action item while an operations staff member writes it down. In many cases, the operations team will have a discussion and decide the course of action to be taken among themselves, while the plant manager listens and offers support when a decision has to be made. Priority must be defined for the actions and defined especially if one function or person has several tasks. Once the DR information exchange is completed, some operations members will want to briefly discuss specific action items to ensure they understand the details and to define a clear action plan. These are brief discussions and conference rooms are rarely needed.

Information Flow

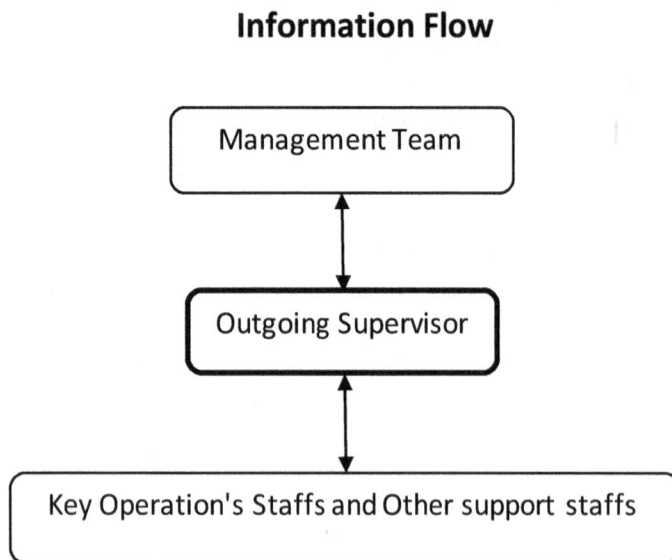

Figure 3. 1 Information Flow Diagram

Table 3. 2 Information Flow - Roles

Management Team	Key Operation's Staff	Other Support Staff
Plant Manager	Planners	Product Engineering
Production Manager	Quality Engineers	Sales
Quality Manager	Manufacturing Engineers	Human Resources
Manufacturing Engineering Manager	Product Engineers	Program or Project Management
Maintenance Manager	Maintenance	Supplier Quality Engineers
Supply Chain, Purchasing, or Materials Manager	Supply Chain	Purchasing

Level 4A, Supervisor to On-Call Management

When a shift ends and there aren't any operations support team members working, the outgoing supervisor still has the responsibility to call or email the plant manager and/or on-call management members. The on-call management may be one or more operations staff. The same type of information will be communicated, although action items may not be captured completely, so the on-call management has the responsibility to clarify and update the operations team upon the next shift start.

Level 5, Function or Department

Depending on the size of the organization, each supporting operation's function should have its own individual function DR before the Level 4 DR meeting. Supporting operation functions are: manufacturing engineering, quality, and supply chain, some companies expand their operation support to include engineering and human resources. It is critical to have a function level 5 DR before attending the Level 4 DR so each member of the function can provide updates from the previous day, such as contacting suppliers, checking sorting status, obtaining feedback from containment activities, updating root cause analysis status, presenting potential concerns, etc. Then, immediately upon completion of the function level 5 DR, some function team members and possibly the function manager attends the Level 4 DR.

The function department manager or designate will start the Level 5 DR on time with a standard agenda. Each function may have a different format or time for starting, but one common item is the status of the previous day's relevant DR Level 4 action items. These action items take precedence over any other agenda item and *must* have an update before going to the level 4 DR. Note: action items status from the previous day is expected to be presented at the Level 4 DR. So, during the Level 5 DR, if there are any open action items, those people responsible must have state an update state. Once all open items have been discussed, each staff member will briefly highlight their high-priority items or top one to five activities for the day or rest of the week.

Other high priority items to bring up at a level 5 DR is a customer, supplier, auditor or other external party upcoming visit. External visits must be communicated when known so everyone is prepared for the visit. At the Level 5 DR, each person should only take a minute or so to verbally state their high important and high urgent tasks. This is a stand-up meeting where everyone is on their feet in close proximity to one another and should be standing near a planning or KPI action board. A Level 5 DR is not a sit-down presentation meeting.

Some companies like to have two large whiteboard monthly calendars in each function's office area or shared among an operation's team, with one showing the current month and the other showing the upcoming month. Staff throughout the day can update important events or issues on the whiteboard using keywords or acronyms (time of day can be included as well). Staff meetings can be held in this area since these calendars can be used to update any significant upcoming events. Once the whiteboard calendar is updated, the electronic shared calendars would be updated as this would be visible to other functions and employees outside the company. Alternatively, monthly staff meetings can be held in sit-down conference rooms with visual presentations provided. An events calendar can be updated during the monthly staff meeting then transferred to the whiteboard in the office area. An example of the function of department DR follows:

Every Monday at a pre-defined meeting time and location:

Individuals present their top one to five issues or activities for the coming week. The individuals would only state the tasks that are to be done that day and week, see Chapter 25, Setting Priorities and Time Management for more information. This is a short one- to two-minute summary, highlighting key points. This meeting is the most important meeting for the function and everyone must have a daily plan and weekly plan. The individual must take time to think and define their top issues, and present them succinctly to the team and their manager. The individual has the responsibility to schedule a meeting with their manager throughout the week to provide updates. Individuals should think about their activities in regard to business and functional strategies, KPIs, current issues, and then prioritize. Starting off the beginning of the week with a functional DR provides greater work efficiency, better communication, and the possibility of working on preventive actions and system activities instead of constantly working in a firefighting mode. Staff should not wait for their managers to define their work.

Functional Level 5 DR on Monday usually takes more time due to the previous week's open issues, past weekend's issues and each staff member's one to five top highlights for the week. This meeting may have to be conducted earlier in the day than the rest of the week, or can even be separated with the open issues and weekend issues being discussed first, then the top one to five items discussed later in the morning, after level 4DR, or even after lunch, but the meeting must be on the first work day of the week. Typically, this meeting would take around 30 minutes. Starting promptly and keeping on track are key.

Each staff member should be reading from their notepad or daily planner, not making unsupported verbal statements. This is so the individual will think about priorities for the day and week. After stating their tasks, they will post these tasks at their desk or work area so they and others can see what they are planning to do. Other staff should listen and, if needed, take notes, especially for items that need support.

<u>Tuesday through Friday at a pre-defined meeting time and location:</u>

Nearly the same as on Monday, after arriving at work, immediately review and obtain a status from the previous day's open issues. Summarize and state the current day's top one to five tasks to be done that day (high importance and high urgency). For the rest of the week, note any deviation from Monday's statements. Throughout the day and week, staff members must stay focused on their top issues. If the manager is not in the office, the manager's delegate will lead the meeting. The DR still has to take place every work day.

By Friday evening, each staff member should be able to easily summarize their weekly activity. Some companies require a weekly, brief, one-page summary report. However, other companies just make a monthly report with these daily activities summarized at month's end. By the end of every week, the individual staff member and manager should have met separately or had a phone call to review the status of their top one to five activities and discuss other issues.

Level 6, General Manager to Corporate
The general manager should have a pre-defined time each day to update the corporate office or their boss if they have one. A daily email blast with an update is fine, as long as it is short, and hits the key highlights. Key highlights can be either favorable or unfavorable. For each favorable or unfavorable item, the general manager should have some statement as to the cause or potential business impact. Also, the statement should have a plan or action that is in process with an expected result. A short phone call often helps to clarify highlights and provides an opportunity for an open dialog.

Off-shift and weekend operations updates or emails are typically not sent, but a summary on Monday for the past weekend is usually expected. If a significant business event occurs anytime during the day or night or even on weekend, a text message, phone call, or email should be sent that briefly defines the issue, actions, and status.

Level 7, Individual Staff DRs

Companies that have DRs for each staff employee operates more efficiently than companies that do not have individual DRs. This is mainly because there are pre-defined activities that should take place and be prioritized for the operations team every day.

Staff coming into work may already be engaged with phone calls, texts or emails, but the most important thing is that they are prepared for their function Level 5 DR. Also, throughout their day, each individual is progressively working through their defined top DR activities. Each individual should have their own specific DR, even if there are several employees doing nearly identical work. This is to ensure there is a clear understanding of tasks and expectations. The following are examples of DRs by position or function:

Daily Routine - Quality Control Engineer

Depending upon the size of the organization at the factory, there could be several quality engineers, each having separate responsibilities, such as quality systems, customer quality, quality control (QC), quality launch for new products, supplier quality (most likely reporting to a supply chain leader or purchasing leader), and various other titles. Or, maybe there is just one Quality Engineer having responsibility for all aspects of Quality. The following is a DR for a quality control engineer in a typical mid-sized manufacturing factory.

The DR for this QC engineer is rather fixed and others are aware of that since it is posted at their work area. On certain days, training, other meetings or other internal QC activities have to be done that change this schedule, but having a defined, published DR at each work area is key to effectiveness and efficiency.

Table 3. 3 Daily Routine – Quality Control Engineer

Time	Activity
Before Level 4 DR	Walk into each work-cell and check:
	All defective and suspect materials have been removed from line, identified and placed into proper locations. If any remaining, take note and immediately remove from line so next shift can run production.
	Check QC data log or database for any new type of defect or defect levels significantly higher than normal. Take note, obtain a sample and bring to Level 4 DR.

Time	Activity
8:30	Attend Level 4 Operations DR and provide any updates from yesterday.
9:15	Prioritize today's work and immediately start working on the priorities; otherwise, go to each work-cell/area, inspect 1st piece parts, confirm any defective or suspect material; prioritize by work-cell(s) and bottleneck process operations. Determine defect cause (if possible) and input data into database; show a sample of the defective material and inspection data to supervisor and lead team member(s). Start root cause and corrective action process.
10:00	Emails and phone calls.
10:15	Walk around factory with supervisor, check operations QC activities and follow up on any concerns. An internal quality audit or layered process audit can also be conducted in a specific area at this time.
11:15	Finish processing defective material analysis and send to appropriate internal operations personnel. If any time remains before lunch, check with other quality personnel for issues or support needed.
12:00 noon	Lunch.
13:00	Attend internal Quality or other functional meeting.
14:00	Analyze defect data (trend). Request meeting to review defect data, prioritize defect(s) for root cause analysis and corrective action. This could be ongoing for a work team to investigate top defect for the month, or some other Pareto sort.
15:00	Perform QC work on factory floor: conduct a reverse PFMEA, check workstation documentation against operator performance, conduct Cpk, Gage R&R, and support operator training with the supervisor.
16:00	Walk around factory with or without supervisor, check operations QC activities and follow-up on any issues.
16:45	Emails and phone calls.
17:00	Finish up any other issues; prepare for evening shift work.
Evening	Personal time to be spent with the family, exercise, community activities, hobbies, and professional development balanced with various work-related tasks such as planning the next days of activities or attending various business teleconferences (especially when suppliers, customers, or division management are in other countries).

Daily Routine - Finance

The following is an example for the Finance function. Typically, a monthly calendar is used to show their main deliverables by a certain day — as opposed to other functions that are typically hourly or shift dependent. The figure shows main deliverables in the left column. The responsibility column and each item in it should have someone's name. Another column can be inserted with a photo of the person responsible, and the staff can change their own photo as appropriate. Within the month, the "dashed blocks" represent dates due. A legend can be added to show typical stoplight colors of red, yellow and green and other symbols for the current day and holidays (e.g., a "star" symbol can indicate the current day, while a "diamond" can indicate a holiday). Also, these symbols can be shown in different colors to standout easier. Alternatively, a "bar" can be drawn to indicate the timing needed to complete the task, such as a start and stop date, although this is usually not needed, since the current monthly checklist should indicate the start and stop dates for each task.

Having a process document checklist or monthly closing book that identifies specific closing tasks with a name and date, including a time for the deadline in many cases, is a fundamental part of the Finance DR. The finance manager and team can review the status every day to check for any deviations from plan and make resource adjustments. The weekly section shows each person on the finance team, including the finance manager. Each member should be updating this calendar each day, especially if the task is in-process, is delayed, or is in jeopardy of being delayed. The staff member can start writing the status on the specific date that problems arise so the manager and other staff member can see potential conflicts or timing for them to provide support.

Having weekly, monthly, and quarterly tasks on one whiteboard may be difficult to see and use, so these segments can be separated into two different boards. If separating into two boards, then a daily task segment can be added.

Daily Routine - Finance

Month -

Weekly	Responsibility	1	2	3	4	5	6	7	8	9	10	11	12	13	14	15	16	17	18	19	20	21	22	23	24	25	26	27	28	29	30	31	Status
Forecast	Bailey																																
Payroll	Sitin																																
Sales	Michelle																																No issues
Expenses	Yu																																
Inventory	Karl																																
General Ledger	Tammy																																
Monthly																																	
Cash Flow																																	
Account Receivable																																	
Capex																																	
Inventory																																	
Balance Sheet																																	
Accounts Payable																																	
Reports	Bailey																																	
KPIs	Bailey																																Analysis on-schedule
Analysis	John																																Audit late tonight and
Audit	Mark																																early tomorrow.
Monthly Meeting																																	
Month end checklist																																	
Distribute closing checklist																																	
Pre-closing meeting																																	
Quarterly																																	
Accrual																																	
Reconcile Tax																																	
Tax Report																																	
Quarterly Report																																	
Analysis																																	
Quarterly Meeting																																	

Figure 3. 2 Daily Routine - Finance function

Daily Routine - Production Operation Supervisor

The Daily Routine for a production operation supervisor has three main segments:

- Start of Shift – See Level 3 DR Supervisor to Supervisor
- During Shift
- End of Shift

During Shift - Supervisor

During the shift, the supervisor should try to break their work into hourly segments so they repeat a defined route throughout their area of responsibility. This hourly route ensures a certain level of confidence in safe work conditions, and that productivity and quality are being monitored regularly. However, due to material, scheduling, labor, quality, machines, and other issues, the hourly segments may be different every day, but during the shift the supervisor should interact in some capacity with all direct labor workers.

Providing face-to-face communication is extremely important for motivating and engaging workers. Daily Routines for supervisors include a review that all team leaders have performed their specific work area checks. Daily Routines for every manufacturing team leader include a confirmation that certain specific activities have been performed according to the documented standards and timing including:

- 5S
- Total Productive Maintenance
- EHS
- First piece approval

- Error proofing/mistake proofing
- Gages and test equipment calibrated
- Operators are wearing proper PPE
- Product Changeover
- Materials processed according to First In First Out (FIFO)
- Inspection frequency and sample is correct
- Master "good" and "no good" parts
- Operators qualified at specific work stations
- Visual Management is clear and practiced
- Work area specific requirements
- Defect or suspect material identified and in defined area
- Reactions conducted timely for special cause situations

Various other activities have to be coordinated during the shift, such as product changeovers, documenting concerns or issues, and taking actions to resolve issues such as the 6Ms: Man, Machine, Material, Measurement, Method, Mother Nature. DRs for supervisors also include other activities such as training, audits, customer visits, improvement opportunity discussions, training coordination of temporary and new workers, training for current workers or the supervisor, employee rotation for work breaks, or changes in work activity.

While the supervisor is making their rounds, they are constantly being informed of productivity and quality in many possible ways: visually on boards displayed in work-cells or around the factory, text messaging, end-of-line tester monitors, etc. When productivity is not meeting the current target, it has to be addressed immediately, including determining a reason for not meeting the target. Documenting these issues and reasons, having a KPI metric such as Overall Equipment Effectiveness (OEE), and using Pareto trending to track these concerns over time can help identify which issues to prioritize, so future improvements in productivity and quality can be made. Note that other operation's support staff will also perform regular frequent factory walks.

When the actual production level starts to miss the planned target, there is often a special cause for this gap, and this has to be addressed immediately by the direct labor worker and possibly with the team leader. If the worker cannot solve the issue promptly and recover to the target level per minute or per hour pace, then maintenance and/or supervisors must be notified so they can provide support to resolve the issue.

If the team leader, maintenance, or supervisor cannot resolve the issue, a decision has to be made whether to:
A. Continue running under the current condition with current or additional resources.
B. Stop the process and identify resources to diagnose and repair.

C. Define some containment actions and then decide to do step A or step B.

D. Escalate the issue further to the management team. This notification can be done within a certain time, such as one hour after missing the target. If the target was missed by two consecutive hours, or some other criteria, then the next escalation level would be contacted. The escalation process should be clear about whom to contact, when to contact, and what information to communicate. See Escalation Matrix in Chapter 27 for more information.

In some cases, when an operator identifies a concern, the operator turns on a signal light, alarm, or other signaling way to inform the team leader, maintenance, or supervisor. This is a convenient and quick way to obtain immediate support. The support team needs to be immediately aware there is an issue at a specific location, then the support team must react quickly and re-prioritize whatever they are doing to help resolve the issue. Then, the support team must respond quickly with a predefined logical method for diagnosing the issue such as use of a fault tree diagram, or work instructions based upon information from the Process Failure Mode and Effects Analysis and Control Plan.

End of Shift - Supervisor

As the production operation supervisor and team are ending their shift, the factory has to be prepared for the next shift's activities. The supervisor must ensure:

- All areas are cleaned of debris, waste, and scrap materials.

- Work areas are clean, organized, and ready for the next shift.

- Materials are prepared and ready at the point of usage.

- Tools and equipment are clean, in their proper location, and ready for use, or turned off if not to be used for the incoming shift. However, some equipment may need to always be turned on whether it is running production or not. Manufacturing Engineering will define the procedure for turning on and off equipment.

- Supporting devices, inspection gages, and equipment are clean and ready for use.

- Work area documentation, production, and quality status have been updated.

- New Hires have been informed of their competency and the next day's activities, time and place to report, and whom to contact.

- Some factories do not have cleaning crews; in these cases, the night shift team may have to clean the bathrooms and dispose of trash or other debris. In addition, the canteen floors, tables, microwaves, and other surfaces have to be cleaned.

- If there is not an incoming shift, the outgoing shift supervisor may have other duties such as ensuring everyone has vacated the building, areas or equipment are turned off and locked, lights turned off, and possibly security is turned on or has been informed.

- Supervisor notepad has been updated for the Level 3 Supervisor to Supervisor DR.

Daily Routine - General Manager or Plant Manager

Having the most-senior manager onsite displaying, promoting, and encouraging all staff to define and follow a DR is clearly a lead-by-example behavior that has so many benefits. The following is an example of a general manager or plant manager DR. Of course, there will be days when the General Manager or Plant Manager cannot perform their DR, such as when they visit customers, participate in customer meetings onsite, or respond to a wide variety of other meetings or issues that need attention. In such cases, a back-up person or deputy manager should perform the DR in order to keep a high-level commitment.

The table below shows how the management team can be aware of the general or plant manager's DR, which allows the management team to define and prioritize their schedule accordingly. Specifically, the general or plant manager would have read some of their emails, checked some KPIs, and/or had some phone calls on the way to work. On arriving at the office, they typically conduct a quick factory walk, which on some days includes a walk around the building perimeter, or even site perimeter if feasible.

When walking around the factory, the senior manager would pay attention to many things beyond observing the displayed production and quality status, such as employee morale, safety practices, potential building infrastructure issues, and any potential environmental issues. The manager has to be mindful of their own attitude and be focused on employee engagement to motivate, encourage, compliment and pay attention to the behaviors of the employees. The manager should also focus attention on the product flow to understand how the physical movements and transformations by worker and machine translate to costs of production and quality.

Table 3. 4 Daily Routine - General Manager

Time	Activity
Before Level 4 DR	Factory walk around entire perimeter and into work-cells; have quick conversations while checking for any significant issues, including 5S or ones that were noticed on the previous day that may need to be addressed at the Level 4 DR.
8:30	Attend Level 4 Operations DR

Time	Activity
9:00	Monday: Sales and Program Management meeting Tuesday: Operations meeting Wednesday: HR meeting Thursday: Supply chain meeting Friday: Individual staff, project or other function's meeting
10:00	Continuation of previous meetings if needed, but try to keep the meetings to one hour. Emails and phone calls soon after the meetings end, then look at today and this week-to-date reports for: sales forecast versus actual, operations production status, inventory and supplier status.
11:00	Finance Manager's DR outputs. Every week or twice a month, Finance should report the forecast of the projected month end closing, including: sales, receivables, outstanding receivables, inventory, obsolescence, payables, and cash flow. This should include a discussion on risks and contingencies. Other managers may need to be called into the meeting for a risks and contingencies discussion.
12:00	Lunch, then walk the perimeter and/or factory, having quick chats along the way.
13:00	Update corporate and/or operations leader on yesterday's and last evening's shift performances as well as any upcoming events, email and/or phone calls.
13:00	Attend internal Quality meeting depending upon the severity noted in the morning's Operation DR. If there is a customer issue, the GM must attend. Internal and supplier issues depend upon the severity. Otherwise, work on other issues and prepare for rest of the day.
14:00	Monday – New business and quote reviews Tuesday – Project Management meeting Wednesday – Sales, Inventory, Operations, and Planning meeting (once a month), Finance Variance Analysis Meeting (once a month), Product Engineering status meeting (balance of the month). Thursday – HR, personal one-on-ones, small group meetings Friday – IT/Manufacturing Engineering, Capacity and Capex plans and status (if needed)
16:00	Open – work on current issues, reflection, future plans, strategy thoughts, follow-up
16:45	Emails and phone calls
17:00	Finish up any other issues, walk around factory if this did not happen at lunchtime. Should try being visible on factory floor at least two times a day, covering possibly two shifts.

Time	Activity
After 17:00	Readiness for evening teleconferences and planning for next day. Personal time to be spent with the family, exercise, community activities, hobbies, and professional development balanced with various work-related tasks. Attend various business teleconferences (especially when suppliers, customers, or division management are in other countries).

Other areas for the General Manager to check

Outside and perimeter walk

- Is there any erosion? Are any trees uprooting?
- Condition of roadway and signage?
- Are tree branches touching fencing, nearby power lines or power transformers?
- Are there any cracks, holes, mold on the building exterior?
- Consider going onto the roof and looking for possible signs of rust or damage to heating, air conditioning, and ventilation units or other rooftop structures.
- Walk or drive from the company entrance to the employee parking areas. Are they well-lit?
- Any pavement or sidewalk issues?
- Are the painted lines for parking, walking, crosswalks, etc., clear?
- Are there potholes or slip areas?
- Does the rainwater runoff flow as it should, or does it pool anywhere?
- Is snow plowing and salting of walkways done before workers arrive and before they depart?

Entrance and lobby walk

Start the walk from where the visitor (customer) would park. Consider how the visitor would walk toward the entranceway and how appealing it is, trying to view the facility through a customer's eyes.

- When entering the lobby, look for areas where the company's products or videos are displayed. Are they the latest?
- How well are the products being marketed in the lobby?
- Does the visitor have to sign in or register in the lobby?
- Do you give the visitor any security or safety protocols?
- Is there a placard announcing the customer's name?
- How long does your customer wait before someone attends to their needs — sharing information about bathroom, coffee, Wi-Fi — and then is properly escorted to a conference room?
- Which would you prefer to have — customer meetings in your conference room, or customer meetings at your customer's facility?

Office area
- When walking into office areas, how are they organized? By workflow? Responsibility? Department/function?
- Is there signage to indicate the different areas?
- Are people's names, titles, high-level responsibilities, email addresses, and mobile numbers posted in their work areas so others can know who resides there?
- Are work areas and table tops relatively clean and organized?
- Are the floors, ceiling, walls clean and areas well-lit?
- Would the customer be impressed?

Warehouse and loading docks
- How are the safety protocols followed in the warehouse or on the way there?
- Do forklift drivers have their safety glasses and seatbelts on?
- Is there a forklift driver check sheet to be sure everything is OK prior to use?
- Is there a checklist for signing a forklift in and out for each shift?
- Is there a specific location for the forklifts when not being used?
- Is there a training matrix that identifies when employees last attended a forklift safety training class?
- Are factory floor lanes painted for forklifts to drive within?
- Is lighting bright with limited shadow areas?
- Are material warehouse racks bolted to the floor?
- Is rack signage easy to read? Are materials stored properly onto pallets, materials labeled, fire extinguishers marked and clearly designated, and is roof secure?
- Have exit doors been opened to check that they can open? Is there a record of dates when alarms are tested?
- Are materials processed First In First Out (FIFO)?
- Are loading docks secured when not in use?
- Are loading docks suitable for use? If they need repair, are they secured?
- Are there any open issues from any previous Environment, Health, Safety, and Security, Layered Process, Internal, or other audits? If so, are they posted?

Final notes for the General Manager DR

The general manager needs to know the KPIs and drivers of the business, share this information with their team, and ensure their team understands. The general manager must also see and hear that those KPIs and drivers are being prioritized by all employees during their daily work.

The general manager needs to spend time speaking with various employees, and not just the staff. Conversations need to be with different employees in different parts of the factory — even spend time with employees during morning, lunch, or dinner breaks. These conversations can be rotated through some sort of a shift schedule matrix where the leader can connect personally with individuals, not just hold a mass town hall meeting. Consider all employees, including security, logistics, finance, warehouse, etc., not just the factory workers. Also, consider scheduling sessions to chat with contractors and temporary worker contract agencies.

Key Steps to Implement a Daily Routine Program

Many people think either their work varies so much every day that they could never have a defined DR, or it is a waste of time to create one since they have been doing the job for several years.

1. The DR is one of the key elements of a factory showcase culture that is led and nurtured by the general manager. Training needs to be conducted on Daily Routines and needs to be attended by all management and staff.

2. Attendees will develop and refine their DRs with their managers, including ensuring the various KPIs are delegated to specific employees. After training, one of the tasks is to write down the key topic that you are working on in 15-minute intervals every day for a week. At the end of the week, you can analyze and categorize the daily activities and determine certain times during the day for those activities to take place the following weeks. Several adjustments will be made by overcoming functional and cross-functional conflicts and finding more effective days and times for conducting certain activities. This iteration may take a few weeks or even a month due to various business happenings.

3. The management team should meet together before reviewing their staff's activities for the week. This is needed to establish specific days and times during the week for cross-functional or project meetings. Also, the management team must review the general or plant manager for their DR plan, and a specific time can be set for the Level 4 DR each day. The management should agree to have at least one person from each function in attendance at the Level 4 DR. Also, shift handover communications should occur when there is a time gap between shifts and during weekends when there is production work.

4. After a month of DR implementation, management should meet to discuss any concerns and improvement ideas, and to agree upon and implement new expectations and refinements, cross-functional operations priorities, modified KPIs or change of data collection and analysis, or modify their own functional DRs. Another month later, more expectations and refinements will be made.

5. This is an ever-evolving process approach for improving operations effectiveness and efficiency. The general or plant manager needs to meet with his management team to ensure each one is working with their staff to define both a functional DR and individual DR. The management team needs to be held accountable for implementing

this system. The general manager should confirm that all levels of the Daily Routines are being conducted on-time and that they are being effectively conducted, sometimes by participating in the various DRs.

Chapter 24 - Setting Priorities and Time Management

Defining priorities, allocating time, and being disciplined and focused are very important business skills. A time management technique such as Eisenhower's Important/Urgent Principle is easy to learn and use. Dwight Eisenhower said, "What is important is seldom urgent and what is urgent is seldom important."

Important means the task is aligned to goals. High importance is related to an individual's KPI, management directing the individual to perform the task, or project team goals. Low importance is related to administrative activities that do not affect functional or business goals. Urgent means the task requires immediate action, while low urgency means there is no deadline.

The priority to work on the various tasks is ranked as:

1. Important and Urgent – tasks to do immediately
2. Important and not Urgent – tasks to schedule (after the above)
3. Not Important but Urgent – tasks to delegate (if possible)
4. Not Important and not Urgent – tasks that don't have to be done any time soon. The thought then becomes why is this task even listed?

Table 3. 5 Setting Priorities and Time Management

	Low Urgent	High Urgent
High Important	2 Tasks to schedule	1 Tasks to do immediately
Low Important	4 Tasks can be postponed	3 Tasks to delegate

It is obvious that you would spend your time on priority 1 and 2 tasks and that with improved planning, there may be fewer priority 1 tasks.

Key Steps to Set Priorities and Improve Time Management

1. Define a list of tasks for the day or week.

2. Identify the ones that are important.

3. If the task is not important, strike a line through the task or place an "X" next to the task, since this task will either be delegated or postponed.

4. Rank the important tasks using the guidelines above.

5. Prioritize the important items by whether they are urgent or not urgent. Urgency can be prioritized by either a crisis or deadline.

6. Rewrite the tasks in order of priority for the current day's work and, if possible, for the week.

7. At week's end, review the tasks completed, evaluate whether they were completed as planned or had to be postponed. If the tasks were postponed or not completed, where in the past week could they have been done? Meaning, could there have been better planning or use of different resources to complete the task?

8. Have a discussion with your manager about your week and upcoming week's work. Reviewing the tasks at the end of the week then discussing them with your manager helps to set the priorities for the coming week. Using this priority and time management practice every day will help plan out work better and improve overall performance.

Chapter 25 - Writing Reports and Audits

Throughout the year, management and staff have to write different types of reports, such as DR summary (weekly or monthly), KPI, project status, Financial, Sales, Inventory, Operations, Planning, and Purchasing (SIOPP), safety incident, internal audit, problem solving, new capital request, business feasibility, supplier related, personal performance appraisal, etc. Also, management and staffs are regularly expected to conduct and participate in a variety of audits: 5S, Layered Process Audits, Quality Systems Audits, Supplier, and Customer.

Writing Reports

Writing reports in the business world is common practice. There are certain guidelines to follow in order to make the report as concise, clear, and complete as possible. Over a career, hundreds of different reports will be written, and all of them will have some common elements, such as:

1. Who is the intended audience? What is the purpose? Why is the audience interested in this information? These are the first questions to answer.
2. What information has to be presented, and how can this be summarized in a simple, easy-to-understand format? Highlight important facts with percentages, numbers, and units with some simple explanations. Consider providing a comparison against previous performance, plan, or budget. Define the next actions to be taken by whom and when. Understand and obtain data from a known source, within the timeframe, once you have personally confirmed the data accuracy. Note: Shift and day data collection may not be the same data sets, since the time clock for a day runs midnight to midnight whereas shifts may work the day date before and after midnight.
3. Is there a predefined format for the report? Are graphs, charts, or tables required? If you unaware of a pre-defined format, ask colleagues or leader. Typically, pre-defined formats already exist and are in a Microsoft PowerPoint, Excel, or Word format. Some creativity may make the information stand out easier, such as use of colors, bold face type, shapes, photos, etc.
4. What feedback, if any, is expected of the audience? By when? It is important to follow up soon after submitting the report in case there are questions or additional information or clarification is required.
5. What is the due date for the reporting? Is it an ongoing, scheduled report? Submitting a report before the deadline is expected, with no accepted excuse for being late. Plans and DRs should be made before the upcoming due reports so there is sufficient time to collect, analyze, and write the report. Following up with the audience after submission is key for improvement on the next report.

Audits

Many types of audits are regularly scheduled throughout the year and each has its own specific objective. The reasoning behind having audits includes providing:

- A snapshot of how well current documented practices comply with

standards, specifications, and procedures. Alternatively, identifies possible non-compliance issues
- Independent validation of the current product, process, or system, especially for customers and registrars
- Means to obtain various internationally recognized certifications, such as ISO9001, IATF19649, VDA 6.X, ISO 14001, AS9100, ISO13485, US FDA 21 CFR 820, ISO/TS22163, TL9000, etc.
- Platform for staff members to gain knowledge
- Sense of confidence among the management and team for compliance with various internal and external documented practices
- Opportunity to improve performance
- Platform for identifying better and best practices
- Supporting system to ensure root causes have been identified and closed via a corrective and preventive action process
- Means of identifying ambiguity, risk, and lack of controls in business processes
- Means to improve customer satisfaction

Illustration – Internal and External Audit Types

The following table summarizes different types of audits.

Table 3. 6 Internal and External Audit Types

Category	Auditor	Scope	Example
Internal	First Party	Product, Process, System	**Layered Process Audit**
External	Second Party	Product, Process, System	Customer, Supplier
External	Third Party	System	International Standards, (ISO9000)

Internal audits are conducted by employees of the company, while external audits are conducted by an entity outside the company.

First Party: an internal audit, typically to determine compliance with your own quality management system documentation. The employees should have participated in an auditing course and at least one employee conducting the audit should be certified as a lead auditor by an external entity. The audit format can be formal or informal.

First Party – Layered Process Audit

Layered Process Audit or LPA is an audit that focuses on a specific product, process, or system elements. The LPA includes employees from all functions in the organization to conduct an audit according to a predefined schedule with defined audit questions.

The benefits of conducting an LPA are:

- Provides a risk assessment and validation. Regularly auditing manufacturing operation activities with high Risk Priority Numbers (RPNs) from the Process Failure Mode and Effects Analysis (PFMEA) validates both the failure occurrence and process controls effectiveness.

- Provides an opportunity to identify continuous improvements.

- Confirms products and processes comply with the required documented standards and practices.

- Provides an opportunity for coaching, training, and recognition by management with the direct labor workers, staff, and supervisors.

Audit findings are documented within the work area. When deviations are observed, they are summarized on the Quick Response Quality Control (QRQC) board so the issue(s) can be immediately corrected. A monthly calendar of the LPA is defined in advance — usually by the Quality function — and is electronically distributed to all staff as well as posted nearby the QRQC board.

The Quality function prepares a list of all operation work areas to ensure an LPA is conducted either by a supervisor, staff, or manager, and this is ideally done each month. Also, the Quality function is responsible for coordinating and compiling a standardized audit questionnaire with individual questions for specific processes. Management is responsible for ensuring LPAs are prioritized within their Daily Routine activities and management should review LPA results during management's monthly operation's review.

Illustration – LPA Monthly Audit Schedule

The following figure illustrates a LPA monthly schedule, showing staff or managers to audit all manufacturing operations (including shipping and receiving being audited once a month). Functional managers and the general manager are typically reserved to conduct an LPA during the second or third week of each month, while staff can cover the remaining days of the month. Each month, a different function can be responsible to ensure the LPA has been completed on-time and can offer their insight into the LPA activities and identify improvement opportunities to the audit structure.

Day	#	A10	A20	A30	B10	B20	C10	C20	C30	C40	D10	D20	M10	M20	M30	M40	M50	M60	S/R	LPA Resp	Staff	Mgr
Monday	1	Q																			Quality	Q	QM
Tuesday	2		ME																		Mfg Engineering	ME	MEM
Wednesday	3			PR																	Production	PR	PRM
Thursday	4				SC																Supply Chain	SC	SCM
Friday	5					FI															Finance	FI	FIM
Saturday	6																				Engineering	EN	ENM
Sunday	7																				Human Resources	HR	HRM
Monday	8						ENM														IT	IT	ITM
Tuesday	9							HRM													Project Manager	PM	
Wednesday	10								ITM												General Manager	GM	
Thursday	11									PM													
Friday	12										GM												
Saturday	13																						
Sunday	14																						
Monday	15											QM											
Tuesday	16												MEM										
Wednesday	17													PRM							LPA Month Leader		
Thursday	18														SCM								
Friday	19															FIM					ME		
Saturday	20																						
Sunday	21																						
Monday	22																EN				LPA Complete		
Tuesday	23																	HR					
Wednesday	24																		IT		LPA Not Complete		
Thursday	25	PM																					
Friday	26		GM																				
Saturday	27																						
Sunday	28																						
Monday	29			Q																			
Tuesday	30				ME																		
Wednesday	31					PR																	

Form XX-XXX-XX Rev 1 — Approved By: Quality

Figure 3. 3 LPA Monthly Audit Schedule

Typically, specific employee names are identified on the LPA calendar by a function representative one to two weeks ahead of time. This is to allow the auditor time to plan their work week, reduce administrative time for follow-up, and this provides an assurance that a specific employee has been identified and has been trained for the upcoming scheduled audit. The LPA leader can place a check mark on the date an LPA has been conducted on-time. If the audit is not completed on-time, a circle can be placed around the date. Every day during the month, the LPA leader needs to contact the function and specific employee that is supposed to conduct the audit to ensure the audit will take place. A reminder can be pre-set in the LPA leader's electronic calendar for contacting and follow ups. Once the LPA audit has been completed by the specified employee, they are responsible to forward the completed audit results to the LPA Monthly leader by the end of their work day. If the auditor has identified any nonconformance, they will address the issue with the supervisor and/or Quality leader of the area before they leave the work area. For any serious non-conformance, the supervisor or Quality person will write the issue on the Quick Response Quality Control board and notify the QRQC team. See Chapter 27 for more information.

Second Party: an external audit conducted of a company by a customer or by a contracted entity on behalf of a customer. For example, a customer can audit your company, your company can audit your supplier, a contracted entity can audit your company on behalf of your customer, or a contracted company can audit your supplier on behalf of your company. The audit format is typically formal with follow-up verifications for corrective actions, although some verifications can be informal.

Third Party: an external audit conducted by a company that has no relationship as a customer or supplier of that company. This audit format is primarily formal, including on-site follow-up verifications for corrective actions.

Four Phases of an Audit
1. Planning
2. Data gathering
3. Reporting
4. Follow-up and closure

1. Planning

Basic questions to answer:

- What type of audit? (e.g., Internal/External, Product, Process, System)
- Which party? (e.g., first, second, third party)
- Who are the auditors and lead auditors?
- When is the audit?
- Where is the audit?
- What is to be audited?
- What is the scope of the audit and its objective?
- How long is the audit and what is the audit agenda?
- Is the audit formal or informal? What additional preparations are needed?
- What audit questionnaire or checklist will be used? Is the lead auditor familiar with this questionnaire or checklist?
- Has the audit agenda been accepted and will it be supported by the people being audited?

2. Data Collecting

This phase starts with the audit opening meeting and ends with the closing meeting (except for LPAs, as there is no need for an opening and closing meeting). The lead auditor typically starts the opening meeting with introductions, then addresses and answers all the questions above. Depending upon the type of audit, the opening meeting attendees will vary, but as a minimum, the general or plant manager and quality manager would attend. Typically, the leaders of the various functions or departments being audited will also participate in the meeting. The lead auditor may present how the auditing findings will be reported, what happens when a non-conformance or concern is identified, and the next steps, including the closing meeting and potential follow-up meeting to confirm the corrective actions have been implemented. In addition, the hosting company may present details regarding the agenda, transportation and logistics, meals, and safety and security protocols, including asking if there are any other questions. After the opening meeting, the audit starts according to the agenda and continues through to the closing meeting. The lead auditor and audit team typically make notes of their observations. Some audits require the auditor to note non-compliance issues, while other audits may note compliance, non-compliance, and opportunities for improvement. The closing meeting typically has the same attendees as the opening meeting. The lead auditor will present the scope and objective of the audit, a summary or overview of the audit, and presentation of each audit finding. The opening and closing meetings should take less than one hour each, unless at the closing meeting there are multiple audit findings.

3. Reporting

The audit report typically can be presented at the closing meeting by the lead auditor. If it is a first-party audit, the report will most likely not be as comprehensive as a second- or third-party audit. The second- or third-party audit report will most likely convey the reason for the audit, contractual information, and auditor introductions and qualifications. The audit report is a confidential document between the parties identified in the audit contract. With first-party audits, the audit report may be published or not. Layered Process Audit findings are typically posted, whereas Internal Quality Management Audits findings may not be posted. The lead auditor may issue the final report upon the follow-up verification to ensure closure of all corrective actions. The audit report is a formal document covering the complete audit, from the opening meeting through to closing meeting and/or verification of the corrective actions implemented. The report will contain information relative to answering the questions in the planning section, including various relevant documents. The report will include some contractual information; introductions and auditor qualifications; and audit findings against standards, procedures, or specifications. The final report would also include the corrective actions needed, along with some documented evidence and dates of implementation.

4. Follow-up and Closure

An on-site follow-up audit may or may not have to occur. This depends on the audit requirements, whether it is contractual, or if the severity of an audit observation requires an on-site verification. Many times, the auditor may just want a copy of the documented evidence showing a corrective action has been implemented. At the next scheduled audit, the auditor will verify the implemented corrective actions on-site.

Key Steps to Pursue Compliance via Auditing

Most companies, when pursuing compliance to customer requirements or to internationally recognized standards such as ISO9001, promote the pursuit and celebrate the success of being awarded certification. Starting the journey to obtain a certification should be a key pillar of an effective operations management team. Some companies have not yet started on this journey, while others have received multiple certifications and are more in a maintenance mode, focusing on ensuring their systems are effective and continuously improving. These companies have already developed and honed their cultures to accept and appreciate the importance of audits. A starting point is needed for companies that do not have these certifications (such as newly formed companies), a company being pressured by their customers to obtain certifications, or companies that need to have a certification to compete in the market.

1. Management discusses the need to pursue compliance to a requirement or standard and to define the expected benefits. This may come from any function, such as sales, marketing, finance, quality, engineering, supply chain, etc. However, it is the general manager's leadership and decision to make the commitment to start the pursuit.

2. Management team needs to assess their current status of meeting the new requirements. Management needs to determine whether an internal or external audit is needed to be performed. In many cases, management does not have a certified lead auditor for the requirement or standard on staff, so an external entity is typically contacted. The external entity can conduct training on the requirements including auditor training. For pursuing specific international standards, the employees wanting to become internal auditors must meet certain personal attributes and be knowledgeable about various company business and manufacturing processes, Total Productive Maintenance, process quality controls, risk analysis, and be trained as an auditor for the specific standard. Personal attributes for an auditor can be found in ISO 19011. If the employee does not meet both the personal attributes and company knowledge, they cannot be an auditor, however they can participate in the audit to gain knowledge. The Quality function should define all the competencies required as well as help to identify and support the training required to the interested employees. This should be a formal process and be a part of the company's appraisal process.

3. The management team should appoint a project leader to start identifying possible entities for both the requirements training and certification process, such as use of consultants or educational organizations.

4. After some research, the project leader can then inform management about different options for training and obtaining certification. If choosing a consultant, the general manager should meet with the consultant to discuss their approach and whether this aligns to the current business culture, as well as to discuss knowledge gaps or other issues, such as resources or training time and costs. If choosing an educational organization, recognize that developing this knowledge in-house will take a longer period of time, as the team will need to attend certain courses. Identifying a high-potential employee to take on an ongoing additional responsibility in auditing may require some time as well. Alternatively, the project leader can pursue both approaches: contract with a consulting company and develop in-house expertise. Meanwhile, the project leader will work with the management team to identify the types of audits to consider doing in-house in specific areas, establish a budget (external training and support), create an initial project timeline, identify a project team if necessary, and define a list of action items to fulfill the requirements.

5. The project leader will regularly meet with their team to implement the new requirements and meet with the management team to provide a status update including performing a preliminary audit on their implementation of the new requirements.

6. The project leader will liaise with management and/or the external entity to coordinate dates for conducting the audit.

7. The project leader will prepare, coordinate, and communicate the 4 phases of the audit internally and externally if needed.

Audit - Questions and Answers

Are upcoming audit schedules posted, and where? What areas will be audited? Functions to be audited? What is the scope, type of audit, and timing?

Audit schedules should be posted in a conspicuous place so all employees can see the upcoming audit schedule. The audit schedule should clearly define the scope, type, function, and timing as well as the company support team member to accompany the auditor, especially if it is an external audit.

Are post-audit findings, corrective actions, and reports posted?

Posting the audit findings, corrective actions, and reports is being transparent and requires a mature, trusting management team. However, certain confidential or sensitive information is not posted.

Does the audit determine effectiveness and performance to the company's objectives, identifying non-compliances, or finding opportunities for improvement?

Internal audits can cover all of these questions, although external audits are typically limited to one of these questions.

Is the audit more internally focused or customer-focused?

Generally, audits are not categorized in this manner. However, both internal and external audits cover both inward and outward assessments. When defining internal audit questions, consider looking with the customer's eyes for value-added activities or to improve customer satisfaction.

Is the audit timing sufficient to comprehensively cover the audit scope?

This is quite subjective and requires an experienced auditor to determine whether the timing is sufficient. Also, the auditor has to manage the time throughout the process to ensure the audit stays on schedule.

How to define an audit schedule to cover all business processes and involve all functions?

A matrix of all business process and functions is needed with a calendar overlay. This is to ensure all business processes and functions can be audited within one calendar year.

Is the audit "horizontal," covering one business process across various functions; "vertical," covering a specific function or area; or combination of "horizontal" and "vertical"?

The audit questions or format may not be specific to horizontal or vertical auditing. The lead auditor uses these approaches to assess the company's effectiveness and performance in different ways.

Who are the auditors and what audit training courses or audit certifications do they have?

A higher quality of audit is expected from experienced, certified auditors. Internal auditors should have participated in audit training and should have some experience as a participant in an audit. External auditors will have various educational and professional credentials, including formal audit training.

Are past audit findings and report included in the scope of the audit?

All audits should consider evaluating the most recent historical audit findings and report.

Chapter 26 - Process Line Stop and Escalation Process

All manufacturing companies experience problems every day; some are more significant than others. It is vitally important for the operations team to have a clearly defined, well-practiced line stop process, escalation process and Quick Response Quality Control System (QRQC). In addition, the staff must have participated in root cause analysis training seminars or classes, and/or have read books such as *Root Cause Analysis: The Core of Problem Solving and Corrective Action,* by Duke Okes. Again, all of these are fundamental and essential for all manufacturing companies.

Process Line Stop

So, what happens when a specific process operation goes out of control? Examples for stopping a line are shown below categorized by the 6Ms: man, machine, material, measurement, method, and mother nature.

Man

- Direct labor worker is not sufficiently trained on a specific process operation. The supervisor checks the training matrix board and confirms that worker has not yet been certified or trained to the appropriate level

- Direct labor worker does not complete the start-of-shift check sheet

- Direct labor worker stops the process because something seems to be wrong, they think they didn't do something correctly some time earlier, or they had to step away from the process due to some event and could not finish their work completely

Machine

- Machine breaks down

- Machine seems to operate or sound differently

- Machine Preventive Maintenance (PM) has not been completed on-time for the current shift

Material

- Defect levels have reached or exceeded that hour's target level

- Raw material looks or feels different

- There is a shortage of raw material

- Material cannot be scanned, material tag has some error, or is a different tag

Measurement

- Gage is reading incorrectly on the master parts

- Gage has been dropped on the floor

- Computer says there is a test software issue, but the computer is still running the program
- Measuring the last part off a production run indicates a defect

Method
- Process method can no longer follow the standardized work due to some issue
- QC chart shows the process is going out of control
- Fixture to place the material is damaged, the fixture is loose, or the tools to be used are damaged or loose
- Changeover process is taking more time than the Standardized Work timing, or a changeover is needed because material for the current product has run out before the expected time

Mother Nature (environment), Health, Safety and Security
- Work space environment has changed — dust collector filters are clogged and are being bypassed, so the workspace has considerable more dust than normal
- Oil is leaking from one of the machine hydraulic hoses and has seeped into the work area, where it became noticeable
- Direct labor worker experienced a near miss or first aid incident
- Outside walkways have a slip hazard or parking lot lighting is not working

The process line stop is a clearly defined procedure where the direct labor worker is given the responsibility and authority to stop a process. The key is that the direct labor worker can stop the process if they "think" or "suspect" there is a problem.

Illustration – Escalation Matrix

The following Escalation matrix can be located in every production work-cell, in the production operations functional staff and manager work areas, supervisor area, break rooms, locker rooms, warehouse, security office, and any other area where there may be a potential HSE, Production, Quality, or manpower issue. Some companies laminate this information and put contact numbers on the lower front part or include on the back side of the document. This document should be a control document and updated accordingly. In addition, some companies provide 6M examples on the back side for further information. This document is also used in training during the Orientation process.

Table 3. 7 Escalation Matrix

Legend: ○ = Verbal | ◉ = Visual Confirmation | ● = Written Report / Analysis Required

	Incident	Trigger	Operator	Team Lead	Production Supervisor	Manager — Prod	Manager — HR	Manager — Quality	General Manager	Additional action activities
Health, Safety, Environmen	Accident	Accident occurs - Injury incurred	○	◉	◉	●	●		●	First Aid. Immediately contact Production Supervisor. Supervisor calls emergency services
	Safety concern	Safety concern outside or inside: - Parking lot, walkways, lighting, etc. - Floors, lighting, ventilation, trip and slip hazards - Machine guard or other machine issue - Material movement, forklift, lifting, placing	○	◉	●	●	●		●	Stop activity. Immediately contact your leader
Production	Downtime	Breakdown at 10 mins	○	◉						Troubleshoot- Man, Machine, Material, Measurement, Method, Mother nature
		Breakdown after 30 mins	○	◉	●	●		◉		Initiate Quick Response Quality Control (QRQC)
		Breakdown after 60 mins	○	◉	◉	●		●	●	Review/Update PFMEA and Control Plan
Quality	1st piece	Part is out of spec, or visual issue	○	◉	◉	●		●		Stop production Quality Control to confirm and escalate
	Reject	Reject more than 5 parts in any hour for any workcell	○	◉	◉	●		●		
	Reject	Reject quantity totals 15 or more parts in any workcell	○	◉	◉	●		●	●	Stop production, QC to confirm and escalate
	Last piece	Part is out of spec, or visual issue	○	◉	◉	●		●		
Manpower	Direct Labor	Headcount less than standard requirement		◉	◉	◉	●		●	Supervisor to prioritize worker location
	Direct Labor	Operator does not meet skill level requirement		◉	●	●		●		Supervisor and Production Manager to define improvement plan
	Direct Labor	Temporary worker in workcell		◉	◉	●				Supervisor to prioritize worker location

Escalation Process

When the worker decides to stop the line, they must inform their team leader or supervisor immediately. The team leader or supervisor then will analyze the situation and determine whether to:

1. Continue the process and make a note of the occurrence for possible follow-up with a technician or an engineer, as well as inform the incoming supervisor. This may be a very minor issue not affecting the form, fit, or function of the part or assembly.

2. Troubleshoot the situation; if the process can return to normal within X amount of time, no further escalation is needed. Many companies attempt to define a time limit of 10 or 15 minutes before escalating the issue to a maintenance or process technician, manufacturing or process engineer, or other supporting staff, such as supply chain or quality.

3. Determine whether recently produced product has to be quarantined and investigated as acceptable or not. Having a good manufacturing traceability program greatly helps to reduce the suspect material quantity and minimize the risk of passing defective material to the next operation or customer. Establishing a "clean," "green" or known good product cut-off date/time, serial number, etc. before the line actually stops is key to ensuring no suspect or defective material is passed to the next operation. Determining whether to investigate previously produced product may be a quality staff responsibility. It should seem obvious, but having a clear description of the problem is key to solving the problem.

4. Have technicians, engineers or support staff, once called, go immediately to the source of the problem and learn about the issue directly from the operator, line leader and supervisor. In most companies, the technicians, engineers and support staff are allowed 10 minutes or less to arrive. If they are late, the supervisor has the responsibility to take note and inform the operations management team. The technicians, engineers or support staff are then allowed up to a certain amount of time to further troubleshoot and fix the problem before escalating the issue to the operations management team, such as the production manager, manufacturing engineering manager, supply chain manager and quality manager.

5. Many companies allow up to one hour for troubleshooting before further escalating the issue to the operations management team. Some companies allow the technicians, engineers and support staff to work out a solution and just text or contact the operations management team with hourly updates. At any point during the process line stop, the supervisor is still the leader and the operations team is in a support capacity unless someone from the operations management team is on site at the problem source. Once the process line stop exceeds a pre-determined time, then the general manager is informed with the details.

6. Some companies require the general manager to be informed via text or phone call if the line is stopped for 30 minutes or more, while other companies escalate issues to the general manager after one or more hours. In any event, the operations management and general manager will receive the daily shift performance after the end of every shift, but having mid-shift notifications is extremely informative, especially if the line has stopped. The escalation process procedure has to be followed consistently during any shift and at any time, including night shift, weekends and holidays. Having a consistent, simple escalation process is key for clear communications. It should be easy to follow and supported by management, especially when there is already stress on the supervisor and operations team to have the line back to normal quickly.

7. A direct labor worker who makes a decision to stop their workstation or line has to be able to contact the line leader as soon as possible, preferably by voice or hand signals along with depressing a switch that turns the work station or line status light from green (running well) to red (line stopped). Many companies have other ways to signal the operations team that there is a problem, such as auto-text messaging to the operations team, loud speaker, or other alarm signaling device. Also, having an electronic operations work-cell or line productivity board within the operations team office would show a color change with a light flashing, or a pop-up message on the operations' teams individual computers. Other ways to signal and alert support is to use two-way radios, mobile phones, or fixed phones located around the factory. This type of communication allows the supervisor to alert specific people, as well as to have a discussion.

8. Regularly auditing and keeping this information current is important because as soon as the operator or supervisor cannot get in touch with someone using that escalation process, the trust in various systems diminishes and frustration level increases. When the support staff can't be contacted due to incorrect names or telephone numbers, the operator and supervisor will make further decisions on their own, such as running the line or bypassing specific operations.

Product and Process Deviation

If the process line can be returned to normal but with some deviated process control or process operation step, the operations team should document the details and have the operations management team's approval before running the line again. In this circumstance, the company may have a deviation process procedure and approval request form to complete. And, some companies may need to obtain customer approval before re-starting the production line.

Process/Product Deviation Form

- Product name and number
- Specific customers affected
- Batch, lot, serial numbers (from/to)
- Reason for deviation with attachments
- Deviation form label on container
- Approval authority signatures and date
- Quality inspection instructions

- Process operations affected
- Start time/date, End time/date
- Color marking on part (yellow dot)
- Color marking on container (yellow dot)
- Tracking method
- Photos of good / no-good situation
- Visually post form for all shifts to see and be trained

Once approvals have been received, the operations team responsible for the area, supervisor, team leader and direct labor workers in that specific area or affected by the deviation will have to understand the deviation details so they can follow the new temporary actions. The operations team would have to prepare new standardized work instructions, conduct any necessary training and validate the product.

Since there is a deviated process, the products may have to be inspected or tested in a different way, and also may have to be checked offline. The deviation approval document and any supporting information should be posted in the area affected and remain there until the deviation has expired. The deviation should be temporary and limited until the process has been corrected and returned to the original state. Quality should be responsible for ensuring that the document is posted in a conspicuous location and that everyone in the area understands the deviated process change. Supervisors and team leaders have the responsibility to ensure the direct workers have been trained and are qualified with the deviation. Since this is a new change, Quality should define an audit schedule to check the product and process on each shift until the deviation has expired. Quality will retain the deviation approval and related documents according to their procedures. If the company currently does not have a deviation process procedure, then this may need to be defined.

Product Changeover

Process line stop and escalation process typically are not initiated for a scheduled product changeover. Product changeover processes should be detailed in a Standardized Work document and the direct labor workers should be qualified to perform the tasks accordingly. If the company has not yet defined Standardized Work for product changeovers, it should at least have a work instruction, especially if a sequence of activities must be performed to move from producing one type of product to producing a different product.

Defining the product changeover process is key to ensuring a consistent quality and time-oriented practice is in place. The practice should be simple, clear and sequential to ensure the work area has been properly cleared and cleaned of old materials, fixtures, gages, tools, machine settings, programs, etc., and then prepared for producing the other product. The team leader and supervisor should ensure that the direct labor worker is qualified to perform the changeover process and is qualified to produce the new product. If the direct worker is not qualified, then follow the current procedure for upgrading an employee's skill capability and attempt to qualify the direct worker. Then, qualify the setup against a standard check sheet to ensure the process has been completed correctly. The first product produced must be inspected and meet all requirements before continuing running production. In some cases, while the first product is being inspected, production would continue, but would be controlled in case the first part does not meet the requirements.

Re-start the line — Qualification

In the event the process line is stopped, it may be necessary to re-qualify the line and/or process to ensure the subsequent product is in specification and the re-started process is stable. The first item produced must be confirmed as acceptable and the following product must be inspected according to the standardized work instructions and control plan requirements.

Key Points to Build a Process Line Stop Culture

A process line stop culture may seem at first to be a simple behavioral system to implement, but it is not simple by any means, due to several interacting and conflicting goals or actions, such as:

- Meeting production targets

- Specific direct labor workers always stopping the line, for known or questionable concerns
- A team leader or supervisor states the line can be stopped, but becomes angry at the direct labor workers when the line is stopped
- Management or support staff always stressing about meeting production targets and not consistently supporting a process line stop culture
- Direct labor workers wanting to stop the line to fix a problem but continue to run the process because they do not want to be singled out as problem workers

Management, supervisor, and team leaders must all understand, accept and support a process line stop behavior culture. When a line stop does occur, the direct labor worker should be thanked and encouraged to help re-start the process. The supporting staff should be evaluating how well the supervisor and team leader are handling the line stop issues. Whenever there is a line stop, everyone's immediate focus is to re-start the process, but it is important to determine the team leader's, supervisor's and support staff's facial expression, voice level, comments, actions, and immediate response as to whether it is help oriented or not.

- Were the leaders upset and frustrated?
- Were the leaders berating the direct labor worker at any time, even after the process line was re-started?

The direct labor workers and others will take notice of how the team leader, supervisor and support staff respond, and then decide for themselves what they will do when they face a similar concern in the future.

When initially building a process line stop culture, it is important to evaluate the team's responses and methods, and determine what improvements, if any, have to be made. At some point, someone will respond in the old behavioral way; this has to be highlighted and addressed immediately with the individual privately. That individual must meet with the affected and related direct labor workers, apologize, and inform them they are still in the midst of changing their behavior.

Key Points to Build an Escalation Process

Starting an Escalation process is significantly much easier than building a line stop culture. However, maintaining and improving upon the response timing and methods are rather challenging, due to the technical aspects of troubleshooting combined with the operation team's competencies and personalities.

The general manager should define the framework for the escalation process, while the operations team should define the details. The framework can be simply stated, such as defining and practicing an escalation process and timing by a certain date for certain conditions, with some examples. Then, the operations team should define who, when and how to respond to the various 6M situations (Man, Machine, Material, Method, Measurement and Mother Nature including Health, Safety and Security). Identifying the various circumstances for escalation helps to define a procedure, flowchart, timing and basis for training direct labor workers, line leaders, supervisors, operations staff, and management.

In addition, each direct labor worker, line leader and supervisor must have escalation notification cards in their notepads (previously mentioned) or at each workstation. The information should be a simple list for each shift, showing whom to contact and a back-up contact in case something happens so a specific person can be contacted for any specific shift, such as:

- Shift A, B, C, D Supervisors
- Team leader and mobile number
- Maintenance technician and mobile number
- Manufacturing engineer and mobile number
- Quality engineer and mobile number
- Supply chain and mobile number
- Health, Safety, Security and Environment and mobile numbers
- Functional managers and mobile numbers
- General or plant manager and mobile number

Some companies make this list into a simple process flowchart with colors or a basic notification table, and insert copies into everyone's notepad or post at every machine or workstation. Keeping the notification information simple, visible, accurate and supported by management is critical for an efficient and effective operations workforce. Support by management requires providing an environment where the direct labor workers and operations team have the responsibility to take action, and the direct labor workers and operations team have a strong sense of empowerment to do what is needed to keep operations running effectively.

Quick Response Quality Control (QRQC)
The QRQC system is an extension of both the process line stop and escalation process but should primarily be concerned with customer complaints or potential customer complaints. The Quality and Sales parts of the organization will ensure all customers have a specific Quality person to contact in the event there is a customer concern, as well as to maintain the communications matrix.

If there is a quality concern with the manufacturing process or from the customer, the Quality organization will take the lead, with the most important step being clearly identifying the problem before any other actions are taken. If there is a quality concern at the supplier end, the supplier quality staff and supplier itself will take the lead to clearly identify the problem.

If a customer reports an issue, it is important to get a clear description of the problem. This may include photos, videos, shipping label information, and serial numbers. It should also include customer locations and customer contact information (phone number and email).

From the initial phone contact with the customer, the clock is ticking to provide feedback as quickly and accurately as possible — waiting for another day or two to pass without any updates will further frustrate the customer. With a QRQC system in place, the team immediately responds with the information collected to clearly understand the problem. The customer may contact Quality, Sales, or Production anytime during the day, night, or weekend, so the company must have a clear, experienced rapid response team in place that is ready to assess and address the customer concern immediately.

The QRQC team will also identify other resources as needed, including staff to support nights or weekends, or external sources for supporting analysis. The QRQC team typically gets together in a specific location on the factory floor or conference room and uses this place as a base of operations until the customer is informed of the corrective action. Some customers may require hourly or daily updates and have expectations that a containment action will be in place within 24 hours and root cause identified within 48 hours. The QRQC team not only has to identify the containment action, root cause and corrective actions, but also has to work with the customer regarding the logistics and identification of defective or suspect material already delivered to the customer or on the way to the customer.

For example, a customer calls a Quality person at the company and informs them of their concern. The Quality person then activates the QRQC team, presents the customer concern, and then starts the Root Cause and Corrective Action (RCCA) process. The customer may not want to use any more of the company's product until a containment action has been approved. The containment action should be discussed and agreed upon with the customer. The product and/or packaging should be identified with markings to clearly show the containment action was taken. To indicate the containment action is taken, the containment action summary, date, time, and Quality approval signature is placed on all of the current finished product that is packaged. In some cases, a green-painted dot may be placed on the product in an agreed-upon location. Current product being produced will also have the containment action conducted on it and the packaging identified with the containment action activity.

The QRQC team will define additional information in support of the containment action, such as a Quality Alert notice posted on the work station where the containment action is taking place. The Quality Alert notice should show the "good" part or feature and the "no-good" part or feature. There should be a clear distinction between the good and the no-good product. Also, note that the containment action may require some offline processing that is outside of the main process work cell such as to conduct some rework operation. The containment action and process to move the materials needs to be very clear. The QRQC team will have to train the direct labor workers and material movement workers to ensure they can meet all the containment action requirements. The first shipment of the product with the containment action must be agreed upon with the customer, with clear identification of the containment action and markings. Subsequent shipments will be identified with the containment action until a corrective action has been implemented.

For the last shipment under the containment action, the product packaging label should denote last containment action shipment along with the other requirements discussed. When the corrective action is implemented, the first shipment under the corrective action will be labeled as "first shipment" with the corrective action title, date and time. Having both containment and corrective action shipments visually identified is to ensure control.

There are several steps necessary to understand the customer concern and identify the root cause or causes to ensure this problem does not recur, even within your company's sister companies, and to update the product and process knowledge to prevent future products or processes from having this problem. Root Cause and Corrective Analysis (RCCA) can also be used for solving problems with health, safety and security, internal and external audit findings, Daily Routine (DR), manufacturing equipment, infrastructure, logistics, warehousing, or any problem where a corrective action is needed.

Many companies recognize the importance of having the operations staff be competent in Root Cause and Corrective Action (RCCA). This will encourage and promote ongoing education and developing skills. RCCA skill set is extremely important in manufacturing and there should be regular, ongoing training classes to upgrade everyone's capability.

The Quality organization can take the lead in defining a regularly occurring RCCA training schedule. Using one RCCA training program helps to ensure nomenclature is common, process steps and objectives are known, and misunderstandings or premature communications can be avoided. However, a RCCA program may not be capable of providing a root cause for all problems, such as in the development of new technologies where knowledge is limited.

The following is a summary of the RCCA steps taken from the book *Root Cause Analysis: The Core of Problem Solving and Corrective Action,* by Duke Okes.

Step 1 – Define the Problem

Step 2 – Understand the Process

Step 3 – Identify Possible Root Causes

Step 4 – Collect the Data

Step 5 – Analyze the Data

Step 6 – Identify Possible Solutions

Step 7 – Select Solution(s) to be Implemented

Step 8 – Implement the Solution(s)

Step 9 – Evaluate the Effect(s)

Step 10 – Institutionalize the Change

Key Points to Build a QRQC System

Every manufacturing company should have a QRQC process that quickly responds to a customer concern. The main benefit of having a QRQC system is to reduce the impact when a defect is identified by a customer. The general manager understands the importance of providing quality products and services to their customers on-time. Also, whenever there is a customer concern or complaint, it has to be corrected immediately.

1. General manager states that a QRQC or Fast Response system is needed and that all functional leaders will fully support this new system, with the Quality Manager taking the lead.

2. Quality Manager defines the QRQC process details as above, and develops a flowchart of the steps, resources, expected timing and escalation process, along with an ad hoc organizational and communications chart. The ad hoc team is only formed when a customer complaint is received or when a potential customer complaint is known; it disbands when the corrective action has been implemented and is effective.

3. Quality Manager presents the new business process to the leadership team for their inputs and approval. In addition, there should be a discussion about how and where both the QRQC documentation and RCCA information will be posted, so management and staff are aware of customer issues and RCCA progress. Also, management and others can understand the details of what went wrong and what is needed to fix the problem. Most companies post the RCCA information on a QRQC or Fast Response board and provide frequent updates until closure.

4. The leadership team will define a plan to roll out the new system and train all operations staff in it. As a minimum requirement, the QRQC team must have participated in RCCA training. After a few customer concerns, the general or plant manager will expect the Quality manager and newly formed ad hoc QRQC

team to review the QRQC process and look for ways improve it, including timing. Ongoing annual improvements will be made to the QRQC through regular internal audits and by participating in QRQC events to identify opportunities.

Chapter 27 - Change Management

Every company has a change management process, whether formal or informal. Companies with formal, automated change management processes are typically more effective and efficient at processing changes than those with informal or manual processes. Changes can be identified as either critical or non-critical. A critical change is something that has a direct impact on the quality, capability, control, or performance of the business. Critical changes can be related to: customer requirements, government compliance, international standards compliance, or other internal requirements. These types of changes typically go through a standardized, structured change management process that is documented, approved, released, with obsolete information removed so that only the current version is available. Also, past critical changes are controlled and are retrievable. The formality ensures that all related functions are aware of a change and can track status for processing the change. A RASIC matrix may be used to identify who has the Responsibility, Accountability, Support, Inform, or Consult activity for each critical change.

Product, Process, People, Project, and Systems

All managers have the responsibility for change management within their functional areas. The Quality function typically has the main responsibility to collect and control critical change items. This is to ensure one change management system is used for all critical changes. The five main areas for change management are:

- Product
- Process
- People
- Project
- Systems

Illustration – Change Management Process

The process for change management has five steps: request for change, change analysis, approve/reject, implement, and effectiveness report. Some companies may have more steps and much greater complexity with swim lane flow diagrams defining the change management process with responsibilities and timing. While other companies are in a transition of using service oriented architecture automation with the beginning steps of artificial intelligence that include: business process flow, responsibilities, timing, alerts, tracking status, various reports, document control, file and revision management, e-signature approval authorization, notifications, audit function capability, embedded analytics, adaptive rules, query tools, and linkages to email, engineering platforms, warranty systems, and other software applications.

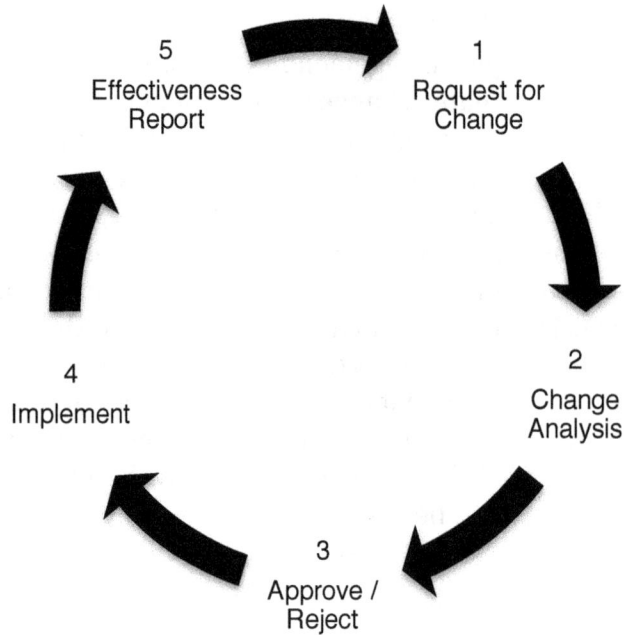

Figure 3. 4 Change Management Process

Key Points to Establish a Change Management System

Depending upon the industry and product maturity, there may or may not be frequent changes that need to be managed. However, with new technology products, there may be changes every day, while in some commodity businesses, there may only be changes a couple of times a year. Either way, having a controlled, formal change management system is essential for an efficient and effective operations management system.

1. Request for Change

Typically, once a product, process, person, project, or system has been defined or is operational, any change would require some management. A product change request may be from a customer, supplier, or internally generated. These changes are typically called engineering change requests (ECR). Once the ECR is approved, the ECR becomes an engineering change notice (ECN). Process changes are typically generated internally from direct labor workers or staff. A similar terminology exists for a process change request (PCR) — once approved, a PCR becomes a process change notice (PCN). However, many companies have combined the product and process change request to become a PPCR, while a product and process change notice is called a PPCN. Finally, some companies may use supplier change requests (SCR) and supplier change notices (SCN) for supplier related matters.

People change requests are typically in the form of a resource request, and the final approval is typically hiring and on-boarding employees or restructuring the organization chart with changes to people and/or their job responsibilities. In other words, requests can be for positions to be filled, eliminated, or restructured.

Project change requests are unique as they can be simple or complex such as using a PPCR, or can be with various combinations including a strategy, plan, and/or organization chart. System change requests are similar to project change requests.

2. Change Analysis

Once a change request has been initiated, the next step is to analyze it. All of the above described change requests will be reviewed internally and can either be approved, approved with modification, or rejected. The review process typically includes an evaluation of cost versus benefits by experienced staff. The review can be simple and informal such as hand carry to various staffs, be a formal meeting, be an automated business process, or be a formal meeting with an automated process. When experienced staff are analyzing the change, they define the impact to the business typically by performing a cost versus benefit analysis with a risk analysis, or for more complicated changes to develop a business case, see Chapter 36 for more information. The staff will have to assess whether the change outweighs the costs by having potentially a higher sales price, higher sales volume, higher productivity (higher throughput, quality and/or up-time), and/or greater customer satisfaction. However, some changes may be required without having any perceived benefit such as compliance to meet safety standards or environment requirements.

Also, some analysis may be quite complicated and require an Ad hoc project team to be formed. Experienced staff may be from engineering, manufacturing engineering, production, quality, sales, supply chain, and possibly include the person originating the change request. The analysis may require a complete new launch of a product or infrastructure project with new process operations, tools, and product testing. The analysis clearly can vary widely in complexity and timing. The key is to have experienced staff who understand the requested change and its related requirements, and who can evaluate a cost-versus-benefit and risk analysis. If experienced staffs are not involved in the change analysis, then the result of the analysis may cause additional costs, delays, and potential loss of business.

3. Approve / Reject

Depending upon the type of change, the experienced staff can either approve, reject, approve with condition, modify the change request and submit to the originator, or may have to submit to management with their recommendation for management to make the final decision. The result should have a reason and be communicated to the originator. Also, if the change request is approved, it may require external approval by the customer, supplier, or regulation entity. All change requests can be negotiated in some way including price and timing.

- If the customer requests a change, the company may approve, reject, or modify the change request and submit to the customer. If the company rejects the change, this may affect and strain the relationship for current and new business. Offering a modification may be a mutual compromise.

- If the request was generated internally and approved, then the customer or supplier may approve, reject, or ask that it be modified and re-negotiated for approval.
- If the supplier requests the change, the company may approve, reject, or have it modified and re-negotiated for approval. This change may also need customer approval.

4. Implement

For change requests that have been approved, they would need some sort of plan to be implemented. Depending upon the duration of the implementation phase, there may be several implementation status reviews to ensure the implementation is progressing according to plan or may not have any implementation reviews at all especially if the implementation was simple and quickly done. However, for both simple and complex changes, the implementation may require resources to be coordinated throughout the entire supply chain. Resources, timing, costs, and reviews are typically defined upfront in the implementation plan and this typically follows a common business process with exceptions defined as required. The implementation must have a clear separation or distinction of the "before the change" versus "after the change". If there is not a clear difference, mistakes or even a catastrophic situation can occur.

5. Effectiveness Report

The effectiveness report is typically performed as an audit once the change has been implemented. However, during the implementation various reports will be generated. A clear tracking system is typically defined for both the "before the change" and "after the change" activities. Both formal and informal systems should have a tracking function to ensure timely implementation and completion of all functional requirements necessary for a successful change. Other functions, such as Finance, may also have to be involved for performing or confirming cost-versus-benefits calculations. Typically, Quality will retain the product and process change request/notices in their quality management system. The tracking system can be automated, can be spreadsheet-based, tracked via visual displays such as a whiteboard, or a combination. A combination of both automation and visual displays work well together. The visual tracking displays can be summary-based, such as number of changes overdue for implementation and status; number of upcoming open changes and status; changes by week/month with savings improvement and status; changes by product line, by customer, by supplier, etc. The key to any implemented change is to conduct a comprehensive audit of the change to verify closure and qualify its expected benefits.

Illustration – Product and Process Change Request

The following shows two diagrams. The first one is the front page while the second diagram is the back page of a Product and Process Change Request. The front page contains all the important information regarding the change, while the back page shows the specific document change, who to contact, approvals, and verification.

Rev. Date: **Product and Process Change Request** PPCR NO. [ ]

Emergency PPCR? Yes / No Initiation Date [ ]

Internal Part Numbers [ ] Internal Part Names [ ]

Customer or Supplier [ ] Customer or Supplier Part [ ]

Initiator Name [ ] Planned Start Change Date [ ]

Problem Statement or Sketch:

Change Reason:

How to verify the change:

Check all appropriate boxes:

☐ Material: A new part, product, or material
☐ Product: Modification required to the part, material, specification, tolerance, or standard
☐ Material or Product: Temporary change to use another material or product.
If Temporary change, define approval process: WHO to approve? What inspection or tests required?

☐ Machine, Method or Measurement: Any change to the manufacturing method or measurement method
If method or measurement change, define approval process: WHO to approve? What inspection or tests required?

☐ New Supplier for material, tooling, or packaging. List the new supplier name:
If new supplier, define approval process: WHO to approve? What inspection or tests required?

☐ Transfer of machine or tooling from customer, supplier or internal

☐ If no boxes selected above, define WHO to approve? What inspections or tests required?

Figure 3. 5 Product and Process Change Request-1

Product and Process Change Request

Rev. Date:

PPCR #

Check all appropriate boxes and provide contact name:

Due Date

Safety
- ☐ Guarding or other safety device   Contact

Manufacturing   Contact
- ☐ Maintenance   ☐ Work Instructions   ☐ PRODUCTION MONITORING

Manufacturing Engineering and Quality   Contact

		PPAP Required
☐ Process Routing	☐ Process Parameters	☐ Fixture drawings
☐ Tool drawings	☐ PFMEA	☐ Process flowchart
☐ Process Control Plan	☐ Machine drawings (elec/mech)	☐ Cutting tool drawings
☐ Mistake Proof Devices	☐ Gage checklist	☐ Standardized work instruction change
☐ Layout	☐ Cycle Time (PART TO PART)	☐ Work standard instruction change
☐ Takt Time	☐ Line Balance	☐ Gage drawing
☐ Packaging (internal/external)	☐ Ergonomics	☐ Define other:
☐ Material Handling	☐ Visual Controls	
☐ Software	☐ Break point required	

Training   Contact
- ☐ Standardized Work Instructions   ☐ New Product or Process   ☐ Define other:
- ☐ Work Standard Instructions   ☐ New Machine
- ☐ CMM   ☐ New Gage, Inspection, or Test

Supply Chain, Production Control   Contact
- ☐ ERP Update   ☐ Kanban/Pull   ☐ Leadtime change
- ☐ Material Routing change   ☐ Packaging   ☐ Min, Max Inventory change
- ☐ Supplier List   ☐ Label   ☐ Define other:

Engineering   Contact:
- ☐ BOM update   ☐ Tester program   ☐ Define other:
- ☐ Master parts list update   ☐ New Tester

Other Functions   Define function and define what needs to be completed
- ☐

Approvals Required	Approval: Printed Name	Approval: Signature
☐ HSE Responsibility		
☐ Manufacturing/Production		
☐ Manufacturing Engineering		
☐ Quality		
☐ Supply Chain		
☐ Production Planner		
☐ Engineering		
☐ Sales		
☐ HR		
☐ Maintenance		
☐ IT		
☐ Others		

Implentation Verification	Approval: Printed Name	Approval: Signature
Quality Audit Date		

Figure 3. 6 Product and Product Change Request-2

Chapter 28 - Total Productive Maintenance (TPM)

Total Productive Maintenance (TPM) is a manufacturing operations system to ensure the workforce (i.e., all workers, including staff and management), manufacturing equipment, tools, gages and infrastructure are always able to perform as intended. The main benefits of TPM include:

- Cost improvements (Quality and Productivity)
- Employee satisfaction (engagement, ownership, morale, pride, spirit)
- Customer satisfaction (delivery performance, quality, and reliability)
- Health, Safety, and Environment improvements

TPM Composition

A TPM system is composed of several broad categories:

1. Collecting, monitoring, and analyzing manufacturing operations data to control various processes
2. Defining and implementing metrics to assess and predict performance and costs
3. Implementing systems to quickly react and respond when unfavorable variances occur
4. Educating direct labors and staff with TPM analytical tools, techniques, systems, and providing a platform for on-going education
5. Engaging and empowering direct labor and staff to take action and be aligned with overall business strategies and plans
6. Building an operations culture that is determined to continuously improve
7. Upgrading detection and prevention systems to ensure equipment is running at ideal state
8. Managing a comprehensive and capable maintenance program including certified staff, maintenance staff, spare part availability
9. Applying TPM techniques to other functions — such as Supply Chain for customer order management, production scheduling, raw material ordering, material movements, and Human Resources for recruiting, on-boarding, and assisting with retaining direct labor and staff.
10. Establishing and executing TPM strategies and plans that are aligned with the company's product and technology roadmaps

Manufacturing Data

Manufacturing data can be collected and analyzed through software programs or can be collected and analyzed manually. Ideally, companies record various data sets into a minimal number of databases for efficiently monitoring and analyzing data. There are databases to consolidate, integrate, link, or auto-create reports from systems such as ERP (Enterprise Resource Planning), CMMS (Computerized Maintenance

Management), employee attendance tracker and skills competencies, Quality inspection results, SPC, defect analysis and prevention, Supplier Quality data, Change Management System, Cloud Computing, Equipment maker data link, and many other software systems. This integration of various software platforms is the next industrial revolution called Industry 4.0, "Smart Factory", and is the start of the 4th Industrial Revolution. The first Industrial Revolution was during the 18th and most of the 19th century and it primarily replaced animal labor with steam power and mechanized production, significantly impacting the coal, iron, railroad, and textile industries. The second industrial revolution started during the latter part of the 19th century up to World War I and used electric power for mass production, including Henry Ford's moving assembly line. The third industrial revolution started during the 1980s using electronics, information technology, internet, Wi-Fi, and renewable energy to automate manufacturing and develop a new Internet of Things (IoT). The 4th Industrial Revolution uses the Internet of Things (IoT) and artificial intelligence to instantly connect and disconnect broad arrays of manufacturing technologies, transforming global economics, governments, and society.

Most companies have various manufacturing operation metrics visually displaying real-time metrics in the operations team office and on the staff's computers. Total Productive Maintenance can be measured by individual metrics or combinations of them. One of the most common combination TPM metrics used in high-volume production is the Overall Equipment Effectiveness (OEE) metric. The TPM metric is calculated as: OEE = Availability x Performance x Quality

Illustration - TPM Categories

The following table shows the TPM categories, metrics, and losses.

Table 3. 8 TPM Factors

TPM Categories	TPM Key Metrics	Losses
Availability	Percentage of production run time	1. Breakdowns 2. Changeovers
Performance	Throughput rate percentage	3. Minor Stops 4. Speed Loss
Quality	Percentage of good product produced	5. Production defects 6. Defects on start-up or changeover
Overall Equipment Effectiveness	OEE = Availability x Performance x Quality	All of the above

Availability

Availability = Percentage of production run time to total planned production time

$$Availability = \frac{(Planned\ production\ time - breakdown\ time - changeover\ time)}{Planned\ production\ time} \times 100\%$$

Availability Loss:

1. Breakdowns can be short term, where the operator can perform the repair, or long term, where maintenance is requested. These are unplanned machine or tooling breakdowns.
2. Changeover, setup, process adjustments, or tooling adjustments are planned production stops. These can also include machine cleaning, machine warm-up, or inspection.

Performance

Performance = Throughput rate or process rate expressed as a percentage, so:

$$Performance = \frac{number\ of\ parts\ produced\ x\ ideal\ cycle\ time}{production\ run\ time} \times 100\%$$

Or:

$$Performance = \frac{production\ run\ time - idle\ time - speed\ losses}{production\ run\ time} \times 100\%$$

The ideal cycle time is the stated time that the operation can run under ideal circumstances. Idle time is when the equipment is running but not producing any product.

Performance Loss:
3. Minor stops, where equipment is running but not producing. This can be due to material flow obstruction, sensors misalignment, a material jam, material misfeed, or material unavailability.
4. Speed loss, where equipment is running at less than the expected or standard rate designed speed. This could be due to the fact that the number of direct labor workers present is less than the number required. Other speed losses can occur when some direct labor workers are in training, machines are running at reduced speeds, machine or work cell cycle time is longer due to poor lubrication or worn out equipment, or even poor environmental conditions (temp too hot/too cold).

Quality

Quality = Percentage of the good product produced versus total number of product produced (the same as First Pass Yield).

Or:

$$\text{Quality} = \frac{\text{total product quantity produced} - \text{defective quantity produced}}{\text{total quantity produced}} \times 100\%$$

Quality Loss:
5. Production defects. This can be due to lower yields, rework, or defective parts resulting in scrap.
6. Defects on startup or changeover. This can be due to incorrect settings, or operators not fully competent.

OEE Example

One work-cell in a manufacturing facility runs 10 hours per day on two shifts. Each shift has a lunch break of 30 minutes and two 15-minute breaks throughout the shift. Each shift has had various equipment breakdowns during the day, with a total of 2.5 hours of downtime (1.5 hours on day shift and 1 hour on night shift) and 20 minutes each shift for changeovers.

The equipment is cleaned twice a shift for 10 minutes and is running at 97% of its designed speed, due to equipment capability. Each shift measures productivity and quality on a per-hour basis.

The day shift had 6 parts rejected for changeover and 10 parts rejected for the whole shift, with a total production quantity of 407, while the night shift had 5 parts rejected at changeover and 16 parts rejected throughout the shift with 421 parts produced.

Availability = %

$$\text{Day shift} = \frac{10 \text{ hours x } 60 \text{ minutes} - 90 \text{ minutes} - 20 \text{ minutes}}{\text{total shift time of } 10 \text{ hours x } 60 \text{ minutes}} = \frac{490}{600} = 82\%$$

$$\text{Night shift} = \frac{10 \text{ hours x } 60 \text{ minutes} - 60 \text{ minutes} - 20 \text{ minutes}}{\text{total shift time of } 10 \text{ hours x } 60 \text{ minutes}} = \frac{520}{600} = 87\%$$

Performance =

Day shift = 407/490 = 83%

Night shift = 421/520 = 81%

Quality =

Day shift = 397/407 = 98%

Night shift = 406/421 = 96%

Overall Equipment Effectiveness (OEE) Metric =

Day shift = 81.7% x 83.1% x 97.5% = 66%

Night shift = 86.7% x 80.9% x 96.4% = 68%

Many companies still track individual metrics as opposed to using OEE because they want to know the details and be able to respond rapidly to an unfavorable metric. However, in a large manufacturing facility with dozens of work-cells, the OEE metric can help reduce the time it takes to narrow down where problems occur, since every shift will have some variation.

In looking at the example above, what questions should be asked, what would be some priorities, what operational metrics are used, and are there any trends? Some specific questions might be:

- Why is downtime 50% greater on the day shift than the night shift? Are there different reasons for downtime? If so, why?
- Has a SMED workshop been performed for changeovers? Why are the changeovers exactly 20 minutes each shift?
- Is there a daily analysis for the shift rejects? Are there any similarities? If not, what are the differences between the 10 parts rejected on the day shift and

16 parts on the night shift? What can be done to reduce the number of rejected parts at changeover?

- What maintenance activities are needed to return the equipment to running at 100%?
- What additional improvements can be made to the cycle time to reduce some of the overtime? How else can overtime be reduced?
- How does this work-cell compare with others regarding Availability, Performance and Quality?

OEE Improvement Opportunities
Availability

Availability can be improved in many different ways, such as:

- Evaluating increasing work within a shift by running the bottleneck operations during breaks
- Ensuring inventory is always available for usage at that operation
- Reducing breakdowns, or adjustments. For reducing breakdowns, using metrics such as mean time to repair (MTTP) and mean time between failures (MTBF) can be effective
- Improving overall tool life management, costs, and tool availability.
- Implementing Single Minute Exchange of Dies (SMED). SMED is presented in detail below
- Ensuring spare parts are readily available and/or have 24-hour service equipment contracts in place
- Ensuring direct labor and maintenance team are competent in diagnosing equipment issues using Fault Tree Analysis or software management tools
- Ensuring Fast Response or other team is quickly alerted and is able to provide immediate resource to troubleshoot, diagnose, repair or replace, and to re-start and validate the process

Performance

Ensure minor stops are minimized and the equipment is running at ideal state with these steps:

- Ensuring start of shift and during shift PM activities are conducted on time and performed correctly
- Providing a method for Direct Labor workers to signal the team leader or supervisor upon recognition of a problem
- Installing various sensors on equipment that detect increase stresses, vibration, leaks, or other potential problems and send alerts to the maintenance staff

- Ensuring direct labor workers are trained and work-cells are correctly staffed
- Ensuring direct labor and staff are actively engaged in productivity improvements

Quality

Ensure a comprehensive Quality Management System is in place and is improving, See Chapter 15 Managing Quality for more information, specific opportunities are:

- Improve process capabilities across all products produced. This can be started by making a Pareto of the products by defect cost and working on those specific causes for improvement
- Ensure Quality inspections are performed on-time and correctly with qualified workers
- Ensure QC Self-checks are in place
- Ensure direct labor follows documented Standardized Work
- Ensure a Layered Process Audit (LPA) system is in place

Key Steps to Implement Single Minute Exchange of Dies (SMED)

SMED is a technique or methodology to reduce changeover time by minimizing the time it takes from producing part A to producing part B. Define all the product changeover times and/or use a matrix, as changeovers may have different times for different combinations of product changeovers.

Illustration – Multiple product changeover times

The following table shows the changeover time in minutes from changing from one product to another. This table assumes that the reverse changeover time is the same, but this may not always be true due to internal/external set-ups.

Table 3. 9 Multiple Product Changeover Times

Changeover (minutes)	A	B	C	D
A	x	5	18	35
B	x	x	22	40
C	x	x	x	25
D	x	x	x	x

Once the longest changeover time is known. The following process steps can be followed:

1. Separate internal from external setups
2. Convert internal to external setups
3. Implement 5S

4. Use functional clamps
5. Use intermediaries
6. Adopt parallel operations
7. Eliminate adjustments
8. Automate

1. Separate internal from external setups

Define the current changeover process activities and timing for a specific work-cell or machine. Detailed information is very important. What activities take place and what happens? Who is doing those activities? How much time does each activity take? Take notes on activities that are repeated. Take videos and photos of the activities (photos showing process steps with timing). Identify whether those activities can be external, which means that they are done while the machine is running. Make a list of all tools, molds, dies, gages, and locations of those devices for each external activity. Collect any documents used for making the changeover.

Look for improvement opportunities:

Preparing parts, tools, jigs, fixtures and gages, as well as their locations and accessibility

- Adjustments and re-adjustments
  Searching for tools, gages, dies, etc.
  Cleaning, inspecting, paperwork

- Excessive movements (walking, hand movements) by operators or technicians

- Changeover validation, quantities, timing, coordination and approvals

- Other actions to support changeover

- Idle time, rework or delays

2. Convert internal to external setups

- Reorganize activity blocks for internal and external

- Try to convert as many internal to external

- Involve experts and others involved in the work-cell

- Reorganize to conduct separate activities

Illustration – Convert internal to external setups

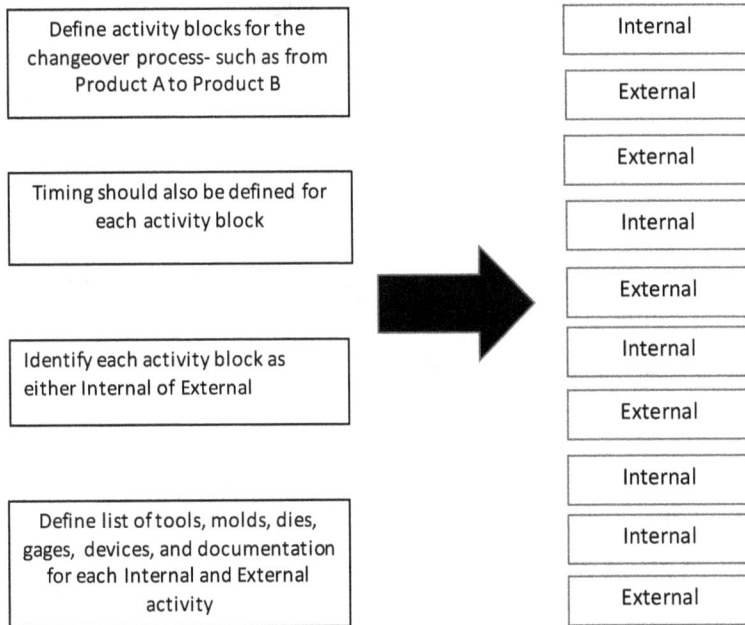

Define activity blocks for the changeover process- such as from Product A to Product B	Internal
	External
	External
Timing should also be defined for each activity block	Internal
	External
	Internal
Identify each activity block as either Internal of External	External
	Internal
Define list of tools, molds, dies, gages, devices, and documentation for each Internal and External activity	Internal
	External

Figure 3. 7 SMED – Separate internal and external activities

Illustration – Changeover time reduction – 1st Analysis

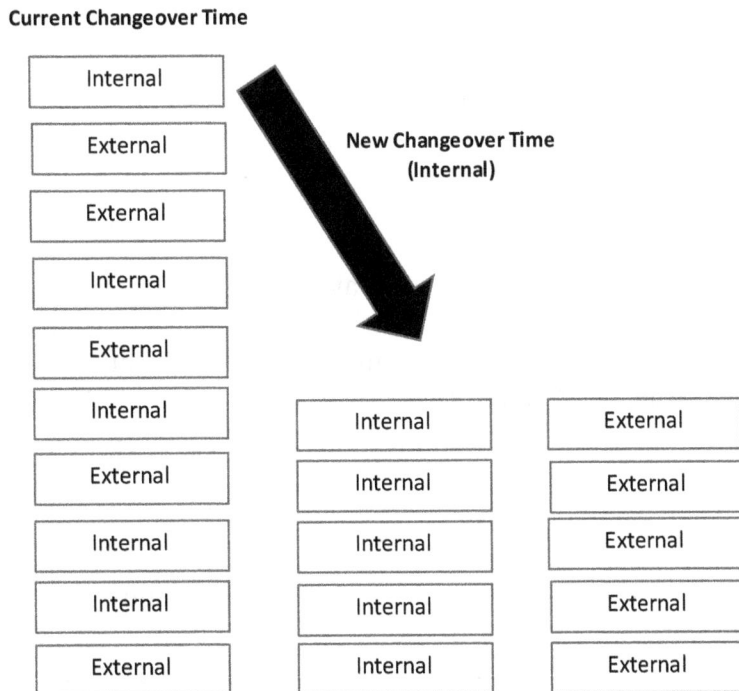

Current Changeover Time

	New Changeover Time (Internal)
Internal	
External	
External	
Internal	
External	

Internal	Internal	External
External	Internal	External
Internal	Internal	External
Internal	Internal	External
External	Internal	External

Figure 3. 8 SMED - Changeover time reduction

3. Implement 5S

- Sort – eliminate unnecessary operations, tools, gages
- Set – arrange the activities, tool, gages, etc., so there is a smooth, efficient flow and make common heights, connection points, or locations for clamping and centering
- Shine – ensure the area is well lit and always clean and organized
- Standardize – use Standardized Work, color standards, visual displays
- Sustain – use Daily Routine, internal audits, praise workers and ensure practices are being done correctly
- Safety and Security – document and enforce

4. Use of functional clamps

- Use of quick connects
- Use of magnetic or spring clamps instead of bolts and nuts
- Interlocking methods
- Pear-shaped holes
- U- or C-shaped washers
- One-touch cams or clamps
- Use of pre-tightening
- Reduce adjustments and use of fixed setting devices
- Check and confirm sequence of clamping and whether there are any gaps between clamp or fixture/jig touchpoint and part

5. Intermediate jigs

- Consider using duplicate jigs and fixtures, or ways to add or remove parts of the jig and fixture to reduce time. Clearly identify the components of the jig or fixture to be added or removed. Have specific pre-defined locations and ease of moving for storing jigs and fixtures
- Use roller racks, carts and hoists, but minimize distance in using hoists

6. Adopt parallel operations

- Typically requires that two or more operators work simultaneously or concurrently on the same activity or different activities or size of equipment; for example, one operator on the left side and another on the right side
- Requires coordination and communication, especially if operations have to be synchronized
- Requires a higher level of safety awareness

7. Eliminate adjustments

- After initial setup, no additional adjustment should be needed — there should be one set of sequences. Team should challenge itself, since this requires a lot of creativity and/or use of external resources
- Use pre-sets, go/no-go gage blocks, or master parts

8. Automate

- Before any automation, thoroughly revisit steps 1–7
- Document and add visuals for each improvement and provide training for all shifts, especially in complicated sequences or for significant changes that separate internal from external activities
- Perform newly established changeovers several times to ensure consistent practice and timing; audit the process activity details and timing
- Identify options for automation and perform a cost/benefit analysis; consider using a simulation or mock-up model of automation for analysis

SMED Summary
Start with the work-cell with the highest changeover time. Alternatively, the start can be with equipment that you have considerable knowledge. Another alternative is to choose the process with the bottleneck or process that has a low OEE metric. Ensure your team consists of a direct labor worker or two from that specific work-cell/equipment, a maintenance person, manufacturing engineer and other support personnel as needed such as a team leader, supervisor or quality engineer.

Discuss among the team as to which machine would have the greatest benefit for reduced changeover time. Obtain current changeover process details for each type of product at a specific machine via videotape, work instructions, checklists, visual aids, inspection sheets, and other documents used. Determine which tools, jigs, dies, molds, machine programs and gages are used, etc. If no documentation exists yet, be sure the team is there to take notes and photos when a changeover is needed. There may be multiple products that are produced on a machine, so multiple changeover processes will need to be documented and photographed.

It may take some time to collect the information, maybe even a couple of days, due to the production schedule. Once information is collected, all of this should be posted onto a wall in a logical sequence so the team can see the different steps of the changeover process clearly. Post the information in order of the changeover process steps and include photos and layouts. Draw or write down where the workers are standing when performing the changeover and who is involved. Then, start with the SMED process step 1 and work your way through the steps. A matrix, checklist, spreadsheet, or other support materials may be needed to ensure the proper sequence, timing, and changeover activity is conducted correctly.

The key is to be specific to one machine to understand and apply the SMED process steps. Once the changeover process timing has been reduced, other products can then be started before moving onto other work-cells or machines. Also, when buying new equipment, be sure a SMED time and Standardized Work (Method) is defined in the contract. Changeover times should be regularly monitored and managed with a system set up to respond when there is an issue.

Upgrading PM to a TPM System

Most companies have a defined Preventive Maintenance (PM) system in place where the maintenance function takes the lead in defining various daily maintenance equipment schedules and performs the maintenance activities. In addition, many companies have direct labor workers perform some basic checks to ensure the manufacturing equipment is operating at the defined condition. Upgrading a PM system to a TPM system involves more than just having the direct labor workers and staff more involved with PM activities. Some companies utilize a Lean Six Sigma approach to upgrade, as TPM is a much broader system than PM. A Lean Six Sigma methodology would involve a team that has been trained in the Lean Six Sigma methodologies by attending courses or being certified to Lean Six Sigma. The certification program typically has courses and different certification levels:

- Process Mapping
- Statistics
- Theory of Constraints
- Visual Management
- Change Management
- Standardized Work
- Continuous Improvement
- Total Productive Maintenance
- 5S

- Waste Identification and Elimination
- Error Proofing
- Root Cause and Corrective Action
- Measurement Systems Analysis
- Team Management
- Potential Failure Mode Effects Analysis

- Single Minute Exchange of Dies

In addition, direct labor workers, staff and maintenance will upgrade the current PM activities so direct labor workers:

- Perform daily maintenance according to defined instructions and check sheets: clean equipment, fixtures, tools; inspect the machines for any issues.
- Perform basic lubrication and conduct various checks as per instructions.
- Identify equipment, fixture and tools for wear or damage.
- Assist maintenance with repairs, replacement or upgrades as needed.
- Perform changeovers and any adjustments.
- Increase their knowledge of the processes and processes.
- Apply their knowledge to ensure processes are running at the standard rate.

- Identify improvements in Availability; Performance; and Quality, including Safety, Health and Environment.
- Participate in Root Cause and Corrective Analysis training.
- Participate in Quick Response Quality Control (QRQC) or Fast Response. Training and get involved when there is a customer concern.
- Actively practice process line stop and escalation process when needed.

While the maintenance staff will:

- Train and evaluate direct labor workers so they are competent at performing daily maintenance as above; identify and respond when equipment parameters are abnormal according to the process line stop procedure.
- Define monthly PM schedule and coordinate with production planning.
- Perform major equipment overhauls, upgrades and any high-risk safety tasks.
- Document equipment maintenance history and generate reports such as Mean Time to Repair (MTTR) and Mean Time between Failures (MTBF).
- Coordinate work with manufacturing engineering and production.
- Upgrade equipment with sensing systems to detect, communicate, and alert maintenance.
- Define and use Fault Tree Diagrams to reduce Mean Time to Repair.
- Respond to predictive process alerts and be actively engaged when the process line stops.
- Most importantly identify and actively reduce process risks

And, other staff will be involved with:

- Integrating software systems
- Creating efficient and timely reports
- Implementing data integrity, security, backups, and uptime reliability
- Implementing advanced analytics
- Implementing human-machine interfaces
- Supply Chain improvements, production planning, and logistics
- Auditing by ensuring compliance to standards and other requirements
- Executing activities to reduce process risks

Key Steps to Upgrade PM to a TPM system

1. Start by understanding the current PM system issues, define specific corrective actions and improvements including new methods, metrics, and tools (analytic software tools, sensors, controls, visual systems, etc.). Understand that the PM system may have several issues, such as: low competencies of operators and maintenance staff, need for specific technical training, old or obsolete software

program, poor method for data collection of machine downtime, and/or categorizing and defining reasons for downtime.

2. Rather than have a meeting in a conference room, go into several work-cells and processes and discuss various current PM issues with the direct labor workers and staff. Take notes regarding their ideas and concerns.

3. Analyze and investigate the equipment breakdown history and repair timing, diagnosis technique and timing (software program faults display, fault tree diagrams, check sheets), repair methods, replace methods, setup methods, and major adjustments that could be simplified.

4. Evaluate 5S in the maintenance area, spare part stores and locations, and identify improvements that can be made. Check whether spare parts are available, identified correctly, or missing from locations, confirm the efficiency of retrieval and lead-time, check for obsolescence or damage such as rust.

5. Establish a work team to review current issues and risks, and define a plan for corrections and improvements. Select a work-cell or process where the Availability, Performance and Quality metrics can be tracked before and after implementation. Review this with direct labor workers and provide any training needed, including for staff.

6. Once a work-cell or process is selected, identify the direct labor workers and staff on all shifts who will support the new system, introduce them to the new system and expectations, then conduct training as per the new system. The new system and expectations should be broader, with some people having greater or more responsibilities, such as: training to add cleaning, lubrication, machine checks, minor adjustments if the process stops or has a fault to the current direct labor worker's responsibility; updating or defining clear troubleshooting guides to help direct labor workers and maintenance staff. New software or a newer version may be needed, with data transferred, as well as training. Improvements may address spare parts storage locations, accessibility, or the process for ordering spare parts.

7. During the training session, the direct labor workers and staff should go to the specific work-cell or processes and perform the following:
    a. Review and perform the current PM duties, identify other checks or inspections that could be performed, and update the instructions accordingly. During the checks, identify any performance, quality or maintenance issues that have to be improved and develop an action plan.
    b. Identify whether the direct labor workers perform the PM activities according to the requirements accurately and timely.
    c. Review the new system requirements and perform the necessary duties. Ensure the direct labor workers and staff fully understand not just the new requirements, but the timing and coordination of the efforts.

    d. Evaluate historic concerns relative to the Work Order management system.

    e. Review the new metrics, including mean time to repair (MTTR) and between failures (MTBF), and discuss how they will be used.

    f. Evaluate historic process line stop and escalation process issues.

8. Within a week after a work-cell or process has implemented the new TPM system, the Availability, Performance and Quality has to be compared to the historic data before implementing the new system into other work-cells or processes, since the implementation may need additional modifications. It is essential to have input and discussions with direct labor workers and staff about data collection and system usage issues and provide any other TPM training needed. If the metrics have not improved, this has to be understood before continuing with the implementation. If data is collected on a per-shift basis and little effort is put into analyzing the data, then improvements probably won't happen.

9. Continue implementation into other work-cells or process areas and ensure the system is being used per plan by conducting an audit to ensure compliance as well as to identify possible improvements.

10. Establish a regular assessment schedule, see Chapter 30 for details.

11. Identify a cross-functional team to study Industry 4.0 or the so called fourth industrial revolution. This team will define and be responsible to implement the manufacturing operation's strategy for the future. Future Annual Operating Plans and Strategic Plans need to define a comprehensive plan from PM to TPM to Industry 4.0. Defining a direction and implementing incremental improvements year-over-year is economical and can keep the company in a competitive posture.

Chapter 29 - Assessing Total Productive Maintenance

Assessing the status of Total Productive Maintenance (TPM) is needed on an annual basis to determine weaknesses, improvement areas, and to ensure alignment to TPM plan or roadmap. The following sets of statements can be used for the assessment with a rank for each statement; these statements can also be used a basis for an audit check sheet. If a rank is used, then each topic can be assessed with a spider chart to show which area needs improvement.

TPM Requirements Assessment

Use the following ranking for each statement:

0 - No system or not yet defined

1 - Training completed by majority of team; implementation started

2 - Lack of a system, but some activities are performed regularly

3 - System defined and practiced daily in some areas, but missing some process steps such as a lack of procedures and check sheets, training or evaluation not regularly performed, lack of regular reviews

4 - System defined, stable, controlled; improvements achieved

5 - System well-defined, complete control, effectively performed, improvements regularly implemented. Demonstrated as a factory showcase, can be a benchmark in some areas

Table 3. 10 TPM Assessment

No.	Topic	Requirements
1	System	Use of computerized maintenance management system (CMMS) or Manufacturing Execution Systems (MES) for TPM implementation
2	System	Yearly overall roadmap assessment to determine system progress from: Run to Failure to Total Productive Maintenance to Industry 4.0 standard
3	System	Daily Routine (DR): responsibilities, issues list, setting priorities, weekly and monthly reviews, weekend and holiday planning (including type of emergency support, contact details)
4	System	Work order management system, database or other system
5	System	Regular online software backups for equipment programs
6	System	Programmable logic controller (PLC) software updated and managed for each PLC
7	System	Safety and security systems: how to check standby plant and equipment, emergency systems, safety valves, alarms, trip devices, machine guards
8	System	Direct Labor worker's PM schedule adherence and timeliness to perform the required PM
9	Metrics	Overall equipment effectiveness (OEE): What is the process for obtaining, displaying and taking action for the OEE metrics? Who is responsible? Where is information posted? Are unfavorable limits defined with immediate actions taken when exceeded? Who analyzes? What is the frequency for analyzing: during shift, end of shift, daily? Which functions review this as a part of their DR?
10	Metrics	Mean time to repair (MTTR) and mean time between failures (MTBF): What is the process for obtaining, displaying and taking action for these metrics? Who is responsible? Where is information posted? Are unfavorable limits defined with immediate actions taken when exceeded? Who analyzes?
11	Metrics	Work Order and Emergency Work Order compliance-accuracy for completion of work, quality of work (no further adjustments), qualified resources utilized, and work orders completed within budgeted time

No.	Topic	Requirements
12	Equipment	Manufacturing equipment is identified with an asset identification number and corresponding location on factory floor layout
13	Equipment	Equipment list showing key spare and serviceable parts, tooling, fixtures, and jigs, identified with an asset identification number and corresponding location identified on factory floor layout
14	Training	Skills matrix of maintenance staff and skill levels for: electrical high/low voltage, mechanical, pneumatic, gas, steam, motors, PLC programming, specific process technologies, CMMS/MES training, total productive maintenance training, and system for maintaining certifications
15	Training	List of monthly maintenance education courses provided in-house or externally with matrix defined for participation
16	Training	Incentives defined for maintaining certification levels and for obtaining new certifications
17	Training	Tracking method and incentives defined for direct labor workers, staff, supervisors, and management to regularly participate in in-house and external maintenance courses
18	Analysis	Equipment maintenance diagnosis capability assessment using Root Cause and Corrective Action (RCCA) techniques
19	Analysis	Repair or replacement responsibility: in-house within 2 hours, local contractor within 8 hours; contractor contact details available on night shift and weekend shifts?
20	Analysis	Documented or software diagnostic Fault Tree Analysis or troubleshooting guide defined for each piece of equipment. List of equipment without diagnostics or FTA available?
21	Analysis	Escalation Matrix for equipment downtime response in the event equipment is down for *x* amount of time (what happens on second shift, weekends)
22	Analysis	Lubrication: analysis, schedule, locations identified with type of lubrication
23	Analysis	Machine Potential Failure Mode and Effects Analysis (Machine PFMEA) documented for all process equipment

No.	Topic	Requirements
24	Analysis	Vibration, stroboscopes, tachometers, infrared camera, electric motor circuit analysis, oil analysis, ultrasonic, visual, and other predictive maintenance tools used on a defined schedule with historical data used for comparison or contractor based with data results, trend, analysis, and recommendations provided for process equipment and list of defined equipment not having predictive maintenance and reason?
25	Documentation	Equipment preventive maintenance check sheet for operator and maintenance team with color photos and clearly identified locations
26	Documentation	General standards and specifications for purchase of new equipment
27	Documentation	Changeover standard operating procedures, including timing and plans to reduce changeover timing
28	Documentation	Machine manuals available and quickly accessible for each machine; supplier contact details updated
29	Planning	Maintenance budget planned yearly, reviewed and updated monthly with actions to meet timing plan
30	Planning	Benchmarking — what specific system, process or activity to benchmark, by whom, how to produce, how to use the data; and assess by skills/labor, costs
31	Audits	Facility condition assessments and action plans
32	Audits	Energy management audits
33	Audits	Regulatory assessments
34	Audits	Safety and security assessment for each machine, process, and piece of manufacturing support equipment, such as air compressors and transformers (can be linked to human resources, health, safety and environment)
35	Audits	Assessment of spare parts storeroom organization, storage, retrieval and obsolescence

No.	Topic	Requirements
36	Audits	Is a contractor assessment performed? How often? What is included? Feedback or response timing? Accuracy of quote, including timing for performing work? Reliability of services performed? Onsite compliance with safety and security requirements? Assessment reviews conducted with contractors to improve their performance?
37	Audits	Participation and maintenance staff's effectiveness in performing Layered Process Audits (LPAs) and Reverse Process Failure Mode and Effects Analysis
38	Cost	Yearly assessment of the previous year's monthly maintenance actual costs versus budget. Actions taken on-time with expected results achieved
39	Cost	Maintenance team's understanding and use of financial variance metrics analysis to operational KPI and activities
40	Strategy	Defined upgrade plans aligned to Industry 4.0 (fourth industrial revolution). Strategy framework defined, plans, budgets, and resources identified

Work Order Activity Assessment

The following questions can be used to determine your organization's quality of work order maintenance activities. Rank each question with a score:

A   All the time
B   Most of the time
C   Some of the time
D   Never

In a Plan, Do, Check, Act cycle with Maintenance, Production, and/or Quality staff, answer the following questions, then analyze the ones ranked as C or D to determine opportunities for improvement. Prioritize, then define plans for improvement. After one year, conduct this survey again, repeating the above PDCA; this time also consider reviewing answers ranked as A or B. Sample 20-30 work orders (including some emergency work orders if available) over the past month or so, then answer and rank the following questions:

1. Are all work orders filled out correctly?
2. Are work orders validated at the machine or place of work?
3. Are supervisors given an opportunity to contribute to planning and scheduling work orders?
4. Is there a documented active response system, feedback, or method for supervisors to contribute to planning and scheduling work orders?
5. Are work order completion times, locations or specific start/stop times scrutinized, confirmed, or validated by production?
6. Are materials and tools prepared in defined staging area with a check sheet noting the list of materials, tools, equipment needed before the work order is fulfilled?
7. Is feedback encouraged and documented from supervisors and production workers regarding quality and timing?
8. Are the minimum number of maintenance people fulfilling the work order?
9. Are uncertified maintenance people fulfilling work orders that require certified maintenance people?
10. Are sketches or specifications made when required before the start of a work order?
11. Is planning of work orders up-to-date (i.e., no backlog of unplanned work orders)?
12. Are recurring jobs analyzed for quality of work performed?
13. Does the work order planning system analyze MTTR and MTBF?
14. Does the work order planning system adjust or make predictions?
15. Are work orders properly coded as to type of work? Is correct authorization obtained?
16. Are errors in coding regularly reviewed with maintenance staff?
17. Are planning and scheduling visits held with various work area personnel and contractors before work is performed?
18. Is factory or equipment shutdown information given to production?
19. Is a monthly calendar of factory or equipment planned-shutdown information provided to production?
20. Are daily and weekly maintenance schedules consistently issued on time to production for planning?
21. Are closed work orders audited to ensure proper work has been conducted?
22. Are contract jobs properly charged to work orders?
23. Are contract jobs bid on by several contractors?
24. Are contract job costs negotiated before work is conducted?
25. Are contractors met with annually to discuss upcoming needs?
26. Do contractors sign and understand the safety and security requirements?
27. Are contract jobs audited for completion of work?
28. Is a full day's work scheduled every day for every maintenance person?
29. Are work orders scheduled according to a priority?
30. If a work order cannot be scheduled within the desired interval, is the originator notified?
31. Are backlogs reviewed regularly to identify overdue work orders and actions?

32. Are arrangements made with human resources and security for special safety or entry permits for external contractors?
33. Are the necessary staff scheduled for minor repairs?
34. Is the effectiveness of the maintenance work time and cost estimates checked after job completion?
35. Are preventive maintenance inspection sheets checked for completion or issues?
36. Is lower-priority unscheduled work included if priority work is completed?
37. Are all TPM work orders properly scheduled according to established frequencies?
38. Is the backlog of corrective work orders under control?

Chapter 30 – Financial Variance Analysis

Management, staff, supervisors, and even direct labor workers evaluate unfavorable variances throughout their work day and try to correct or improve the situation. Generally, a variance is the difference between an actual result versus a plan or between an actual result versus standard. Finance defines a variance as the difference between actual costs of production and the standard cost of production. Standard costs, budgets, or rates are based upon historical production data or estimated costs when developing a business case study. Standard rates are established yearly on a per unit basis. Standard rates are utilized in establishing the annual operating plan; see Chapter 37 for more information.

Variances are related to product sales, product being produced, direct related manufacturing materials, tools, supplies, procurement costs of raw materials, and various direct related work activities to transform raw materials to a saleable product. Each function has a responsibility to evaluate variances, determine root causes, implement corrective actions, improve their KPIs, as well as to perform their work responsibilities with the underlying principle being Plan, Do, Check, Act.

The Plan, Do, Check, Act (PDCA) model is also known as the Deming or Shewhart cycle. This model is a 4-step management iterative method for control and continuous improvement. A simple description of the model follows:

- Plan – identify, define, or revise a plan to make an improvement
- Do – test the improvement on a small scale
- Check – analyze or measure the effectiveness
- Act – determine whether the "Do" phase is an improvement or not. If successful, then implement the change or improvement, if not consider the "Plan" phase once again.

Financial Variance Analysis Metric Reviews

Financial variance metrics are calculated and distributed by the finance function to various management and some support staff. Metrics are presented by any or all of the following: by product family, by product name/number, by product name/number and customer. Reviews of both significant favorable and unfavorable metric results are analyzed. Reviews can be formal or informal with reasons or action items defined. Operations and other functions will identify special causes for the significant unfavorable variances and perform a root cause and corrective action.

Each month finance will report the actual results, annual monthly budget amount, and a flexed budget amount. A flexed budget amount adjusts the original plan/budget for changes in the volume or amount of activity that can be compared to the actual results. The flexed budget amounts only vary with items that vary with output, so fixed overhead is not adjusted. A flexed budget is based upon standard rates. The main items in a flex budget are:

- Sales
- Direct Material
- Direct Labor
- Variable Overhead

Illustration – Income Statement Plan, Flex, and Actual

The following figure shows a typical manufacturing monthly income statement for a specific month with the annual operating plan, flex budget, actual results, actual less flex, and a favorable or unfavorable status for each line item.

Table 3. 11 Income Statement

Month and Year - XX

Income Statement	Annual Operating Plan	Flex Budget	Actual Results	Actual - Flex	Status
Total Sales	**$791,224**	**$783,557**	**$780,838**	**($2,719)**	Unfavorable
Cost of Goods Sold:					
Direct Material	$269,533	$282,074	$295,237	**$13,163**	Unfavorable
Direct Labor	139,050	145,507	152,284	**$6,777**	Unfavorable
Variable Overhead	61,949	64,875	67,948	**$3,074**	Unfavorable
Total Cost of Goods Sold	$470,532	$492,456	$515,469	**$23,014**	Unfavorable
Depreciation and Amortization	25,000	25,000	25,000	**$0**	-
Fixed Overhead	176,150	176,150	175,603	**($547)**	Favorable
Operating Income	**$119,541**	**$89,952**	**$64,766**	**($25,186)**	Unfavorable
Income Tax	39,449	29,684	21,373	**($8,311)**	-
Net Profit	**$80,093**	**$60,268**	**$43,393**	**($16,874)**	Unfavorable

For month XX, the Annual Operating Plan sales shows $791,224 and the actual sales results are $780,838. Adjusting the flex budget using standard price and actual quantities show flex budget sales of $783,557. Actual sales less flex sales shows ($2,719). Since actual sales are less than Flex Budget, the status is shown as unfavorable. All other line items are defined in the same way showing either a favorable or unfavorable status. Further analysis of the income statement requires a cost accounting system that has defined standard costs by product family or product name/number. Each finished good product has a specific bill of material that is itemized showing the amount or quantities of raw materials, components, sub-assemblies, and other direct materials.

Illustration – Favorable or Unfavorable Status

The following figure shows a Favorable or Unfavorable indicator when analyzing actual costs and standard or budgeted costs. When actual costs are less than standard or budgeted costs, the status is Favorable. Alternatively, when actual costs are greater than budget or standard, the status is Unfavorable. The opposite is true for sales, operating income, and net profit. When actual sales, operating income, or net profit are greater than standard or flex budget, the status is Favorable.

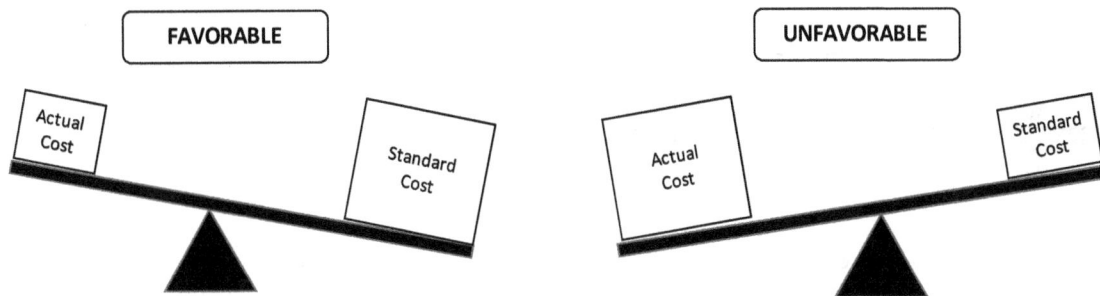

Figure 3. 9 Favorable or Unfavorable Costs

Financial Variance Metrics

- Sales Variance – Price, Volume, Mix, and Quantity
- Direct Material Variance – Price, Usage, Mix, and Yield
- Direct Labor Rate Variance – Rate, Efficiency, and Idle Time
- Variable Overhead Variance – Spending and Efficiency
- Fixed Overhead Variance – Spending and Volume

Illustration – Standard and actual product details

The following illustration is a breakdown of the above income statement into standard and actual details for specific product families. There 5 different product families, namely A, B, C, D, and E. The tables are defined as:

- Standard sales price and quantity sold
- Standard costs per unit
- Actual sales price and quantity sold
- Actual costs per unit

Table 3. 12 Standard and actual product details

Product Family	Qty / month	Sale Price	Total Sales	DM	DL	VOH	Contribution Margin/Unit	Total Contribution Margin	Standard Mix ratio
	Standard sales price and quantity sold				Standard costs per unit				
A	13,000	$23.99	$311,870	$8.40	$4.32	$2.16	$9.11	$118,430	47.0%
B	12,000	$24.99	$299,880	$9.25	$4.25	$1.50	$9.99	$119,880	43.4%
C	2,000	$59.99	$119,980	$16.80	$9.60	$4.80	$28.79	$57,580	7.2%
D	500	$79.99	$39,995	$12.00	$11.20	$6.56	$50.23	$25,115	1.8%
E	150	$129.99	$19,499	$19.50	$18.20	$3.90	$88.39	$13,259	0.5%
		Std Total	$791,224						

Product Family	Qty / month	Sale Price	Total Sales	DM	DL	VOH	Actual Mix ratio
	Actual sales price and quantity Sold				Actual costs per unit sold		
A	12,667	$23.99	$303,881	$8.89	$4.57	$2.29	46.8%
B	11,552	$24.99	$288,684	$9.63	$4.42	$1.56	42.7%
C	2,118	$58.99	$124,941	$17.22	$9.84	$4.92	7.8%
D	601	$78.99	$47,473	$12.60	$11.76	$6.89	2.2%
E	122	$129.99	$15,859	$20.19	$18.85	$4.04	0.5%
		Act Total	$780,838				

Illustration – Sales Variance

The following table shows the sales variance ratios for each product family.

Table 3. 13 Sales Variance

Product Family	SPV	SVV @ Std Price	SVV @ CM	SMV	SQV
	Sales Variance Analysis				
A	$0	($7,989)	($3,034)	($231)	($1,426)
B	$0	($11,196)	($4,476)	($808)	($1,942)
C	($2,118)	$7,079	$3,397	$366	$245
D	($601)	$8,079	$5,073	$121	$91
E	$0	($3,640)	($2,475)	$0	($12)
Total	($2,719)	($1,514)	($552)	($552)	($3,045)

Sales Price Variance = SPV

SPV = actual price x actual units sold – standard price x actual units sold

SPV is the change of sales between actual and standard price. A positive sales price variance is favorable and a negative number is unfavorable. A positive variance may be due to inflation, market conditions, or sales team influence. However, having a higher actual sales price than standard sales price may result in lower overall sales as demand may reduce. The SPV for product family A and C is calculated as:

SPV_A = $23.99 x 12,667 - $23.99 x 12,667 = 0

$SPV_C = \$58.99 \times 2{,}118 - \$59.99 \times 2{,}118 = (\$2{,}118)$

Product A standard and actual prices are the same, but Product C actual sale price is $1 lower, resulting in a negative SPV. Overall SPV for the month for all products is unfavorable by ($2,719). The cause for lower sale prices needs to be analyzed and determined. The sales function should define the causes and determine the impact on forecasted sales. Lower sales prices may be needed to increase sales volume or prevent competitors from making a sale.

Sales Volume Variance = SVV

SVV = (actual units sold – budgeted unit quantities sold) x standard unit price

Alternative for marginal costs and profit reconciliation:

SVV = (actual units sold – budgeted unit quantities sold) x standard contribution margin

Or:

SVV = (actual units sold – budgeted unit quantities sold) x profit per unit

SVV is the change in revenue, profit, or contribution caused by the difference between actual and budgeted sales quantity.

$$\text{Contribution margin per unit} = \frac{\text{total revenue} - \text{total variable costs}}{\text{total units sold}}$$

Or:

Unit sale price – Direct Material cost – Direct Labor cost – Variable Overhead cost. Contribution Margin (CM) is the amount by which sales exceeds variable costs. The higher the contribution margin or profit, the better. Having a very low or negative contribution margin indicates the product is not profitable. Management may use CM when making pricing decisions, especially when discounted pricing or special pricing is needed to make a sale.

SVV Product $A_{StdPrice}$ = (12,667-13,000) x $23.99 = ($7,989)

SVV Product A_{CM} = (12,667 – 13,000) x $9.12 = ($3,034)

SVV Product $C_{StdPrice}$ = (2,118 – 2,000) x $59.99 = $7,079

SVV Product C_{CM} = (2,118 – 2,000) x $28.80 = $3,397

Product A sales quantities are lower than plan by 333 units and Product C sales quantity are higher than plan by 118 units. Overall SVV for all products at standard price is unfavorable by ($1,514), whereas SVV at contribution margin is ($552). Product B SVV is the most unfavorable amount at ($11,196) and ($4,476) for standard price and contribution margin respectively. The causes for Product A, B, and D lower sale quantities need to be analyzed and known. The sales function should define the causes and determine the impact on forecasted sales.

Sales Mix Variance = SMV

SMV = actual units sold x (actual sales mix % - budgeted sales mix %) x budgeted contribution margin per unit. SMV is the change in contribution caused by the variation in the proportion of different products sold from the standard mix as individual product profitability and unit sales quantities are different for each product. A change in the sales mix of the different products sold can alter the overall net profit, even when the total sales are flat or relatively the same.

SMV Product A = 12,667 x (46.8% - 47.0%) x $9.12 = ($231)

Overall SMV for all products is unfavorable by ($552). The sales function needs to analyze the sales mix ratio and determine the cause. Management should regularly review the sales mix variance against the sales commission structure and make plans for improvement, such as incentivizing higher profitable product families.

Sales Quantity Variance

SQV = (actual quantity sold – budgeted quantity sold) x budgeted sales mix % x budgeted contribution margin per unit. SQV is the change in standard contribution due to actual and budgeted number of units sold.

SQV Product A = (12,667 – 13,000) x 47.0% x $9.12 = ($1,426)

Overall SQV for all products is unfavorable by ($3,045), with Product Family A and B contributing negatively by ($3,368). Sales function needs to analyze SQV and its causes. Possible causes can be market driven or competitor driven. Other possible causes can be related to the sales commission structure, price changes of different products, or the fact that the company recently released a new product impacting current sales quantities of a more established product.

Illustration – Direct Material Variance

The following table shows the Direct Material variance ratios, along with the Quality yield %, material consumed, and revised standard for each product family. The variance ratios are defined with examples below the table. Quality yield % defines the standard quality yield and the actual yield for the product sold. Actual yield % may change from time period to time period, but the standard yield is fixed according to the annual operating plan. Material consumed is calculated as the actual quantity sold divided by the standard quality yield. For example: Product A material standard consumed is 12,667 / 96.5% = 13,126, and actual material consumed is 12,667 / 91.11% = 13,903. Revised standard quantity is calculated as actual material consumed multiplied by the standard quality yield %. Therefore, Product A revised standard quantity is 13,903 x 96.5% = 13,416.

Table 3. 14 Direct Material Variance

| Direct Material Variance Analysis | | | | | | | | |
| Direct Material Variance Ratios | | | | Quality Yield % | | Material consumed | | Revised |
Product Family	DMPV	DMUV	DMMV	DMYV	Std	Act	Std	Act	Std
A	$6,812	$6,527	$4,091	($6,292)	96.50%	91.11%	13,126	13,903	13,416
B	$4,749	$4,579	$4,338	($4,403)	96.25%	92.44%	12,002	12,497	12,028
C	$974	$974	$2,453	($907)	93.71%	91.39%	2,260	2,318	2,172
D	$407	$384	$576	($360)	92.95%	88.50%	647	679	631
E	$96	$98	$254	($78)	90.82%	87.70%	134	139	126
Total	$13,038	$12,561	$11,711	($12,040)			28,169	29,536	

Direct Material Price Variance

DMPV= actual quantity x actual cost – actual quantity x standard material cost

DMPV Product A = 13,903 x $8.89 – 13,903 x $8.40 = $6,812

DMPV is the change between actual cost of direct material and the standard cost of quantity purchase. A positive variance is unfavorable. An unfavorable variance may be due to raw material and component market price increases, a company's decision to use a higher priced raw material, higher priced component supplier, a company's inability to buy at the standard rate, increased negotiating power by suppliers, or loss of pricing discounts due to lower procurement volumes.

Direct Material Usage Variance

DMUV = (actual quantity – standard quantity) x standard material cost

DMUV Product A = (13,903 – 13,126) x $8.40 = $6,527

DMUV is the change between actual quantity of material used and the standard consumption material of material for a specific quantity. A positive variance is unfavorable. An unfavorable variance may be due to higher production scrap as a result of worker's lower capabilities due to training or supervision, lower raw material or component quality, or lower production process quality capabilities.

Direct Material Mix Variance

DMMV = (actual mix quantity - standard mix quantity) x standard material cost

DMMV Product A = (13,903 – 13,416) x $8.40 = $4,091

DMMV is the change between cost of actual proportion of materials and the standard proportion of materials consumed. A positive variance is unfavorable. An unfavorable variance may be due to a use of a higher cost ratio mix compared to standard, or higher production scrap due to a different mix ratio than standard.

Direct Material Yield Variance

DMYV = (actual yield – standard yield) x standard material cost

DMYV Product A = (12,667 – 13,416) x $8.40 = ($6,292)

DMYV is the difference between actual amount of material used and the standard amount expected to be used for a given level of input, which is then multiplied by the standard cost of materials. A positive variance is unfavorable. An unfavorable variance typically is in the form of production material scrap, material quality level change, material spoilage due to handling or storage, and material losses due to a logistics issue.

Illustration – Direct Labor Variance

The following table shows the Direct Labor variance.

Table 3. 15 Direct Labor Variance

Direct Labor Variance Analysis				Labor Hours			Cost per hour	
Product Family	DLRV	DLEV	DLITV	Std	Act	IDLE Hrs	Std	Act
A	($14,868)	$3,348	$13,198	2,624	2,779	611		
B	($13,150)	$2,095	$10,087	2,361	2,458	467		
C	($5,511)	$562	$2,894	1,004	1,030	134	$21.60	$16.25
D	($1,883)	$367	$907	335	352	42		
E	($626)	$86	$238	113	117	11		
Total	(36,038)	$6,458	$27,324	6,437	6,736	1,265		

Direct Labor Rate Variance

DLRV = actual hours x actual rate – actual hours x standard rate

DLRV Product A = 2,779 x $16.25 – 2,779 x $21.60 = ($14,868)

DLRV is a change between actual cost of direct labor and the standard cost of direct labor used. A negative variance is favorable. Having a favorable rate can be due to the use of a strong temporary direct labor work force. Also, the standard labor rate could have been set high during annual planning due to a high cost, long-term labor work force.

Direct Labor Efficiency Variance

DLEV = actual hours x standard rate – standard hours x standard rate

DLEV Product A = 2,779 x $21.60 – 2,624 x $21.60 = $3,348

DLEV is a change between standard cost of actual number of direct labor hours used and the same standard hours of direct labor hours. A positive variance is unfavorable. An unfavorable variance is caused by workers not meeting the productivity expectations. There are many possibilities for not meeting expectations, such as: poor supervision, poor training, low morale, low skilled workers, poor material movement coordination, lower quality materials resulting in handling more materials, poor production planning, not enough manpower to operate efficiently, and lower machine capacity or capability due to equipment issues.

Direct Labor Idle Time Variance

DLITV = total number of idle hours x standard labor rate

DLITV Product A = 611 x $21.60 = $13,198

DLITV is the cost of idle time of direct labor that could have been used in production but was not due to downtime. A positive variance is unfavorable. An unfavorable variance may be due to the same factors as direct labor efficiency variance.

Illustration – Variable Overhead Variance

Table 3. 16 Variable Overhead Efficiency

Variable O/H Var. Analysis				Cost/hour
Product Family	VOESV	VOEV	Act Cost	Std
A	$5,060	$1,491	$31,794	
B	($4,136)	933	$19,510	
C	$1,496	250	$11,405	$9.62
D	$1,292	164	$4,678	
E	($564)	38	$562	
Total	$3,149	$2,876	$67,949	

Variable Overhead Spending Variance

VOSV = actual manufacturing variable overhead expenditure – actual hours x standard variable overhead rate per hour

VOSV Product A = $31,794 – 2,779 x $9.62 = $5,060

VOSV is the change between variable production overhead expenses incurred and the standard variable overhead expenditure. A positive variance is unfavorable. An unfavorable expense may be due to indirect materials and supply price increases, equipment continuously remaining on when the equipment is planned to be off, process operations requiring increased indirect materials and supplies due to product or production changes, increased waste of indirect materials and supplies, improper cost allocation, a higher mix of indirect labor costs above standard, lack of indirect controls in purchasing and production usage, or production part repair costs higher than standard.

Variable Overhead Efficiency Variance

VOEV = actual hours x standard variable overhead rate per hour – standard hours x standard variable overhead rate per hour

VOEV Product A = 2,779 x $9.62 – 2,624 x $9.62 = $1,491

VOEV is a change between standard variable overhead due to difference between standard number of manufacturing hours and actual hours worked. A positive variance is unfavorable. An unfavorable variance can be due to low total productive maintenance capabilities, low employee motivation, low worker and supervisor skillset, use of different direct or indirect material causing higher defect rates or longer time to process.

Illustration- Fixed Overhead Variance

Table 3. 17 Fixed Overhead

Fixed Overhead Var. Analysis			
FOSV	FOVV	FOTV	FOAR
($547)	$8,544	($8,997)	$6.25

Fixed Overhead Spending Variance

FOSV = actual fixed overhead expenditure – budgeted fixed overhead

FOSV = $175,603 - $176,150 = ($547)

FOSV is a change between budgeted and actual fixed production overhead. A negative number is favorable. A favorable variance can be due to any one of the fixed expenses that were not realized to the full amount as budgeted. Fixed expenses can be management, indirect staff, and supervisor salaries, benefits, insurance, building lease, long term automobile rental expense, utilities, building maintenance, security, and any other factory related expenses that do not vary with production volume.

Fixed Overhead Volume Variance

FOVV = absorbed fixed overhead – budgeted fixed overhead

FOVV = 29,536 x $6.25 – 28,169 x $6.25 = $8,544

FOVV is a change between absorbed fixed overhead and budgeted fixed overhead. Absorbed fixed overhead is the amount of fixed overhead costs applied to the production. Absorbed fixed overhead = actual production quantity x fixed overhead absorption rate.

Fixed Overhead Absorption Rate

Fixed overhead absorption rate (FOAR)

$$= \frac{\text{budgeted fixed overhead}}{\text{budgeted production quantity}}$$

FOAR can also be defined using labor hours or machine hours instead of production quantities — this depends upon the company's manufacturing strategy of being more machine or labor based. A positive variance is favorable. A favorable variance indicates that more fixed costs were applied towards production quantity than budgeted.

Fixed Overhead Total Variance

FOTV = actual fixed overhead – absorbed fixed overhead

FOTV = $ 175,603 – 29,536 x $6.25 = ($8,997)

FOTV is a change between actual fixed overhead and absorbed fixed overhead production. A negative variance is favorable.

Key Steps to Establish Financial Variance Analysis Reviews

1. General manager and finance manager determine the financial variance metrics to evaluate the company's performance and decide the meeting frequency to review the variance analysis metrics. They also decide the method to present the variance metric, such as by product name, by product family, or by product and customer. If there has not been any previous Financial Variance Analysis (FVA) metrics or meetings, the general manager and finance manager should select a few metrics to start this activity.

2. General manager and finance manager to determine whether they have the component parts of the metric, such as the budgeted or standard rates for the variance metrics selected and the ability to obtain reliable accurate and timely actual data. For new parts, the business case costs can be used. For more information on Business Case, see Chapter 36, Pursuing New Business. For parts already in production, the standard or budgeted rates can be based upon historical average costs with a defined set of logic parameters and methodology. The logic parameters and methodology are unique to every company as long as the standard rate calculation is clear, consistent, meets Generally Accepted Accounting Practices (GAAP), and has supporting details. A master file containing standard rate details, logic parameters, methodology, and notes to be saved for the subsequent planning years.

3. General manager, finance manager, and assigned support staff define the business process activities for extracting actual data and define the reporting

scheme. An audit of the business process and report needs to be conducted to ensure the information to be reported is correct.

4. The general manager and finance manager decide which staff to participate in the evaluation of the Financial Variance metrics. Responsibilities for each metric need to be defined. Responsibilities for each variance metric can be determined using a RASIC matrix. Specific RASIC roles are to be defined for preparing the financial variance metrics and gathering supporting information for significant variance issues, including defining the issue/problem statement, defining the root cause, containment, corrective, and preventive action.

5. Finance defines a monthly calendar for distributing the FVA report and defines a date and time for a meeting to discuss the variance details, issues, and action plans. The calendar needs to be fixed, such as once a month — perhaps the second or third Wednesday every month following management's Daily Routine activities. Finance should update their functional Daily Routine to include the business process activities and timing each month.

6. Finance provides training to functional managers and support staff, as they must understand the metric definition, formula, possible causes for unfavorable and favorable variances, their role, and expectations. Finance conducts training by describing the details for each of the financial statements, namely the Income Statement, Balance Sheet, and Cash Flow Statement. The bulk of the training consists of real company examples using each of the FVA metrics, RASIC matrix, and relating the FVA metric to operational KPIs and other activities. Also, the training should include the monthly FVA meeting format, objective, and expectations.

7. Prior to the FVA meeting, finance should make the FVA report showing the budget, flex budget, actual results, and highlighting significant variance amounts. In addition, finance is to plot the variances on a month-to-month graph to show possible trends, with significant trends highlighted. The general manager and finance manager should identify the definition of a significant variance, such as any variance over a certain dollar amount needs to be investigated, or an unfavorable trend over a specific time period.

8. Finance leads the Financial Variance Analysis (FVA) meeting and presents the FVA report. Functional managers and staff present their supporting information and have a discussion on significant variances to determine what actions to take. Both significant favorable and unfavorable variances need to be analyzed.

9. Functional managers and staff need to match individual significant variance metric details to historic operation's activities. The ERP (Enterprise Resource Planning), MES (Manufacturing Execution System), MOM (Manufacturing Operations Management) or other related production and Quality databases may have the ability of easily extracting these details with detailed descriptions of the performance issues.

10. Management and staff decipher historic process record details to identify the trigger point(s) at which the process started the unfavorable trend. Then, study the situation, identify solution(s), and implement in a way that the historic event does not recur.

Financial Variance Analysis Questions

Why is it difficult to match a significant FVA metric to historic operation's data?

Many companies have this concern. This can be improved by training and investing into improved operational controls, methods and systems. Management can delegate a team to study the FVA metric and business process activities, or delegate a team to initiate a 90 Day Challenge (see Chapter 38 for more information). Also, companies tend to have an abundance of operation's data, but it may not be organized for identifying financial improvement opportunities. The main difficulty is that there is no proper data link between a FVA metric and operation KPI, activity, or that the link is so broad that the system shows an unfiltered and excessive amount of raw data. So, the employee spends more time extracting and filtering data than analyzing it.

Is it really that important to match FVA metrics to operation's KPIs and activities?

It is absolutely necessary to match FVA metrics to operation's KPIs and activities to determine the profitability and control at the lowest common denominator, such as for an individual product. By understanding the profitability at the lowest level, other business decisions can be made, such as pursuit of similar business or to work on specific projects to become more profitable.

Why not just concentrate on improving and controlling operational KPIs?

Concentrating on improving operational KPIs is extremely important. However, just concentrating on improving operational KPIs does not necessarily mean the company is profitable or will remain profitable. If all products' profitability is known, then future operation projects can be ranked by impact to overall profitability. However, if the individual product profitability are unknown for the coming months, how does the company decide which projects to undertake? Or, in other words, what criteria is used to undertake projects?

How much time should be spent on FVA metric data collection and analysis?

In most companies the raw data collection for matching an FVA metric to an historic metric takes much longer than the analysis. Use the 7 Basic Quality Tools defined in Chapter 8 to analyze the data sets. If your company already has a query database, auto-generated reports, or other swift means to match significant FVA metrics to operation's KPIs and activities, then analyzing all products in depth as to the cause(s) would take a very short amount of time. Defining a plan to improve the situation may take considerably longer than the analysis, as the plan may have to cover multiple products over multiple shifts and days. If your company does not have a query database or other swift means to match the data, then it may take hours to collect the data and the data may not be accurate or comprehensive. Spending hours collecting this historic data is a waste of time, as it means plans or actions are not being undertaken. Consider studying the amount of time to collect and match the FVA metrics to KPIs and operation activities — this may be a future high priority project.

How do you know the standard rate or budget is right or correct?

The correct way to establish a standard rate or budgeted amounts is to use known historic information with some logic applied. Or, for new products, the business case amounts are used. Defining the standard rate or budget will involve some probability or estimate. Each month comparisons are made between actual and standard rates. Some months there may be favorable or unfavorable financial metrics even though the volumes may be the same. Also, note that standard rates and budgets are defined for the upcoming year. Standard rates and budgets are used to develop the annual operating plan. Over the course of the coming year, many changes occur in the market and in operations, but the standard rates and budgets will not change until the next planning cycle.

What happens when you cannot explain the variance?

Most significant favorable and unfavorable FVA metric results can be explained by an assessment of the historic data with a special cause(s) identified. When the special cause is identified, a corrective action must be put in place. However, in some cases a special cause cannot be identified for an unfavorable financial variance. This may be due to the operation's performance is within the running range of acceptance. Or, in other words, there may be several operational factors that all are within specification but occur in a certain unfavorable financial way. In these cases, there may be no particular reason to generate an action item. However, if the specific FVA metric shows an unfavorable trend, then a more detailed investigation may be needed resulting in tighter operational control specifications being implemented, or communication response timings are to be faster. In addition, more sophisticated analytical tools may need to be utilized.

Chapter 31 - People

Each of the following topics are related to working with people. As a manager or staff member, you will gain many different experiences over your career regarding the following:

- Resource Gap Analysis
- Attracting, Recruiting and Interviewing
- On-boarding, Mentoring and Promoting
- Challenge, Confrontation and Compromise
- Warning, Discipline and Termination
- Transitions and Re-structuring
- Interim Assignments and Projects
- Performance Appraisals and Pay for Performance
- Exit Interviews
- Becoming a Leader

Resource Gap Analysis

There are several templates and human resource assessment tools available to determine whether an increase or decrease in staff is needed. More staff may be needed during a busy time of year. Alternatively, fewer workers may be needed if there is a downturn in sales or when a new process technology is introduced. Each month the Income Statement (Profit and Loss Statement) shows the variable and fixed labor costs. Understanding how labor impacts profitability, customer service and quality is very important. For example, adding a staff position increases fixed labor costs. Management needs to justify this staff position so profitability, customer service, quality, or other business metrics are not affected in an unfavorable way. However, note that initial costs may increase especially for new projects being industrialized but long term metrics become more favorable.

When work is not being done or not done well, the manager has to understand the root cause and implement both a short-term and long-term containment action and corrective action. The manager should seek out support and/or escalate this issue when weekly work starts to fall behind.

This can be noticed and discussed during and after the DR functional reviews. While this is not an immediate cause for hiring new people, it could be an opportunity for changing some people's responsibilities. Searching for additional staff, interviewing, on-boarding and training require significant time from the manager and staff, so changing responsibilities or improving an internal process is most likely a better short-term solution. When hiring due to attrition, the same applies: Can responsibilities change or an internal process be improved? If so, then a replacement is not needed. Responsibilities can be adjusted or a replacement can be hired, but remember that significant effort is needed to bring on additional staff. Also, the

271

reason for attrition should be tracked over time to determine whether there is a systemic problem with a function or manager.

Attracting, Recruiting, and Interviewing

If your company has well-known products or a great reputation, people are generally more inclined to be attracted to it. Recruiting these people is relatively easy, whether through a recruiting agency or jobsite posting. The key is to know what you are looking for, and how to know when you have found the right fit or almost the right fit.

If your company is not well-recognized, how do you attract talent? There are several characteristics that may attract potential employees: location, position title, responsibilities, product, processes, technologies, salary and benefits, professional development support, colleague reference or networking. If you interview applicants, describe your work environment, culture, and employee expectations. Initially interviewing by phone to narrow down selections is helpful before face-to-face interviews with facility tours, etc. The first section of this book discussed the onboarding process in detail.

How do you know you found the right or almost-right candidate, and what is next?

Attracting and recruiting can be done via online jobsite postings, recruiting agencies and advertising displays around your company. Once you start receiving résumés, someone will have to screen the potential candidates. This person has to assess whether the candidate fulfills the basic requirements. You may need several rounds of screenings, depending upon the number of résumés received for a specific position, or the hiring manager may want to perform all the screenings. Screenings usually consist of confirming or checking degrees, qualifications, experience that meets the requirements and references. These days, online social media and professional website postings also should be reviewed, such as Twitter, Facebook and LinkedIn activity.

After screening, the selected potential hires should be scheduled for interviews in a defined block of time, such as within one week, so a clear, fair assessment of all candidates can be made. One way to ensure you have found the right candidate is to have more than one interviewer participate and ask a variety of questions, including specific standard ones, such as:

What contributions or value would you bring to this company?

In what ways are you passionate about what you do?

Why are you leaving your current job?

Also, ask abstract and practical questions to observe the interviewee's composure, quick thinking ability, critical thought, sincerity, and understand their quality and safety mindset.

Some companies have standard interview questions with a rating scale and a comments section for each question, others do a post-interview assessment, and still others are less-formal — they just write notes on the résumés and discuss their opinions.

Some companies hold training sessions to prepare interviewers in proper techniques, and some require group interviews to educate junior staff on interviewing techniques. The interviewee assessment form should include the interviewer name, interviewee name, date, open position title and notes regarding the interview, such as:

- Personality
- Customer service orientation
- Interest in the position
- Company and product knowledge
- Overall impression

- Communication assessment
- Maturity
- Motivation level
- Potential concerns

- Strengths

While the interviewee is responding, the interviewer should be writing an evaluation using a standard template. Be sure to have the interviewee speak more than the interviewers. After each phone interview, face-to-face interview and follow-up interviews, an assessment of the candidate has to be made. Each interviewer should define how they connected with the interviewee. It is important that both the interviewers and interviewee make connections where there is some chemistry, similar past learning experiences, sense of interest and passion for the position work, and whether the interviewee would work well in the culture of the company.

On-boarding, Mentoring, and Promoting

The first day and week for a new hire have already been discussed in Orientation. Once the new employee is on board, the company and new employee should work to identify a mentor or two. A mentor can be the employee's manager, but ideally, others should be sought out to give the employee knowledge in other functions as well as in management. A mentor should have mature experience with the company in order to give advice and orientation to the new hire.

The company should encourage long-term management and staff to seek out and advise junior staff and new employees. The company can encourage mentoring and advising as part of its culture of professional development through short discussions after the functional DR, regular weekly or monthly meetings, specific technical training sessions, private one-on-one discussions, or involvement in projects. Mentoring does not have to be a formal process with objectives set, but in some cases, this is needed. This is true especially when a promotion is on the horizon or change in responsibilities is impending, such as a new project or temporary assignment.

Typically, some people's salaries, benefits, position titles and change of responsibilities occur after annual personnel reviews. Companies with formal employee reviews have standardized evaluation criteria that are completed by both manager and employee that result in sharing a statement, scores, recommended actions or other communications with the employee so they know how they performed previously and what the upcoming objectives are in the future. This process also gives the employee critical feedback on their performance that they can reflect upon and ideally use to modify or improve their results for the next review cycle.

Promoting people based on a performance review process is far better than promoting based upon seniority, opinion, or other informal ways. Employees prefer to have clear, unbiased structure and requirements to fulfill for being considered for a promotion. Managers and staff should reflect on and think about their professional growth opportunities, as well as investigate online or local courses to upgrade skills or increase their functional and technical expertise. Promoting an employee should involve greater responsibilities and clear objectives defined for a certain time period, such as 100 days, so a near-term review can be conducted to ensure the promotion was a success for both the employee and organization. During the performance review, it is the employee's responsibility to demonstrate how their accomplishments align with the company vision, individual and functional KPIs.

Challenge, Confrontation, and Compromise
Going to work and doing the same old thing day in and day out is not so challenging. When the slightest challenge comes about, most people feel energized and engaged. Since everyone is different, management needs to find the balance to motivate and challenge each of their employees. Management should identify the employees who love challenges and those who need a little encouragement. All employees like to receive praise; this needs to be given often both individually and in a group — praise given in groups provides the greatest motivation.

For employees not wanting a challenge and who are not performing well, management has to understand their personal and professional situations and determine whether advice, help or other issues are affecting their interest and commitment. If the employee does not have a special circumstance, perhaps it is time for that employee to look for work elsewhere. It is management's responsibility to identify the low-performing, low-engagement, non-committed employee(s) and work out an exit plan.

When challenged to perform better, some people immediately can get on board, while some need time to contemplate or ask questions, and others may object to the new demand. Challenges or discussions are good as long as they remain positive and not personal. There is a difference between challenge and conflict, and the fuel for the conflict usually is someone's ego. Employees do not want to constantly be in conflict with management, but they do understand and can accept heated debates as long as these do not become constant bickering.

When the challenge becomes a conflict, someone needs to handle it so the organization is not affected. When conflicts are not escalated, poor performance results, positive culture sours, and employees become discouraged and possibly pursue other work.

During the challenge discussions, compromises may evolve. Compromises can help toward achieving objectives and reduce continual conflict, but compromises do not work well when egos are involved. When the stronger personality or more politically connected employee's opinion outweighs the other's opinion, a less-than-optimal solution results. If the same person is always giving in and accepting a compromise, it is unfair to the organization and ultimately has a negative effect on the organization's performance. A keen manager would recognize this before the conflict takes place and provide a more-open positive forum, ask questions and suggest different ideas.

The manager might even accept the leading ego idea to ease tension but modify it by asking questions and providing a window of opportunity for that person or others to develop an even better solution.

Warning, Discipline, and Termination

Organizations have rules; when these are compromised, the people involved have to be reprimanded immediately. Depending on the offense, severity and occurrence, the immediate manager may issue a verbal warning or written warning, or process a termination. Employees and management must fully understand and promptly enforce all rules with an unbiased, fair and consistent approach. When rules are broken and recourse is not immediate, employees get confused and may want to test other rules or argue about the enforcement timing and criteria.

When verbal or written warnings are issued, other employees should notice that a disciplinary action is being taken but should not be aware of the details — this should be private between the manager and employee, possibly with a human resource representative present. Sometimes rules are broken and the culprit(s) may not be known, which is unacceptable. Within a day, a general meeting or shift meetings for employees should take place so everyone knows the situation. This reinforces the rules and gives notice about the disciplinary actions to be taken. This would be the case if an empty beer can is found in the lunch room garbage can. If the rule states no alcoholic beverages on campus, this would be cause for immediate termination. The rules and disciplinary actions should be clear for warnings, discipline, and termination. Terminating an employee should especially be very clear with instructions for management to follow. Depending upon the termination cause, the employee may not return to their work area, security may need to be aware or present, and human resources and/or IT may need to be involved.

A probationary period should be defined for all new employees. Each week, or at least once a month, the manager should evaluate a new hire and determine whether there is a true fit — if the new hire is trainable, works well within the team and shows a passion for their new position. The probationary period varies by company and reviews can be conducted at 30/60/90 day intervals specifically for salary and staff. The manager and colleagues should spend enough time with new hires to ensure they are adapting and excelling in their new positions. If a new hire is not meeting these minimum expectations, the sooner they are discharged, the better. However, before discharge, management should analyze whether the potential discharge is due to the manager not providing a proper orientation with clear responsibilities and expectations, rather than the new hire being incompetent.

There is no need to bring a new person on board if there is no proper orientation program defined and followed. As previously mentioned, companies should define and share the rules in employee handbooks and, where appropriate, signage throughout the work space. Sometimes it is necessary to update or add additional rules. When this happens, all employees have to be immediately made aware of the change. Additional postings and verbal statements during the DR are necessary for communication.

Transitions and Re-structuring
There are many situations where the organization will have a transition and restructure, such as: consolidation, product line/value stream change, growth, acquisition, merger, transfer, greenfield startup or brownfield closure, among others. Senior executives will have an overall business plan with interrelated functional supporting plans, with human resources having an integral role in identifying position titles, number of people, timing, budgeted costs, objectives, responsibilities and KPIs. Developing this organizational plan requires much thought to make sure the new aspects do not disrupt current production, quality and customer service. These "people" plans have to be somewhat confidential and communicated or developed with only a few senior management, but can be rolled out in phases or with other details, such as milestones and investments.

This organization transition and restructure information should be entered into a spreadsheet and include defining different time periods or phases, such as: phase 1 current period, phase 2–4/ transition periods or milestones, and final phase/end state, such as one year after the new regime. Other factors to include can be sales, product types, volumes, volume percent change, various financial KPIs, headcount ratios, internal staff versus external hires, expected outputs with lead person identified, risks and contingencies.

Each column of the spreadsheet should have a milestone header (project phase), timing, and short objective description to clearly separate the different project phases. In addition, a matrix of people has to be defined to ensure staff and direct workers are accounted for. Use a column to identify when and how the transition affects each individual, including whether they stay, change function, change responsibilities or location, or are terminated.

Senior management should define a project leader, have frequent follow-up meetings to assess the current status of the plan and modify the plan as needed. Senior management should work with a legal advisor to ensure they are fulfilling all legal requirements. Senior management and/or a project leader should make regular announcements and hold update meetings with all concerned staff and direct workers. One-on-one meetings and interviews should be held with key members to discuss their current situations and near-term changes.

The project manager will need to hold various working meetings throughout the phased implementation plan with current management staff and the final phase management staff; in some cases, these may be the same people, but the meetings will have different objectives. During each of the transition meetings, the risks and expected outputs or changes in these factors should be the top priority to discuss instead of reviewing the sequenced timing plan. As mentioned earlier, the project leader should keep to a fixed meeting schedule and only highlight key or significant changes. Supplemental working meetings may be needed to further analyze status and options or refine more details of the plan.

One additional aspect of some organization changes is that the plan may require using new IT platforms or adapting to new factory conditions. So, timing for specialized training has to be included and personnel identified to participate in the training. Some plans may overlook the need for a higher set of technical competence and performance requirements, so the various functional managers will need to provide their input to the project manager.

Interim Assignments

An Interim Assignment (IA) is typically needed when a very skilled staff or manager has left the company and there is no one readily available to fill that position. That's when you can use interim external staff or temporary current employee assignments to fill the gap. Interim external staff or temporary current employee assignments are similar in nature to a project. Interim assignments end when either a full-time replacement comes on board, the position does not need to be filled, or work and responsibilities have been allocated to other employees. IAs and projects are typically short-term but can last up to a few years. In some cases, an IA may turn into a permanent position at the same location or at various locations. The IA may be a staff position, project manager, or even a functional management position.

For example, an external interim staff can be hired to be a project manager. They may have staff either directly or indirectly reporting to them, depending upon the scale of the project, priority, scope, and organizational culture. IAs have planned start and end dates, expectations, and KPIs. Projects typically have teams and these teams are disbanded once the project is completed. However, other projects might start or be underway and would require resources so typically previous project staff members would just move onto the new project. Some companies may never have IAs, but all companies will undertake projects.

The hiring process for IAs and projects is similar, but not the same. In larger companies, the IA or project is posted online at the same location, or at all company locations, for internal candidates to bid. Some companies may consider opening the position for external candidates, especially in the case of a manager replacement, where a consultant can fit and assume the role in a very short time compared to hiring someone for a permanent position.

Many companies use external consultants in this way to minimize disruptions and keep the business operations running with the same momentum. The other benefit of bringing a consultant on board is that they can also provide training to various functional staff to upgrade their skills and provide a different perspective on the business.

The selection and interviewing process would be similar for any new position, except the onboarding process may be truncated when an internal candidate or consultant is selected. However, if an external candidate is selected, there would be a full onboarding process according to the company Orientation process.

Both interim assignment and project personnel would define expectations, objectives, KPIs, timing and budget with management as well as establish a regular review meeting. In the case of an IA, management must determine whether they need to search for a full-time replacement.

Performance Appraisals and Pay for Performance

Nearly every company has an assessment process, typically one time a year to determine whether staff have met, exceeded or need improvement for their functional objectives and individual KPIs. Management typically aligns the vision statement to defined business objectives and KPIs in their annual operating plan and then translates this into functional and individual KPIs. Management at the senior most level must be aligned via the vision statement, business objectives, and highest level KPIs. Management should ensure that each individual's KPIs are understood and in-line with their job description and responsibilities. This is to reduce potential failures, reduce management variability on decision making, reduces potential barriers, and reduce overall company risks.

These objectives and KPIs are usually rolled out just before the new year starts and rarely modified in the coming year. Some companies have quarterly or semi-annual personnel reviews to ensure that individuals are developing themselves and working toward achieving the various expectations.

There are several benefits of an assessment process. Managers should be trained to conduct them effectively, since they might involve some uncomfortable dialogue. The benefits for the individual and for the company include the following:

Individual

- Meet with their immediate supervisor or manager
- Discuss accomplishments, KPIs, areas of improvement and concerns, if any
- Discuss professional development and upcoming training programs of interest
- Obtain a rating score or level; receive feedback, motivation, recognition or reward — for individuals who performed poorly, there may be a written or unwritten practice for dismissal
- Understand expectation of receiving higher pay for higher performance

Company

- Ensure the overall business objectives and KPIs are linked to individuals
- Ensure individuals are aligned to the objectives and KPIs, and have accountability for the previous year and responsibility for the upcoming year
- Provides a common platform for everyone to be rated against and documents poor performance in case of potential legal action
- Identify possible succession planning possibilities

There are, of course, disadvantages of a performance appraisal, such as:

- Not all managers will conduct them in the same way, since they have different opinions
- Managers may not be adequately trained in how to conduct appraisals, so there are varying degrees of reviews
- Reviews may be more qualitative than quantitative. This may be due to KPIs not being tied directly to individuals
- Reviews may be discouraging or demotivating. This may be due to company politics or lack of transparency

- Performance appraisals and pay for performance should be cohesively aligned so a higher appraisal would equal higher pay and vice versa. However, when the employee receives a mid to low performance appraisal, this typically does not result in a lower salary.

Exit Interviews

In many companies, the human resources function will require any departing staff to have an exit interview. Departing personnel have no real obligation to participate or provide any information, but their responses will keep the door open for any future opportunity.

HR usually has a standard exit questionnaire to be completed for their records. The exit interview should occur before the last day of work, but in some companies the interview occurs by phone a week or so after the departing employee's last day of work. Sometimes HR will contract with a third party, who will contact the individual using the company's standardized format in an unbiased way.

It can be challenging for HR to determine the real root cause of a resigning employee. The most-common reasons for employees leaving are higher pay, better benefits, location closer to home, flexible work schedule, or poor management. The resigning employee may not state poor management as the reason due to future potential retribution, or frustration with the company. The real root cause for someone to initially start looking for other employment may never be identified. However, if detected at an early stage, there may be a chance to keep the employee by changing the function or department, or identifying the manager and taking action with the manager such as training, issue a warning notice, or re-assignment.

In any case, HR will collect and analyze the responses, then generate a report to present to senior management for possible changes or improvements. For the individual, the exit interview should not be a time to release stress — that can be done at the gym. The individual should always be professional, courteous and non-confrontational.

Should companies hold exit interviews? If the company is just going to file a report or make a presentation, but not take it seriously, then it is a waste of time. However, if senior management wants to improve the environment and culture, then an exit interview should be conducted properly and professionally. This could even be done through an independent company such as a temporary worker agency that is used for sourcing direct labor.

Becoming a Leader

First-time managers typically question their decisions, are not confident in their actions, and do not use their staff or colleagues optimally in many situations. They also are quick to criticize individuals and provide little ongoing praise. Good managers quickly learn to praise individuals and team performance or, when needed, critique their team or function as a whole instead of calling out an individual.

Good managers also have a way of delegating by way of persuasion and suggestion, or asking their staff for ideas and guiding them, as opposed to issuing direct orders. By asking questions about the staff's ideas, you can tweak as necessary or collectively define a completely different alternative. This is a fast way to get their buy-in.

Follow up with their ideas and ask about their plans and status. This can be done at the functional DR as well as one-on-one. However, be cautious of being a micromanager and checking their status so much that staff get annoyed or upset. The follow-up can be done in the form of praise, support or a functional group update. Always respect your staff and be a partner of the team — a partner with decision-making authority.

Over time, your staff and colleagues should recognize your level of commitment or passion about work and how deeply you care about work and them. They will also learn of your strengths and weaknesses, and ideally recognize your maturation as a leader. As opportunities are presented and assessed, and actions taken, your staff and colleagues will watch how you interact and support them, as well as measure your individual contributions.

The deeper the passion you exhibit, the greater possibility of respect you will earn. When mistakes happen or an opportunity becomes a major risk or loss, your staff and colleagues will want to continue to support you and won't continuously belabor the failure. Reflecting upon mistakes is helpful, but not to the point that you are always looking at those past mistakes — the future is where the business will be a success or not.

Having a mentor can improve the first-time manager's capabilities. When the manager is confronted with a certain situation, they can think what their response is as well as think what response their mentor might make. Simulating how the mentor would handle certain situations can better develop the manager. Also, the manager can discuss with the mentor; ways to approach and conduct themselves in a specific situation, discuss a specific situation that happened to see if things could have been handled differently. Senior managers should be available and should have some input and advice for the first-time manager. This is important and should be formalized to ensure the first-time manager is open to accepting critique and advice from senior management, as well as establish regular, frequent meetings or reviews.

Having a review and discussion about decisions and behaviors is useful, but it is far better to work on improving performance. Being a first-time manager will be challenging on all fronts. Establishing a DR and using visual boards will help the first-time manager understand the team's concerns, work capabilities and priorities, and can be used as a management development tool as well. This will help the first-time manager gain business knowledge, establish an open communication system and develop an effective way to delegate your team. The DR and visual aid boards can provide the means to communicate vertically upward, downward and horizontally to peers.

First-time managers through senior experienced managers have to observe and develop individual staff capabilities when they are managing their activities and projects. Guiding individual staff on their management capabilities is critical for the staff's professional development and enhancement of their competence. This is the main ingredient for organic promotion. With this organic management promotion model, by default, management is learning and applying leadership abilities — but being a manager doesn't mean you are a leader. Being a leader is a characteristic earned over time, where people value your opinion and want to be part of your activities.

There are many characteristics of being a leader. Most can be learned and practiced from reading, emulating bosses you admire, practicing an array of behaviors, getting feedback, reflecting and challenging yourself to continual improvement. The key is to practice and refine various leadership characteristics, observe the result, analyze for improvement, and repeat. The general manager should periodically have one-on-one leadership development meetings with their management team.

Leadership characteristics to develop over time are:

- Integrity
- Listening before speaking
- Adaptiveness
- Dependability
- Delegation
- Empathy
- Emotional stability
- Innovation
- Positivity
- Trust
- Flexibility
- Confidence
- Decisive
- Encouragement
- Empowerment
- Honesty
- Leading by example
- Vision

Senior staff and managers should be tapped for knowledge and experience with business strategies and with market, customer, product, technical, operations, financial and supplier matters. Experienced managers can refine these above characteristics, as well as work with junior management and staff, on applying various new technologies.

Finally, many companies have an unwritten "handbook" of language for managers and leaders to use — or not use. Learning to understand and avoid culturally insensitive words or behaviors can only help. When speaking or writing, use professional business language or words that have been used in previous correspondence or meetings. This will ensure your idea is at least heard or read without the listener immediately rejecting you or your message. It can take time to identify sensitive words and understand why they might be an issue unless you have a mentor who can directly tell you what words or phrases not to use. This is even more important when the company is multi-national or where there are employees from different cultures.

Chapter 32 - Personal Health and Work-Life Balance

Many of you have already read several personal-development, management, technical and other professional books, but have you actually assessed yourself with personal health and work-life balance in mind? What is personal health and work-life balance, and why is it important?

Factors

Understanding various factors of your life and setting priorities or allocating time to each of them is work-life balance. These factors may change somewhat throughout the year, and most definitely will change throughout the rest of your life. The factors are personal health, mental health, spirituality, family, friends, hobbies, social wellbeing, financial wellbeing, work benefits, job satisfaction, work/career, and any other influences affecting your quality of life. You may have other factors to include or you might want to break down some of these factors into sub-factors for ease of planning and executing.

Assessing the factors by priority and by time allocated each week or month is balancing. Balancing these factors is unique to each person, so there is no ideal priority or time allocation. Each individual can use these factors to measure their quality of life and make adjustments to attain a certain level of satisfaction. On a subconscious level, everyone already prioritizes and allocates time to these factors, but some people consciously make more of an effort to plan, execute, reflect and make adjustments to improve the balance between their personal health and work lives. Some things cannot be changed or adjusted easily, such as hereditary issues. Other positive and negative activities can have an effect on this process, such as preventive medicine, nutrition, sleep, fitness, substance abuse, and tobacco and alcohol use.

The key is to determine whether you want to understand and possibly improve your current personal health and work-life balance. Just because you understand the meaning of priorities and time allocation does not necessarily mean you have the self-control and power to make changes due to your personality, current responsibilities and commitments. This is just a guide to help you understand what gives you satisfaction, quality of life, and provide a basic roadmap for self-improvement. Also, this information can help you and your company develop a more open dialogue to personal health and work life balance.

Nutrition

Having good nutrition, diet, exercise and sleep help to maintain high levels of energy and reduce mood swings throughout the work day. Having these factors under control can lower blood pressure and bad cholesterol; control weight; improve concentration, alertness and productivity; and reduce absenteeism and risks of getting sick or having heart disease, diabetes, etc.

If you love what you do, or even just really need to keep doing it for financial reasons, why risk being absent from work? Take note of your daily food consumption, exercise and sleep patterns, and make an effort to prioritize and plan these factors into your Daily Routine to strengthen your immune system and improve your overall personal health and work life. After a few days or weeks, review this information and establish daily goals. It's especially good to study this on the weekends and prepare for the coming week.

Healthy food choices have a direct impact on cognitive capabilities and sustained performance levels. Eating foods with low glycemic index numbers gradually releases glucose into the bloodstream, maintaining a level blood sugar level, while foods with high glycemic index numbers cause glucose spikes. Try to plan your lunch or dinner times rather than waiting until the last second to eat or skipping meals. Making food choices when you are hungry and have limited time reduces your ability to make healthy choices and increases the likelihood of consuming sugary, salty and processed related foods. Snacks during the day or shift, such as vegetables with peanut butter, yogurt, or protein bars, can help you maintain a constant glucose level and reduce the spikes or drops in blood sugar levels when you finally do eat a meal.

Exercise and Recovery
What is your daily exercise routine? Do you have an overall weekly plan for exercise? Taking brisk walks several times a day in and out of the factory sets a foundation for more advanced workouts before work, during lunch, after work and/or on weekends. Gyms and fitness centers, clubs and other social groups have various fitness programs. Either you make time for it now, or a lack of exercise eventually will catch up with you in unsatisfactory ways.

Everyone needs a different amount of sleep time to be their most productive. When working on shift rotations, you will need significantly more time to sleep to be energized on some days than on others. Enough sleep time is important, but the quality of sleep is more important, especially if you travel a lot —sleeping on an airplane or hotel room, or napping in taxi, takes a toll on your overall health. At some point, you will need to find a place where you feel comfortable and safe, so you can take the necessary time to rejuvenate.

Wellness Opportunity
To encourage colleagues and employees to start developing their own personal health and work-life balance plan; consider making wellness lectures or provide informational booklets combined with discussions during lunches or between shifts. The lectures can be presented by internal or external sources and should take 15 to 30 minutes, with a focus on a variety of personal health and business topics. Also, having computers or TVs in lunch or break rooms that show different daily positive life choices can help change the culture. Consider establishing a group walk or jogging

route, offering fitness or yoga classes, sponsoring or providing discounts on gym memberships, and improving food and snack choices in vending machines. See if someone is willing to take responsibility for writing a daily personal health and work-life balance note to be posted on a whiteboard or other display near the cafeteria — that will help educate and remind people that this is important. Not everyone will take advantage of all these things, but morale will improve, employees will feel more engaged, overall healthcare costs might even drop and absenteeism might go down as well.

Part 3 - Conditioning Summary

Most people think of Conditioning as daily physical exercises performed at some level of intensity, or as a measure of fitness. The fitness program called CrossFit has their definition of fitness as: to forge a broad, general and inclusive fitness supported by measurable, observable, and repeatable results. In the contents of this section, I have taken this general definition of Conditioning together with the aim of CrossFit and have applied this into a manufacturing operation's business. Conditioning in a business sense is to have employees actively engaged in various work capacities to promote profitability, productivity, quality, safety, delivery, servicing, product and process innovation, morale, personal health, personal development, and work-life balance with an improvement-oriented mind-set. This improvement-oriented mind-set strengthens the company and underlies having a Factory Showcase Culture.

A Daily Routine is a fundamental business activity, and the highest priority that all management, staff, and direct labor workers must perform every day at the start of their work day. The balance of the section discusses many techniques, tools, and systems regarding data analysis, auditing, reporting, coordinating resources, and responding to inputs using analytics with some time element. Finally, Personal Health and Work-life Balance is extremely important to ensure each person comes to work healthy and ready to tackle mental and physical work-loads and stresses every day. Many academic journal articles are published every year supporting the importance of health and work-life balance. Also, many general media such as television, newspapers, magazines, podcasts, books, and E-books discuss and advertise the benefits of having a daily regime of healthy eating, physical exercise, and work-life balance. So, it is important for the general manager and management team to realize their employees are bombarded by this information, and lead by example to promote personal health and achieve work-life balance.

Part 4 - Competitiveness

Competitiveness is the way that a company is profitable when compared with other businesses in the same field. A company becomes competitive by demonstrating its advantages in executing short-term plans aligned to a vision with long-term investments and producing higher quality products. Some companies have certain competitive advantages and understand them so well that they can maximize their profitability year after year.

These competitive advantages lie in (1) producing a product at a lower cost and offering a price lower than competitors and (2) offering a different advantage such as a unique product; advanced technology, innovativeness, research and development (R&D), and engineering capability; strong brand identity; superior customer delivery and servicing; high-quality and reliable products; or quick-to-market offerings.

Chapter 33 - Competitive Advantage

Competitive advantage can be defined in many different ways. Excellent leaders are able to identify and exploit those advantages. Leaders must take a comprehensive view of the company, industry and market and then create, communicate, and execute a plan to achieve those advantages with a committed, disciplined management team. The key is that the leader and management team be aligned with a coherent mission with various short- and long-term plans. This section will explore how to establish and improve a company's competitiveness via plans, systems and practices. By developing a factory showcase culture of high standards with a focus on customer expectations and profitability, companies will set themselves above their competition.

Prior to developing a long-term strategic plan and an annual operating plan, senior management should review their mission and value statements, and spend time with key customers to understand their interests better. Senior management must evaluate their mission and values with their staff — both formally and informally. This is to gain the staff's perspectives about the company's mission and value statements, the company's capabilities, and the belief for a solid future for the staff and company. Identifying the reasons the employees believe in certain things helps to identify what needs to be modified and validates senior management perspectives. When the employees have positive thoughts about the company's capabilities and future, the greater the likelihood for success.

The review of the mission and value statements is also prompted when significant company transformations have recently been made, or when there has been dramatic industry changes such as mergers, bankruptcies, rising of new competitors, or other economic or political country changes such as currency valuation risks. In many cases the mission(s) might change, and in some cases the values are modified or aligned when there is a merger, consolidation, or other significant business event change.

Chapter 34 - Strategic and Annual Operating Plans

Understanding your company's current position in its industry and market, and on a global scale, year after year is usually achieved through strategic and annual operations planning. Many companies create strategic long-term plans and annual operating plans (AOPs) and then manage their businesses against those plans and forecasts periodically, while other companies loosely define plans and manage their business accordingly.

Within the long-term strategic and annual plans, new business opportunities are created in detail with existing business financials, which cover capital investments, capacity planning, workforce, timing, and various KPIs (key performance indicators). Strategic plans are high-level, and long term used to evaluate the company's current position in the industry and various international markets against its competitors, assess comparative advantages using SWOT/SCOT (strength, weakness/challenge, opportunity, threat) analysis, and define strategic initiatives and financial targets. Strategic plans may also include a product and technology roadmap with a comparison against competitors' technology, their customers, and their capabilities. A product and technology roadmap visually shows the linkages of the technologies over time including investments, capabilities, volumes, and other business drivers. There may be multiple levels, dimensions, models, and ways to display the information. Annual Operating Plans are a derivative of strategic plans in one-year increments. Annual operating plans detail current and new business projects, product volumes, financials, functional budgets and plans, and KPIs on a monthly basis for the upcoming year. The following section defines the major elements of a strategic plan, and those of an annual operating plan.

Strategic Planning

Strategic plans are created by senior management and/or with the executive management team. They may include inputs from the board of directors and from other management. Senior management creates a calendar of events for starting and finishing the strategic and annual operating planning process and creates a calendar for evaluating monthly and quarterly performance.

Strategic plan timing starts and ends prior to starting the annual planning process. The annual planning process must end and be communicated to the organization before the end of the company's year-end fiscal calendar. The fiscal calendar may or may not be the same as the calendar year (Jan. 1 through Dec. 31). For example, if the company's financial year is from January through December, the strategic planning workshop can start as early as July, while the annual planning process can start in August. This provides several months for the board of directors' approval and for fine-tuning.

Preparation for a Strategic Planning Workshop

One person on the executive management team should be responsible for the strategic plan. One of the best ways to develop a strategic plan is by having a workshop with the executive management team and other select members as needed. The management team may also choose board members, an external consultant, or an adviser to facilitate the workshop.

Who should attend the workshop?

The most senior executive should define the workshop participants. If the company has several business divisions or units, each business division or unit should have their own strategic planning workshop, especially if the business divisions and units have dissimilar products and different customers. Not all senior management may be invited to attend. Additionally, lower-level leaders such as an R&D manager, product engineering manager, sales manager, or plant manager may be invited. The goal is to have a diverse group to stimulate thinking.

Where is the workshop taking place?

The location, venue, and logistics are important to ensure that interruptions are minimized and discussions are open, candid, and productive. Having the workshop in a neutral, off-site location is typically preferred. This provides an environment where people can be creative, allows attendees to get away from their daily responsibilities, and also useful for team building.

When are the dates for the workshop?

It is important to plan months in advance, so personal and professional preparations can be made. In addition, this provides time for potential conflicts to be managed early enough to ensure all participants can attend.

What is the agenda?

An example of a one-day workshop agenda is provided below. Strategic planning sessions can be combined with quarterly reviews or a major business activity, such as a new product launch. Also, strategic planning can be longer than one day, depending on the amount of discussions, data analysis, and planning activities. If longer than one day, then consider having smaller groups or assigning the participants to certain specific tasks to be done in advance of the workshop.

What are the objectives and expected deliverables?

The objectives and expected deliverables need to be clearly stated when scheduling and inviting the participants. Revisit goals just prior to the strategic planning event for preparation work, and thoroughly review them at beginning of the workshop. Also, make it clear that at the end of the workshop, a few key initiatives will be outlined with details — as opposed to having multiple initiatives without clarity. Note that having multiple initiatives dilutes the effectiveness of management, especially if the initiatives are not clearly defined or if everyone is not aligned or committed to achieve them. An example of an objective and expected deliverable can be a broad requirement such as:

- Increase sales by "x" percent in "y" years.
- Design and market product "z" by year "y" (with some delineated new features, technology, cost target, and so on).
- Capture "x" percent of the market in "y" years.
- Decide on a specific direction to go in or an innovative pursuit to undertake.
- Define a SCOT analysis in simple, short statements, with a ranking or priority within each category. Designate a team and define a specific date for completion.
- Create one to five strategic initiatives with a budget, financial performance expectations, key milestone plans, project leader, resources required, risks and contingencies, and scheduled follow-up date(s).

What material preparations are expected?

The strategic planning leader should ask participants to bring relevant information. Such information can be historical sales, customer feedback surveys, market and industry data, customer and competitor profiles and financials, internal functional staff feedback, and engineering technology reviews. In addition, participants should have information relative to the questions below.

What is a SWOT/SCOT Analysis?

A SWOT/SCOT stands for: Strength; Weakness or Challenge; Opportunity; Threat. A SWOT/SCOT analysis is a powerful tool to define your company's competitive position against its competitors in a simple framework that is used as a basis for creating strategies or initiatives. The analysis should focus on where your company is today versus the future. Each of the categories should have a few simple, clear statements that can be either factual or a perception of your company against its competitors.

- Strength — something positive to maintain, grow or build; or existing capabilities. Example- higher market share in all markets, engineering and test in-house capabilities, engineers available on-site at customers, manufacturing plants in all major market areas, short order fulfillment lead-time, lean six sigma function in every facility, strong project management

- Weakness/Challenge — something inadequate, flawed, defective, poor or a short coming. Example – Quality issues are more than competitors, delivery performance weaker than competitors, slow to launch new products and often with quality problems, ERP system and supply chain is not global-each market operates independently, no strategic planning and no long-term product technology roadmap, plant managers have low skilled operation's teams.

- Opportunity — possible future favorable business venture, advancement or circumstance. Example - Customers-customer (consumer) interested in aftermarket products and servicing, possibility to offer some products into the premium market, higher available capacity to potentially outsource.

- Threat — some possible current or future unfavorable business concern, risk or effect that causes damage to the company. Example - Poor Quality affecting new business wins, past few years of low investment into R&D causing competitors to catch up, low priced competitor products may impact current market share, social media affecting brand name

During the Strategic Planning Workshop

<u>Define current position</u>

What are your company's products, volumes, and prices being produced? For which customers (including Internet sales)?

What is your company's current market share by total sales globally or regionally versus competitors?

What is your company's current market share by product family globally or regionally versus competitors?

Where are the markets or geography for the current year and for the next year?

<u>Define your customer perception of your products (Strengths, Challenges, Weaknesses)</u>

What is your customer's perception of your products? Or, why are your products chosen over those of your competitors? (Look for new business win and loss reasons.)

What are your perceived advantages or strengths? List by product, by market, and by region.

What are your customer concerns, perceived weaknesses, or challenges? Include warranty, field failures, service calls, customer surveys, and internet feedback. List by product, by market, and by region.

What is the expected volume change rate or growth rate of your products in the various markets and geography over the next five years?

What are the total sales by product, by market, and by region over the next five years?

What comparisons can be made of your KPI performance versus the competitors' performance in the different markets or regions?

<u>Define future products, technologies, and possible trends (Opportunities)</u>

Future products or technologies should include some technical information to clearly distinguish technical directions or market expectations.

What are the future products of your R&D?

What are the future products of your competitors?

What are the future product desires of your customers?

Who are some prospective customers based upon some future product you are developing?

What are some upcoming technologies and possible trends that your products are related to? Do similar products exist? What are the risks of your products becoming obsolete?

How are digital technologies affecting your company, competitors and customers?

What is the product technology roadmap of your products versus your competitors' products?

<u>Define competitors and market (Threats)</u>

Who are your main competitors? List by product, by sales or volume, and by market or region.

Does each competitor recognize you as a major competitor or a minor competitor?

What is the market size for those products?

Where are all the markets for each product (by region or geography)?

Are your suppliers developing technologies that may compete with or may advance ahead of your products?

How do customers perceive your competitors' products?

How does E-commerce affect the market? What E-commerce strategies have your competitors pursued?

<u>Where are we going?</u>

Define the new digital technologies or strategies (including E-commerce) to pursue and define current gaps.

Summarize each section above with action item statements, goals, KPIs, leader to take ownership of the action item, and timing.

Prioritize all action item statements. Priorities can be defined in a variety of ways, such as cost versus opportunity, business loss versus opportunity, or cost versus risk. Prioritizing actions should be defined in a quantitative way.

How fast will we get there?

Prior to leaving the workshop, the leader should define timing for follow-up meetings to ensure action items are closed on-time. The leader and strategic planning team should regularly meet to determine whether to continue the initiative or not, define investment budgets and return expectations, define resources required, and define project planning milestones. If the strategic planning team agrees to pursue an initiative, then regular follow-up meetings are expected, with more planning details, action items, and status reports. This will ensure the strategic plan is not just shelved until the next year. Follow-up meetings need to occur frequently throughout the coming year to ensure organizational alignment is supported by executive management. In addition, if economics or markets change, the direction of the initiative may be altered or even be canceled, so frequent meetings are needed to make adjustments. Then, when the following strategic planning session is held a year later, the initiative status can be presented, with successes, redirections, or reason(s) for discontinuation.

Strategic Planning Workshop Agenda

The following table shows an example of an agenda for a company's first strategic planning workshop. If the company has already completed a strategic plan in a previous year, then after all teams have presented their SCOT presentation, the previous year's SCOT analysis can be shown and critiqued. Alternatively, the latest SCOT can be evaluated and edited in a large group setting. It is important to review the historical SCOT analysis over the years to evaluate any changes, issues, or improvements for each segment and determine what the drivers of the change were. It is crucial to examine the drivers for any change and determine courses of action. The first topic should be "who are we?" by evaluating the company's values and mission statements. Senior management alignment for both values and mission statements is critical to develop coherent strategic plans, and to define and prioritize KPIs. All senior management must conduct this introspective and critical evaluation. If there is a debate or if a refinement needs to be made, time should be extended as clarifying the statements are a key objective. Note that prior to this workshop, senior management should already have met with their customers and staff to have a good idea as to any refinements to their values and mission statements.

The next topic is "Tomorrow's world" where one or more short presentations are made showing new technologies. The objective is to promote creativity by setting a spark inside the minds of management for linking new technologies with the next topic of Strengths, Challenges, Opportunities, and Threats (SCOT).

The rest of the day is devoted to using the SCOT information as a baseline to generate strategic initiatives. If a company has already completed a strategic plan in a previous year, the previous year's SCOT analysis can be critiqued. Alternatively, the latest SCOT analysis can be evaluated and edited in a large-group setting or with breakout teams and should require less time than shown in the table. The reason to review the historical SCOT analyses over the years is to evaluate any changes, issues or improvements for each segment and the drivers of the changes. It is crucial to examine the drivers of any change and determine a course of action. At the end of the workshop, a summary of the key initiatives is generated and provided to each senior manager.

Table 4. 1 Strategic planning workshop agenda

Topic	Responsibility	Time	Objective
Welcome, introduction, rules, agenda	Senior executive, workshop facilitator	8:00–8:15	Establish expectations; see Meeting in "Orientations"
Who are we?	Facilitator	8:15–9:00	Reassess company's values and mission statements
Tomorrow's world	Facilitator	9:00–9:20	Promote creativity, present new technologies across industries
SCOT	Facilitator and teams	9:20–11:30	Define SCOTs
Lunch		11:30–12:15	Working lunch
SCOT presentation	Teams	12:15–12:45	Present each team's SCOT
Initiatives	Facilitator	12:45–13:45	Summarize SCOT, delineate key initiatives
Initiative planning	Teams	13:45–15:30	Scope initiatives, determine direction
Critique; identify leader, priorities, goals	All	15:30–17:00	Evaluate and gain commitment for each initiative
Summary and next steps	Facilitator	17:00–18:00	Summarize and select dates for reviews

Strategic and Annual Operating Plan Format

Both the strategic and annual operating plans are confidential and should not be shared externally. They should be controlled internally, with access to details only for key personnel.

Plans can be presented using different formats, the most common format is using Microsoft PowerPoint. The plans would include spreadsheets with embedded or pasted information into the presentation. Charts can be presented as four-panel displays, with each page broken into four equal sections. Three sections can be used to display trend charts, Pareto charts, tables, graphs, and one section can be for a text summary. Also, each presentation slide should include a summary statement — in other words, explain the importance of the slide. Companies typically define a standard presentation format for ease of data compilation, as several people from different functions will provide input. Finance or a planning function can prepare the standard format template so contributors can copy and paste their information, and graphs into it.

Annual Operating Plan

The Annual Operating Plan (AOP) is prepared by management with inputs from all functions. The plan is then presented to senior management for approval. Once approved the AOP then is communicated to the company. The AOP is prepared one time per year. The AOP is different than the strategic plan, as it is used on a monthly basis throughout the upcoming year to compare actual results against forecasted data. After the financial closing every month, there should be a review of the company's performance against the AOP and against a forecast made in previous months. The forecast should be updated each month for the remaining months of the upcoming year; however, the AOP numbers remain fixed, so comparisons can be made. For example, when the first-month financial closing occurs, there will be a review and the forecast will be made for the subsequent months. Comparisons and updates should occur after each month, such as 1+11. Then, after the second-month financial closing, 2+10 will be reviewed, and so on. The Financial Variance Analysis in Chapter 31 presented the different metrics used for the comparisons.

The AOP should be cash flow- and profit-driven, with other key deliverables embedded, such as sales, quality, safety and delivery. If the business has more than one manufacturing company or location, a briefing on each company is needed that includes geographic location, products, volumes, capacity, processes, head count and ratios, union issues, main customers, customer awards, certifications, and key financial highlights over time, including inventory. A SCOT summary should be in the beginning of the presentation.

Annual Operating Plan Input

The AOP should include the following:

- Yearly financial highlights — historic and forecasted — shown in a combination of tables and graphs, with a focus on profitability
- Current year-to-date plan versus actual financial highlights with overall year-to-date trends, and a summary of unfavorable issues
- Strategic initiatives summary with SCOT summary and explanation of where this AOP fits
- Next year's monthly financial forecast summary with highlights and executive summary
- Key projects, timing, organization charts and competitor financial ratio comparison
- Sales and marketing analysis by product and by region (geographic economics and industry trends)
- New business win-loss analysis, win percentage, percentage of sales volume wins and reasons for loss
- New business win details — product, customer, sales, volume, profit percentage, capital expenditure amount, start of production timing and manufacturing plant location

- Committed sales targets for the upcoming year — by product, customer, sales amount, and volume
- Prospective sales and confidence percentage for the win (estimated win award) — by product, customer, sales amount, profit percentage and volume
- E-commerce strategy — management of and plans for website improvements, mobile application, online ordering and online marketing
- Pricing strategy — by product, by customer, by volume, by online sales, etc.
- Next year's financial income statement forecast by month, with favorable/unfavorable figures highlighted (consider showing product volumes and main takeaway)
- Favorable explanations, with details and timing
- Unfavorable explanations with details, risks, contingencies and timing
- List of new product project plans, value analysis/value engineering, Lean Six Sigma, productivity and quality improvement projects, summary, financial contributions, responsibility, and timing
- Project name, project leader and team names, product, customer, capital expenditures, sales, volume, project planning stage, project plan status, key milestones, issues, risks, contingency, and summary
- Individual project plan summaries (one page per project)
- Capital expenditure plan
- Facility infrastructure repairs and improvement costs
- IT hardware and software, including maintenance and upgrades. All functions will have some sort of hardware and software requirements and needs.
- Balance sheet summary
- Cash-flow summary
- Supply chain and inventory changes, by quarter or month
- Raw materials — economic and industry trends by commodity; purchase amount and volume by geography; issues and risks
- Raw material plan, issues, risks and contingency plans
- Management and functional organization charts and changes; summary of head count for direct and indirect workers (each business unit, value stream, or functional organization should be shown with a chart and with key highlights and changes)
- R&D project summary
- All functional KPIs, historical performance via a graph, functional specific plans and initiatives.
- Summary of key business drivers and highlights

Annual Operating Plan Development

As the AOP is being developed, senior management may want to review specific parts of the plan and make changes before consolidation. Once the AOP has been consolidated into one presentation, there may be several rounds of preliminary reviews with management before the final formal presentation review is conducted.

Management must challenge, question, and scrutinize the sales forecast, as this is the driver for the AOP. Over the past year, the sales team should have presented a monthly sales forecast whereby the accuracy has been evaluated each month and subsequent months, such as: month +1, month +2, or month +3 basis with exceptions and variances analyzed and reported. Also, an expectation should be that the sales business process has been audited at least once, and the sales forecasting process has been refined either from the variance analysis study, auditing findings, digital technology enhancements, a modification to the analytics, metrics timing improvement, or use of new data input sources. The sales forecasting process should be constantly evaluated to improve the accuracy and timeliness so the management team's confidence level increases over time. The sales planning process should be clearly defined with inputs, flow, responsibilities, timing, analysis techniques, data sources defined, and data consolidation streamlined and automated to reduce errors. Also, the process or system should be defined so that the customer's buying behaviors or customer's buying process and practices are incorporated — this should include customer feedback, assumptions and ways in which the forecasted sales can be qualified or confidence level can be indicated.

Having digital technology features is helpful to reduce the sale department's administrative time so they can focus their time with customers. No matter how accurate the sales plan is, there will still be uncertainties and unexpected events to occur. The key to having a more accurate sales forecast is how quickly the management team understands the changes, uncertainties, unexpected events, and then reacts or takes actions based upon the new information.

Annual Operating Plan Executive Approval and Communication
During the executive and board AOP review, there may be several modifications to the plan before being approved. Then the senior management team can communicate certain non-confidential details of the plan to the rest of the company. Some companies openly present the entire plan, while other companies present specific parts of the plan. Having transparency and showing the entire plan to all staff members (except for specific human resources changes or other highly sensitive and confidential details) demonstrates a high level of trust and shared commitment to the success of the business. Also, showing the AOP to the staff and having them participate in reviewing the actual monthly performance against the AOP month and against forecast helps with their engagement, commitment and professional development.

Chapter 35 - Pursuing New Business

Another business process that the sales organization or function leads is that of pursuing new business. Companies should have a clear process to continually gain new business sales (win contracts) and remain profitable. It is important for companies to promote innovations and pursue new business opportunities. Those companies that don't vigorously manage this tend to get left behind such as; Kodak versus the digital age, or Blockbuster versus Netflix. Companies pursue this in a range of ways. Some companies have well-defined and agile processes, some have rigid bureaucratic processes, and other companies have poor business processes.

When a new business opportunity is identified, resources and investments are needed, and having a well-defined process — including responsibilities, timings, and fulfillment of data expectation — typically have greater success of gaining the new business. Moreover, if customers do not purchase or are not interested, the company is able to analyze their loss so they can be more competitive for the next venture. Companies with a looser process for pursuing new business typically pursue a diverse range of products in different markets over time. This requires various manufacturing and administrative processes that are difficult to manage, making it harder to compete in one particular market, resulting in lower profits year-over-year. So, having defined process steps is a key element to remain competitive. Even though the process of pursuing new business varies for each manufacturing company, there are 10 main activities:

1. Identification of a new business opportunity
2. Qualification of a new business opportunity
3. Business pursuit decision analysis
4. Business case development
5. Risks and assumptions
6. Business case analysis and decision
7. Quote submission
8. Customer presentation
9. Win/loss status and analysis
10. Project kickoff

1. Identification of a New Business Opportunity

New business opportunities may come from identifying new products or ways to add value to customers by; development of new products, use of technologies in different ways, use of new technologies, an expansion into current markets with pricing and marketing strategies, or enlarging current markets with greater customer value-add, pricing, and market strategies.

Define a target market by researching potential customers both consumer and businesses; their demographics, buying habits, buying frequency, wants or needs they are fulfilling, products they have bought, and potential products they are interested in. Market strategies can then be developed with direct customer contact. Customers can be pitched various market strategies with social media such as Instagram, Facebook, LinkedIn; directly by sending emails; face-to-face contacts; and indirectly through websites. Eventually targeted potential customers are identified. In addition, developing an advertising scheme can also cultivate potential customers. For current customers, build upon the relationship to expand business with other products or present products that your company has the capability to make that they would be interested. Building upon existing relationships is vitally important — it creates a barrier to your competition and can develop into strategic alliances.

Business opportunities may be identified in various international marketplaces and may require an international sales and support services team whether directly a part of your company or through a sales representative organization. The key is to ensure the international group understands your marketing materials; product, process, and service capabilities; and business pursuit strategies. Schedule regular new business pursuit meetings, including several face-to-face meetings with the international sales team and customers (both potential and current). Ensure that international sales teams are focused on your strategies and that their new business proposals are meeting the customer qualification requirements.

Business opportunities should be regularly reviewed and each opportunity should have a status (such as active or closed). Active opportunities should be further classified as to the business process step name below with updated action items. This is to ensure the opportunity is moving in a favorable direction. Some companies have weekly reviews for all new business opportunities, whereas others may have reviews only once a month.

2. Qualification of a New Business Opportunity

To understanding the customer's wants and needs, determine who the buyers and decision makers are. Having this knowledge helps to better assess how real the opportunity is, and further defines the customer profile and customer assessment qualification. The assessment criteria should have several components, such as:

- Fits customer pursuit strategies
- Has a solid sales growth rate
- Fits within the project development timing window
- Has a high initial confidence rating to win the business

- Meets sales targets
- Has a desired profitability rate
- Meets the current product and process capabilities
- Can provide a clear reason to pursue the opportunity

For customers that are businesses, a basic customer profile should be created, including business name, business sales size, types of main products, locations or possible ship-to locations, and key contact information.

If the customer provides a Request For Quote (RFQ), then the above information can be readily compiled, or the customer can be contacted to provide missing information. However, if there is no RFQ, then either the customer and/or sales team will need to define these requirements. Having a close relationship with the customer and defining these requirements jointly can better position the company to win the business. By writing your own specifications and standards, you create a barrier for your competitor. Also, if your products are highly transaction oriented, standardized, commodity based, or are readily available in the market, then the customer qualification process does not need to be so complex or rigid.

Every year, the sales, marketing, and senior management team should evaluate and update the customer assessment qualification criteria, then train all sales teams on any revisions. Reviewing and editing this every year will ensure you are not missing out on trends, threats, or other opportunities.

3. Business Pursuit Decision Analysis

As mentioned, every week there should be a new business review meeting. During this meeting, discuss all prospective and current new business opportunities and plan appropriate actions.

The first decision to made is whether to pursue the business opportunity or not. Sales will have completed their potential customer assessment qualification information requirements and be available to discuss or answer any questions about this new prospective customer, products, current suppliers, competitors, etc. The sales manager should define a fixed time each week and have sufficient time to cover all opportunities. The decision makers may be a team that includes sales, marketing, finance, engineering, general manager, and others as needed.

The decision-making team should have some guidelines and "go" or "no-go" criteria when deciding whether to pursue the opportunity or not. The guidelines or criteria can be quite flexible but should be directional or aligned to current business strategies and capabilities. Most likely, the sales manager would take the lead and present each opportunity. The four typical decisions are:

- Need more information
- Wait until "X"
- Agree to pursue
- Agree not to pursue

Whatever the decision, document the reason for the decision for future analysis — the opportunity may be presented again as economics, markets, and industry status change. In some cases, the decision to pursue may be quick, especially if it relates to a current or strategic customer. In other cases, the decision to pursue may be rejected quickly due to a competitor alliance.

4. Business Case Development

Once the decision is made to pursue the opportunity, the Business Case (BC) development process begins. Typically, someone from finance or a project leader is nominated. The business case leader coordinates gathering data from various functions. The leader and team quickly needs to process a lot of information quickly, as the timeframe to respond to the customer can be anywhere for a couple days to a couple weeks.

When the business case is quite complex, the BC leader should have a one to two-day workshop with a cross-functional team that can work out all the details of the business case. During the workshop, the team should address refining the sales volume, developing a mock-up or simulation of the material flow, manufacturing process and quality requirements, and product validation tests to estimate the various costs. Also, the workshop should include what-if scenarios to ensure the business case addresses risks, assumptions, terms and conditions. Some scenarios to consider are:

- If the volume is never realized on a per-month basis, what are the conditions written in the offer to the customer or the contingencies to salvage the loss of investment?

- Alternatively, are there conditions on volume, such as certain prices corresponding to a certain range of volumes?

- Can current production capacity and capability meet the RFQ requirements?

- Are incremental investments needed to achieve the volumes over time?

Developing the business case in a workshop with an experienced cross-functional team discussing and challenging ideas is far better than asking for inputs via an emailed spreadsheet template or having this developed by one person. However, for less complex projects, a business case workshop is not needed and spreadsheet templates can be completed by various functional staff members, or even by one person. Staff would enter information into a spreadsheet template, then the business case leader would compile and perform a sensitivity analysis using various prices, volumes and investments over certain time periods. Typically, the business case leader will have a cross-functional meeting and review the customer profile, qualification assessment, timing details, spreadsheet templates needed to be completed, and answer questions. Then, the leader would identify who is responsible for obtaining the various costs. In some cases, the BC leader may have to make cost assumptions and prepare the analysis for the decision-makers to review. The cost assumptions should be defined with both the BC leader and the functional staff member responsible for that line item. The functional staff members define assumptions, so it is up to the BC leader to challenge and to use historic quote information to obtain a compromised estimated cost.

Input factors to prepare a business case

The following shows a detailed list of the many input factors to determine whether the business opportunity would be worthwhile to pursue and be financially viable. Make sure all involved functions understand the customer requirements. Sometimes such specific requirements are on the customer's online portals or referenced as statements in the RFQ. The following is a comprehensive list of factors that may or may not apply to all RFQs.

- Expected due date for submission to customer
- Product type and volumes per period
- Customer profile and qualification assessment
- Customer requirements, work scope and RFQ details
- CAD drawings, specifications, standards and any software or testing requirements
- Cost of materials
- Raw material sourcing, qualification and timing
- Components or write specifications that may have been designed by Engineering
- Costs and timing for engineering design, development testing and production testing
- Evaluation of the new business pursuit against the product technology roadmap and manufacturing footprint
- Manufacturing equipment needed, manufacturing process flow, routing details, cycle times, changeover timing, equipment utilization, and manufacturing equipment configuration
- Manufacturing process costs and estimated scrap costs
- Internal tooling requirements, costs and timing
- Supplier tooling costs, qualification requirements and timing
- Quality inspection and testing requirements, equipment, timing and costs. Some quality and test equipment will be within the manufacturing workspace and other quality and test equipment may be in inspection rooms, laboratories or other places.
- Capital expenditure cost (Capex) summary of the above, including building, infrastructure, information technology (IT) systems and timing
- Direct labor timing and costs
- Indirect labor timing and costs
- Material handling requirements, costs, labor requirement, and timing
- Manufacturing expenses, such as supplies and perishable tooling
- Manufacturing space requirements and other infrastructure needs

- Equipment and building maintenance expenses
- Engineering product and software development requirements and timing, including testing
- Packaging requirements for suppliers and customer
- Logistics requirements for suppliers and customer, freight costs, customs duties, and Value Added Taxes (VAT)
- Allocation costs, including overhead, selling, general and administrative expenses
- Inventory amounts (raw, in-process and finished goods) and resulting cash-flow requirements
- Prototype price, preproduction price, and production price, if applicable
- Revenue estimates using different pricing and volumes
- Targeted price variation explanation

Next Steps

Once this information has been entered into a financial analysis spreadsheet and summarized, a sensitivity analysis can be made by different volumes, prices or investments. Also, this opportunity can be compared with other completed projects or other current business opportunities. A sensitivity analysis is a method of evaluating different scenarios with differing inputs. Probabilities can be assigned to certain prices and volumes; see below table for an example.

Table 4. 2 Sales, volume, price, and probability table

Volume per month	Probability	Volume x Probability
18,000	0.6	10,800
20,000	0.25	5,000
22,000	0.15	3,300
Estimated volume		19,100

Price ($/unit)	Probability	Price x Probability
27	0.2	5.4
26	0.5	13
25	0.3	7.5
Estimated price		$25.90
Estimated monthly revenue		**$494,690**

The above example shows how probability can be used for defining both a volume and price. These probabilities can come from an analysis of current products in the market, discussions with the customer, or internal discussions. There is no correct or exact volume and price to use, and using probabilities based on some known market intelligence is far better than guessing. Also, note that the volume is on a monthly, not yearly, basis. A finer breakdown for the first year may be needed for production ramp-up, supply chain fulfillment, market penetration, for determining initial cash-flow requirements, and for estimating monthly financial budgets.

Once estimated volume, price, and estimated revenues have been defined, the business case leader can inform the various functional staff responsible for collecting the BC factors. The information collected can be summarized into a pro forma income statement for an entire year, for the next several years, or for the life of the project. Also, these statements can be incrementally added to or analyzed against the company's full financial statements.

Using the financial calculation for Net Present Value (NPV) can help compare profitability and internal rates of return (IRR) for each of the different business cases. The business case with the highest NPV and IRR percentage is the best choice. The NPV formula is shown below, and the IRR formula is when the Rate of Return (R) yields an NPV = 0.

$$NPV = \sum_{t=0}^{T} \frac{\text{Profit each time period}}{(1+R)t} - \text{Initial Investment}$$

where R = the rate of return, and t is the number of time periods

An example follows:

A company has a potential new business opportunity and requires an investment of $1,329,900. Over the course of 5 years, the project is expected to generate a profit of ($235,442) for the first year, $483,802 for the second year, $537,296 for the third year, $639,769 for the fourth year, and $739,168 for the fifth year with a cost of capital of 10%. A pro-forma Income Statement is shown:

Table 4. 3 Income statement

Income Statement	Year 1	Year 2	Year 3	Year 4	Year 5
Revenue	$298,140	$5,936,280	$6,216,000	$6,216,000	$6,216,000
Cost of Goods Sold:					
Direct Material	$74,929	$2,360,859	$2,454,113	$2,380,490	$2,309,075
Direct Labor	63,890	1,439,548	1,494,220	1,449,393	1,405,912
Variable Overhead	296,814	963,510	1,002,050	971,989	942,829
Total Cost of Goods Sold	$435,633	$4,763,917	$4,950,383	$4,801,872	$4,657,816
Gross Profit	($137,493)	$1,172,363	$1,265,617	$1,414,128	$1,558,184
Depreciation and Amortization	-	269,367	269,367		
Fixed Operating Expenses	97,949	201,834	217,560		
Total Operating Expenses	97,949	471,201	486,927	486,927	486,927
Operating Income	($235,442)	$701,162	$778,690	$927,201	$1,071,257
Income tax		$217,360	$241,394	$287,432	$332,090
Net Profit	($235,442)	$483,802	$537,296	$639,769	$739,168

NPV@5 years = [($235,442/1.10^1) + ($483,802/1.10^2) + ($537,296/1.10^3) + ($639,769/1.10^4) + ($739,168/1.10^5)] - $1,329,900 = $583,589. This assumes year 4 and 5 sales remain the same as year 3. Also, material, labor, and variable overhead productivity have a 3% improvement year over year starting at year 4. Operating expenses for years 4 and 5 remain the same as year 3.

To calculate the Internal Rate of Return (IRR), use the same NPV formula, where NPV = 0.

$$\sum_{t=0}^{T} \frac{C_n}{(1+R)^t} = 0$$

where C_n is the profit for each period.

NPV = 0 = ($1,329,900) + ($235,442)/1+R^1) + ($483,802/1+R^2) + ($537,296/1 + R^3) + ($639,769/1+R^4) +($739,168/1+R^5)

IRR = 23%.

Finance may also prepare other financial statements such as Cash Flow and Balance Sheet, and compute some financial ratios such as Payback Period and Return on Assets. Typically, projects will be compared using the NPV as the main criteria with secondary criteria being IRR, Payback Period, Return on Assets, and other non-quantitative reasons. In addition, risks and assumptions need to be defined, as the risks may be too high to accept even though the NPV and other financial ratios are acceptable.

5. Risks and Assumptions

Risks and assumptions need to be collected from the various staff that are collecting and preparing factors and details of the business case. The BC leader should provide a summary of the Risks and Assumptions with the business case. The business case and Risks and Assumptions are to be presented to the decision makers. The Risks and Assumptions may be edited during the BC development and during the BC presentation. If possible a scenario of best case and worst case can be calculated by identifying the risk drivers and the probability of occurrence (a business case risk FMEA) using the risk criteria below:

- Define assumptions for probabilities for both volume and price, especially for new customers.
- If the opportunity is in a different industry, there may be different product development, quality, testing, delivery, or warranty requirements that may be unknown or uncertain, so this needs to be highlighted as a significant risk.
- Are familiar raw materials being processed? If so, processing timing, tooling and scrap are relatively known. If little to no experience in processing these materials, then this needs to be highlighted as a significant risk. The lack of experience could be a major problem and this could cause rejection of the BC opportunity.

- Are product quality, performance and dimensional requirements within the current process range and within the process capability requirements? If the requirements are tighter or beyond the range of the current process capabilities, then this would be a significant risk and should be highlighted. This could lead to rejection of the BC.
- Does the timing for product and process development meet the customer's requirements? If not, can options be defined and presented to the decision makers? This needs to be highlighted and may lead to rejection of the BC.
- Are any customer requirements not available? Is any other information missing? If financial estimations are made, a list of these estimations is needed and presented to the decision makers.
- How does the cash-flow requirement affect the company's financials, with and without this new business opportunity? Are there ways in which the cash-flow requirements could be managed to reduce risk, such as pushing some investments into year two or waiting until certain volumes are attained?
- Are there other opportunities with better or similar NPV/IRR values with less risk?
- If the company does not pursue this opportunity, what advantages do your competitors gain?

6. Business Case - Analysis and Decision

Once the Business Case (BC) leader has collected information, analyzed factors, and prepared a summary of the BC, then a review meeting can be held. Typically, these meetings are held once a week. The BC review meeting agenda, review expectations, decision-making quorum and decision-making criteria should be fixed and aligned to strategic initiatives.

A presentation should be made beginning with a business summary. The summary will include details on the customer/consumer, and the product. The presentation will also cover prices, volumes, and profit. Risks and Assumptions would be the next part of the presentation. The decision makers may also want to make some modifications to the BC — such as using a different pricing, volume or investment — to see the effect. Thus, the financial model needs to be flexible and quickly able to show these modifications and reveal how corresponding details are affected, such as changes to NPV and IRR.

Based upon this review and sensitivity analysis, the decision makers will then decide on a price and submit a quote to the customer, reject the business case for more information needed, or reject the business pursuit with a documented reason. If the decision is to pursue the business, the decision makers should at this point discuss and define any conditions to be added to the quote.

Once the BC review meeting is over, the BC leader will write up the decisions and actions defined and then distribute the meeting minutes to the decision leaders. The BC leader can use a spreadsheet to summarize all the BCs, including the file names for the business cases, and a worksheet that summarizes all the action items. Each BC will have its own set of data files and should be stored and filed in such a way that it is easy to retrieve for future reference. Files should be named by product type to clearly indicate what is within the file.

7. Quote Submission

A quote will be prepared only for a business case that has been approved for pursuit. The customer typically has a RFQ (request for quote) document template for filling in the blanks and attaching information. Some E-commerce companies offer their quote templates online. Some templates are quite simple, while others can be quite complex to navigate. Keep in contact with the customer frequently and let them know your intentions as you prepare the RFQ. As mentioned, RFQs could require information such as the following:

- Prototype, preproduction, and production unit prices
- R&D and validation costs
- Part number, revisions and drawings
- Timing plan for product and process development
- Statement-of-work agreement
- Quality certifications, licenses or other certifications, especially those involving hazardous materials
- Non-Disclosure Agreement
- Company registration, tax identification, DUNS (Data Universal Numbering System) number, NAICS (North American Industry Classification System) number, or Standard Industrial Classification (SIC) code
- Contact list or high-level organization chart

The key is to submit the RFQ on time, with all documentation completed. Once the RFQ is submitted, a follow-up call should be made to request a time for formal review. Follow-up calls are necessary and especially important for new customers.

8. Customer Presentation

A customer presentation may occur over the phone, online or in person. The meeting may also have customer representatives from Purchasing, Quality, and Engineering. A detailed understanding of your quote is needed, including from a technical perspective. Based on the meeting result, you may have a follow-up meeting, your quote may be rejected, you may have to modify the quote in some ways for further negotiations, or your quote may be accepted as is and be nominated for a business award.

9. Win/Loss Status and Analysis

At some point, you will know whether you have won or lost this business opportunity. Either way, you should contact the customer. Offer thanks for the opportunity and discuss the reason(s) you were selected or not, as this information is vital for future opportunity pursuits. If the new business venture is awarded to your company, a meeting with the decision-makers should take place to define a project kickoff announcement and identify a project leader. This meeting can occur during a routine business pursuit meeting. If the business is not awarded to your company, the business case is closed with notes made about the reason(s) for loss.

10. Project Kickoff

Only for new business that is won, a project kickoff takes place. The business case leader would identify specific managers and staff to review the new business win details. In addition, the finance department would immediately update the financial forecasts with the new business venture details.

Business Pursuit Meetings – General

New business pursuit meetings are held at least once a month, with many companies having them on a weekly basis. During the new business pursuit meeting, the status of each project is reviewed with updated action items to ensure the project is active and moving in a favorable direction. The meeting is to provide an update, it is not intended to be a business case working meeting. Business case meetings are typically held according to the business case leader's schedule. The new business pursuit meetings are for steps 7–9, from Quote submission to Win/Loss status and analysis.

Chapter 36 – Purchasing, Sourcing, and Supply Chain

Purchasing, sourcing, and supply chain activities have been discussed throughout this book. These activities are an integral part of all manufacturing companies, and many companies define and use these terms, roles, and activities differently. The Council of Supply Chain Management Professionals (CSCMP) has defined various terms, including logistics and supply chain management. Logistics have been discussed in detail in Chapter 20. According to CSCMP, the definition of supply chain is "supply chain management encompasses the planning and management of all activities involved in sourcing and procurement, conversion, and all logistics management activities."

Illustration – Industry 4.0 Supply Chain

Manufacturing companies are becoming more sophisticated in developing their "smart factory" with supply chain strategies aligned to Industry 4.0 digitalization technologies and concepts. The following diagram shows Deming's Plan-Do-Check-Act cycle with Industry 4.0 Supply Chain objectives and main activities. Supply Chain objectives and detailed activities need to be included in the Annual Operating Plan and Strategic Plans.

Reduce costs, lead-times, variations, & risks
Improve supply chain reliability, effectiveness, and efficiency

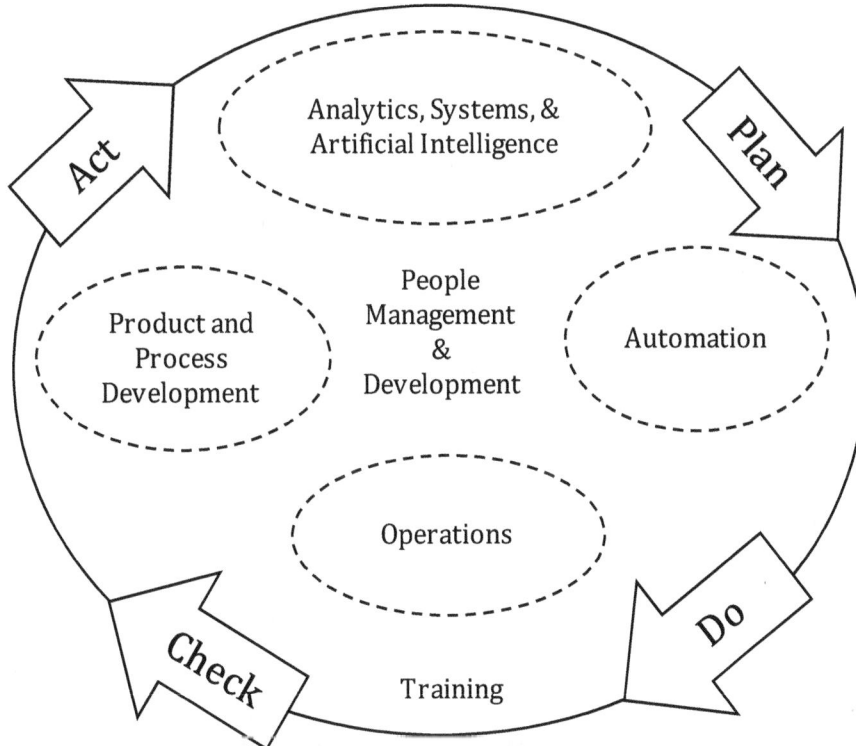

Figure 4. 1 Industry 4.0 Supply Chain

Analytics, Systems, and Artificial Intelligence

- Agile business process management workflow and KPIs
- Forecasting capabilities, planning, and reactions to changes — market, customers, and suppliers
- Product lifecycle management system
- Data communication's linkages — entire supply chain and logistics
- Business case development costs, timing, and options sensitivity analysis
- Advanced notification system
- Change management system
- System compliance and auditing effectiveness

Automation

- Various administrative tasks, operations and quality activities, decision making, and physical material flows
- Human-machine interfaces — data collection, analysis, reporting, and visualization
- Access and use of supply chain knowledge library for training, career advancement, and industrialization developments
- Customer, government, international standards, and internal requirements management

Operations

- Order fulfillment — production planning, processing, servicing, ordering, inventory management, and revenue
- Means to continuously optimize logistics
- Financial Variance Analysis capability and timing
- Total Productive Maintenance

Product and Process Development

- Confidence of flawless product launches
- Supplier development and supplier management processes
- Root Cause and Corrective Analysis system — alerts, automation, diagnostics, read-across to other products, root cause validation, containment and corrective action effectiveness, linkage to engineering knowledge library
- Product reliability and warranty management, and link to engineering knowledge library

Purchasing, sourcing and supply chain are roles within all manufacturing companies that are tactical, strategic, and can be a persuasive competitive advantage. Sourcing is both strategic and tactical. Strategic sourcing is a long-term activity based on the total cost of ownership and risk. It requires building relationships with suppliers and partners. It begins early in the product development process and builds and develops value chains to establish low costs and low risks over the long term. Strategic sourcing uses both quantitative and qualitative measures for evaluating and developing suppliers; such qualitative measures include culture, scalability, innovativeness, and agility. Tactical sourcing is a short-term, cost cutting, transactional activity where price is driven by negotiation. This approach assumes "low cost countries" are always the preferred choice and uses only quantitative measures for evaluating suppliers. Manufacturing companies may sometimes use both strategic and tactical approaches for their supplier base, depending upon the strategy and business situation.

Sourcing process for manufacturing companies consists of the following for procurement:

- Direct materials — material directly utilized to manufacture a finished goods product that are defined in the bill of materials for the finished product.

- Indirect materials, perishable tooling, and supplies — items that do not become a part of the finished goods product

- Supplier tooling

- Capital expenditures

- Services, such as: customer support services, grounds keeping, engineering, human resources, information technology (IT), logistics, maintenance, marketing, quality, security, and supply chain

Illustration – Sourcing Process

The following illustration expands upon the Supplier Quality activities defined in Chapter 15 to include activities specifically for sourcing activities. Manufacturing companies are evolving their documented business processes into work flow digital management systems to incorporate various business functions.

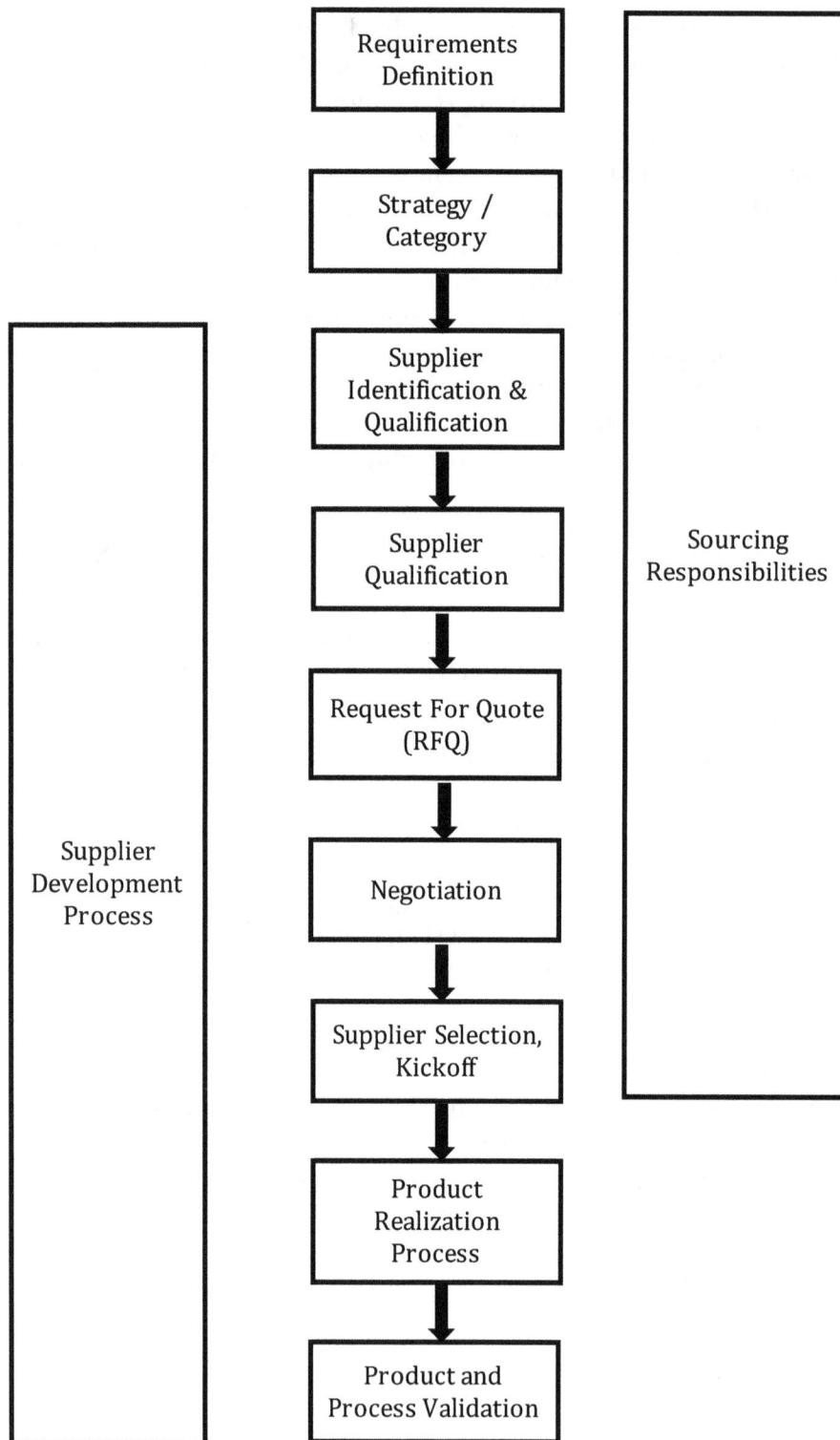

Figure 4. 2 Sourcing Process

Key items to evaluate the effectiveness of purchasing, sourcing, and supply chain:

1. Define and understand the entire supply chain relative to various KPIs, such as: costs, quality, delivery, lead-time improvements, cost reductions, flawless launch confidence and result, forecasting capability, and many others

2. Regularly assess and improve the supply chain value stream

3. Continuously invest in new supply chain technologies

4. Promote, engage, and continuously train people

5. Openly communicate and visually display supply chain issues, plans, and actions

6. Conduct self-critical external audits of internal operations

7. Conduct audits throughout supply chain

8. Evaluate performance against the annual operating plan and strategic plan

Chapter 37 - Capacity Planning

Capacity planning is an evaluation of the current manufacturing process utilization over a certain forecasted period. It is a part of the manufacturing footprint and usually defined in a spreadsheet for long-term strategic and annual planning, analyzing new business opportunities, and for forecasting production needs. Capacity is defined as the maximum amount or number of good products produced, or the throughput rate for a specific manufacturing process, line, work-cell, work station or equipment for a specific period.

For long-term strategic and annual planning, capacity typically is defined in units per year with a corresponding utilization rate and/or available capacity amount for several forecasted years. For evaluating new business opportunities, the customer RFQ is typically expressed in units per year for several years. The capacity planning template needs to show both the current capacity and utilization rate for several forecasted years. Some of the manufacturing equipment may be shared amongst products; as volumes change or a new manufacturing process equipment is installed, capacity plans may help to identify opportunities for cross-utilization or cost reduction opportunities. Also, when contracts expire, current utilization rates will be affected. In addition, the capacity planning template can show the number of direct laborers planned based on product volumes for specific work-cells. This information is useful for Production management to ensure they have qualified direct labor workers. Some difficulties arise when developing multiple business cases using manufacturing equipment with available capacity. Some companies note this within the capacity planning module so several business cases can be viewed at one time to see the impact on overall capacity and possibility of future investments needs — especially in the event the customer awards the business and it affects more than one business case or submitted RFQ.

Capacity - Short Term

Capacity can be changed in the short term or temporarily increased to meet production needs. To increase capacity in the short term, the following can be used:

- Use overtime
- Add part-time or full-time shifts
- Use suppliers to contract work
- Change shift working hours
- Change shift work scheme
- Add labor during breaks

Capacity – Long Term

To increase capacity in the long term, a structural or significant change is needed to the existing operations, facility, and/or layout. Some of the above short-term changes can be permanent as well, including the following:

- Change product and process design to use less process time
- Purchase new equipment
- Continuously conduct productivity projects
- Outsource lower profit products, then use that available capacity

Capacity Formula and Analysis

There are several factors to define the capacity for each specific machine, process work-cell, or process line. Capacity can be defined annually, but for production planning purposes, capacity by shift, day, or week is more useful.

C_{mach} = Capacity of a specific machine, work-cell or process line expressed as a quantity per time period. For short processing times, measuring in seconds or tenths of seconds is used. Use the same time units for each factor and express capacity in common units across the manufacturing processes for ease of use and comparison.

AWT = Available work time in seconds or minutes, which is time available to run production on a specific machine, work-cell, or line. AWT is calculated by taking the total work time minus time for scheduled breaks, lunch, and dinners (including beginning of shift, end of shift breaks for cleaning, or for Daily Routine meetings).

DT = Downtime in seconds or minutes, including planned and unplanned downtime such as tool changeovers, setups, inspections and Preventive Maintenance (PM).

CT = Cycle Time expressed in seconds or minutes.

TC = Tool Change expressed in seconds or minutes, but typically in seconds. The tool change time represents time that the machine is not able to process a part. In other words, capacity is affected as the process is not running. Alternatively, if a tool has to be changed but the machine is still processing, this time is not affecting capacity and therefore not included in the tool change time. This variable is separately defined as some companies have multiple tool changes — some of which are online — affecting capacity. However, online tool change may not affect capacity if there is an automatic tool changing system that is timed for changing while another tool is in process. Offline tool changes — whether manual or automatic — should be performed so they do not affect processing time. These offline tool changes do not affect capacity.

QR = Quality Rate is the percent of acceptable parts yielded at a specific process for a continuous production run of a specific product type. Product that needs to be reworked and returned to the production line is not included in this calculation.

QR = (1 – Number of parts defective or rejected at the specific process)/total number of parts produced at that specific process of a specific product type × 100% (or number of acceptable parts produced/total number of parts produced × 100%). This number can be averaged over time or estimated based on process capability studies, or estimated based on similar process quality rates. Typically, set-up parts during start-up or changeover are not included in the Quality Rate. Reworked parts are not included in this calculation. The calculation only considers first-time produced parts with "good" status. Note that the cycle of rejecting parts, then reworking or inspecting/testing as "good" or "no good" is not included. Handling of rejected parts at a specific process may increase cycle time, and as a result, lower capacity. Typically, this cycle time increase is overlooked in most companies and not included in the calculation of cycle time, downtime, or quality rate, but it should be.

Capacity = (Available Work Time – Downtime)/Cycle Time × Quality Rate.

Note: The units of time may be different and should be converted to the same units.

$C_{mach} = (AWT - DT) / CT \times QR$

AWT_{Day} = Shifts per day × (hours per shift × 60_{min} – Scheduled breaks$_{min\ per\ shift}$ – $DR_{min\ per\ shift}$ – Operator $PM_{min\ per\ shift}$)

Note: $AWT_{Week} = AWT_{Day} \times$ Production planned work days/week

DR = Daily Routine time for shift start briefing

Operator PM = Preventive Maintenance time for checking machine readiness

$Downtime_{Day}$ = Historic average unscheduled DT/day + Historic average Preventive Maintenance/day + (average time per TC/average number of pcs between TC) × average number of parts produced/day.

Note: Some companies calculate Operator PM as a part of scheduled breaks within the Availability Work Time metric while others calculate Operator PM under Downtime. Also, there may be more than one type of tool that is used in this specific process and the time to change and the number of pieces between tool changes may be different. Changeover time per part = Changeover time/number of parts produced. Typically, this is expressed in seconds, but some companies may express it in minutes. For determining downtime related to changeover or tool changes, this can also be defined using the average changeover time per day. So, the formula can be re-stated as: $Downtime_{Day}$ = Historic average unscheduled downtime/day + Historic average Preventive Maintenance/day + Average changeover time/day.

CT = MT + AT

$Cycle\ Time_{Observed}$ = Manual $Time_{Sec}$ + Automatic $Time_{Sec}$

Manual time is the time the direct labor worker is engaged in manufacturing the product. Automatic time is the time the direct labor worker is not engaged in manufacturing the product — in other words, a machine is performing some manufacturing operation. These times should be computed over several parts being produced and then averaged. For accuracy, observe 10 or more parts or a production run of a certain amount of time. This calculation is used whenever one person works at more than one machine or station. When one person is working at one machine or station, then the cycle time can be computed from measuring the time it takes to finish making one product to the time it takes to producing the next product at the same machine or station.

$T_{takt} = AWT_{Day}/D_{Daily\ Demand}$

Takt Time is the pace of production that matches customer demand. A more detailed definition is the average time from the start of producing one finished good to the start of producing the next finished good part that matches the customer's rate of demand. Takt time cannot be calculated using a stopwatch, as takt is based upon the rate of customer demand. However, cycle time is calculated using a stopwatch.

Maximum Capacity for a process

The *maximum capacity for a process* is equivalent to the process step with the lowest capacity. The process may consist of one or many machines processing product. In other words, for any product, the process step with the lowest capacity limits the entire process from producing more product.

$C_{proc} = \min\{C_{mach1}, C_{mach2}, C_{mach3}, ...\}$, where C_{machX} = Capacity of each machine

Number of Direct Labor Workers for a process

An estimate of the *number of direct labor operators for a specific process* can be calculated by taking the process step with the lowest capacity multiplied by the total walking time and manual work times of the entire process. The Available Work Time (AWT) usually is calculated on a per-shift basis but can also be on a per-day basis. This is expressed as:

$DL_{number} = C_{proc} \times (T_{walk} + T_{manual}) / AWT_{Shift}$

Where T_{walk} = Time to walk in between machines or stations when no work is being performed. If one operator is at one machine or station, then there is no walking time. However, if the operator works in a work-cell with two or more machines or stations, then this time to walk between the machines is collected. And, T_{manual} is the time that the operator is performing some process operation step. If the operator is working at a machine and the operator unloads and reloads a machine, the unloading and loading time is collected; if the operator then inspects the part or does any other work (such as deburring or recording any quality or traceability information), this time is also collected. For assembly operations, the time required for the direct labor worker to load a part into an assembly jig, then perform manual assembly operations, then unload the part is calculated as the cycle time and would be the manual time. However, there are assembly work-cells where some work stations have a machine or automated time. Since the automated time is not manual time, the automated time is not used in the calculation unless the station requires the direct labor worker to remain at the station for the machine to run (for example, depressing two palm buttons or using ergonomic touch buttons).

Number of Direct Labor workers to match Takt Time

$$DL_{Takt} = (T_{walk} + T_{manual})/T_{takt}$$

For example:

A manufacturing company has 2 shifts, 10 hours each shift, 5 days a week, with a total of a 1-hour break for lunch and other rest times. Several similar products are produced on work-cell A1. The demand has increased from 4,000 parts a week to 4,200 parts per week. The work-cell on average produces 800 parts per day, just meeting the current demand. Typically, maintenance performs their work on production off hours and on weekends when there is no production running. And, each operator performs a machine check and station cleaning for 10 minutes each shift. Also, prior to starting the shift, the Supervisor meets with all operators for 10 minutes for the Daily Routine meeting.

Manufacturing assembly work cell HH-1 has three stations: A, B and C. Station A is a hydraulic press machine, station B is an assembly station, and station C is a test and label-printing station. The work-cell has 2 direct labor workers. Typically, one direct labor worker performs Station A and Station C work, while the second direct labor worker mainly works at Station B.

At Station A, one direct labor worker takes 2 parts and fits them together into a jig then depresses a two-hand button to activate a hydraulic press; the load and unload times is 5 seconds each, and the machine cycle time is 18 seconds to press the parts together. Typically, there is no tool change, as all similar products use the same fixture and die. However, the defect rate is 1.5%, where most of the time the parts are not reworked, they are scrapped. The unplanned downtime averages 30 minutes per shift. The operator then moves this sub-assembly to the Work-In-Process (WIP) table at the next station and continues to fill the WIP table until it is full. Then, the operator moves to Station C. While moving to Station C, they check whether Station B needs any components or materials. This operator stocks Station B components and removes empty component containers. This allows Station B operator to stay at their station performing the assembly work uninterruptedly.

At Station B, the direct labor worker picks up the sub-assembly from the WIP table and places it into a jig, then installs various components and torques several screws to hold the assembly together and then moves the assembly to the WIP table at Station C. The Station B worker has to change the tool bit every 200 parts because of tool wear. The tool change takes 20 seconds when there are available spare tool tips available at the station. It takes 5 seconds to load and unload each assembly from the jig and 60 seconds to perform the manual assembly. The unplanned downtime for station B averages 20 minutes per shift and the defect rate is 0.5%.

At Station C, the direct labor worker tests the assembly and if the assembly is acceptable the direct labor worker puts a label on the assembly and puts it into a box. If the assembly is rejected, the tester automatically makes a small indent on the part and automatically removes it to the back side of the station. No label is placed on the assembly. The direct labor tests several of these assemblies before returning back to Station A to repeat the process. Station C load and unload is 5 seconds each, the test cycle time is 10 seconds, and applying the label is 5 seconds. The average unplanned downtime is 10 minutes per day and the reject rate is 0.5%.

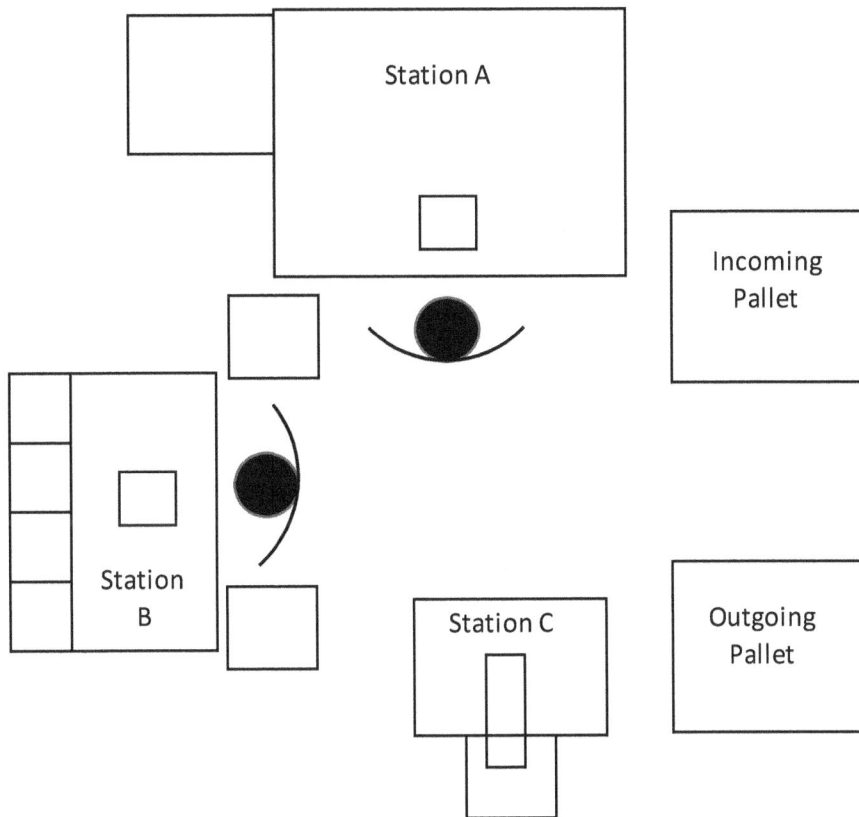

Figure 4. 3 Manufacturing work cell HH-1

To determine the maximum capacity per day for work-cell HH-1, calculate capacity for stations A, B, and C. The lowest capacity number of the 3 stations is the maximum capacity for the work cell. See the following calculation: C_{HH-1} = min ($C_{HH-1 \text{ station A}}$, $C_{HH-1 \text{ station B}}$, $C_{HH-1 \text{ station C}}$).

C_{HH-1} = min ($C_{HH-1 \text{ station A}}$ = (AWT – DT)/CT × QR, $C_{HH-1 \text{ station B}}$ (AWT - DT) / CT × QR, $C_{HH-1 \text{ station C}}$ (AWT - DT) / CT × QR

Station A

$C_{HH\text{-}1\ station\ A}$ = AWT = AWT_{day} = Shifts per day × (hours per shift × 60_{min} – Scheduled breaks$_{min\ per\ shift}$ – $DR_{min\ per\ shift}$) = 2 x (10 x 60 – 60 – 10) = 1,060 minutes

$DT_{HH\text{-}1\ station\ A}$ = Downtime$_{Day}$ = Historic average unscheduled Downtime/day + Historic average Preventive Maintenance/day + (average time per TC / average # of pieces between TC) × Average number of parts produced/day

$DT_{HH\text{-}1\ station\ A}$ = Downtime$_{Day}$ = 2 shifts x 30 min unplanned DT + 2 shifts x 10 Operator PM = 80 minutes

$CT_{HH\text{-}1\ station\ A}$ = Cycle Time$_{Observed}$ = Manual Time$_{Sec}$ + Automatic Time$_{Sec}$ = 10 + 18 = 28 seconds

$QR_{HH\text{-}1\ station\ A}$ = 98.5% good parts

$C_{HH\text{-}1\ station\ A\ per\ day}$ = (1,060 minutes – 80 minutes) / 28 seconds x 98.5% x 60 minutes = 2,069 parts per day

Station B

$C_{HH\text{-}1\ station\ B}$ = 2 x (10 x 60 – 60 – 10) = 1,060 minutes

$DT_{HH\text{-}1\ station\ B}$ = 2 x 20 + 2 x 10 + (20 sec / 60 / 200) x 800 = 61 minutes

$CT_{HH\text{-}1\ station\ B}$ = 10+60 = 70 seconds

$QR_{HH\text{-}1station\ B}$ = 99.5% good parts

$C_{HH\text{-}1\ station\ B\ per\ day}$ = (1,060 – 61)/70 x 99.5% x 60 = 853 parts per day

Station C

$C_{HH\text{-}1\ station\ C}$ = 2 x (10 x 60 – 60 – 10) = 1,060 minutes

$DT_{HH\text{-}1station\ C}$ = 2 x 10 + 2 x 10 = 40 minutes

$CT_{HH\text{-}1station\ C}$ = 10 + 10 + 5 = 25 seconds

$QR_{HH\text{-}1station\ C}$ = 99.5% good parts

$C_{HH\text{-}1\ station\ C\ per\ day}$ = (1,060 – 40) / 25 x 99.5% x 60 = 2,436 parts per day

Capacity of HH-1 work-cell

$C_{HH\text{-}1}$ = min ($C_{HH\text{-}1\ station\ A}$, $C_{HH\text{-}1\ station\ B}$, $C_{HH\text{-}1\ station\ C}$)

$C_{HH\text{-}1}$ = min (Station A = 2,069, Station B = 853, Station C= 2,436)

Capacity of HH-1 work cell is 853 parts per day, or 427 parts per shift

Takt Time

Old T_{takt} = AWT_{day}/$D_{Daily\ Demand}$ = 1,060 x 60 / (4,000 / 5) = 80 seconds per part

New T_{takt} = 1,060 x 60 / (4,200 / 5) = 76 seconds per part

Number of Direct Labor workers

$DL_{number} = C_{proc} \times (T_{walk} + T_{manual})/AWT_{shift} = 427 \times (28+70+15) / (1{,}060 / 2 \times 60) = 1.5$ operators per shift. Station A press time requires the operator to remain at the station, so the entire cycle time is computed, and Station B is completely manual assembly, so the entire cycle time is computed. However, Station C test time is automated, so this time is not included. Alternatively, takt can be calculated as follows:

Old $DL_{takt} = (T_{walk} + T_{manual})/T_{takt} = (28+70+15) / 80 = 1.4$ operators

New $DL_{takt} = 113 / 76 = 1.5$ operators

The direct labor calculation shows 1.4 or 1.5 direct labor workers are needed. However, it is not possible to have a partial worker, so 2 workers are needed to meet the direct labor requirement. In other words, the number should always be rounded up. However, prior to rounding up, the work elements at each station should be analyzed further, as work elements can be automated, re-distributed, consolidated into other stations, or waste can be eliminated for each work element. By analyzing the work elements, the total walk plus manual time may be reduced, thus resulting in higher capacity with less direct labor. This allows the planners and supervisors to move direct labor to other work areas.

Based upon the above calculations, going from a demand of 4,000 to 4,200 parts per week (or from 800 to 840 per day) is an issue because the average number of parts produced per day is currently only 800 with a rated capacity of 853 parts. It is questionable as to whether this work-cell can meet the new demand as-is, so an improvement must be implemented. Historical production, quality and maintenance records need to be analyzed to confirm the above numbers; a discussion with the line supervisor and a review of the data with the supervisor are also needed. Having the supervisor on each shift aware of the productivity every hour is very important. Training the supervisors to be roaming or routed on the floor will be challenging at first, as the supervisors will come up with a variety of reasons for not wanting to work in this new way. Also, the supervisors may state valid reasons for not meeting the daily production requirement, such as the direct labor workers were spending time trying to rework parts. In reality, the supervisor and direct labor workers inherently know that station B is the bottleneck, but in practice every hour of everyday, does the Station B operator stay focused and attentive to operating their station and meeting the takt time and productivity per hour? For example, station B operator may process station C work or even stock their own station with parts. Or due to fatigue, operator at station B may slow down during a 10-hour shift. The supervisor should be sure the direct labor workers are trained and certified for the work they are performing. The supervisor along with manufacturing engineering staff should define a rotation time between the two operators to reduce fatigue. There are many reasons why the production may not meet the requirements, and both a quantitative and qualitative study, with valuable input from direct labor and supervisors, may be needed to determine the cause(s). One of the first studies that can be jointly conducted is to develop Standardized Work for the work-cell, see "Standardized Work" for more information. By defining the work elements for each station, a Line Balance exercise can be conducted. It may be possible to move some work elements from Station B to Station A, resulting in a higher capacity for Station B and for the work-cell.

Finally, if the work-cell does not have an hourly productivity chart showing the number of parts being produced per hour, one could be created. Studying this chart over a few weeks can help validate the downtime, cycle time and quality rate. In addition, workers may be able to identify improvements needed to meet new demands. They may suggest simple fixes, such as doing a line balance, changing the component part presentation so it is easier to assemble, finding a more efficient way of assembling the components, or reducing unplanned downtime. The unplanned downtime for Station B of 40 min/day contributes to a possible 34 parts that could be produced (DT 40 min x 60 sec / CT 70 sec). The operators know the issues and opportunities in their work-cells — they just need a forum and culture that allows them to define improvements and ultimately implement them. Depending upon management's maturity and interest in developing manufacturing competence, management may want to have the work-cell direct labor workers participate in a 90 Day Challenge. See 90 Day Challenge for more information, as it is positively oriented and overall beneficial to the company.

Manufacturing is highly complex, with many variables to understand and control (or at least minimize the variability). There is no single analytical tool or industrial practice that will solve all manufacturing problems. The keys are to:

1. Improve understanding of your processes using various analytical tools
2. Learn and develop mathematical understandings of the processes with direct labor workers, supervisors and staff
3. Coordinate resources to voice improvement ideas
4. Manage, engage, empower, and motivate people
5. Conduct improvement workshops and use 90 Day Challenges
6. Define risks and implement corrective actions
7. Define and implement annual plans and strategies

Chapter 38 – 90 Day Challenge

Many companies have yearly campaigns or slogans, typically launched several months into the New Year, with stretch KPIs. For several months, the initiative is hot and active; however, towards the fourth quarter of the year, the campaign often takes a backseat to next year's plans. A 90 Day Challenge provides a more-focused, intense initiative. This can be started any time during the year. It can be broad based, functionally specific, or project specific. During the annual planning session, one section of discussion should be on major projects for the coming year — most of which should be project based — but some will be infrastructure, productivity based, or have a quality focus. Of course, there are projects that focus on safety, employee welfare, employee engagement and factory showcase culture, customer visits, community events, and various operation upgrades. Any topic in this book can be pursued within 90 days with a diligent and committed team, and improvements will be made. Sustaining those improvements or continuing on the improvement path after the 90 days may require a different approach, but it is still important for senior management to recognize team members involved and continue to provide support for their efforts.

Who to involve with a 90 Day Challenge?

Ideally, having a small group or functional team is best to work on a specific project. A senior manager should be involved to mentor or support the project in the event a resource or conflict issue happens. The team can be comprised of a mix of different functions, including factory workers. Also, the team can include suppliers, customers, or external resources such as trainers or consultants. The group and senior manager should identify a project leader. The project leader typically is a staff member, but there are projects where a Direct Labor worker can be the lead. Another benefit for having 90 Day Challenges is to develop employee's leadership abilities. Some difficulties arise when direct labor workers from the night of off-shifts are on the team. The project leader must find ways to engage them.

When is the best time to start these 90 Day Challenges?

The best time to start a 90 Day Challenge is soon after one has been completed, or anytime during the year when a team and manager can be engaged. A manufacturing factory always has issues and projects, so everyone will always be busy doing something. Having a team focus on one specific challenge helps the business in many ways, including boosting morale. Upon completion of the project, recognizing the team and support members is critical to boost morale. It is easier to get involvement from others if a snack, hat, or plaque in the cafeteria is awarded. Another way to encourage participation is to post and promote an announcement or highlight the challenge in a company online newsletter.

How to start a 90 Day Challenge?

There are many different ways to start a 90 Day Challenge. One common way is that the Plant Manager identifies a specific project. Then, the project background information is posted in the cafeteria and break areas. Meanwhile, functional managers, supervisors and staff discuss how to support the project. Typically, one function takes the lead and will start recruiting candidates to participate. Once a kickoff date is defined, typically the Plant Manager will launch the Challenge by having an initial meeting with all participants. The Plant Manager will state the importance of the project and provide information about the background of the project. Then, the Plant manager would utilize their Lean 6 sigma function, certified black belt employees, project managers, or in some cases different function managers on a rotating basis to act as a project leader. These types of leaders are experienced with assembling a group and are qualified to provide some training to the Challenge participants. Some other companies are embracing Agile methodology. Agile is an iterative approach whose objective is to accelerate innovation, add value to the customers, and develop the organization from top-down hierarchies to self-organizing teams. Agile at this time is still in its infancy, but is slowly gaining traction across all industries.

What if the challenge is completed before the 90 days or after 90 days?

The team and the senior manager should be working towards a project timing schedule. Peer and management pressure should provide some stress to keep the project on schedule; in some cases, it may be completed before the deadline, or extended beyond the deadline. Fixating on the completion time is not nearly as important as the task. Management should have weekly, short reviews of the project to ensure the right resources are available and project direction matches the intended challenge. Having the project extend beyond 90 days gives less credibility to these challenges and warrants the senior management to be more engaged throughout the project. So, it is critical during the reviews to be sure the challenge is completed on or before 90 days. However, the same celebration should happen whether the challenge is completed according to schedule, before the 90 days, or later.

What happens if the challenge does not meet the intended goals?

The team should establish a reasonable but challenging goal. Throughout the weekly reviews of the challenge, management should assess the probability of achieving the goal and expected benefits, including morale. Sacrificing and accepting a lesser goal by management may be the best option, as the team would gain invaluable knowledge about their project, work as a group, and gain experience with making presentations to management. If management recognizes there is a very low probability of achieving the goal, the team and management should reassess their project and determine whether to modify the project challenge or modify the goal. The team should not be allowed to disband without some achievement.

How many 90 Day Challenges should be undertaken at any one time?

Management needs to assess having more than one active 90 Day Challenge at a time. Initially, starting one challenge and ending it with a celebration as defined above gives management an understanding of how these challenges evolve, efforts required by various resources (including management's time for reviews and assessments), and gives management an understanding of when to initiate a second or third challenge while one is under way. As one 90 Day Challenge nears its completion, another 90 Day Challenge project can be posted for people to participate in.

Chapter 39 - Building a Factory Showcase Culture

Building a factory showcase culture begins when the general manager and management team accept that the current culture is too traditional or old school and needs to modernize. Once these leaders make the decision to turn the facility into a factory showcase culture, they need to assess their competencies in the sections of Orientation, Foundation, Conditioning, and Competitiveness, and at minimum, to take action on the following:

- Improve physical infrastructure
- Positively change behaviors
- Kick-off committees
- Use social media
- Enhance employee's careers
- Seek feedback and analyze to improve

Improve Physical Infrastructure

Several physical infrastructure improvements can be made to show workers that the culture is in the process of changing. These physical changes provide an impetus for improving other aspects of the business. Physical upgrades of the cafeteria, restrooms and lounge areas are the most direct way for workers to notice that changes are being made. Cafeteria improvements, for example, might include painting walls, installing new vending machines with a greater variety of choices, ensuring food trucks are available during breaks, and providing disposable plates and utensils. Post daily/weekly/monthly factory KPIs or bulletins, implementing new cleanliness standards, and start to openly discuss ways to improve morale.

Positively Change Behaviors

Cultural shifts can also form by implementing Daily Routines, having layered process audits, and having weekly management meet-and-greets. It is imperative that management and staff be on the factory floor every day to help work out issues, listen, and engage workers to express their ideas. Management should have monthly birthday recognition lunches for employees, offer a variety of information during lunch time, and promote knowledge development during shift and after work with internal courses, online programs, or other training programs, including college courses. These opportunities are to provide management and workers "face time" to discuss current business activities and other things, including local community events. Making the conversations personal, even in a group setting, helps to unify, strengthen and align acceptance of changes. Management should also participate in external workshops to learn what are acceptable and not acceptable behaviors, as well as to learn how to cultivate the new behaviors. Management should also schedule reviews of their management culture and of themselves with an external consultant.

Kick-off Committees

A complete review and possibly an overhaul of the company handbook and manufacturing operation's controls are necessary to convey a change in culture. Committees can be formed to discuss and refine company rules and behavior expectations, business processes, manufacturing quality practices, nutrition and wellness, mental health programs, and eventually roles, responsibilities and organization structures. Committee meetings can be oriented to training, open dialogue, or geared towards working on various projects. It is very important that the organization be trained by external trainers in the establishment and promotion of active committees. Committees should be small groups formed from a cross-section of the factory workforce, including manufacturing operators, supervisors and staff, and not directed just by the management team. Committees can post their specific topics and provide updates by posting the status in or near the cafeteria, so every worker can learn about what is going on and consider participating. The goal of developing committees is to have participants experience greater autonomy with more authority.

Implementing a factory showcase culture can start with small focused groups, even though it may be a company-wide initiative. The groups are tasked with defining an objective and working towards meeting that expectation. Each group may focus on a specific work area or topic in this book, such as Daily Routines. Every company or facility chooses its own path and timing to have a factory showcase culture. The chapters in this book define many tools and techniques, some of which your company may already have implemented well, while others may need significant effort. This is an ongoing, evolving process.

Use Social Media

Broadcasting the development of a factory showcase culture can be achieved with redefining posted slogans, providing new, ergonomic smart clothes for direct labor workers, regularly updating the company intra-website, and most importantly, use of social media such as Facebook, Twitter, Instagram and LinkedIn. Social media is vital for connecting people inside and outside the company by showing workers activities, accomplishments, projects, and even innovations. Also, social media can be used for announcing new products, presenting product promotion sales, and broadcasting partner products and services. Moreover, social media can be used for congratulating individuals and the entire workforce on achievements and for a variety of other company announcements with photos and videos. The frequent use of both internal and external social media broadens the connections to potential customers and promotes the company in many positive ways. Social media can also be detrimental to a company, as former distraught employees may use this against the company. However, in the long run, employees gain more satisfaction when recognized and people outside the company recognize and become familiar with the company and its products and services.

Enhance Employee's Careers

There are many ways to enhance employee's careers, beginning with mentorship programs, and by encouraging them to participate in committees, projects, and 90 Day Challenges. Engaging employees to nurture a passion for company improvement requires an adept, altruistic, mission- and vision-focused leadership team. Management, staff, and direct labor workers need to put effort into educating themselves individually and as a group. Employees should be encouraged to participate in different committees and projects, provide their ideas, and build their knowledge.

Another visible way to enhance employee's careers is to start broadcasting when model temporary workers are promoted to full-time, permanent workers. Putting barriers between permanent and temporary workers negatively affects overall performance. There is no reason to exclude temporary and contract workers from factory happenings and opportunities, including job openings and promotions. How these workers are treated day to day by management should be recognized internally and externally. If the treatment is positive, that behavior becomes part of the factory showcase culture.

Seek Feedback and Analyze to Improve

Customer feedback can be gained from internal and external sources including customers visiting the factory. Feedback can be obtained from: sales, customer service department, quality, supply chain, marketing, surveys, and various online social media comments.

Factory visitors can be customers, suppliers, members of the community, potential new hires, government officials and others. Whenever visitors come to the factory, it is essential they review and acknowledge safety and security rules. Visitors are expected to wear a displayed identification or barcoded badge and wear fluorescent-colored safety vests. Different colored vests may be used to indicate the type of visitor or the area(s) they are allowed to visit. A policy should be in place to ensure that visitors have escorts — this is for their own and for others' safety, and to ensure that propriety information is not at risk. Visitor tours in and around the factory can be conducted with guides using a script. Requiring guides to use a script ensures there is a standard for conveying information at the right time and right place throughout a tour. There may be different scripts, including some tailored to specific visitor's interests. The script may cover a wide variety of topics, such as KPIs, capacities, plans, projects, innovative accomplishments, products, process technologies, quality systems, laboratories, test facilities, warehousing, distribution services, IT systems, and factory showcase culture. More than one person may lead a tour so specific content can be delivered by knowledgeable and experienced people, or a tour leader could stop and invite staff to chime in about their responsibilities and work activities; in some areas, factory workers may be asked questions. The tour should have a defined route with various stopping points for observing factory operations.

The length of the tour and time to start the tour should be determined beforehand and agreed on with visitors so internal operations are not affected, workers are prepared, and the overall visit stays on schedule. During the tour, the visitor may be observing, taking notes, asking questions, or just listening and trying to learn. It is important to ask the visitor questions about the tour experience with a follow-up questionnaire or survey, whether on leaving or shortly after the visit. Some visitors may point out concerns, offer compliments, or even give ideas for improvement. Concerns should be addressed quickly, especially in the case of a potential safety or a near-miss issue. Less urgent concerns can be written down and photographed, then directed to others for follow-up after the tour. Compliments are always nice to hear and they need to be broadcasted to the entire organization. Ideas for improvement should be discussed after the tour. Other tours may consist of showing how customer concerns are managed; these are best handled by showing an actual recent customer concern and walking through the root cause and corrective action process. The tour guide may walk to the specific location on the factory where customer issues are posted and then discuss the issue, process, activities, timing and results.

Even though the destination is having a factory showcase culture, it by no means is an end point. The culture should always be adapting, growing, and innovating. Having an environment where the employees can develop themselves and self-organize will encourage innovation and add value to customers. Analyzing feedback from customers, full-time employees, temporary, and contract workers is needed to identify strengths, weaknesses, opportunities, and threats (SWOT). In addition, it is vital to respond to customer online comments and seek out visitor feedback. Finally, evaluating KPIs and understanding their link to the culture is just as important as financial variance analysis. At least once a year, there should be a formal review of the culture such as during the strategic planning process. Finally, implementing the tools, methods and practices in this book will direct your company to have a factory showcase culture.

Chapter 40 - Assessment

After reading this book, you may want to consider assessing your company to see how well your company is using these tools and techniques. Making this book available to many of your staff, including supervisors, will help educate them to become more productive and help them advance their careers. Students who learn these tools and techniques will have more to offer their future employers.

Initially performing an assessment once a year will help to identify improvement areas and subsequent years may need twice-a-year assessments due to the velocity of changes. The assessment must involve a cross-functional team reviewing each chapter's main topics and applying a score, as well as determining improvement opportunities and actions. The scoring should use the following guideline:

- 0 - No system or not yet defined
- 1 - Training completed by majority of team; implementation started
- 2 - Lack of a comprehensive system but some activities performed
- 3 - System defined and practiced nearly every day or when expected, however lacking some process activities or steps (lack of procedures, check sheets, training, auditing not regularly performed). Analysis weakly performed with few reports; corrective actions sporadically implemented or not completely effective
- 4 - System defined and managed; Analysis performed for special causes with effective corrective actions implemented.
- 5 - System well-executed and efficiently performed; innovations and improvements regularly occur; demonstrated as a factory showcase — can be a benchmark

Spider or radar charts can be used to show areas of strengths and areas needing improvement. Multiple assessments can be shown on the same chart differentiated by colors to representing the different assessment dates. Each of the four sections of this book should have its own spider or radar chart. These four charts can be placed on one page, or assembled on a four-panel chart for presentation, so they can be easily shared among management and staff for discussions and planning.

The main takeaway from analyzing the charts is to identify both strengths and improvement areas, as well as areas in which some favorable or unfavorable change has occurred, including where actions were taken but the score remained unchanged. Management and staff should evaluate the reasons for unfavorable changes or for unchanged scores. After the introspective evaluation, management should create its new set of challenges and action plans. Once you have reached achieved the highest rating of 5, do not rest! In order to always be competitive, you need to go through the cycle of Orientation, Foundation, Conditioning, and Competitiveness in a regular, yearly evaluation with all employees aware of the status and improvement plans. This helps to keep the employees engaged, updated, and minimizes the risk of working with outdated tools and processes.

Illustration – Building a Showcase Culture – Assessment

The following figure shows an example of a company's first assessment summary of "Building a Showcase Culture". Each of the 4 main sections is shown with a rating for each chapter title. The company management team needs to assess each section and chapter details to analyze the strengths and weaknesses. The low rating scores need to have a clear improvement plan. The detailed improvement plan needs to be included in the Annual Operating Plan so the status and updates can be reviewed during the monthly operation's reviews.

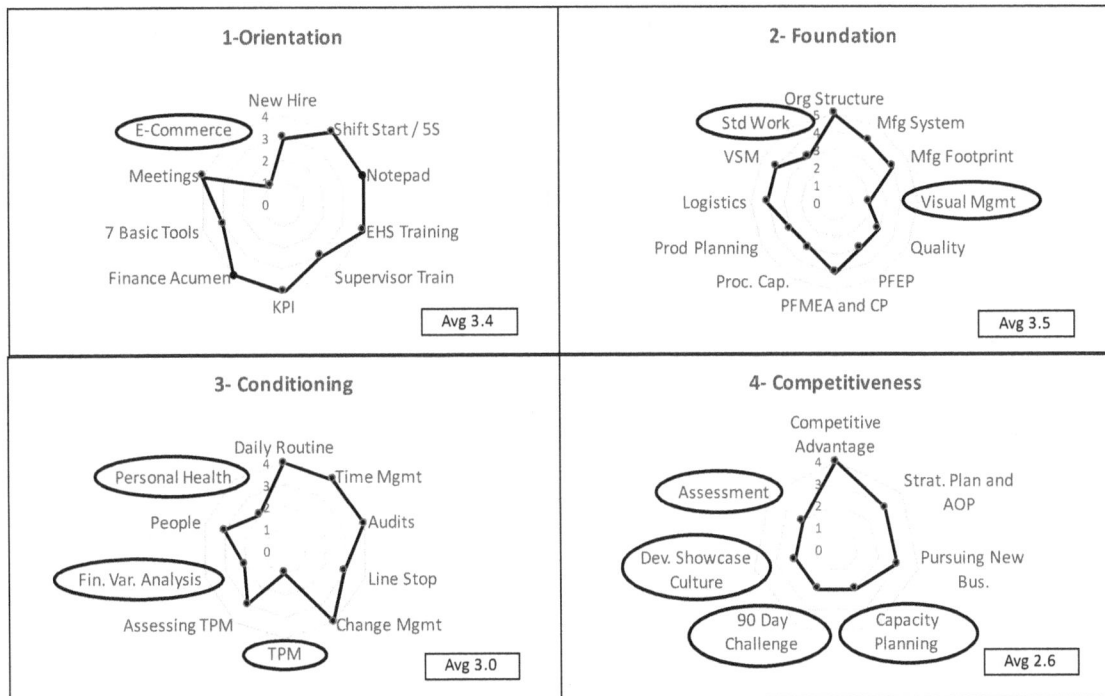

Figure 4. 4 Building a Showcase Culture Assessment

Part 4 - Competitiveness Summary

The final section of this book focused on Competitiveness. Many business books, podcasts, and other media present competitiveness in a generic sense and rarely provide the development and conversion details from a strategy to tactical plans to specific business opportunity assessments. This section starts with the development of a strategic plan to confirm the company's mission and value statements. Then, as a workshop breakout session, teams define the company's strengths, challenges, opportunities, and threats. Upon review of the SCOT, the team evaluates, critiques, and prioritizes various initiatives. The next step is to develop an annual operating plan. The annual operating plan (AOP) also known as a yearly plan or operating plan is a monthly cash flow and operating plan for an entire year. It is profit-driven showing key deliverables with financials, resources, and timing, including a summary with key business drivers and highlights. Information to develop a detailed AOP is listed along with a brief business process to approve the plan.

One of the key components of an AOP is outlining all current and new business opportunities awarded that will have an impact on the AOP planning period. An entire chapter discusses pursuing new business with 10 main process activities. Each activity is defined with an emphasis on developing a business case with various input factors, risks, assumptions, analysis, and decisions to proceed with presenting a customer with a quote.

Other chapters in this section are: Capacity Planning, 90 Day Challenge, Developing a Factory Showcase Culture, and an Assessment chapter that covers the entire book. Capacity planning is necessary as part of the manufacturing footprint and is used in both long-term and annual planning. A 90 Day Challenge is a focused, intense initiative to accomplish a specific objective within 90 days. Developing a Factory Showcase Culture has been discussed throughout each section of the book with some new key elements in this chapter. This chapter outlines how to start the culture change and evaluate progress. The final chapter is Assessment. After reading this book, the general manager and management team may want to assess the company's relative strength with each section and then make a detailed assessment of strength relative to each chapter's requirements. Radar or spider charts can be used to show the strengths and improvement areas, and to track progress over several assessment periods.

Next Steps

I truly enjoyed writing this book, and I think there is a need for an expansion of each section into a separate book. Expanded sections in separate books would encompass real-life examples with figures to show the use of a tool, technique, or management method. And, perhaps the books may include an audit or strength rating section. The expanded sections could also come from other people's experiences that have read this book and want to share their insights.

If you would like to share your experiences — both negative and positive — with the various tools, techniques, and management methods described in this book, please email them to me at mark.lado@global-mfgservices.com. I'd also like your input on other topics to include in subsequent books.

Also, I am considering the development of a Factory Showcase Culture certification program specifically for Plant Managers and functional managers. After having many discussions with company owners and senior executives, I've realized that there is a clear need for a certified educational platform to develop managers into factory showcase leaders. Company owners and executives regularly mentor their plant managers, but these managers lack necessary and specific materials to educate themselves and to use as references. Also, if the plant managers have these materials on hand, they can discuss and share them easily with their staff. When both the Plant managers and other functional managers have the same reference materials, key concepts and acronyms are understood in the same way. Plant managers can attend college courses, attend various online programs, and read a variety of books to learn and gain a broad understanding, but these types of trainings tend to be too general and lack sufficient key steps. In addition, when Plant Managers can readily access this book, they are more likely to implement a new business process activity with the "Plan, Do, Check, Act" philosophy in mind. Eventually, the Plant Manager becomes more confident with implementing new business practices and these successes ultimately lead to the building of a Factory Showcase Culture. I am also interested in participating in the 4th industrial revolution, helping to build factory showcases for the next phase of technology linkages. There are many manufacturing and information technologies that will soon be linked on a global scale.

My other next steps: I will continue doing CrossFit and competing in Olympic Lifting. I will try to spend more time with Panjai, touring around the USA and visiting other places around the world. And, of course, I will continue to do consulting, training, writing, and accepting interim assignments nearly anywhere in the world. I truly enjoy visiting and helping to improve manufacturing operations.

Thank you very much for reading this book, I hope it has been valuable for you.

Biography

Mark Lado is a consultant, advisor, writer, entrepreneur, world business leader, and US Navy veteran. He was born in Utica, New York, and currently lives in Baldwinsville, New York. Mark earned a BS in Industrial Engineering from SUNY Polytechnic and an MBA from University of North Florida.

His work experiences and job titles have been quite broad and has held nearly every job title in a manufacturing facility. He probably did not meet the minimum experience requirements for some positions he has held, but the company leaders believed he had the right positive mindset, work-hard ethic, personal confidence, desire to achieve goals, and they knew he had a keen interest to make the business successful. He thrives on being put into a high-risk business situation with little to no knowledge of that situation and just the belief that he can manage that challenge and make improvements. After many years of honing that trait, he decided to start his own consulting company and that is when his life opened up to even more opportunities, including spending several years at home with his wife raising their kids.

Mark has lived and worked in several Asian countries for over 13 years, including Thailand, Malaysia, China, South Korea, and Australia. Also, he has lived in the UK and Germany and several US states. He loves living and visiting many different places seeing and experiencing the sites, cultures, foods, drinks, languages, and making friends. He has friends all over the world and is always looking to make more friends, especially ones that like healthy living. In his spare time, Mark is a master CrossFitter, and master Olympic weightlifter. He is also a former CrossFit gym owner and former PADI scuba divemaster.

Mark admires people with similar interests, such as Mike Rowe from Dirty Jobs, Marcus Lemonis from The Profit, Andrew Zimmern from Bizzare Foods, Bear Grylls from Man vs. Wild, and Joe Teti and the other experts from Dual Survivor. He is sure there are many others too, as they all have a similar trait, and one he shares — they all seem to experience great satisfaction from getting into a new situation, learning about it, adapting to it, and overcoming or accomplishing a challenge.

Mark enjoys several TV shows, including How It's Made, Extreme Engineering, Top Gear, Fast N' Loud, Through the Wormhole, Wonders of the Universe, Physics of the Impossible, and Star Talk. For him, these shows provide a forum to think, be creative, explore the unknown, and fantasize about it.

Acknowledgements

Courtney Calderwood, MSc

Steve Chirello, Owner, Steve Chirello Advertising

CrossFit 315 and 315 Weightlifting, coaches and members

Bryce Currie, Vice President & General Manager, GE Aviation Delivery Operations

Ed Diodato, Mentor, retired – GE Aerospace

Jim Farfaglia, Author of numerous books

Terry Goff, Mentor, retired – Engineer and Entrepreneur

Hugh Goodridge, MVP Project Manager, Eaton Crouse-Hinds

Mitch Graves, Project Manager, Anoplate

Alex Grimshaw, Consultant and Co-founder, PPS International Limited

Jeffrey Gu, General Manager, Mestron

John Jasinski, Mentor, retired- GE Aerospace

Ed Kopkowski, PE, COO, Dexter Axle Company

Nick Kousmanidis, President, Accredited Business Consultants

Jason Lado, Outside Sales Engineer, KJ Electric

Ron Lado, Retired Plant Manager, Mechanical Engineer

Terry Larcombe, General Manager, Magna Powertrain

Karl Lindenberg, Owner, Linshan Consulting

Heather McCoy, Graphic and Web Designer, Marketing Consultant, 315 Designs

Steven Mettrick, Plant Quality Manager, ZF TRW Automotive

KenYip Ng, Senior Director, Automotive Quality Asia, Harman International

Jack Phillion, Senior Manager North America Supplier Development, Cooper Standard

Duke Okes, Author, Owner & Knowledge Architect, APLOMET

Meg Schader, Freelance Editor

Todd Sheppelman, CEO, ABC Group

Sanjay Singh, CTO and Executive Vice President, Dura Automotive

George Strampp, Mentor, CEO Automotive Manufacturing Solutions

XingYuan Sun, retired- CEO, Scientist, and Entrepreneur

Ruth E. Thaler-Carter, Freelance Writer, Editor, Proofreader, Speaker, Author

Gwendolyn Tolliver, Administrator

Bibliography

Beeson, John. *The Unwritten Rules: The Six Skills You Need to Get Promoted to the Executive Level.* Jossey-Bass; First Edition, October 19, 2010. ISBN-10: 0470585781, ISBN-13: 978-0470585788

Burkhammer, Steve. *Leading and Managing Manufacturing: Proven Concepts and Processes From The School Of Hard Knocks.* CreateSpace Independent Publishing Platform, September 30, 2013. ISBN-10: 1491246456, ISBN-13: 978-1491246450

Defeo, Joseph A. *Juran's Quality Handbook, Seventh Edition.* New York: McGraw-Hill Education, November 3, 2016. ISBN-10: 1259643611, ISBN-13: 978-1259643613

Eichenbaum David A. *The Business Rules: The Seven Irrefutable Laws That Determine All Business Success.* Entrepreneur Media. January 17, 2017. ISBN-10: 1-59918-061-8, ISBN-13: 978-15-9918061-8

Holstein, William J. *Why GM Matters: Inside the Race to Transform an American Icon.* New York, NY: Walker Publishing Company. February 3, 2009. ISBN-10: 0-8027-1818-7, ISBN-13: 978-0-8027-1718-4

Hopp, Wallace J. Spearman, Mark L. *Factory Physics.* New York, New York, McGraw Hill/Irwin. 2008. ISBN: 10-007-282403-4, ISBN-13: 978-0-07-282403-2

Ittelson, Thomas R. *Financial Statements: A Step by Step Guide to Understanding and Creating Financial Reports.* Franklin Lakes, NJ: Career Press. August 15, 2009. ISBN-10: 1601630239, ISBN-13: 978-1601630230

Jones, Dan, and Jim Womack. *Seeing the Whole: Mapping the Extended Value Stream.* Cambridge, MA: The Lean Enterprise Institute. November 1, 2002. ISBN-10: 0966784359, ISBN-13: 978-0966784350

Kotter, John P. *What Leaders Really Do.* Harvard Business Review Press; First Edition March 18, 1999. ISBN-10: 0875848974, ISBN-13: 978-0875848976

Larco, Jorge, Elena Bortolan, and Michael H. Studley. *Lean Manufacturing in Build to Order, Complex and Variable Environments.* Richmond, VA: Oaklea Press. January 1, 2008. ISBN-10: 1-892538-41-5, ISBN-13: 978-1-892538-41-3

Liker, Jeffrey K. *The Toyota Way: 14 Management Principles*. New York, NY: McGraw Hill. January 7, 2004. ISBN-10: 0071392319, ISBN-13: 978-0071392310

Louis, Raymond S. *Custom Kanban: Designing the System to Meet the Needs of Your Environment.* Boca Raton, FL: Productivity Press. September 11, 2006. ISBN-10: 1563273454, ISBN-13: 978-1563273452

Monden, Yasuhiro. *Toyota Production System: An integrated Approach to Just-In-Time (Fourth Edition)*. Boca Raton, FL: Productivity Press. October 5, 2011. ISBN-10: 143982097X, ISBN-13: 978-1439820971

Okes, Duke. *Root Cause Analysis: The Core of Problem Solving and Corrective Action.* Milwaukee, WI: ASQ Quality Press. March 10, 2009. ISBN-10: 0873897641, ISBN-13: 978-0-87389-764-8

Rochas-Lona, Luis, Jose Arturo Garza-Reyes, and Vikas Kumar. *Building Quality Management Systems: Selecting the Right Methods and Tools.* Boca Raton, FL: Productivity Press. June 27, 1013. ISBN-10: 1466564992, ISBN-13: 9781466564992

Rother, Mike, and John Shook. *Learning to See: Value-Stream Mapping to Create Value and Eliminate Muda.* Cambridge, MA: The Lean Enterprise Institute. June 1, 1999. ISBN-10: 0966784308, ISBN-13: 978-0966784305

Rothfeder, Jeffrey. *Driving Honda: Inside the World's Most Innovative Company*. New York, NY: Penguin Group. September 29, 2015, ISBN-10: 1591847974, ISBN-13: 9781591847977

Ruffa, Stephen A. *Going Lean: How the Best Companies Apply Lean Manufacturing Principles to Shatter Uncertainty, Drive Innovation, and Maximize Profits.* New York, NY: Amacom. June 23, 2008. ISBN-10: 081441057X, ISBN-13: 9780814410578

Index